SEVEN THOUSAND DAYS IN SIBERIA

TRANSLATED BY

JOEL AGEE

WITH AN INTRODUCTION BY

DANILO KIŠ

FARRAR STRAUS GIROUX

NEW YORK

SEVEN THOUSAND DAYS IN SIBERIA

KARLO ŠTAJNER

English translation copyright © 1988 by
Farrar, Straus and Giroux, Inc.
All rights reserved
Originally published in Serbo-Croatian as
7000 Dana u Sibiru © 1971 by Karlo Štajner and Globus
This edition translated from the German
Siebentausend Tage in Sibirien © 1975 by Europa Verlag
Introduction by Danilo Kiš originally published in
Sept mille jours en Siberie © 1983 by Editions Gallimard
Printed in the United States of America
Published simultaneously in Canada by
Collins Publishers, Toronto
First American edition, 1988
Designed by Cynthia Krupat

Library of Congress Cataloging-in-Publication Data
Štajner, Karlo.
Seven thousand days in Siberia.
Translation of: 7000 dana u Sibiru.
1. Štajner, Karlo. 2. Political prisoners—
Soviet Union—Biography. 3. Communists—Yugoslavia—
Biography. 4. Prisoners—Russian S.F.S.R.—Siberia.
I. Title. II. Title: 7,000 days in Siberia.
HV8959.S65S7213 1988 365'.45'0924 [B] 87-21206

CONTENTS

ALEXANDROVSKY TSENTRAL

AMONG WAR CRIMINALS

LIVING IN EXILE

AUTHOR'S NOTE

I was born Karl Steiner on January 15, 1902, in Vienna. After moving to Zagreb, the capital of the Yugoslav Republic of Croatia, in 1922, I adopted the Serbo-Croation spelling of my name, Karlo Štajner. In 1932, I emigrated to the Soviet Union, where I remained until 1956. Because of my Austrian origin, I was accused of being a Nazi agent and condemned to ten years at hard labor; a second ten-year term was later added to my sentence. After my release from prison in 1956, I returned to Yugoslavia and continued calling myself by my Serbo-Croatian name: Karlo Štajner.

K.S.

KARLO ŠTAJNER, WITNESS FOR THE PROSECUTION

Dead souls

In June 1956, the most senior representatives of the Yugoslav and Soviet governments—Tito and Khrushchev, accompanied by their chiefs of staff—sit in one of the parlor cars of the special train that shuttles between Moscow and Kiev. There is no need for an interpreter. Since their schedule is overburdened (the meeting's purpose is to smooth out the numerous ideological differences that had accumulated during the Yugoslav "schism"), little time remains for ancillary matters. However, taking advantage of a moment of good humor on the part of the master of the revels (Khrushchev), Tito proffers him, from across the table, as one proffers a menu to a diner, the list of dead souls. The scene is Gogolian. "Here, this is the list of our hundred and thirteen former officials who were in the Soviet Union. What became of them?" Khrushchev glances at the list of dead souls, then hands it to an aide. "I will answer you in two days." Exactly two days later, at the point in a meeting when drinks and cigars have replaced the official conversation, Khrushchev announces suddenly, point-blank, while drumming on a piece of paper with his pudgy fingers: *"Tochno sto nyetu"* ("Exactly one hundred are no longer of this world").

Then, under orders from the highest authorities, the monstrous machinery of the KGB puts itself in gear to find, somewhere in the immensity of Siberia, the thirteen surviving Yugoslav communists. And it is thus that among these living dead, in the faraway city of Krasnoyarsk, Karlo Štajner is discovered. A decision by the Ministry of State Security had condemned him, after twenty years of prison and camp, to internal exile for life. (He was what they called a "freed man"!)

Štajner: "I knew only that Tito was alive . . . The news had reached us. In exile, in Maklakovo, I had gone to the movies. Khrushchev had already made his trip to Belgrade and had admitted what he had admitted. In the newsreel, they showed some clips from Yugoslavia. And I thought I recognized Djuro Cvijič somewhere on a reviewing stand. I wondered what his position could be now. He must be at least a member of the Politburo. We had known each other well, and I had addressed myself to him in a letter I had written to the Yugoslav embassy in Moscow . . ." (Interview of March 1981). In this Gogolian universe of dead souls, irony mixes with tragedy: this childhood friend, formerly a party official, had been dead eighteen years when Štajner wrote him his letter! Declared a traitor, he had been killed—either in a Siberian camp or in the Butyrki prison.

Without scars

In 1976, at the bar of the International Hotel in Zagreb, I get ready to meet the famous survivor of the Gulag, the author of the celebrated book *Seven Thousand Days in Siberia*—which had been an invaluable guide for me as I wrote my own *A Tomb for Boris Davidovich*. I had dedicated one of the stories in the collection to him. A solidly built man of medium height, with a ruddy, brisk appearance and closely cut hair, came up to our table, his hat in his hand. No, it's not him! That *cannot* be him! "Štajner." Though twenty years had passed since his return from Siberia—sufficiently long for the wounds to turn to scars— where, I asked myself, are the scars? Just as the mark of the murderer is, as Solzhenitsyn tells us, imprinted on the face of the murderer in the form of a vertical line at the corner of the lips, there must be a mark, a scar, visible on the faces of the victims, like the wound on Christ's palm.

"Somewhere in *A Tomb for Boris Davidovich*," says this gentle man, without malice or pity, "your hero strolls around the Kremlin at night. You should correct that in the next edition . . . Anyone—especially any foreigner, like your hero—who prowled around the Kremlin during that time would have been arrested immediately." I promise to make the correction in the next edition, as well as a few others he suggests. I ask him what he would like to drink. He says it is all the same to him. "I'll have a vodka." Štajner, like someone who, though troubled, does not want to offend, replies: "Ah! No, thank you. Anything you like, except vodka. It is twenty years since I've had a single drop. And I'm not prepared to do so now. And in your book, at one point, you speak of colored paper," he continues as we opt for a French brandy (in memory of the good old days). "Ah! Young man"—Štajner lifts his hands toward the sky—"what colored paper was there in Russia in those days!" I try to explain that I found a mention of colored paper in an encyclopedia and that I used it precisely because it was so bizarre, because it *seemed* an anachronism. Again, Štajner raises his hands to the sky, like a man not used to being believed even on weightier matters. (But where are the scars, I ask myself, looking into those sincere, gentle eyes. Where are the scars?)

"La femme est l'avenir de l'homme"

During a subsequent meeting in Zagreb, Karlo introduces me to his wife, Sonya, a Russian. He dedicated his book to her: "This book is dedicated to my wife, Sonya, who waited faithfully for me." Any comparison, any association with the mythical Penelope would be *offensive*. In fact, while the Greek Penelope spun at her loom for twenty years, quietly, under the clement skies of Greece, and, to universal admiration, sent away her numerous admirers, in the modern Soviet version of the myth Sonya was the "wife of an enemy of the people," humiliated, mocked, tortured. And that was the destiny of those women who did not repudiate their husbands: "Many women had been arrested for having 'connections with an enemy of the people' . . . The children of arrested parents were put in special NKVD homes." Or: "Most of the men had left wives and children behind

and knew how difficult their lives were—since the wives and children of
political convicts were regarded as 'enemies of the people' and were
treated accordingly. This term can have little meaning for someone who
has not felt its harsh impact on his own life. The women were dismissed
from their jobs; the children thrown out of school . . . their apartments
were taken away and possessions confiscated. Relatives rarely dared
offer them refuge, as that would expose them to the risk of arrest. Thousands of women divorced their jailed husbands. Every day, the newspaper carried notices by women disowning their husbands, children
disowning their parents, because they had been branded 'enemies of
the people.' "

Eyes as deep as pits
We don't know what supported Sonya during her twenty-year wait. We
know only the part that is told in Karlo Štajner's book. When he was
arrested, Sonya was in the last month of her pregnancy. The little girl
who was due to be born died—of misery, of cold, of illness. Afterwards
came the long days of waiting: there was no cloth to weave, but rather
lines, proceedings, the round of the ministries, the fear of the knock on
the door, the wait for a rare letter, economizing down to the last kopeck
so as to be able to send a small sum or a package to Karlo . . . I repeat:
any comparison with the mythic Penelope would be too facile, an offense
against Sonya Štajner.

I look at Madam Štajner and lower my eyes. This look is unsustain-
able! No, Sonya Marmeladova exemplified an altogether *human* suffering;
she was a literary character—in the worst sense of the term—made up
of paper, of poetry, and of joie de vivre. But in the eyes of that other
Sonya, Sonya Štajner, in those eyes riveted in that beautiful face (that
face that had remained beautiful), I discover something I had never seen
before: dead eyes! They are not like the eyes of the blind, not blind eyes,
but eyes that no writer has ever described and that few people have seen,
dead eyes in a living face. (And I remain helpless before that look, since
no one has ever described anything like it; so I speak of something the
reader cannot recognize, and psychological explanations are no help.)
Sonya Štajner's eyes are not void of expression, they are dead as the eyes
of the dead are dead: the glassy look, the petrified look. These are eyes
in which nothing remains but the ash from what had been live coals, a
burning cinder, deep pits rather than whirlpools, where the light of the
sun never penetrates. These are eyes as deep as two pits, where, bending
toward them, one sees only the immobility of somber green, stagnant
water, pits that reflect only dead stars in a dead sky. And between them,
a deep furrow—the mark of the martyr.

And it is now, only just now, that, indirectly, I recognize in Karlo
Štajner what I had been searching for: those twenty years, more than
seven thousand days, that he spent in the farthest reaches of Siberia,

above the Arctic circle. The humiliation, the blows, the fear, the hunger, the cold, the death.

Short biography

Karlo Štajner's biography resembles that of thousands of others in Europe, particularly in Central Europe. The outline is well known: a son of a proletarian family follows the great road of the struggle and of ideals and finally finds himself in "the Third Rome," in Moscow. Here is how Štajner himself, in a typewritten note, sums up his youth: "Born at the beginning of this century, in Austria, he was, from the end of the First World War, a typesetter and a member of the directorate of the Communist Youth League. He worked at the Youth Section of the International. In the twenties, he enjoyed excellent relations with Yugoslav communists and came to work in Yugoslavia. In Zagreb, following party orders, he founded and directed the printing press which issued the party's clandestine publications. He collaborated with a number of the revolutionaries of the period, carried out different missions, traveled, was imprisoned in Zagreb, Paris, and Vienna, worked for the Comintern in Berlin, and finally, in 1932, under orders from the Yugoslav Communist Party, left for the U.S.S.R. A month after his arrival in Moscow, where he immediately presented himself to the Balkan section of the Comintern, he was named director of the printing press and publishing house of the Communist International. He worked there for four years, and still held that post when, in 1936, he was arrested."

The rest is known. The rest constitutes the plot of the book called *Seven Thousand Days in Siberia*.

A book's fate

"In the dungeons of the NKVD, in the icy wastes of the extreme north— wherever my suffering had passed beyond the limits of endurance—I held fast to one resolution: to survive, in order someday to tell the world and especially my party comrades about my terrible experience." Štajner's manuscript was ready in 1958, two years after his return from Siberia and the same year as Solzhenitsyn's *Gulag Archipelago*. What befell Štajner's manuscript until 1972; that is, during the ensuing fourteen years? That also constitutes a story, but one which Štajner never wrote. Recently, however, in an interview, he revealed a small part of this mystery: "The manuscript languished for several years. It could not be published. Publishers were willing to go ahead, but someone seemed to be obstructing the publication . . . I had given one copy to Zagreb . . . and another to Belgrade . . . and both copies disappeared . . . Yes, they disappeared! Quite simply, there wasn't a trace of them. That's what they told me . . . But the original had been kept in a safe place, at my brother's home in Lyons . . . Siberia taught me a few things . . ." But because world politics also depends on the conscience of individuals and their initiative, the manuscript was accepted for publication in 1971, evidently with Tito's personal consent . . . When it was released, *Seven Thousand Days in Siberia* received one of Yugoslavia's most important literary awards: the Book of the Year prize, which bears the name of the Yugoslav poet, partisan, and martyr Ivan Goran Kovačić. Four years passed between this first edition of the book and its initial foreign publication in Germany. And, outside of the French edition, that was the only translation of Štajner's seminal book. I know that as a mark of his gratitude to Tito (whose intercession saved his life), and in the name of that party *discipline* which he has still, visibly, never renounced (as a member since 1919, he is one of the oldest adherents of the Yugoslav Communist Party), Štajner refused an offer of American publication because it came from Djilas's publisher. That is what his party comrades had advised him to do. And Sonya, too, whose eyes—those two deep pits full of fear—said: "Karlo, be careful!" As for foreign publishers, they could not publish the book before it came out in Yugoslavia. "After all, I wanted it to come out here first," said Štajner in the same interview. And after the book's publication, mysterious intrigues circulated around him. The Yugoslav Authors' Agency, which serves as an intermediary with foreign publishers, received option requests from a number of Western European and American publishers. Štajner says that, by letter, the Agency declared itself happy to inform him that foreign publishers were interested in his book. And Štajner went to Belgrade. "For an event of such importance, I made the trip." And there he was told by an employee of the Agency: "I've been ordered to stay out of this affair, and I advise you to sever all contact with foreign publishers." (Sonya: "Karlo, be careful!") Thus, the translated manuscript also begins to get mislaid in foreign publishing houses. "It was the same with the Italians . . . I had gone to a meeting in Florence. They took me to a house in the suburbs. That day I said to myself, 'Take courage. If you get out alive, it will be a second Norilsk! I had the impression of being with killers. They were seated, smoking. And I was supposedly with a publisher. It had been a long time, I admit, since I had been so afraid. Still, I left the book there. That it was 'lost' afterwards does not surprise me. No one knows whom I talked with. Neither I nor anyone else . . . When I inquired at the publishing house, they informed me that the individuals in question did not work for them . . . As for me, I haven't the slightest doubt as to the identities of the people mixed up in this" (interview, 1981).

Trust your own sense
In 1977, during a public appearance before the youth of Belgrade, a young leftist asked Štajner: "Did you remain faithful to your earlier ideals during the twenty years of your imprisonment?" Štajner replied: "We the prisoners were just livestock, men reduced to their basest biological instincts, to their most elementary existential needs. There was no place for ide-

ology; the only 'ideology' was to survive." Many of the people present—among whom were Austrian, German, French, and Italian students—began to stir in protest. Štajner had not uttered the phrase which had been suggested by the question and which frees teleological consciences, corrupted by ideology, from their sense of guilt. Štajner had more confidence in his own reason, in his *biological* experience, than in any politicized consciousness. He showed himself "spiritually superior," in that moral sense Kant gave the term: "Knowledge is spiritual superiority; its motto is, 'Have courage to trust your own sense!' "

Danilo Kiš

Translated from the French by David Rieff

FOREWORD

In the dungeons of the NKVD, in the icy wastes of the extreme north—wherever my suffering had passed beyond the limits of endurance—I held fast to one resolution: to survive, in order someday to tell the world and especially my party comrades about my terrible experience.

As soon as I was out of the MVD's reach, I began to put my resolve into practice. I knew my task would be difficult. I was particularly worried that my book might be dismissed as one of the usual anti-Soviet books and that the events described in it would not be believed. I also wanted to prevent my book from being used as a weapon against socialism. I have tried to show, therefore, that developments in the Soviet Union had nothing to do with socialism; that, on the contrary, it was the counter-revolution led by Stalin in 1936, an attack primarily directed against socialism itself, that brought them about.

This is proven by the extermination of the old party leadership in 1936–39. It is proven by the pact concluded between Stalin and Hitler against socialism and democracy in 1939. It is proven by the betrayal and abandonment of German communists to the Gestapo.

After the war, Stalin provided another proof: the newly founded People's Democracies were subjugated and exploited in a manner recalling the most implacable imperialism.

This book is only a partial account. To tell everything I experienced during those twenty years—and with me tens of thousands of others—would require superhuman memory and fill dozens of volumes.

Most of the names in this book are not invented; but in a few instances I did change names in order to protect certain individuals.

I have generally abstained from analysis. My intention is to describe events in their nakedness and allow the reader to form his own opinion.

K.S.

ARREST
INTERROGATION
MILITARY TRIBUNAL

MOSCOW, 1936

It all began on November 4, 1936, in Moscow, at 67/69 Novoslobodskaya Street, apartment 44.

I was asleep when I heard the doorbell. At the same moment, I felt my wife's hand on my shoulder. I woke up, heard the bell ring again, turned on the light, looked at the clock: it was a quarter to three. Who would be visiting us at this time, I wondered . . .

It must be . . .

Another, furious ring. I went to the door: "Who's there?" A voice answered: "Comrade Steiner, please open the door, this is the superintendent!" I turned the lock and peered through the crack. The superintendent stood before me. "There's a leak in your kitchen, it's flooding the apartment below yours, I have to take a look," he said uneasily, a little too quickly.

"Everything's in order here," I replied.

"Open up, I have to look," he insisted.

I opened the door, and the next instant three uniformed men appeared, an officer and two soldiers. One of the soldiers stayed outside; the other walked in, together with the officer and the superintendent. None of them said a word.

With a swift movement of his hand, the officer opened his coat and showed me the insignia of a lieutenant colonel in the NKVD. "Are you armed?" he asked. "No," I replied, surprised at my own calm. My fear of the unknown had vanished; the danger was here and now, and it was known.

The officer searched me. I looked at him: he was blond, well built, with a peasant's features, about thirty. His face was expressionless.

Then he drew a piece of paper from his pocket and handed it to me. I read the heading: "Order of Arrest." I handed the sheet back to the officer. He ordered me to sit down and went into the other room. Pointing at my wife, who was lying in bed, he asked: "Who is that?"

"My wife."

"Get up," he said.

"My wife is in her last month of pregnancy," I said. "Please let her lie there; she shouldn't get too upset."

"Get up!" he shouted.

My wife stood up. I wanted to help her.

"Stay in your seat, don't move!"

I didn't listen. I went to the bed to help my wife get dressed. He rushed to the bed, threw sheets, blankets, and pillows to the floor, and ordered us again not to move. He searched the entire apartment, while the soldier watched us. I tried to console my distraught wife, but the officer forbade me to talk to her. He examined every single object and put aside all foreign-language books. He did this for two hours. Finally, he told me to get dressed. I tried to calm down my wife, ignoring his orders.

"What will you take with you?" she asked.

"I don't want to take anything. This is obviously a mistake; I'll be back soon."

"Move!" shouted the officer, and walked ahead. The soldier followed behind me.

I heard my wife's loud crying.

The door shut behind us. The third NKVD man joined us on the stairs. I was shoved into a car that was waiting in front of the house. A soldier sat on my right and one on my left; the officer sat in front, next to the driver.

"Go!"

We drove swiftly through the dark streets of Moscow. I tried to collect my thoughts and get a grasp on what had happened. But I didn't have much time to think.

LUBYANKA—NKVD HEADQUARTERS

After about ten minutes, the car stopped in front of the main NKVD building on Lubyanka Street. A large gate opened, and the car drove in. One of the two soldiers ordered me to get out. We stood in a narrow courtyard surrounded by five-story buildings with barred windows. I was pushed through a narrow door into a large room where some thirty men and women sat waiting on benches along the walls. Some had bundles with them; others, valises. Some were staring into space; others were dozing. No one said a word. The silence was suddenly broken by a young girl's sobs. I thought of my wife. Every fifteen minutes, a door would open and a soldier would call out a name. My turn came after two hours. I was led into the next room. It looked like a general store—everywhere you looked, suitcases, baskets, and bundles were piled up on shelves, and there was a counter. Behind it stood several uniformed men and women, the latter wearing white blouses.

A noncommissioned officer stepped up to me and asked for my name. I responded.

"Do you have any money?"

I drew out my wallet and handed it to him. He counted my money and told me the amount.

"Any valuables?"

"My watch."

He gave me a receipt for the money and another one for the watch. Then I had to take off all my clothes. After a thorough search, I was told to get dressed again. A soldier led me along several corridors and stairs to a hallway with numerous doors, and left me with a guard who was carrying a bundle of keys. The guard used two of his keys to open a door and pushed me inside.

I found myself in a stinking, suffocatingly airless room about five meters long and three meters wide. Thirty or forty men were lying on the floor, some on top of their coats, others using their coats as blankets. A few heads rose when I entered; I saw tired, sleepy faces. A man with a long blond beard moved over and invited me to lie down next to him. Carefully and with some difficulty, I stepped over the bodies on the floor and lay down by his side.

"You must be a foreigner," he said. "I can tell. Our people are much more decisive."

I didn't respond. Seeing how upset I was, he didn't insist on an answer. "Get some rest," he said. "We'll talk about it tomorrow."

He asked me one more question: what time it was. I shrugged. He said nothing more.

I looked around. Some were sleeping, others were watching me. I was lying on the bare floor, wearing a suit and a thin coat. It was warm in the room, but I felt cold and was shivering. I tried to think: What will happen next? What do they want of me? Will I have to stay here long? What will happen to my wife? Did someone denounce me? I couldn't concentrate. I closed my eyes and tried to sleep. I couldn't. Over and over, the same questions pursued me. The few hours until daybreak felt like an eternity.

"Toilet!"

Everyone stood up. I followed mechanically as we were led into a room with several stalls. Some men squatted; others washed in a long tin basin. I, too, washed. The water was icy; that made me feel better. After a few minutes, the guard led us back to our cells. My cellmates surrounded me, plying me with questions. I answered somewhat reluctantly. Whereupon, several of them tried to console me: "You're not the only one. The prisons are overflowing. We don't know why we're here either."

After a while, the guard brought thirty-four portions of black bread on a wooden platter, about half a kilogram for each man, and two tin pails with hot water. Each prisoner fetched his aluminum bowl and served himself hot water from a pitcher that was on the floor next to the pails. I hadn't been given my bowl yet, but I had no desire for food or drink. The others were cutting their bread into two or three pieces; they used a thread for this, since there were no knives. I noticed how greedily most of them ate. Any crumbs that fell to the ground were carefully picked up and eaten. There was complete silence during the meal, as if it were a ritual. The uneaten bread was carefully put away in rags or bundles: one ration for midday, another for the evening.

My bearded neighbor asked me why I wasn't eating.

"I'm not hungry," I said.

My bread lay there, untouched, and I saw the other prisoners devouring it with their eyes. I asked my neighbor if he wanted my bread, but he suggested I keep it. "We don't get enough to eat here," he said. I finally persuaded him to take at least half. He accepted it, chewed it with pleasure, and told me that he had been brought here from Vladivostok and had been waiting in the *sobachnik* (the doghouse—that's what this cell was called in prison lingo) for four months but hadn't been called to a hearing yet. He'd been arrested nine months ago. During the revolutionary period, from 1917 to 1920, he had commanded a partisan group in the war against the Japanese. After that, he had been a manager in the canned-fish industry in the Far East. Now he was being accused of having planned an uprising against the Soviet government, with the aim of helping Japan to annex the Far East regions of the Soviet Union.

I was shocked to find myself lying next to a man who had contemplated such a terrible deed. I asked him how, as a revolutionary, he could have done such a thing. He laughed aloud and said he had never even dreamed of it; it was pure fantasy on the part of the NKVD. He was laughing so hard that his long blond beard and broad shoulders shook. It felt as if the Far East tundras themselves were laughing at my naïveté. I gaped at him.

Now the bearded fellow asked me what I was accused of. I told him I had no idea. Other prisoners sat down next to us and asked me where I was from. I told them I was a political immigrant and had been in the Soviet Union since 1932. My replies were vague and disjointed. There was one question that crowded out all other thoughts: Why am I here? I felt trapped in a bad dream. I couldn't pay full attention to the questions I was being asked.

Lunch consisted of half a liter of herb soup and a dipperful of peas; I left the soup untouched but ate the peas. My appetite had returned. In the evening, we were given another portion of peas. At around ten, the light was turned on and off three times in the hallway: that meant it was time to go to sleep. Most of the inmates spread their jackets or coats on the floor and lay down. I followed their example. I was tired and fell asleep quickly. But I hadn't been asleep long when the door opened and I heard one of the prisoners being summoned to a hearing. It took me a while to fall asleep again.

Suddenly I was awakened. "Your turn!" said the guard, standing in the doorway. I stood up, put on my shoes, and stepped out into the hall. There stood a young blond woman in an NKVD uniform; she was wearing a beret with a cockade and was holding a printed sheet of paper in her hand. "What is your name?" she asked.

I replied.

"Move!"

We passed through several iron gates, went up to the second floor, then down to the courtyard and into a large building. An elevator took us to the fifth floor.

The woman led me to a large room. Behind a desk sat a man of medium height, about forty years old, with graying hair and an English-style mustache. He was wearing the uniform of an NKVD captain. The female officer handed him the piece of paper, which he signed. I was standing by the door. When the woman left the room, the officer scrutinized me for a minute. Then he pointed to a chair and said: "Sit down. My name is Revzin. I'm your interrogator. What language shall we speak, German or Russian?"

"Either one," I said.

He handed me a piece of paper. "Read this and sign it."

I read:

1. You are accused of belonging to the counterrevolutionary organization that murdered the Secretary of the Central Committee of the Communist Party of the Soviet Union and of the Leningrad Regional Committee, S. M. Kirov.
2. You are accused of being a Gestapo agent.

I smiled when I read that.

"Don't laugh," Revzin said. "These are serious charges."

I took a deep breath in relief. I thought to myself: I was right, it's all a mistake. I suddenly felt confident and in good spirits. "There's a misunderstanding here, I have nothing whatsoever to do with these things," I said.

"There is no misunderstanding at all, we have all the proof we need, and you'll be much better off if you admit everything honestly."

"For God's sake, what are you saying? I'm completely innocent! I've always been a good communist, always served the party as best I could!"

Revzin stood up. "We won't talk any further today. Go back to your cell, think it over, we'll continue tomorrow."

At that moment, the female officer returned and led me back to my cell. As soon as the door closed, my cellmates surrounded me, asking questions. I told them about Revzin's fantastic accusation. "It's unbelievable, they made the whole thing up," I said.

"Sure," several voices commented. "He's a foreigner, so he's a spy."

"For heaven's sake, I have nothing to do with this!"

"Do you think we have anything to do with the crimes we're accused of? We would never even dream of them!"

The guard knocked on the door with his keys, demanding quiet. We returned to our places and lay down. I couldn't sleep; I kept thinking about the words I had read on that sheet of paper. What did it all mean? Why should I get dragged into this kind of affair? I consoled myself with the thought that sooner or later everything would turn out to have been a mistake, and that I would be released.

A new day began. Once again, we got bread in the morning, soup and peas for lunch, gruel for dinner. In between meals, we discussed my hearing. Each man told his own story. Half the inmates didn't even know why they had been arrested; the others talked about the outlandish charges that had been leveled against them.

One peasant boy had been accused of terrorism because he had quarreled with the chairman of his collective farm and had threatened to kill him. Only one of the prisoners was charged with having engaged in counterrevolutionary talk. His own brother had testified against him. When they were confronted in court, his brother had stated that the NKVD had ordered him to report everything he heard his brother say about the Soviet state. Later I learned that this man—his name was Smirnov—was condemned to eight years in a detention camp by the Troika. That was the name given the commission, made up of three NKVD officers, which judged a portion of the inmates without bringing them to trial.

Several days passed and I was not called to another hearing. I was transferred to another cell on the fifth floor. Here, in contrast to the *sobachnik*, there were iron beds with straw sacks, pillows, and even sheets. It was a single cell, but there were three beds in it; the floor was painted and remarkably clean. I spent four days alone in that cell. On the fifth day, two other prisoners joined me.

On the fourteenth day, I was taken to Revzin's office. He apologized: he said he hadn't been able to call for me sooner, he'd been very busy; but tomorrow he would be sure to give me a hearing. That was all he had to say. I now remembered something the prisoners in the *sobachnik* had told me: the NKVD liked to use the promise of an imminent hearing as a means of keeping the prisoners in a state of nervous agitation.

I got to know my new cellmates. Larionov, an old Bolshevik, a tall, imposing man of about forty-two, had been director of a chemical works in Kemerovo in the Urals. He was accused of having sabotaged the plant he directed. He swore it was a complete fabrication, and that he'd refuse to sign anything. One night, Larionov was summoned to a hearing and didn't return for five days. For five days and nights, he had been forced to stand in a corner, with just a single meal per day, consisting of some soup and bread. This vigorous man, who had faced all sorts of dangers fighting on the side of the Red Army in the Civil War, had broken down under this torture and confessed to everything he was accused of. Three weeks later, he was removed from our cell; I never saw him again.

Goldman was about thirty-five years old. He had been Rykov's personal secretary at the time when Rykov was still chairman of the Council of People's Commissars. He stubbornly refused to admit that his boss had hired him as a Gestapo agent.

One night—the hearings were usually conducted at night—Goldman was summoned to a hearing and was brought back with broken ribs, around four in the morning. He lay groaning on his cot from Saturday until Monday morning, when the prison doctor finally came and asked him what was the matter. He just stammered: "Those bastards . . . bastards . . ."

Two hours later, two guards came with a stretcher and carried him away. I was left alone with my habitual questions: Why? How long will it go on? What's happening to my Sonya? Does she have any idea what I'm accused of? That thought haunted me more than all the others.

The next day, three men were brought into my cell, among them one who had spent two days with me in the *sobachnik*. The other two had been arrested recently. One of them was a sixty-five-year-old man named Schab, born in Moscow of German parents. He told me he had worked for nearly fifty years in an armory in Moscow. Two days after his first hearing, he was informed that he was a Gestapo agent. The old man was deeply grieved by this accusation; he swore he was completely innocent and asked my advice as to what he could do to refute the charge.

What advice could I give him? I had need of advice myself!

One day, the old man was questioned for nearly forty-eight hours. The interrogator, a very young man, insulted him in the vilest manner: "You old whore, you son of a bitch, we know your sort well, you served the capitalists for fifty years, we'll teach you what stuff the NKVD's made of, you'd better sign this confession in forty-eight hours or we'll make mincemeat out of you, dirty old dog . . ." While he was telling me this, the old man wept bitterly. One night, he woke me up and asked me a favor: if I ever got out, would I tell his wife, who lived on Baumann Street in Moscow, that he was completely innocent? The next day, he refused to accept any food; after five days, he was barely conscious. On the sixth day, he was carried out of the cell.

Several years later, in Norilsk, I met a prisoner named Nechamkin who had been in the same prison hospital ward with Schab. Nechamkin told me that Schab had died without regaining consciousness. Unfortunately, I was not able to carry out my comrade's last wish.

While I had gotten close to Schab very quickly, I was not at all successful with Vishniakov. He had been the director of the industrial academy in Moscow; he was about sixty years old. He refused to talk to anybody. Every time we tried to engage him in conversation, he said he would have no dealings with counterrevolutionary elements. One day I told him that I, too, was a communist; that I had been a party member since 1919, had been repeatedly jailed for my activities as a communist, and was now accused of espionage and terrorism.

"The NKVD does not arrest innocent people" was his curt reply.

"In that case," I asked, "why were you arrested?"

"It was a misunderstanding," Vishniakov replied, and turned his back to me.

Several days passed. Then a prison official in a white smock came and said: "Whoever has receipts for money can buy bread, sugar, marmalade, herring, and cigarettes in the prison shop." He gave us three pieces of paper on which to write our requests. Vishniakov had no money, but he was a smoker; although I was a nonsmoker, I ordered three packs of cigarettes and a piece of soap. The next day, when my purchase was delivered, I offered the cigarettes and the soap to Vishniakov. "How dare you offer me anything!" he screamed. "You, an enemy of the people!" I put the cigarettes and the soap on the table and said nothing.

Several days passed. Then—at night, as usual—the door hatch opened and the NKVD man on duty in the hall said: "Psst, psst."

I was the first to hear it and lifted my head. He summoned me to the door with his index finger. "Is the guy with the initial V here?" he whispered. (It was a rule in NKVD prisons for the guards never to call out a complete name, so that, in case of a slip-up, the prisoners would not know who was in the next cell.)

I awakened Vishniakov.

"Get dressed," said the NKVD man, "and *bez veshchei*—leave your stuff."

At around eight in the morning, Vishniakov came back from his hearing, groaning. "Ah! Ah! . . . What's happening here! They called me a bandit, a parasite, an enemy of the people, a Trotskyite, they threatened to beat me to death if I didn't admit everything."

I opened a pack of cigarettes and offered it to him. "Have a smoke," I said. "It'll calm you down." The old man burst into tears, took a cigarette, and lit it. After he had smoked it to the end, he walked up to the door and knocked. When the guard came and asked what he wanted, Vishniakov said: "Give me paper and ink. I want to write to Comrade Stalin to inform him of what's going on here."

"You'll have to ask your interrogator for paper and ink. We have nothing," the guard shouted through the door, and walked away.

Vishniakov sat on his bed, lit a second cigarette, and stared into space. When the time came for our daily walk, he stayed sitting there.

Every day, we were allowed a fifteen-minute walk, either in the very narrow courtyard or on the flat roof of the prison building. We walked single file, with our hands behind our backs; we were not permitted to look left, right, or above us. A breach of this ordinance was punishable by up to five days without the right to enjoy fifteen minutes of fresh air, or to buy anything from the prison shop. A virtual torrent of sanctions showered down on us for even the slightest infractions. An especially close watch was kept to prevent anyone's retaining the piece of paper he was given each morning and evening as he stepped into the toilet room. The guard was constantly checking through the peephole to make sure the paper was used, or, if unused, returned.

After a long interval, I was called to another hearing, and from then on, I met with Revzin nearly every night. I would usually be fetched at about 11 p.m., and the hearing would last until two or three in the morning. Sometimes forty-eight hours would pass before I was led back to my cell. For the first few days, Revzin interrogated me in a polite and formal manner. He began by advising me to admit everything, so that I would have a chance of eventually rejoining the party and perhaps even earning a decoration or two. I asked him to tell me specifically what I was accused of.

"We know you are an agent of the Gestapo, we know you are a member of the counterrevolutionary organization that killed Kirov," Revzin said.

"That's all made up out of whole cloth. The NKVD cannot possibly have any evidence of my guilt, since I have never in my life had anything to do with people or organizations that do such terrible things," I replied.

"The NKVD would never have arrested you without evidence. This evidence was first presented to the Executive Committee of the Comintern, because you were an employee of the Comintern apparatus, and the Executive Committee ratified your arrest. After that, the case against you had to be presented to the Chief Prosecutor of the U.S.S.R., Vyshinsky, and he also approved your arrest." Revzin said this very cold-bloodedly, very deliberately, as if reading a text.

I demanded to see the warrant for my arrest. He showed it to me. On the upper left, it said: *"Arest odobryayu.* Vyshinsky." (Arrest approved. Vyshinsky.)

"I don't understand any of this," I said. "I repeat, I have had nothing to do with this, and I am convinced that the NKVD will have to come to the same conclusion."

Hearings were rarely held on weekends, but one Saturday night I was unexpectedly called to Revzin's office. As usual, he addressed me with affected politeness. "You see, Steiner, I'm even sacrificing my Saturday night for you. In your own interest, I would like to bring this matter to an end without further delay. All it takes is your cooperation, and we can close this case once and for all."

"I'm prepared to do everything in my power to do just that. I assure you, I am extremely eager to get out as soon as possible."

"Good," said the interrogating officer. "In that case, we can start talking seriously."

Revzin drew out a printed sheet of paper with the heading: *Protokol Doprosa.* After the usual questions—first and last name, birth date, etc.—he asked: "Do you declare yourself guilty of being a member of the counterrevolutionary organization that murdered the Secretary of the Central Committee of the Communist Party of the Soviet Union and of the Leningrad Regional Committee, S. M. Kirov?"

"I can only repeat that I have no connection with this matter whatsoever and that I am completely innocent."

Revzin put down his pen. "You won't achieve anything that way, you have to confess everything."

"I have nothing to confess. I'm innocent."

We continued in this manner all night. Revzin urged me to be reasonable and admit everything. I swore for the hundredth time that I was innocent. Revzin looked at his watch and pressed a button.

As I waited for the soldier who would escort me back to my cell, Revzin said: "I want you to go over this carefully. I'll have you brought back here tomorrow. But I can tell you one thing in advance. If you keep on stubbornly denying your guilt, things will come to a bad end with you, do you understand? A very bad end . . ."

I said nothing.

On Monday, I was called for another hearing. This time, there was a second NKVD officer in addition to Revzin.

"This is the man who thinks he can lead us around by the nose. I've lost patience with him. See what you can do. But don't try too hard. If he refuses to give in, we'll just put him up against the wall. All right, I'm leaving." Those were the words with which Revzin introduced me to my new interrogator.

"Sit down," he said. He pulled a pack of cigarettes from his pocket and offered me one.

"Thanks, I don't smoke."

He lit a cigarette and began to leaf through some papers. I observed him. He was a big man, with broad shoulders. He had slickly combed, unparted hair and symmetrical features. He wasn't wearing a uniform, just the usual party shirt and civilian trousers, with a wide belt. When he finished smoking his cigarette, he asked me: "Are you hungry?"

"No."

"Then let's have a cup of tea together later."

I said nothing.

He initiated a relaxed conversation, asking me who I was and how I had come to the Soviet Union. I told him I was Austrian and had lived in Yugoslavia for a long time, and that the persecution of communists by the police there had forced me to flee the country. I had lived in France for a while, I explained, but eventually I had to leave that country as well, again because of my communist activities.

He listened carefully. Then he rang a bell. A girl appeared, and he said: "Bring us two glasses of tea and two hundred-gram portions of sausage."

She returned after a few minutes. He pushed the tea and sausage toward me, saying: "Eat, you must be hungry."

We both ate and drank. When he finished his meal, he quickly lit another cigarette, and said: "You've told me the story of your life. I now ask myself how a man who from his earliest youth has been a functionary of the communist movement could turn into a dangerous agent of a foreign power."

I gave him a quizzical look.

"You are a rational human being. Listen to my advice. Confess. Name the persons who recruited you. Tell us the nature of your assignments, who were the people you recruited, and what were your activities."

"I am completely innocent, no one recruited me, nor did I recruit anyone," I replied.

The interrogating officer leapt up, shouting: "Do you know Eimike?"

"Yes," I replied.

"Tell me where and when you got to know Eimike."

"I was sitting with an acquaintance in the Metropol Café in Moscow— that was in 1934—when a man came to our table and greeted my acquaintance. We were introduced, and he joined us at the table. I learned from that conversation that Eimike ran an animal import–export business in Berlin and had dealings with similar organizations in the Soviet Union. He exported wild animals from tropical countries to the Soviet Union, and in exchange he received animals from northern Siberia. I saw Eimike two other times on the street in Moscow; we greeted each other from afar without exchanging any words. That's all."

"You are lying! I am going to prove that you met with Eimike several times in a hotel, and that you received assignments for espionage from him."

"Now I know for a fact that all this is an invention. I happen to know that the NKVD carefully watches the guests of the Metropol and therefore knows very well that I was never in a hotel room with Eimike."

I hadn't quite finished when the interrogator jumped up, banging his fist on the table with such force that the inkwell tipped over and a glass of tea fell to the floor, shattering.

"Now I see what a dangerous character you are! Who do you think you're dealing with? The Austrian police? The NKVD will bring you to your senses soon enough!" he roared.

I stood up. "Please have me brought back to my cell. There's no point in tormenting me. I am not inclined to let myself be treated like a dog."

That set off an even bigger explosion. "Sit down, and don't you dare stand up without my permission! Or no, go and stand facing the wall over there!"

I stood facing the wall for about two hours. Then he ordered me to sit down and began to write the report on my interrogation. Both the questions he had asked me and the answers I had given him were recorded quite accurately. He did try to sneak in a few formulations that distorted my meaning, but after a lot of back-and-forthing, he consented to write my words down as I intended.

For almost two weeks, I was interrogated nearly every day, but nothing changed. Always the same questions, and almost the identical answers from me. During one of the hearings, when I had the impression that Grushevsky (that was the second interrogator's name) was in a good mood, I asked whether he had any idea how my wife was doing.

He laughed. "Of course I do. We watch every step your wife takes, and I can assure you, she's having a ball; no sooner were you arrested than she was sleeping with other men."

This answer infuriated me so that I forgot I was in the clutches of the NKVD. I shouted at him: "You have no right to talk about my wife in this manner! These are fascist methods! From now on, I refuse to say another word to you!"

My shouting was so loud that another officer came in from the room next door. When I finally quieted down, I said: "My wife was about to give birth and is probably in the hospital by now. I am concerned; I need to know how she is. I thought I was dealing with a person who could put aside the fact that I am prisoner, at least for a moment, and answer me as one human being to another. I see now that I was mistaken."

Grushevsky acted as if nothing had happened and promised to inquire after my wife's condition and let me know the next day. Then he had me taken back to my cell.

In the cell, I burst into tears. My cellmates were not surprised when I told them what had happened. They knew that the NKVD would use any means to demoralize its prisoners.

A week later, I was called to the prison's administrative office and informed that my wife had given birth to a baby daughter and that both mother and child were doing well. I was very happy, especially since I now knew that my wife had not been arrested. In most cases, the wives of arrested men were locked up even if they were pregnant or nursing a baby. As many as three hundred pregnant or nursing mothers were locked up in the Butyrki prison every year. As soon as the children were a year old, they were taken away from their mothers and put in an NKVD child-care center. Heartrending scenes took place there. Sometimes the mothers screamed so loud that you could hear it all over the prison: "Don't take my baby! Give me back my baby!"

Those words still echo in my ears.

BUTYRKI FORTRESS

In mid-December 1936, the guard came and told me to "pack my stuff." My heart began to pound. What did this mean? Was I being released?

I took leave of my cellmates. The guard led me to an empty room on the ground floor, where I was made to strip and submit to a thorough search. After that was over, the warden told me to get dressed again. He led me into the same courtyard I had seen when I arrived. A delivery van stood there, with a single word painted on it in four languages: *Khleb— Pain—Bread—Brot*.

An NKVD man opened the door of the "bread truck" and ordered me in. It was a prison van with many small compartments; I was squeezed into one of them. You couldn't move in there, you could hardly breathe;

I noticed that some of the other cells were already occupied. More prisoners kept climbing in. I tried without success to attract my neighbor's attention by coughing; we had been told to stay absolutely silent, and a guard sent along to supervise us kept stern watch over our every move.

The gate slammed shut behind us, and the van with its multilingual inscription tore through the streets of Moscow. Who would have suspected the NKVD of hiding its victims behind such a slogan?

After fifteen or twenty minutes, we arrived at the Butyrki, the largest NKVD prison in Moscow. Two gates opened, and we were ordered to step out. I noticed right away that this would be a rougher place than NKVD headquarters. In the Lubyanka, the guards and officials had maintained a modicum of officious decorum, and some of them were even polite. But these NKVD soldiers cursed and pushed us constantly. Everything had to be done in a hurry. "Hands on your back!" was the first command I was given, right after being unloaded from the "bread truck."

A massive door opened, and behind it a second, iron door. We were led into a long hall that reminded me of a railway station. There were many doors without handles on either side of the hall. One of these doors was opened for me, and I was shoved inside. The "room" was a concrete box containing nothing but a bench, which was fastened to the wall. No window. I sat down and listened to the sound of doors opening and closing behind the other prisoners. Some of them tried to ask questions but were answered only with shouts: "Quiet! Not a word!"

After a long wait, I was led to a shower. I was given a piece of soap, and I washed myself with pleasure. After twenty or twenty-five minutes, the guard knocked on the door. "Get dressed!" I got dressed and waited. It was very hot in the shower room. I must have waited for almost an hour. My clothes stuck to my skin; sweat poured down my body. Finally, the guard came and led me across the large courtyard into a three-story building. We stopped on the first floor, in front of cell number 61. The guard ordered me to take off my clothes. When I objected that I was drenched in sweat, he screamed at me and started to tear off my clothes. He examined them minutely for about half an hour, while I stood stark naked on a stone floor in the middle of December, at a temperature of at least minus twenty-five degrees Celsius. I was sure I would catch pneumonia; fortunately, I only got a cold.

The guard opened the cell door. I didn't trust my eyes—had I landed in hell? A room about eight meters long by five meters wide, densely filled with half-naked bodies. Some of them had trousers on; others, only underpants; but everyone's chest was bare. Some were lying on long bunks attached to the walls, while those who couldn't fit on the bunks sat, squatted, or lay on the floor. It was impossible to step in without treading on somebody.

Hundreds of eyes were staring at me. I stood rooted to the ground. A man in the middle of the room made an effort to approach me; he asked the others to make room for him; finally, he reached me. "You'll have to settle down over here for the time being," he said, pointing at a spot next to a *parasha*, a latrine pail. "Tomorrow or the day after, I'll assign you a better place." This man was the cell's elder.

There were two large *parashas*, one on either side of the door, each of them covered with a lid. The prisoners were allowed only two visits to the toilet, in the morning and in the evening; in between, those buckets were used.

I squatted down next to one of the *parashas*. A number of prisoners immediately crowded in on me, asking where I came from, why I had been arrested, and so on. When they learned that I was a foreigner, they told me there were several foreigners in the cell. It wasn't long before I got to know some of them.

The cell had been built to hold roughly twenty-four prisoners. Two hundred and five men were crammed into that room; at times, there were as many as two hundred and fifty. Since the cell was only rarely aired, a horrible stench pervaded it. The heat was so intense that prisoners frequently fainted.

At 5 a.m., the cell would come to life; the door would open—time to go to the latrine. Many waited with great impatience for this moment, for in the course of the night the *parashas* filled up and became unusable. Four men were assigned to empty the buckets each day; it was their job as well to keep order in the cell.

Since there weren't enough latrines for all the inmates to use at the same time, we were taken there in three groups. There were basins in the latrine where one could wash up. Only a few men had towels. Most of us dried ourselves with a handkerchief or with our shirts.

At eight, we were given breakfast—bread in boxes, four hundred grams for each prisoner. The guard would deliver the bread, and the *starosta*, the man elected elder by the other prisoners, would distribute it. In addition to bread we had "tea," which usually consisted either of hot water or of some kind of coffee substitute. Lunch as a rule consisted of half a liter of herb soup and a hundred fifty grams of millet or low-grade barley gruel. Dinner consisted of half a liter of soup.

The food was unpalatable by any standard, but for most prisoners, eating it was the only way to stay alive. In the beginning, I had to overcome a certain repugnance at mealtimes. Those prisoners who had money could buy various staples in the prison shop every ten days—bread, herring, margarine, sometimes butter and sugar as well. Smokers could buy tobacco and cigarettes. Shopping days were always a big event, not just because of what you could buy but because they broke up the monotony of prison life. Even those who had no money looked forward to the next shopping day, because they knew that they would receive some gifts. Most cells had organized a *kombed*—an aid committee for the poor. It was illegal to do so, since no solidarity among prisoners was allowed, not even this simple form of charity. Usually, everyone who could buy provisions sacrificed ten percent of his purchases for those who had no money.

Each prisoner was permitted to spend up to fifty rubles at a time; that was the monthly allotment he was allowed to receive from his relatives. The elder would go to the store with a shopping list, accompanied by five or six prisoners carrying sacks or large pieces of cloth. The shop was in an adjacent building. Purchases were made by weight, but of course there were no scales in the cell, so everything was divided into equal piles, and each prisoner would get approximately the amount he had ordered. For about five days after a shopping day, a good mood would prevail in the cell, until the provisions ran out and people began to wait impatiently for the next shopping day.

In the evening, after the signal for silence, the problem would be where to lie down. We lay in such densely packed rows that we could hardly breathe. You couldn't turn over unless the entire row did it with you. Those who found room on a bunk were fortunate; most of us had to sleep on the floor. The most difficult thing, at night, was reaching the *parasha* and finding your way back to your place.

Every day, we had a fifteen-minute walk. Since the prison was overcrowded, the day wasn't long enough, and prisoners were taken for walks at night as well. We were frequently awakened at two or three in the morning and led outside. Once a month, all the prisoners were herded into another cell. There they were made to undress, and every piece of clothing was examined with the utmost thoroughness. Forbidden items like needles and pieces of tin or metal, which were always of use to the prisoners, were confiscated. The search would usually last four or five hours. We were often led to the baths at night; while we were bathing, our clothes would be disinfected.

The first foreigner I got to know in the Butyrki was the Hungarian communist Lantos. When I arrived in cell 61, I was shown a man sitting in a corner, who, I was told, did not want to speak to anybody. He was an intellectual type, wore spectacles, and was skeletally thin. The expression on his face was not an agreeable one. I approached him and greeted him in Russian. He looked at me but didn't answer. I didn't want to impose, so I withdrew. However, the next day, by chance, we got into a conversation. The first thing I noticed was that Lantos spoke hardly a word of Russian; but he did speak German. I learned that he came from Budapest. I wasn't able to find out anything more about him; but he seemed to enjoy listening to me tell my own story.

Several days passed. Then Lantos, who had been in the Butyrki for four months, was suddenly called to a hearing; he didn't come back until the following afternoon. He didn't say a word, but everyone could tell he had been beaten. I tried to talk to him, but he evaded all my questions and finally told me roughly to mind my own business.

One day, I was called to a hearing again, at 11 p.m., as usual. When

I stepped into the hearing room, Revzin, Grushevsky, and two young men were sitting there. Grushevsky was in charge of taking down the evidence. He asked questions; I answered them. He didn't like my answers. Once again, he "encouraged" me to admit that I was a Gestapo agent, and I repeated that I was innocent and would never sign such a statement. Thereupon, the two young officials, who had been silent until then, assailed me with a flood of the most vulgar insults—"fascist," "traitor," and "spawn of a whore" being the mildest—and simultaneously started to tear the clothes off my body.

I had an idea what was to come. I turned to Revzin. "Give me one more day. I want to think it over."

Revzin told his young henchmen to leave me be. He and Grushevsky once again appealed to my good sense. "You can't fool around with the NKVD."

I was taken back to my cell.

The next evening, when I was called again to the hearing, I refused to go. The guard was surprised and didn't know what to do. He pondered for a little while; then he roared at me, but I didn't pay any attention and crawled off to the farthermost corner of the room.

The guard left. Ten minutes later, he came back with the chief guard. "Come here, you son of a bitch!" he shouted, stepping in the door. I didn't budge. The chief guard continued threatening and cursing.

"I will not go to a hearing until the Public Prosecutor comes here in person."

The chief guard multiplied his threats; then he plied me with promises. I refused to budge from my place. The chief guard left. After an hour, the door opened again; outside stood the prison warden with a small detachment of NKVD soldiers.

"Get over here this minute, who the hell do you think you are? Do you think we're playing games here?"

"I'll go if the Public Prosecutor comes, and that's all I've got to say," I replied from my corner.

It was impossible to reach me in the overcrowded cell. The warden ordered the cell cleared. Ten minutes later, I was sitting alone in the corner of the cell. On the warden's order, the soldiers rushed at me, put me in a straitjacket, dragged me like a sack into the cellar, and dumped me in the "cooler."

This dungeon was two stories deep in the ground. There was a row of twelve cells in a long corridor—single cells and cells for four to six men. I was put in a single cell; but there were four men in there with me. A bunk was fastened to the wall. Two men could manage to sleep on it with some effort; the others had to sleep on the floor. An electric light burned day and night over the door. Compared to the mass quarters, this cell was comfortable, since the four inmates could at least turn around and walk two or three steps. A small tin bucket stood in the corner—the *parasha*. Every day, we were given three hundred grams of bread and a pot of warm water—that was all. I was tormented by hunger. In the mass cell, the heat had been unendurable; this cell was bitter cold.

After five days, I was brought back to cell 61. Lantos asked me why I, a communist, was creating such problems for the prison administration. In his opinion, a communist in Soviet Russia must act like a communist even in prison.

"The interrogator and the administration are using fascist methods against me, and I will defend myself as effectively as I can," I replied.

Thereupon, Lantos began to expound on the theory that communists had to make sacrifices if the party demanded it of them. I could not understand what possible advantage the workers' movement and the communist state could derive from my allowing myself to be beaten half to death if I didn't confess.

Finally, Lantos began to tell his own story. He had been the secretary of the clandestine Hungarian Communist Party. For two years, he had lived illegally in Budapest, where, together with a few others, he had led the Hungarian communist movement. An opposition group had developed among the leadership; Lantos disagreed with its line. Instead of working on the organization of the masses, day after day was spent in sterile disputation about various fine points of orthodoxy. Finally, they decided to make a telephone call to the highest authority, the Executive Committee of the Communist International in Moscow. Hungary's representative in that body was Béla Kun, former chairman of the Council of People's Commissars of the Hungarian Soviet Republic. Béla Kun accused Lantos of forming a dissident faction and summoned him to Moscow. Lantos went, and was immediately arrested, incarcerated, abused, and brutalized. Eventually, he confessed to having infiltrated the Communist Party as a spy for the Horthy regime, subverting the party and delivering many honest communists to the Horthy police.

I asked Lantos whether there wasn't at least a grain of truth in these charges.

"Everything in my signed confession is a lie. I am convinced that the group that accused me of these crimes is in the employ of the Horthy police," he replied.

A second foreigner I got to know in cell 61 was a butcher from Mukachevo in Carpathian Russia. He was always called by his first name, Mishka; that's why I've forgotten his surname. I couldn't determine his nationality either—he was equally fluent in Rumanian, Yiddish, Hungarian, and Ukrainian. Mishka was perhaps the only guilty man in the entire cell. He said he had been a member of the Communist Party in Carpathian Russia, which at that time was part of Czechoslovakia. It became apparent that an informer had infiltrated Mishka's organization, for the police knew all about its activities. Suspicion fell on a Jewish girl who had fled from Poland to escape persecution by the police there. This girl had only recently joined the Communist Party of Mukachevo.

On the party secretary's insistence, a resolution was passed to "liquidate" the girl; i.e., to murder her. The assignment fell to Mishka. He asked the Polish girl to accompany him to a river, under the pretext of carrying out a mission for the party. Having led her to a secluded spot, he strangled her and threw her body in the river. But the girl was merely stunned, not dead; she regained consciousness in the cold water. To his horror, Mishka saw the girl swimming to the other bank. He ran across the railway bridge to the other side and caught up with his victim. The girl pleaded with Mishka to let her live, and he promised to release her if she would admit to being an informer. She insisted on her innocence. Now Mishka carried out his assignment more thoroughly. He pulled out a knife and stabbed the girl.

After a while, the corpse was found, but the police could not determine the identity of either the murderer or his victim. Later it turned out that the girl had been innocent and that the informer had been the party secretary himself. He had ordered the girl's "liquidation" to clear himself of suspicion.

In the end, the police caught scent of Mishka's part in the crime. He fled to the Soviet Union and lived there for a while. When the real informer of the Mukachevo organization was unmasked and the Polish girl's innocence was proved, Mishka was arrested by the NKVD. In his defense, he maintained that he had carried out the assassination on the party secretary's orders.

A group of prisoners was brought in from a provincial prison; they were to be confronted with prisoners in Moscow. One of them, a young engineer named Misha Levikinov, was put into our cell. When he learned that we were all political prisoners, he was very frightened. He had never been politically active, he said; he was only interested in his work and in his young wife and infant son. Levikinov could talk for hours about his wife and child.

His wife did not know that he had been arrested; he had been away from home on a professional assignment and was expected to return in five days. His wife would be waiting at the train station with their child, and he wouldn't be there! What would she think? Surely she would suspect an accident; that would be the main thing she would worry about. His wife loved him very much, but she wished he was in a different line of work, because of the danger. One high-voltage shock and it would be all over. But Misha hoped he'd be able to clear everything up by Saturday; maybe he'd be able to return home before then.

Several days passed, and Misha Levikinov's name was not called. Saturday came, and he still didn't know why he had been arrested. I asked him whether he remembered saying something he shouldn't have said. He thought about it for a long time, but couldn't remember anything.

On Sunday morning, he came to me. "You know, I spent the whole night thinking about this. All I can remember is getting mad because I was sent some defective insulation material. Do you really think anyone could get arrested for that?" He looked at me expectantly.

"What can I tell you? Everything is possible here."

Finally, Misha was called to a hearing. After two hours, he returned to his cell. His livid face revealed that something terrible had happened to him. Without saying a word, he sat down in a corner and began to cry, quietly at first, and then loudly. I tried to console him—in vain.

Some of the men called out to him: "You should be ashamed of yourself, blubbering like a woman. Don't be a sissy!"

When Misha finally calmed down, he told us that the interrogator had shouted at him as he entered the room: "You Trotskyite swine, you snake, tell us about your Trotskyite activities, you bastard son of a bitch!"

After abusing him in this manner for some time, the interrogator dismissed him, telling him to think the matter over very carefully and confess. Otherwise, his wife, too, would be arrested, and his child would be an orphan. Misha's despair was boundless. He ate almost nothing, and at night you could hear him sobbing and crying. After fourteen days, he was skinny as a rail. He brooded constantly, wondering what all this meant, since he wasn't conscious of having done anything wrong. One evening, about twenty minutes after the signal for sleeping had been given—we were already lying down—the *kormushka,* the door hatch, was pushed open, and the guard called quietly: "Levikinov!"

Misha leapt up in a fright. "What, what?" he shouted, without even noticing who it was that had called him. Finally, he went to the door.

"Get ready for your hearing."

Misha got dressed and went to the door, where he was received by the soldier who would accompany him to the hearing room. Misha returned in the morning. We had kept his bread for him; the *kipyatok*— the pot full of hot water—stood on the table. Misha didn't want to eat, all he had was two mugs of hot water.

No one dared ask Misha what he had been through. He began telling his story of his own accord: "The first thing he asked was: 'Tell us about your counterrevolutionary Trotskyite activities.' I told him what my life was like, all the things I did in my free time. He listened to everything without interrupting me. Then, suddenly, he asks me: 'Were you ever a member of the Komsomol [the Communist Youth League]?' I told him that when I was very young I had been a member of the Komsomol. 'Name some people who belonged to that Trotskyite organization.' I told him it wasn't a Trotskyite organization, and that today, ten years later, I had only a dim memory of those people's names. 'Trotskyite dog, give me the names of those bandits or I'll make mincemeat out of you!' I swore that I had never been a Trotskyite and that I couldn't remember the names of the other Komsomol members. The interrogator read a few names off a list. Then I remembered them. 'You see,' he says, 'now that you remember the names, go ahead and remember how you used to run around praising Trotsky.' I couldn't remember anything like that. At that moment, four people were called in who told me to my face that I was one of the people who had signed a resolution in support of Trotsky. I said that I *had* signed the resolution, along with most of my friends, but that I'd had no dealings with Trotskyites. The interrogator wrote a report on our session, and I signed it. It said I was a member of a Trotskyite organization."

Six weeks later, Levikinov was taken from our cell. A few days later, we found some words scrawled on the wall of the bathroom: "Misha Levikinov—ten years camp."

Several days after I returned from confinement in the cellar, I was called to another interrogation. This time, only Grushevsky was present. When I stepped into the room, he welcomed me with a smile and asked me why I had refused to come to the earlier hearing. He assured me that no one wished to hurt me. When I asked him why the men had torn my clothes off, he said they had been doctors and had intended to give me a "medical examination." I just looked at him, but he pretended to be absorbed in paperwork.

After a while, he stood up, walked back and forth in the room, and tried to prove to me that my stubborn refusal to sign a confession was unreasonable and would have unfortunate consequences for me.

"You can chop me to pieces," I said, "but I will not sign a false confession."

"None of this will be of any use to you. Whether you sign a confession or not, you will not be able to get out of here. But if you sign, you'll be granted certain advantages. If you don't sign, you'll have a very difficult time in the camp, take my word for it."

The years I spent in prisons and labor camps have proved Grushevsky right. Prisoners were punished not only according to the paragraph that determined their crime but also according to the "degree of danger" they represented. A character analysis by the interrogating officer accompanied each convict to the camp he was assigned to.

The case of Vorobyov is an example of the way the NKVD extracted confessions from its victims. He was my bunk neighbor, and he told me how he had been forced to sign his confession.

Vorobyov, an engineer and party member, had gone to England with a Soviet import delegation to purchase various factory equipment. When he returned, he was arrested and accused of sabotage. His interrogator wanted him to confess to having deliberately bought the wrong machinery in order to impede the development of socialism in Russia. Vorobyov was told that he had acted on orders from the British bourgeoisie, who wanted to prevent Russia from industrializing. Vorobyov firmly refused to "confess" to this absurd accusation. One night, he was called to an interrogation; two hours later, he returned a broken man to his cell. We couldn't get anything more specific from him than a single brief statement: "I signed everything."

The next day, when he had recovered, Vorobyov told us how his "confession" was obtained. "I was led into the interrogator's room as usual. The interrogator asked whether I was finally ready to confess everything, and I replied that I hadn't committed any crimes and therefore had nothing to confess. Whereupon the interrogator said: 'I recommend that you sign everything immediately, because we have to close your case today.' Again I refused. Whereupon the interrogator made a telephone call and said, 'Bring in the witnesses against Vorobyov.' I was quite surprised at that. I wondered: What sort of witnesses? After a few minutes, I heard some loud crying. I recognized my wife's voice. The door opened, and in came my wife, my nine-year-old daughter, and my twelve-year-old son. When they saw me, they all began to cry loudly, rushed over to me, embraced and kissed me, and said: 'Papa, Papa, sign it, don't ruin our lives. If you sign, they'll let you come home. If you don't, they'll lock us up, too!' Before I could say anything, the interrogator butted in: 'Aren't you ashamed of yourself? Your wife and children are begging you to admit your guilt, and still you deny it! Just sign, and in three days you'll be able to join your family.' Again, the children begged me to sign. I just couldn't bear it. I signed."

Vorobyov was given ten years in a camp. His wife was sent into exile.

LEFORTOVO

Several months passed. Finally, in August 1937, I was summoned. "Leave your stuff!" it was a hearing.

I was led into the courtyard and toward the gate, and there I saw the familiar NKVD bread truck. I thought I was being taken to a hearing at the Lubyanka and wondered why the trip was taking so long. When the truck stopped and I got out, I didn't know where I was. I could see this was a large prison, though, since I was surrounded by buildings with barred windows. I was led to a door, where an NKVD officer received me. A soldier stood by his side. The officer asked for my first and last name and the year of my birth. Then he told the soldier to search me. I had to strip, my clothes were thoroughly examined, and after I got dressed again, the soldier shackled my hands and feet. "Move!"

I walked with difficulty, prodded along by the soldier. We climbed several flights of stairs. Then he opened a heavy iron gate and pushed me in. I was in a bare stone cell, with no more than a square meter to move around in. There was a stool in one corner, cemented onto the floor: I sat down and tried to think.

Several hours passed. I was hungry, so it had to be time for the evening soup; I had left the Butyrki shortly after lunch. But no food came;

I waited a while longer, and finally knocked on the door. The peephole opened, and the guard asked me what I wanted. I asked whether I had been forgotten at mealtime.

"What mealtime? It's one o'clock in the morning!" The lid dropped over the peephole.

I sat down. What now? What did they plan to do with me? A long time passed; I could no longer sit up, so I lay down on the concrete floor. I fell asleep. After a while, I woke up but felt too weak to stand. Again, a long time passed. Then the door opened and a soldier ordered me to come out.

I mustered all my strength and walked out into the hallway, but I was dizzy. Two soldiers held me under the arms and led me across another courtyard into a different building and up a flight of stairs to the second floor. There the soldiers opened a door; I stood in a long, brightly lit room with padded doors on right and left. I had to wait for a few minutes and looked around. There were pictures of Stalin, Molotov, Kaganovich, and Beria on the walls. The hands of a clock pointed to ten after two. So it was night.

After a while, I was taken to another room. A man in civilian clothes sat behind a desk. Next to him stood a man in an NKVD uniform. To my right, next to the wall, sat a man whose features seemed familiar. His face was covered with beard stubble. "This is a confrontation. Do not ask the witness any questions without my permission," said the man at the desk. "Do you know this man?" he asked.

"He looks familiar."

"Who is he?" asked the interrogator.

"I don't remember."

"Think."

I tried, but I wasn't able to recall where I had seen him before.

The interrogator turned to the witness and asked him, pointing at me: "Do you know this man?"

"Yes."

"Who is he?"

"That is Steiner."

"How did you get to know Steiner?"

"I got to know him through Eimike."

"Who is Eimike?" the interrogator asked.

"Eimike is the chief agent of the Gestapo in the Soviet Union."

"What do you know about Steiner?"

"Eimike told me that Steiner is also a Gestapo agent."

"Steiner, what do you have to say about that?"

"This man is either insane or else he's a provocateur."

At this, the interrogator leapt up and rushed at me, punched me several times in the face, and showered me with the most vile abuse. Blood spurted from my nose; I blacked out. When I recovered consciousness, a soldier was standing in front of me with a glass of water and a towel. He wiped the blood from my face. Someone brought me a glass of tea and forced me to drink it. The interrogator gave an order to have my shackles removed. Only then did I notice that the witness was no longer in the room.

The commissar had him brought back in. "Schütz, do you affirm the statements you have just made?" the commissar asked.

When I heard the name Schütz, I remembered who he was. This was the coffeehouse acquaintance who had sat at the table with me in the Metropol Café and introduced me to Eimike. I had hardly known him then, and his pre-trial detention had changed his appearance considerably.

He didn't immediately answer the interrogator's question. The interrogator leapt up and roared at him, asking if he wanted to go back to the punishment cell. Thereupon, Schütz said very softly, almost inaudibly: "Yes, I affirm everything." He stood up, leaned over the desk, and signed the deposition.

Again, the interrogator tried to break me down with a barrage of insults. Then the uniformed NKVD officer went to the door, called in a soldier, and said, pointing at me: "Get this animal out of here!"

I was led back to the tiny stone cell. Solitude now felt like a blessing. About an hour later, I was led into an ordinary cell—a single cell, with an iron bed that was folded up against the wall during the day.

Morning came, and I was given a piece of bread—about half a kilogram—and hot water. I felt better after eating. I could move again. I walked back and forth in the cell a few times, but got tired quickly. I sat down on the bench, laid my head on the little table, and went to sleep. "No sleeping!" That was the guard's voice calling through the door hatch.

I wasn't alone for very long. On the fourth day, a man was brought in whose name I've forgotten. All I remember is his telling me that he was the secretary of a member of the Academy named Gubkin, and that he had been brought here from the Butyrki. He was accused of being a Trotskyite. I found out from him that we were in a military prison called Lefortovo. That evening, he was called to a hearing; he didn't come back to the cell.

Lefortovo, where I was for two weeks, deserves to be called a hell. At night, you could hear horrible screams from all sides. Interrogation rooms and cells faced each other, separated only by the width of a corridor. There wasn't a quiet minute; if you weren't being tortured yourself, you had to endure the indescribable pain of listening to other people's suffering.

Women were treated with particular harshness. Most of them weren't locked up for their own "crimes"; they were accused of having been their husbands' accomplices. Beatings, solitary confinement, and other forms of torture were used to force the women to implicate their husbands.

Many women had been arrested for having "connections with an enemy of the people"—that is, with their own husbands. The punishment for this was usually ten years in a camp in the extreme northern latitudes of Russia, or banishment to Siberia. The children of arrested parents were put in special NKVD homes, unless relatives volunteered to adopt them—but that, too, could incur suspicion of having "connections with an enemy of the people"; that is why many people chose to conceal their family relationship to victims of the NKVD.

Several days later, I was brought before the same interrogator. He asked his stereotype question: Had I finally decided to sign my confession? I repeated that I was innocent. Thereupon, he said he would give me fifteen minutes to think it over, and if I didn't sign then, I would be shot. I was taken back to my cell, just a few steps down the hall. Fifteen minutes later, I was brought back to his room.

The interrogator asked: "All right now, will you sign, or won't you?"

"I've thought this over carefully. I would rather die than sign a false confession," I replied.

The interrogator pulled out a pocket watch. "I'll give you another five minutes."

I said nothing.

After a while, he pressed a button. A soldier came in.

"Bring in the lieutenant."

A young officer appeared.

"Eliminate this man, he's another stubborn case, I have nothing more to say to him," said the interrogator to the young lieutenant.

The lieutenant tore off my clothes and threw them in a corner. Then he went to the telephone and shouted into the speaker: "Two men in full gear, third floor, room 314!" Two soldiers came in with rifles and mounted bayonets.

I was shivering from head to toe. Not that I was cold; sweat was running down my forehead. The soldiers took me by the arms. The young lieutenant ordered: "Forward march!"

I couldn't walk. The soldiers propelled me along several corridors and then down to the cellar. Another officer approached us there. He asked the young lieutenant where I was being taken. The lieutenant reported: "He refuses to confess. We're going to execute him."

"Take him back. Give it one more try."

I was taken back to the cell. My clothes were there. I lay down on the bed and covered myself, but I couldn't calm down. My teeth were chattering, my whole body was shivering.

I was never called back for another hearing. Three days later, I was brought before the prison warden. He handed me a typewritten sheet of paper and told me to read and sign it. It said:

INDICTMENT
It has come to the attention of the NKVD of the U.S.S.R. that the
political immigrant Karl Steiner was recruited by the Gestapo, that
he was active as a German spy, and that he planned acts of sabotage.
Toward these ends, the accused cultivated extensive contacts with
foreigners and Soviet citizens. In addition, Steiner belonged to the
organized group that assassinated the Secretary of the Central Committee of the Communist Party of the Soviet Union, Sergei Miron-
ovich Kirov. Despite obstinate denials on the part of the accused,
his crime has been proven by the testimony of witnesses. Charges
are brought against the accused, therefore, in accordance with Article
58, paragraphs 6, 8, and 9. In accordance with the decree of 1 December 1935, the accused is herewith transferred to the jurisdiction
of the Military Tribunal of the Supreme Court of the U.S.S.R.

Chief Prosecutor of the U.S.S.R.
Vyshinsky

At the sight of this indictment, I lost all my illusions about the
possibility of being released. I saw how right those people were who had
said: Once you're arrested by the NKVD, you'll never get out. According
to NKVD principles, everyone who is arrested is guilty. The court procedure is a mere formality designed to maintain the appearance of prin-
cipled legal procedure. It didn't take long for me to find that out.

BEFORE THE MILITARY TRIBUNAL

On the night of September 6, 1937, I was removed from my cell and
locked up in the concrete box I had been in before. In contrast to the
first time, when I had not been fed at all, I was now given roughly four
hundred grams of bread and a pot of hot water twice a day. Two days
later, my door was opened at 11 p.m., and four soldiers ordered me to
follow them. Two of them walked ahead of me; the other two, behind
me. We went up several flights of stairs, to a room roughly thirty square
meters in size. In it was a large table covered with green cloth, and near
it a smaller table. A soldier ordered me to sit down.

A few minutes later, an officer marched in briskly and shouted:
"Attention, the court is arriving!"

Three high-ranking officers stepped in and took seats at the green
table. A young uniformed man sat down at the smaller table: the court
stenographer.

The officer who was sitting in the middle announced: "The Military
Court of the Soviet Union opens procedures against Karl Steiner, accused
of committing crimes punishable according to Article 58, paragraphs 6,
8, and 9, of the Penal Code. Accused, rise to your feet. Do you confess
your guilt?"

"No, I am completely innocent."

"How did you come to Russia?" asked the chairman.

I had scarcely begun to speak when he interrupted me: "Speed it up!"

I tried to continue but was interrupted again. "Do you wish to say anything by way of a conclusion?"

I had barely opened my mouth when the chairman interrupted me again: "We know all that. Enough!"

I tried once again to profess my innocence. The chairman turned his head to one side, then to the other, mumbling a few words to the two officers next to him, after which all three stood up and left the room. A soldier ordered me to sit down.

After a short time, the judges returned. Again I was told to stand up. The chairman read something off a piece of paper he held in his hand. All I heard was: "Ten years' isolation, under severe regime!"

The trial had lasted no more than twenty minutes. Neither a public prosecutor nor a defense attorney had been present. I was led out of the "courtroom." A soldier opened a cell just a few feet down the hall and shoved me in. I was among the condemned.

The cell was full of people who had been sentenced on the same day by this same military tribunal, eighteen men altogether—all in the course of four hours. Among them were workers, peasants, engineers, party functionaries, even a circus director. When I stepped into the cell, I wasn't asked how many years I had gotten. They all knew. Everyone who had been brought into that cell before me and after me was given a ten-year sentence. The same procedure, the same judgment. That, at least, is what I was told by the other condemned men; I had no way of verifying it, since no one was given a written copy of the judgment. Such a document would have been useless in any case, for there was no way to appeal the sentence, or to ask for clemency.

That is how justice was practiced under Stalin by his henchmen Vyshinsky, Smirnov, Ulrich, Matulevich, and others.

EN ROUTE TO SIBERIA

On September 7, 1937, around eight o'clock in the evening, we were all led into the prison courtyard. A transport truck was waiting there, already half filled with other prisoners who had been sentenced the previous day. We were thirty-two altogether. We were first taken to the transit quarters of the Butyrki prison. The initial procedure was identical to the one I had been subjected to as a pre-trial detainee: the same thorough search, the same soft soap, the same shouts: "Hurry up! Move!"

There was a church in the middle of the large courtyard. During the tsarist period, prisoners attended religious services there. Now the building served as a transit station. There were three floors, equipped with cells of all sizes. Most of these cells had a triple tier of bunks. All of the rooms were overcrowded. Cells originally built for thirty or forty prisoners were used to hold as many as ten times that amount. Not surprisingly, the hygienic conditions were abominable beyond description. There were no latrines at all, only two large wooden *parashas*.

There were no bunks in our cell; we had to sleep on the floor. But at least there was a table. I had the good fortune of finding a place on the top of the table, which I had to share with another prisoner. It was already fall, and it was cold, especially at night. We on the table were envied by the others, who had to sleep on the stone floor. In the morning, we were given a pail filled with water. That had to suffice for eighteen men to wash their hands and faces.

Our life was quiet during the ten days we spent there. Having been sentenced, we were no longer called to nocturnal hearings. We passed the time telling each other the plots of books we'd read.

Next to me was Vasily Mikhailovich Chuprakov, chief engineer of a Moscow factory called Kompressor. He was a tall, powerfully built man with blond hair and blue eyes, a classic Russian type, born in the northern Russian city of Kotlas. Vasily couldn't spend a moment without performing some kind of work; he was always busy. Now he was mending the other prisoners' clothes.

Almost every man told the story of his life. Only Yefim Morozov, the circus director, did not say a word. He sat in a corner, sighing and groaning.

One day, it was my turn. I told the story of my arrival in Moscow, and of my life there during the four years preceding my arrest.

It was September 14, 1932, when I first set foot in the capital of the country where, I believed, my ideals had become a reality. I had traveled there from Berlin, via Lithuania. I remember the pouring rain as I stepped out of the train station and rushed toward the car that was waiting for me on the open square. The next day, following the instructions I had been given by Georgi Dmitrov, the representative of the Executive Committee of the Communist International in Berlin, I promptly reported to the director of the OMS (the Communist International's Department of International Relations), a man named Abramov. Abramov's assistant conducted me through the various barriers and controls. Abramov called Chernomordik, the organization's economic manager, and instructed him to arrange for my room and board. And he told his secretary to give me five hundred rubles pocket money. "Rest for a few days, then come back to see me," said Abramov.

I wandered around Moscow for a month, getting to know the city. Then boredom began to set in, and I decided to visit Abramov. The NKVD official checking me in at the offices of the Comintern's Executive Committee gave me a suspicious look when I mentioned Abramov's name;

then he made a phone call. Fifteen minutes later, I was given a *propusk,* a pass, to visit Abramov. Finally, I arrived at Abramov's waiting room. The secretary greeted me like an old acquaintance, asked me how I liked Moscow and how I was feeling. Almost an hour passed before the secretary led me into Abramov's office.

Abramov's diminutive figure was almost swallowed up by his big armchair. A pair of sharp eyes gazed at me through gold-framed glasses. Abramov asked me a few questions, which I answered. The last of these questions was: "Do you consider yourself capable of directing a *special* sort of print shop and publishing outfit?" He stressed the word "special."

I replied that I had sufficient experience of that sort.

"Very well, then. Report to Comrade Kolarov tomorrow. I shall talk to him in the meantime."

Kolarov was the director of the Communist International's Balkan division. His office was in the former palace of the Russian industrialist Morozov, at 14 Vozdvizhenka Street (now Kalinin Prospect). The doorman—he was wearing an NKVD uniform—asked my name, searched for it on a list, and said: "Just a moment!"

I was about to sit down when the chief of Kolarov's secretariat appeared. He introduced himself: "Stepan Adamovich Bergmann. Comrade Kolarov is waiting for you."

I entered Kolarov's room, accompanied by Bergmann. Kolarov remained seated in his armchair as he held out his hand to me. In contrast to Abramov, he appeared amiable. Of medium height, somewhat corpulent, with a bald head and a short neck, he looked more like a merchant than the old radical who had dynamited the Cathedral of Sofia, Bulgaria, in 1922, killing hundreds of people, among them ministers of state, generals, and high officials.

Kolarov rang a bell. A young girl appeared in the doorway. Kolarov said: "Order three glasses of tea."

While we drank the aromatic tea, Kolarov asked me questions about my trip, about Berlin, about how Comrade Dmitrov was doing. He also wanted to know my opinion about the political situation in Germany. The general expectation there, I said, is that Hitler will seize power in a matter of weeks, or months at the most.

"We won't allow that to happen," Kolarov said. And turning to Bergmann, he said: "Take care of the rest of the matter with Comrade Steiner."

I took leave of Kolarov and followed Bergmann to his office. After discussing my future work with him for almost two hours, he led me from department to department and introduced me to the various department heads: the Bulgarians Goryev, Selesov, and Boykikyev; the Yugoslavians Filipovic, Copič (Senko), and Vujovič (Gregor); the Rumanians Anna Pauker and Mironescu. There were some Poles, too, like Verski and Mikhailchuk, as well as people from the Baltic countries. The Balkan

department, which took up the entire Morozov Palace, also occupied a
new three-story building in the compound. That was where the International Agrarian Institute (MAI) printed and published its work.

In the course of the following two weeks, I became acquainted with
most of the multinational personnel that worked there. Right at the beginning, I made an unpleasant discovery. The dining room was divided
in two: a larger dining room for "ordinary" workers and employees, and
a smaller one for management. The large dining hall had a self-service
buffet that offered relatively simple fare; the small dining room resembled
an elegant restaurant, with waiters serving the finest cuisine.

Soon after I began working in my new office, I ordered the same
cuisine served in both dining halls at the same prices. This led to my first
clash with the Balkan department's troika, consisting of a representative
of management, the party secretary, and the secretary of the union. These
three men criticized my "schematic egalitarianism" and ordered me to
reverse my decision.

My second clash with the leadership occurred when I arranged to
have the Moscow meat combine supply us with three tons of tripe every
Saturday, in exchange for which we would do some printing for them.
For two weeks, on Saturdays, the workers received two to three kilograms
of meat to take home for themselves and their families. When Bergmann
noticed this, he asked the chief cook where the meat came from, and
learned of my deal with the meat combine. Bergmann reported this to
Kolarov, who had me summoned to his office and advised me to put a
stop to the distribution of meat. In his opinion, one group of workers
should not receive any rations in excess of what others were granted on
their ration cards.

In Vsevyatskoye, a suburb of Moscow, we had an apartment building
for our printers. There were mainly unmarried workers there; only a few
had families living with them. The furnishings were very primitive, and
the apartments hadn't been renovated in years: floors were rotting; paint
was peeling off walls and ceilings. Only after a good deal of arguing could
I persuade Kolarov and Bergmann of the need for a thorough renovation
of that building.

My predecessor, the Hungarian Ferencz (appointed by Béla Kun),
had been neglectful in his management of the company. I immediately
set about reorganizing it, and succeeded in turning this losing enterprise
into a profit-making one. Not surprisingly, I earned the respect of the
workers and employees. During a party purge in 1935, when I stepped
up to the podium to respond to the questions of the party commission,
the entire staff rose to their feet and, to my surprise, applauded me
enthusiastically.

The representative of the Yugoslav Communist Party, Vujovič, and
the representative of the Austrian Communist Party, Grossmann, spoke
of me as a courageous revolutionary. Various workers and employees stood

up to praise my activities in the plant. I was receiving so much unqualified praise that the chairman of the party commission, a Red Army general, specifically declared that he wished to hear only critical testimony against me. No one spoke up.

Several days later, the chairman of the party commission announced, to the applause of the entire assembly, that the commission had unanimously agreed to accept me as a member of the CPSU (Communist Party of the Soviet Union). I was also required to take part in public activities. I was taken to conferences and meetings where, as a "representative of the foreign proletariat," I had to tell the Russian workers how hard the lives of workers are in the capitalist countries.

One day, I was addressing the students of the Institute for Foreign Languages. Among the many young women I met there was a girl who eventually became my wife. Soon we found an apartment and lived there happily together.

Our friends were mainly emigrants from various European countries. Although most of them were disappointed by conditions in the Soviet Union, they tried not to be critical, and sought to explain them as vestiges of tsarist tyranny. Only rarely was some slight criticism expressed.

In August 1935, I returned from a vacation in the Caucasus and met with two surprising changes. My adjunct in the publishing house, Nikolai Markovich Lyubarsky, had been arrested—for "Trotskyism," as I learned at the party meeting later. The next surprise was the presence of a second adjunct in the print shop. Since I didn't need this second adjunct, I went to Kolarov and asked him to explain why this man had been appointed in my absence and without my approval. Kolarov as well as Bergmann proffered reassuring explanations: I was overworked, and besides there were plans to expand the company, after which I would definitely need a second assistant.

It soon turned out that my new adjunct, Smirnov, was a confidant of the NKVD. At first, he seemed modest and self-effacing; later he tried to take measures which I could not tolerate and therefore overrode. Little by little, Smirnov became more and more presumptuous. He began to criticize my decisions, always appealing to the authority of his superiors. Once, at a party meeting, he claimed that a "bourgeois spirit" prevailed in our company. I didn't have to respond: several workers repudiated the accusation.

On May Day 1936, I was given a citation and a large monetary award for "contributions toward the building of socialism in the U.S.S.R." My wife was especially pleased with the windfall, since we were expecting a child.

How different life was in Moscow! I regularly attended party meetings; they were always monotonous. Usually someone gave a lecture, and no matter what its title was, the content was always the same: the usual panegyric to Stalin and his "wise policies." Only rarely were matters of practical substance discussed. The discussions, too, were always the same; everyone knew that he had to mention Stalin's name at least once.

I often participated in company meetings as well. At first, I didn't know that the thesis of each speech had to be presented to the party secretary beforehand, and that he would insert whatever issues were of particular importance to the party at the time.

I did not have much private contact with my colleagues. Russians only rarely dared to have private dealings with foreigners. Relations between foreign and Russian communists were limited to their common participation in party meetings. My wife's relatives remained virtual strangers to me. None of them dared visit us. When her relatives learned of our plan to marry, Sonya was warned by all of them, and always for the same reason: "He's a foreigner!" Sonya's objection that I was a member of the party didn't assuage anyone's fears.

Once, at the park on Tverskoi Boulevard, I got into a conversation with a man I had not met before. We talked about harmless things, but as soon as he realized that I was a foreigner, he stood up and excused himself with these words: "You are a nice man, but it's better if I leave." And he walked off in a hurry.

A young girl named Tanya worked in the company; she was the secretary of the company's Komsomol group. One day, she invited me to visit her where she lived with her parents. I went. The parents and Tanya's married sister were very pleased to have me come. When I left, I promised to return. Several weeks later, I paid them a second visit. This time, Tanya's brother-in-law, a marine officer, was there, too. I immediately noticed how constrained the atmosphere was. Right after tea, I excused myself, saying that I had to attend a meeting, and left. The next day, Tanya told me she was sorry I had had to leave so early but that I had done the right thing, since her brother-in-law did not approve of having a foreigner in the apartment.

If I didn't want to lead a hermit's life, I had to content myself with the company of foreigners. Sometimes I would get together with friends and acquaintances visiting Moscow for a short time. I was always glad to learn from them what was happening in the outside world, and I was beginning to dream of leaving the country.

One day in 1934, I was sitting together with two friends, the former Comintern representative in Austria, Baral, and the director of the largest department store in Moscow, Vischnitz. We were talking about conditions in the Soviet Union, and I said: "The Austrian Social Democrats weren't able to convince me in fifteen years, but after a single day in Moscow I could see that their criticism was justified."

"Is that so?" Baral said. "We really ought to tell the Central Committee about that." Vischnitz agreed with a nod.

About a month after this conversation, I was summoned to the

Comintern's personnel division. The head of the division said: "Where do you think you are, sitting in a coffeehouse, chattering like that? Vienna?"

November 7, 1936, was approaching—the anniversary of the Revolution. Sonya and I had invited some friends to celebrate with us.

On November 4, I went to work as usual. The head of the planning commission brought me the report on the production quotas for the month of October: the plan had been overfulfilled by 29 percent. I called the department heads into my office and asked for the names of workers who should be rewarded with premiums. At lunchtime I went with Filipovic, commonly known as Boshkovic, to the cafeteria for Comintern officials that had recently opened in a wing of the Kremlin hospital.

"This beats Kempinski, wouldn't you say?" said Boshkovic. Kempinski was a famous restaurant in Berlin. I could neither confirm nor deny it, since I had never set foot in Kempinski.

In the afternoon, I went to the central administrative office of the polygraphy industry on Taganka Square to order materials for the coming year. After returning to work, I received a visit from the principal of the school that our company was patron of; she asked me for some money for the school and invited me to attend their celebration of the victory of the revolution on November 6. I promised to come. The chief bookkeeper objected to the amount I had set down as a holiday gift for the children of our employees. But after lengthy negotiations he gave his consent.

It was 6 p.m. by now. Before going home, I went to the dentist. I got home at eight. After dinner, I went for a walk with my wife. We went to bed at eleven.

That night, I was arrested.

When I finished my story, there was a long silence. To relieve the oppressiveness, the Ukrainian engineer Nemirovsky told of a tragicomic experience he had had during a cure in Kislovodsk in the Caucasus.

"When I showed up at the main desk and asked for a room, they told me there weren't any rooms available at the moment but I could share a room with another guest; and I was expressly told that my partner would be a 'very quiet and solid individual.' I was exhausted from my long trip, so I fell asleep right away. In my dreams I felt a strange anxiety and I woke up. In front of me stood my roommate with his arms stretched out as if about to strangle me. 'What do you want?' I asked him. Quivering from head to toe, he screamed: 'I know who you are! You're the one who's supposed to kill me! You've been following me for weeks! You're the one who threw a beer bottle at me in the coffeehouse yesterday!' I jumped out of bed and tried to reach the door, but the man barred my way. The noise woke up several neighbors. A male nurse came hurrying in as well.

The next morning, I learned that the man was suffering from a persecution mania and had been taken to a mental hospital."

On September 17, 1937, we were transported, under heavy escort, to the train station at Kursk. Two third-class passenger cars with barred windows were waiting for us on a sidetrack. One by one, we were taken from the transport truck and led into the train. There were about eighty men in each car. We had to sit quietly and converse in whispers. The big guessing game began: Where are they taking us?

Some of us tried to find out by asking the guards, but none of them dared answer. The cars stood in the station for two hours. Through the windows, we could see freight trains being shunted from track to track. The railroad workers looked at us curiously. Most of them showed signs of pity; some, especially the women, waved. Even though such transports were a daily occurrence, you could see how people, as soon as they noticed us behind barred windows, would try to pass by our cars as often as possible. Maybe they hoped to discover some relatives among us. Some women were known to search the train stations for weeks after accidentally learning that their husbands had been sentenced. I thought of Sonya and imagined how wonderful it would be to spot her among the searching women. How was she? Was she in good health? How was our child? I didn't know anything. Surely, I thought, she has searched all the prisons in Moscow to find some trace of me, and she probably still doesn't know anything.

Finally, our cars were coupled to a passenger train. Enviously, we watched people who were still able to move about at liberty, chatting over beer and wine in the railway café. Most of them had no idea that many among them would suffer the same fate as us. A whistle blew, and the train rolled out of the station. My heart contracted. Now we were leaving the city where I had worked for years, where my wife lived, and my child.

Where are we going? Will we ever come back?

My companions were in the same emotional state I was in; all were silent, some were crying. The train passed the suburbs of Moscow; we were heading southeast. At each end of the car stood a guard who observed all our movements. We were allowed to converse only in a low voice. In the Butyrki, we had been given provisions for two days: twelve hundred kilograms of bread, two salted fish, and two lumps of sugar.

Next to me sat Chuprakov and Mareyev. Mareyev had been the head of a large petroleum company in Moscow. He was short, broad-shouldered, with a round face, a potato nose, and blue-gray eyes—a typical Russian peasant. He was chewing on his bread and grinning. I gave him a questioning look.

"Nothing special," he said. "I was remembering my boss in the Ministry, a real party-liner. He was constantly saying that anyone who deviated from the party line should have a firecracker stuck up his ass. Well, the NKVD stuck a firecracker up his ass, and up mine too, and when they confronted us in prison, he told them I'd tried to recruit him for some counterrevolutionary organization. He's probably nibbling on a scrap of bread right now."

Suddenly our conversation was interrupted. A newspaper had been found under a bench, a copy of *Izvestia*. Maybe one of the guards had left it behind. I hadn't seen a newspaper in over a year, and had heard only fragments of rumors about the world outside. For us, this newspaper was like bread to a starving man. We read it with greedy curiosity, though we had to be very careful to keep the guards from noticing. We studied the *Izvestia* for an hour; then the soldiers realized what was going on and called their superior officer. We weren't able to hide the paper in time, and he took it away from us.

But now we had something to talk about, and time passed quickly. It was late afternoon when the train pulled into a station. We looked out the window and read: Vladimir.

THE VLADIMIR TRANSIT PRISON

The train was shunted onto a sidetrack, our cars were detached, and the train moved on. After a short time, three trucks arrived. Twenty-five prisoners were loaded into each one. I waited with the others while the first shipment drove off; half an hour later, the trucks returned for the rest of us. As we climbed into the trucks, an officer shouted: "Anyone who tries to escape will be shot!"

It was five in the morning when we drove through the empty streets of Vladimir. The prison stood on a hill just outside the city. We stepped off the trucks and joined the other prisoners, who were kneeling in front of the prison gate. We waited, kneeling, for more than two hours. Finally, the gate was opened.

"Attention, prisoners! Stand up!"

We were glad to be allowed to stand up. We were told to line up in rows of five and march through the gate. Then each man had to step forward and call out his first and last name, his patronymic, his birth date, the paragraph according to which he was sentenced, and the length of the sentence. Then we were taken to a room where we were not permitted to smoke or eat. This was strictly enforced. After a long wait, we were called out, one by one. Finally, it was my turn. I entered a room where I was stripped and searched. A soldier inspected every orifice in my body. He stuck his fingers so deep into my throat that I instinctively pushed his hand away, whereupon he called me a fascist. Later we were taken to a shower room, where the pleasantly warm water assuaged somewhat the humiliation of the body search.

Then, in another room, we were given new clothes made of dark blue cotton: a pair of pants, a shirt, and a short padded coat, called a *bushlat*, with brown patches on the elbows and knees. Each man also received a cap and a pair of pig-leather shoes with rubber soles. None of the clothes fit—some were too large; others too small. When we returned to our cells in our new clothes and with our heads shorn, we could scarcely recognize one another.

The Vladimir prison, about three hundred kilometers from Moscow, was a hundred and fifty years old, and it had always served as a transit station for prisoners on their way to labor camps in Siberia. It consisted of three buildings with mass cells, and a fourth, newer building, with the number 1912 chiseled into its red façade; that building had single cells. And there were some smaller buildings: a hospital, a bath, and a kitchen.

Our cell was on the ground floor. Light came into the room through the top of the windows—the lower half was walled up. But we never had sunlight, since the windows faced north. The bunks were arranged in two rows: seven in one row, six in the other. Between them was a table about the length of one of the iron bunks. Each man was given a sack filled with straw; a smaller, pillow-sized sack, also stuffed with straw; and a blanket. We had steam heat, but it didn't work well, so it was always cold. The cell was narrow; only two or three people could move about in the space between the bunks. The bunks and the table were cemented into the floor. In the corner was a tin *parasha*.

Most of the prisoners consoled themselves with the hope that from now on, cruel and unjust though our sentences were, we would at least not be tormented any longer with interrogations and solitary confinement. Every one of us yearned for a newspaper; everyone looked forward to the day when he would finally be allowed to write to his closest relatives and receive their replies. But how great was our disappointment! The reign of terror that prevailed here destroyed any lingering hope of rest or humane treatment. In some ways, it was worse than the Butyrki.

Twice a day, we were led to the toilet; but it was impossible for thirteen people to relieve themselves in the five to six minutes we were given. The guards chased us out before we could button our pants. We were constantly hungry: five hundred grams of bread, and slightly sweetened tea in the morning; herb or potato soup, with a tablespoon of gruel, for lunch; and the same again in the evening. The daily walk was a torment as well. The inmates of several cells were led out at the same time. To prevent these different groups from seeing one another, wooden walls divided the yard into small sections, one for each cell. Thirteen men would rotate in one such cubicle for a quarter of an hour, like mice on a treadmill, single file, with their hands on their backs and their eyes fastened on the ground. Anyone who raised his head went straight to the punishment cell. The warden who supervised our walks objected constantly to one thing or another: one man wasn't holding his hands properly on his back; another had glanced to the side. In the end, you were glad to be back in your cell, however much you needed the fresh air.

We were told that we could write two letters a month to our closest relatives. We were given postcards on which we could note our address and ask for money. After a week, I got a letter from my wife, with a photograph of our daughter. I wept for joy. Five days later, I received fifty rubles and bought myself bread, salt fish, sugar, and onions in the prison shop. Everyone who received money shared his provisions with the others, whether they had money or not.

We particularly enjoyed the books that were brought into our cell one day—each of us took one book. The prison had an excellent library—one of the few rays of light in the place. Reading Balzac, Dostoevsky, Tolstoy, or any of various technical and scientific works helped you forget the sad reality for a while.

A month after we arrived, the prison warden came to inspect our cell. He was powerfully built, a black-haired man with a large mustache and brutal features. Several prisoners asked him questions; he answered each with an insult. When the engineer Silenko asked whether he could work instead of just lying around idle, the warden said: "We can get along without you." (When the NKVD director Yezhov was liquidated, the warden of the Vladimir prison was arrested and shot—merely because he had been appointed by Yezhov.)

Either because of a cold or because of spoiled food, I got sick with diarrhea. At first, I thought it would go away by itself, but it got worse, so I asked to be taken to the prison doctor. His office was in a room on the ground floor, near our cell. I described my discomfort to the doctor; he didn't reply. I repeated my request for help—still no answer. The guard who had brought me in roared: "That's enough, shut up now!"

That made me so angry that I shouted back—even though I knew he was one of the worst bullies in the prison—telling him to leave me in peace, that I was sick and had to talk to the doctor. He was speechless with astonishment.

So I was taken back to my cell without having had a word from the doctor. When I told my comrades in the cell about it, they all agreed that my clash with the guard would land me in the punishment cell. But several days passed and I was not punished. Perhaps the guard hadn't reported my behavior to the warden. The nurse came into the cell, gave me medication, and said the doctor had prescribed a diet of white bread, bouillon, and stewed fruit.

The nurse was the only person in the prison who treated the inmates with human kindness. The rest of the personnel, from the warden to the guards, did not miss an opportunity to show their contempt. Consequently, the nurse was very much appreciated by everyone; the prisoners all liked to ask favors of her. She always had a friendly expression on her face, and when she smiled, you could see her beautiful white teeth. To this day, I find pleasure in remembering that noble presence in our midst.

When I received my first dietary ration, I was surprised at the lovely piece of white bread and the tasty stewed fruit; the bouillon, on the other hand, was unpalatable—a few dabs of grease swimming about on the surface of some lukewarm water. The next day, I didn't get the white bread, only the water-soup and a small portion of stewed fruit. I asked the guard why I wasn't getting any white bread.

"You eat what you get," he said.

I asked to speak to the chief guard. After a long wait, he came, and I said: "The doctor prescribed a diet for me, but instead of bouillon, I'm getting dishwater."

The chief guard dragged me out of the cell without saying a word; in the hall, the other guard grabbed me and twisted my arm. I screamed in pain, and also in protest. The chief guard covered my mouth with his hand, but I succeeded in twisting my head away and continued screaming as loud as I could. That persuaded the two men to let me go; quickly, they opened the cell and shoved me inside.

My cellmates urged me to be reasonable. It was useless to fight against monsters like that, they said; you'd always end up losing. I knew that myself, but at the moment I didn't care, I couldn't have acted any differently.

How great was my surprise the next day when, instead of being punished, I received a bowl of bouillon, as good as any homemade soup, and a pot full of stewed fruit and a goodly piece of white bread. We couldn't think of an explanation for this turn of events. We finally came to the conclusion that the guards were as terrorized by the warden as we were by them, and that they didn't dare report me, for fear of suffering reprisals themselves. I was served the special diet for two more days; after six days, I was well again, but I was so weak that I had to lie down several times during the day; this, however, was forbidden. The guard saw me lying on my back, opened the door, and told me to get up. I said I was feeling weak and asked for permission to lie on my back for another ten minutes. The guard called the chief guard and told him that I had been insubordinate.

The chief guard ordered me to follow him, led me to the other end of the hall, opened a heavy iron door, and shoved me inside. I was in the cooler!

This cell was no different from a cage for wild animals. The only objects on the stone floor were a stool and a pail to be used as a toilet. At midnight the guard, who constantly paced back and forth in front of the cell, shoved in a broad platform. I was supposed to lie on this object until six o'clock in the morning. But it was very cold, and I couldn't fall asleep; so I stood up and tried to warm up by moving around. The guard on duty that night had a human heart. He stepped up to the bars and asked me softly why I had been put in the punishment cell. He was no longer young, a gray-haired man of medium height, with good-natured features. In a whisper, he said to me: "Listen, my friend, I advise you to calm down, you don't seem to realize what a terrible place this is."

A little later, he brought me a piece of bread and some salt fish. After eating, I lay down and tried to fall asleep. But after a short while I felt sick and threw up. The next morning, the good man told the warden that I was seriously ill. Thanks to this kind man, I was taken to the doctor that same afternoon, and he ordered my return to the mass cell.

Several days later, we were told to gather up our personal belongings and were taken to a large room, where we presumed the usual search would take place. Instead, some two hundred prisoners were crammed together, among them many whom we knew from the Butyrki and from Lefortovo. We were allowed to converse freely, which surprised us greatly. Clearly, something unusual was about to take place. Soldiers carried in the bundles that had been taken from us the day we arrived. The warden told us to throw our prison garments in a pile and put on the clothing we had been wearing when we arrived from Lefortovo.

We were leaving Vladimir. We were glad of that; perhaps the next place would be better. But some feared that it might be worse. A guard detail took charge of us; they were to take us to our next destination. The commander of the guard checked our identities, comparing each face with a photograph in the prisoner's dossier. Then we were loaded on trucks and driven to the train station. There a train was waiting for us.

The trip was relatively pleasant; we were allowed to talk, even to sing softly. The guards were very decent—none of the usual harassment, and no cursing. Naturally, we would have liked to know where we were being taken, but the officer whom we asked only said: "You'll be better off there than in Vladimir. Only prisoners serving twenty-five-year sentences go to Vladimir now. You're probably going to a camp."

We were surprised to learn that there were twenty-five-year sentences. "That's right," said the officer, "Don't be so surprised. A law was passed in October. The maximum penalty's twenty-five years now, instead of ten." So we had been sentenced in the nick of time. Just a month later, the same "crimes" were punishable with twenty-five years. Only in rare exceptions were the sentences reduced to twenty or fifteen years.

During the trip, which lasted two days and two nights, each of us was given two portions of canned fish, two kilograms of black bread, and fifty grams of sugar. Whenever the train stopped for any length of time, the soldiers brought us hot water in pails.

When we reached Moscow and drove out from the Kursk station in the direction of Leningrad, we realized that we were heading for the subarctic. In Karelia, there were large camps for prisoners who were building the White Sea Canal and laying a second set of tracks for the Murmansk Railway. Hundreds of thousands of other prisoners were employed as woodcutters.

About halfway between Leningrad and Murmansk lies the station of Kem. That's where our train stopped. Our cars were detached and shunted onto a sidetrack. It was early morning. A gray, unfriendly landscape surrounded us: woods on one side, the White Sea on the other. A few houses alongside the tracks; many goats, but few people. A group of about eighty prisoners approached us, accompanied by armed guards. They passed close by our car. We could see their tired, sunken faces. When they looked in our direction, the soldier shouted at them. That's what we're in for, we thought.

Through the barred windows, we looked out at the eerily quiet gray sea. There was scarcely any movement; only once in a while did we see a gull or some driftwood by the shore. Suddenly a dark speck appeared in the distance. We stared at it as it got bigger, coming closer. It must be a ship, some prisoners assumed, and soon we could make it out: it was, in fact, a ship. Someone remarked: "Now we're going to the place where the devils say good night."

We grew more and more agitated as the ship approached. Many surmised that we would be taken to the notorious Solovetsk Islands. Finally, the ship dropped anchor. It wasn't far away, we could read the inscription: SLON (*Solovetsky lager osoboyo naznacheniya*—Solovetsk Islands Special Camp). Now there was no doubt . . .

The commander went from car to car; finally he reached us, stopped in front of the door, and shouted: "Attention, prisoners, prepare to exit with all your possessions! Any movement to the right or left is forbidden. Offenders will be shot!"

We stepped out one by one. Soldiers with submachine guns at the ready formed a corridor leading from the train to the ship. We marched single file down the steep corridor to the shore and onto the ship. It was a small freighter; we were put into the lower deck, where the freight would usually have been stowed.

When we were all on board, the commander of the guard went over our names. After this, the soldiers and officers left the lower deck, and we were by ourselves. We squatted on the ground, since there were no benches or chairs. A glum and irritated mood prevailed. Suddenly, one of the prisoners, a man named Gluchkov who had once been secretary of the Murmansk regional committee, said: "Boys, we're heading out to sea to be sunk along with this old boat. It wouldn't be the first time the NKVD gets rid of its prisoners that way. It's a clean job and doesn't leave any traces."

The men howled with rage and fear and attacked Gluchkov with their fists. Several more reasonable men succeeded in restoring order. I admit that I, too, was inclined to believe Gluchkov.

After a short while, we felt a gentle rocking motion and heard the anchor being raised. The boat set out, and at that moment many prisoners turned ashen, and some burst into tears. The date was December 2, 1937. The little steamship made slow progress, for the water was partially frozen near the shore. Frequently, the ship had to back off and then advance anew before the ice shoals would give way. The trip took seven or eight hours.

We were taken from the lower deck one by one. This time, we had to climb up a very steep path. It was dark, and there were lights everywhere. The island commander, who was also the prison warden, stood in front of a little house with a group of assistants. They called out our names from a stack of dossiers, and the commander inspected each prisoner from head to toe. Our treatment here was completely different from what we had experienced in Vladimir. The guards comported themselves correctly; there was no cursing, no pushing.

I looked around in the darkness; the electric lights lit up only my immediate surroundings. All I could make out was the large wall of the kremlin (the fortified part of the town). We were on the main island of the Solovetsk archipelago.

Once again, we were called up by name and ordered to assemble in rows of five. Then, escorted by soldiers, we marched forward. The gate opened and we entered the fortress.

ON THE
SOLOVETSK
ISLANDS

THE KREMLIN

The Solovetsk Islands are situated in the southwest corner of the White Sea, seventy kilometers east of the railway station of Kem. Their total surface comprises 6,573 acres. They have been inhabited since the fifteenth century, when monks built a monastery and a church there. These institutions played an important cultural and economic role, so that eventually Solovetsk became a citadel of the Grand Duchy of Moscow. In 1584, the islands were fortified to give them protection against the frequent attacks they were subject to.

In Soviet times, these islands were transformed into one of the first and most feared concentration camps. This is where the first political prisoners and the especially dangerous criminals were sent. Many of the prisoners had once been monks at the Solovetsk monastery.

There were fifty thousand prisoners on the Solovetsk Islands. Only some were locked up in cells; most had to work. One of the principal industries was livestock farming. Unusually fine hay was produced there as well—huge amounts were transported to the mainland each day. The large forests yielded excellent wood, the famous Karelian birch. There was an extensive fishing industry, too. Herring caught in this region sold at spectacular prices on the world market. There was also a large brick factory, which not only met the needs of the islands but exported part of its products to the mainland.

In 1937, a halt was called to the exploitation of the islands' natural resources. The camps were disbanded, the prisoners transferred to other camps. Only political prisoners remained, and they were locked up, not put to work. All available rooms on the island were converted into cells. In December 1937, when we arrived, there was room for forty-eight hundred prisoners. From then on, Solovetsk was run as a military prison for political convicts, and its management was immediately subordinate to the Ministry of the Interior.

We were put into the second section, a two-story building which, like all the other old buildings there, had once served as living quarters for the monks. Except for the bars on the windows, the cell was no different from an ordinary living room. In contrast to the other Soviet prisons I had seen so far, the floors here were made of wood instead of concrete. A large tile stove supplied ample heat. Our cell housed ten prisoners.

After we had made ourselves "comfortable," the hatch in the door opened, and each of us was given a large piece of bread and a tin bowl filled with hot potato soup. We liked the food. We thought it was all we would get, but then we received a bowl of porridge with lard. We were glad to be here.

When the signal for bed was sounded, we lay down on straw sacks that were redolent of hay. We covered ourselves with warm blankets and fell asleep quickly. At 6 a.m., we were awakened. We were led out into the hall, where there was a sink; we could wash without being rushed or bullied. Breakfast consisted of six hundred grams of bread, tea, and nine grams of sugar.

At 10 a.m., we were led out into the yard for a thirty-minute walk. It was a little graveyard, with centuries-old tombstones bearing the names and the birth and death dates of the monks who were buried there. As we walked, we got to know our surroundings. There were six other two- and three-story buildings in the kremlin, all of them serving as prisons. In the middle of the graveyard stood a mighty church building, once the monks' cathedral; now it was filled with crates and barrels and sacks full of flour and other provisions. The phrase "poor as a church mouse" lost its meaning here, for rats and mice could eat to their heart's content in this place.

Not far from our prison was the bathhouse, an old, ramshackle building, ripe for demolition. There was a real sauna there, just as in any Russian bathhouse. Soon after our arrival, a new bath with single stalls and showers was built.

We were well fed. Lunch consisted of two courses—soup and porridge—and there was a one-course dinner. Three times a week, we were served a large piece of salt fish. In other respects, too, the regimen wasn't especially severe.

We lived in the kremlin for a week. Then we were transferred to the island of Muksulma, ten kilometers away. Muksulma was connected to the kremlin by a land bridge: you could walk or drive from one island to the other. We walked to Muksulma, and it was a lovely walk. We were able to admire at least part of this large and beautiful island. We could see several lakes (they were frozen) and a very beautiful forest. We also saw what had once been a silver-fox farm. (The farm had been closed down to provide room for prisoners.)

MUKSULMA

We reached Muksulma in the afternoon. The prison there consisted of a large two-story building and three smaller, adjacent structures—the kitchen, bath, and administration building. There were dozens of similar small island prisons on the Solovetsk archipelago.

The minute we stepped into the prison yard, we knew a stricter regime prevailed here than in the kremlin. The prison warden and an NKVD representative, Bardin, were waiting for us. Bardin, we soon found out, had a very clear understanding of what Stalin and his government expected of him—the physical and moral destruction of political prisoners. To this end, he exerted all his energy, and it was solely due to his efforts that hundreds of prisoners found their graves at the bottom of the White Sea.

We were herded into an empty room and told to strip. As soon as we were naked, a band of soldiers literally attacked us with head-shaving equipment. Since these peasant boys had no training in the use of shavers, there was as much tearing as cutting of hair. Then we were chased across the courtyard—stark naked at minus thirty degrees Celsius—to the bath-house. As I entered the building, I thought for a moment I had landed in hell. There was a large iron vessel over a blazing bonfire; that was where the water was heated. On the right was a cubicle for dressing and undressing. Fifty or sixty men were shoved into the next room. Each man was given a wooden bowl filled with hot water. Not knowing that this was our entire ration of water, we soaped our bodies; but scarcely had we begun to wash when the soldiers yelled at us to finish up. We asked for more water to wash off the soap; there was none. We had to get dressed without drying. Each of us was given new prison clothes and underwear. I dressed quickly; it was cold and my teeth were chattering.

Then we were led into a room containing eighteen wooden bunks. Each man was given a blanket, a straw sack, and a pillow. Though we were very tired, most of us were too dismayed and cold to sleep. That was our introduction to life in Muksulma.

I knew some of my seventeen cellmates from Moscow: Vasily Chuprakov, for example, a Moscow engineer, a close friend to this day. He was a good and generous comrade, and had a calming influence on all of us. That was very important in prison, where the atmosphere was fraught with tension on the point of exploding. Chuprakov also entertained us with lectures on modern technology, about which he knew a great deal.

Yefim Morozov, director of the Moscow circus, had lost his fat belly; in the bath, you could see his skin hanging off him in folds. This man played a sad part in my second trial.

Mareyev, former director of the Glavnev Trust in Moscow, had only one concern: whether he would be readmitted to the Communist Party after he had served his ten years.

The electrical engineer Nemirovsky, born in the slums of Odessa, was serving a ten-year sentence for receiving food packages from some American Jewish organization during the severe food shortages in the Ukraine between 1930 and 1932—proof of secret contacts with the foreign bourgeoisie. He eventually died under miserable circumstances in Norilsk.

Sorokin, a Red Army major, had been given ten years for praising Trotsky.

Selesny, secretary of the communist youth organization in the Ukraine, was an extremely taciturn man—or rather, he was utterly depressed and discouraged.

A newcomer in our group was Samoida, once the foreign-policy editor

48

of the Ukrainian newspaper *Kommunist;* he was still defending the party line.

Heated discussions divided the prisoners into two camps. One group, led by Samoida, maintained that all prisoners must remain loyal to the party, even if they had been unjustly convicted. Stalin was a genius—and whoever doubted this was in danger of being denounced by Samoida. The majority supported my view; those were people who now understood how little Stalin's regime had to do with socialism, and who thought it questionable that a state that practiced the most brutal despotism could be called "progressive."

Once, when Samoida attacked me one more time for saying something about the hypocrisy of Stalin's regime, a violent dispute erupted. Samoida vowed that he would continue to defend everything that Stalin and the party considered correct, and in the course of his vituperations he boasted of his part in the deception of Edouard Herriot, the leader of the French radicals.

Herriot had visited the Soviet Union in 1934; he had wanted to know, among other things, whether religious freedom existed there. In order to show Herriot that the Soviet Union did not suppress religious freedom and that anyone who wished to attend religious services could do so, several churches which had been converted into warehouses or movie theaters were turned into churches again. One of the largest churches of Kiev, ordinarily used as a warehouse for a brewery, was cleared out a week before Herriot's arrival: more than two hundred workers were used for this strange restoration. When Herriot came to Kiev, a mock service was held for his benefit. The "faithful" were NKVD agents and their wives. Samoida played the priest. Since Orthodox priests have beards and Samoida was clean-shaven, he was taken to a theatrical makeup artist, who equipped him with a false beard. It was a thoroughly successful performance. Herriot was delighted, and after returning to France, he reported that everyone in the Soviet Union was quite free to go to church if he wished.

When Samoida finished his story, I asked him: "Do you really think that's defensible, putting on this sort of charade?"

"Yes, I do think it's all right."

"It's pure deception, to my way of thinking!"

"But tell me, why shouldn't we communists deceive a member of the foreign bourgeoisie?"

"Herriot is not a member of the bourgeoisie. A great many French workers vote for him."

"That doesn't matter. Those who vote for Herriot are, in effect, supporters of the bourgeoisie."

"Even if what you say were true, it wouldn't justify that kind of imposture. You have to attack religion with reason, not with deception."

"Go to hell, you're impossible to talk to!" That was Samoida's final argument.

I often wondered why innocent people condemned to long years of imprisonment—and, worse, forced to witness their families' misfortune—would continue to support Stalin's regime. I once talked about this with Yegorov, the former mayor of Stalingrad. In Yegorov's opinion, most of those people were only pretending to like the regime. They defended it to protect their relatives who hadn't been arrested yet.

There was peace and quiet only when there was something to read; everyone appreciated the opportunity to lose sight of reality by losing himself in the pages of a book. The bad food and the brief walk in the courtyard did not offer any real break in the monotony of our days. A letter was a genuine event, but letters arrived rarely, since the prisoners' relatives feared being accused of "association with an enemy of the people." Only a few had the courage to write and send some rubles. But when letters did come, the news was mostly bad: an arrest, a death in the family. Of course you couldn't report an arrest outright in a letter, but a secret language had evolved, and everyone knew what was meant by: "Your brother Petya has gone on a long trip."

The money we occasionally received didn't offer much solace either, since we knew that our relatives were depriving themselves of food to help us.

Bardin, the NKVD representative, had his hands full. He was constantly sneaking around the hall, quietly opening the "wolf's eye" on the door to see if one of us was committing a "crime." This young blond hangman could find criminality in the most harmless acts. Laughing, walking back and forth with your shoes on, reading aloud—these infractions were all punished by a denial of the right to a daily walk, of the right to correspond with one's relatives, of the right to buy provisions in the prison shop, and of course by confinement in the punishment cell.

In March 1938, the authorities decided to regroup the prisoners; I was transferred to another cell, where there were only foreigners. The cell was small and held only eight men. Here I met the German communist Werner Hirsch—Ernst Thälmann's "right-hand man." Thälmann had been a faithful adherent of Moscow's policies but didn't have the theoretical knowledge needed by a leader of a large workers' party. To make up for this deficiency, he was provided with a highly educated Marxist as an assistant.

Werner told me he had lived next door to Thälmann, and whenever Thälmann needed something, he'd just knock on the wall and Werner would come over. Whatever the issue—theses for a party congress or a resolution to be proposed at a meeting—Werner Hirsch supplied the goods, not only to Thälmann's satisfaction but to Moscow's. But even though Werner was a docile servant of the Stalin regime, he was not above suspicion. On November 4, 1936, the NKVD arrested him in Moscow, where he had been living since Hitler's seizure of power in Germany. The Troika sentenced him to ten years in prison.

I had differences of opinion with Werner concerning the German Communist Party's policy before Hitler's accession to power. Nevertheless, we were good friends. I admired Werner's heroic struggle against the murderous regime on the Solovetsk Islands.

Werner received no financial help; he was unable to buy food to satisfy his constant hunger. In addition, he was a smoker. I helped him as much as I could. Although I had little money for my own needs, I bought Werner about ten packs of cigarettes a month and also shared bread with him to the extent that I could.

His health was deteriorating visibly. Werner applied to the prison warden for larger rations, explaining that he had no money to buy food from the prison shop. He never received a reply. Whereupon Werner began a hunger strike, which he broke off after five days, on my recommendation. Like many others, he couldn't understand that methods that are effective in a civilized country were useless here. Of what use is a hunger strike in a place where a sick man is advised to just curl up and die, instead of being given medical aid?

The direct result of Werner's hunger strike was that he became the NKVD's preferred target. He was sent to the punishment cell for the pettiest reasons. During the year I lived with him in Muksulma, he spent a hundred and five days in the punishment cell. During the last weeks of our time together, he could hardly move; he was so weak that he had to give up the daily walk in the courtyard.

Although Werner still believed in Stalin's version of socialism, he dreamed of building a little house somewhere in Europe and living there, far from any political involvement. He loved to tell me about his wife and children. He didn't know where they were, or even if they were still alive.

In December 1938, I was separated from Hirsch. I asked about him in various other prisons and camps, but I never learned what happened to him. Only once did I hear that he had been seen in the prison of Orel shortly before the beginning of the Russo–German War.

The other striking personality in my new cell was Sasha Weber, former People's Commissar for Popular Education in the Volga–German Republic. Sasha was forty years old, of medium height, with a round face and a bald head. During an argument, I called him a thickheaded peasant, and he wasn't at all insulted. "Yes, I have a peasant mind!" he answered proudly. Like most men in this cell, Weber had no money, but he refused to accept any support from me. "I cannot accept help from people who don't agree with me politically," he said.

Weber steeped himself in books; if there were none, he would sit quietly in a corner and rarely say a word. Once in a while, he would mention his eight-year-old son, who had been left somewhere after the death of his mother.

The story of Gould-Verschoyle is of particular interest. This young Irishman had joined the Republican Army as a volunteer during the Spanish Civil War and worked as a radio technician for the Barcelona radio station. When he noticed that the NKVD was gaining more and more influence in the Republican Army, he reported to his commander and told him he was a republican but not a communist, and since he now appeared to be fighting for a communist, not a republican Spain, he asked to be released from service. The commander told him he would have to wait a few days until a replacement was found.

Several days later, a soldier approached him and asked him to come to the harbor, where there was a ship with defective radio equipment. Gould-Verschoyle took his tool bag and boarded the ship; it was a Soviet freighter. He had scarcely stepped into the cabin where the defective equipment was supposed to be when the door shut behind him and he found himself in the company of two members of the Communist Youth League. The ship departed and didn't stop until it reached the harbor of Sevastopol. There the Irishman and the two Komsomol members were arrested by the NKVD and taken to jail. Later they were transported to Moscow, where they were accused of being British spies and were sentenced to eight years in prison.

Another cellmate was Pfeifer, formerly a member of the staff of the *Deutsche Zentralzeitung,* a German-language newspaper in Moscow. He was as quiet as a mouse—very different from what he must have been like in the past, when he was active as a communist agitator in Wuppertal. He was a pleasant cellmate.

The other three were German communists who had worked in various Soviet factories and had been sentenced to ten years for being "Gestapo agents."

Despite our strict isolation, we managed to make contact with several other cells. There was a petroleum lamp in the toilet room; one day, we noticed that the lamp seemed to be hanging askew. When the guard stepped away from the door for a moment, I examined the lamp and—there was a note in it! I quickly stuck it in my mouth, for we were often searched as we left the toilets. After returning to the cell, I turned my back to the door, facing a corner, and read the note.

"Dear Comrades," it said, "Cell 102 has 20 men . . ." and there followed twenty names. We wrote an answer and hid it in the same lamp in the toilet room. In this way, we had some contact for a while, not just with cell 102 but with two other cells. We supplied one another with news, especially of new trials and arrests. Once, we even found a piece of newspaper in the lamp. It was smeared with excrement; we concluded that one of the guards must have used it and thrown it away, and that our neighbors had found it. From that little piece of paper, we learned of the fighting between the Russians and the Japanese on Lake Hasan.

One day, we were all thoroughly searched as we left the toilets, and the "regular mail" from the neighbors' cell was found in my possession. I was taken to Bardin, who wanted to know where I had got the piece of paper.

"I found it in the toilet."

Bardin did not believe me and sent me to the punishment cell for ten days—in two installments, with a twenty-four-hour interval, since he wasn't allowed to administer more than five days of solitary confinement without special permission from his superiors. Our relations with the other cells came to an end after that. We found out later that the cell next to ours had been punished as well.

When I returned from isolation, my comrades told me that money had arrived for me. Since I had not received anything from my wife for a long time, I was very happy; for a long time, gifts of money were the only communication I received from Sonya; only rarely did I get a letter. When the chief guard came into the cell, I asked him for a receipt for the hundred rubles that had come for me.

"No money came for you," he said. Later I learned from my wife that several times the money she sent was returned to her.

Bardin was responsible for that. Finally, I did get a letter from my wife; but it gave me no pleasure. It contained the last photograph taken of our daughter and the news that she had died. I never met this child, who was born a month after my arrest. That letter reached me without any delay; it was the kind of information Bardin didn't mind passing on.

I didn't hear from my wife for the rest of my stay on the Solovetsk Islands.

Bardin was always searching for new ways to torment the prisoners. That's how he came upon the idea of rationing the air in our cells: he gave an order to ventilate the rooms only twice a day for fifteen minutes. The prisoners weren't allowed to open the windows; only the guard could do that. The heat in the cell became unbearable. We weren't allowed to take off our shirts; often, we were bathed in sweat. All our requests to leave the windows open a little longer were refused. Sometimes the air was so stale that people fainted.

Out of sheer desperation, I decided to take action. When we were led out on our walk, I claimed I was sick and asked to be left in the cell. After everyone left, I took the water pot and shattered the window with it, sending a rain of broken glass down into the yard. The sound of it was tremendous; it echoed through the quiet island like a cannon shot.

Right after, the door opened and about fifteen soldiers hurled themselves on me and dragged me off to the punishment cell. Bardin was not on the island at the time and didn't return until two hours later. I was taken out of the punishment cell and led to his office.

Sitting behind his desk with his legs spread apart, he asked: "What was that, a signal for a revolt?"

I was surprised and must have looked it.

"Out with it, admit it! I know everything, anyway!"

"What are you talking about, what revolt?"

"You gave the signal for a revolt. You'd better admit it. Otherwise, I'll have you sent to Sekirnaya Gora." (We were constantly threatened with Sekirnaya Gora, a remote island that had nothing on it but a lighthouse. Executions were carried out there and the corpses thrown into the sea.)

"You can do whatever you like, you're in power," I said. "I'm telling you that I did not give a signal for a revolt. I simply did not want to suffocate in my cell. I wanted more air, the air which you are denying us."

Bardin continued trying to extract a confession from me. Finally, he wrote a report on the incident and had me taken back to the punishment cell. When I rejoined my cellmates five days later, everyone congratulated me and said I had been lucky. They had expected something much worse. After that, we were permitted to open the top window whenever we felt the need. This success was very gratifying for all of us; even Weber came up to me and gave me a firm handshake.

Nearly three months passed. One night, I was suddenly awakened; the guard told me to get dressed and come with him. I was sure that my last hour had struck. We were in the middle of a period of massive state terror, shortly after the trials of Bukharin, Rykov, Pyatakov, and others, when tens of thousands of people were shot in prisons and camps.

I was taken out to the yard. There was a truck, and next to it stood the prison warden and several soldiers. I was told to climb onto the truck. Four soldiers followed me with submachine guns. I had to lie down and was covered with a tarpaulin. During the ride, I thought of my poor wife, who had had to endure such terrible things. Our daughter had just died, and now she would be notified of my death. Probably she would be told that I had died of some illness. Then I thought it didn't matter what they told my wife—the main thing was that all my suffering would be over. I tried to maintain my composure, but I found it difficult. It must be a long way yet, I thought. First, we had to drive to the kremlin, and then go on by motorboat to Sekirnaya Gora. But it was dark, I realized; they couldn't put out to sea at night. Then it occurred to me that they could simply throw me into the sea; why bother transporting me such a long distance?

Finally, the car stopped. The tarpaulin was pulled off. A soldier kicked me with his boot, shouting: "Get up!"

I remained on my back. He repeated the command. I didn't have the strength to get up.

"Hey, you, did you crap out?"

I remained silent.

Then two soldiers took me by the head and feet and dragged me off the truck. The man who had my feet let go, and the other one dragged me by the collar into a brightly lit room and left me lying there. My eyes were shut. I felt relieved. I tried to fall asleep and not think of anything.

Day was breaking when I was awakened. I stood up. In front of me was the prison warden who had received us when we arrived in 1937. He was holding a piece of paper and read off to me a resolution passed by the central prison administration in Moscow. I was being given twenty days in the punishment cell for my unruly behavior and for insulting an NKVD representative, and I was to pay 44 rubles for the window I had broken. I had to sign the document. Then I was taken out into the yard. Now I knew that I was in the kremlin. I was led to section 4, which had about twenty "coolers" on the ground floor. I was stripped to my underwear and was given *lapti*, sandals woven of bark, to replace my shoes. The lower part of an iron gate was opened, and I had to crawl in on my hands and knees.

The cell was very small, as most punishment cells are in Russian prisons. It had a stone floor and no windows. A small electric bulb glowed above the door. A guard watched me constantly. It was very damp and cold; I wasn't able to sit for long on the stool (which was cemented onto the floor)—I was too cold. So I stood and paced back and forth. That wasn't enough; I had to swing my arms. That helped a bit, but I soon grew tired.

I was glad when day finally came and the guard brought me the day's ration—three hundred grams of bread and a pitcherful of hot water. The water warmed me so much that my back felt damp. Every five days, I was given a quart of soup. At night, I was allowed to lie on the narrow bunk, but I was so cold I couldn't sleep. Once, I pulled my undershirt over my head, to warm myself with my own breath; the door hatch opened and a voice shouted: "What's that supposed to be, a scarecrow?"

It was Bardin.

"I'm freezing. I pulled the shirt over my head to get a little warmth," I said.

"That's why it's called a cooler. Now pull down your shirt, or I'll have you stripped naked!"

On the eleventh day the entire door opened, and in came several high NKVD officers, every one of them a colonel or a general, accompanied by the warden. They asked me why I was in the punishment cell. I told them everything that had been building up in me for the past eleven days: that I was a foreign communist and had been imprisoned in several countries because of my communist activities, and that I had never experienced or heard of anything even remotely like this in any country.

One of the generals said: "Very well, we will see." He advised me not to violate the prison regulations.

After they left, I felt relieved; at least I had been able to confront my hangmen with the full force of my rage. A few hours later, I was taken out of my cell and led to another cell along the same hallway. This was a punishment cell too, but what a difference! The floor was wood, and there was a little window that let sunlight in, and the room was twice as big. I almost felt at home. I served the rest of my twenty-day sentence there.

On the twentieth day I expected to be taken out, but there was no sound. I knocked on the door. It happened that the meanest of the guards was on duty that day. He asked what I wanted. I told him my twenty days were over and it was time to let me out of the punishment cell.

"All right, all right, stop knocking," he said.

This put me into such a rage that I began to scream.

"Stop hollering, or we'll put you in a straitjacket!"

But I wouldn't calm down. I kept insisting on being let out. The officer on duty heard my shouts and came to ask what was the matter. I explained.

"Have some patience. We'll see what we can do."

Soon after that, the officer returned with a bowl of soup and a piece of bread.

"Here's something to eat for the time being. There's no one in the office, but I'll try to find out later why no one told me to let you out."

He didn't come back till later that night. He let me out of the punishment cell and took me to the second floor. He opened up a cell with eight iron beds, one of which was covered with a sheet and a blanket. "Go to sleep here." I lay down on the bed and immediately fell asleep.

Then someone was shaking me. I opened my eyes with an effort. The same officer was standing before me. He told me to get dressed. It was still dark outside; I asked the officer why I wasn't being allowed to sleep.

"You'll have lots of time to sleep."

He led me to a soldier, saying: "He's yours. Take him."

Now I realized why I hadn't been released on time. I was an "outsider," having been brought to the kremlin from Muksulma—I didn't belong here; and in Muksulma I had evidently been "forgotten." If I hadn't energetically demanded my release, I would have stayed in the punishment cell for a long time.

"What's the matter with you?" the soldier asked. "Just look at you!"

I didn't say anything.

"All right, let's go."

A horse and wagon were waiting in the courtyard. I had to lie down on the wagon, and the soldier covered me with a tarpaulin.

I wondered why I was being escorted by only one soldier. He wasn't even armed. The wagon moved slowly. After a long while, it stopped. The soldier pulled the tarpaulin from my head and asked me in a friendly tone how I was feeling and whether I was hungry. I was so moved I couldn't utter a sound.

The soldier handed me a big piece of bread. "There, eat!"

I took the bread and ate, my tears wetting the bread. I sat up until we could see Muksulma in the distance. Then the soldier said to me: "Now you have to lie down. Someone could see and I would get in trouble."

I lay down and the kindhearted soldier covered me. When I returned to my cell, it was empty because my cellmates had been taken to the toilets. When they came back, they were surprised to find a new convict in the cell, and were about to ask me the usual questions, when they suddenly recognized me. They were horrified by my appearance: my face was sunken, bearded, caked with filth; I hadn't been given a drop of water to wash myself for the past twenty days. My legs were swollen to elephantine proportions.

When the bread came, everyone broke off a portion and offered it to me. I thanked them and told them about the friendly soldier who had given me bread. They told me how they had tried to guess what had happened to me. Most of them had been convinced I'd been sent to Sekirnaya Gora; others thought I had been released and sent back to my country. I wasn't surprised; long-term prisoners always imagine an extreme solution to their problems—death or freedom.

The joy of reunion didn't last long. That same day, I was taken back to the kremlin. But before leaving, I was permitted the great pleasure of taking a shower. Also, my head and face were shaved.

The new cell was small; only two other men were in there, both Yugoslavians. One of them, Stanko Dragic, I already knew from Zagreb. I had met him in 1923, when he was director of a shoe factory where illegal communist meetings were held. Dragic was a fanatical revolutionary. He came from Bosnia and had a lively temperament. He was an indefatigable organizer, undaunted even when his actions had no chance of success. In 1927, he fled from Yugoslavia to escape police persecution. He lived in Moscow for a long time and studied at the University of the Western Peoples, a school which trained communist officials for work in the Western countries.

Like most of the students of that school, Dragic was given a three-year sentence by the NKVD's Troika. After serving the three years, he was not released; instead, he was informed that the Troika had sentenced him to another three years. Dragic protested vehemently and was subjected to disciplinary measures.

This string of punishments had turned the once powerful Dragic into a cripple. He was always complaining of intestinal pains; he could barely eat the prison food and lived on soup, tea, and a little bread. Because of his unruly behavior, the officers frequently threatened to send him to Sekirnaya Gora; he knew what that meant. I tried in vain to persuade him to be reasonable and not give the authorities a pretext to kill him. He kept saying he didn't care; he preferred to die honorably. And he did die honorably. In December 1938, when he was informed that he had been sentenced to still another three years, he cursed the officer who read the verdict. That cost him ten days in the punishment cell. When he returned to our cell, he climbed onto the high windowsill and shouted at the top of his lungs: "Comrades, if you ever regain your freedom, tell the world that the Yugoslavian communist Dragic was innocent and that he was tortured in prison!"

Soon after that, the warden, Korchkov, came with Bardin and two soldiers. Dragic was put into chains and led away. His last words to us were: "Farewell, comrades!" The NKVD kept their word. Dragic was taken to the island of Sekirnaya Gora, murdered, and thrown into the sea.

The other Yugoslavian's name was Anton (I no longer remember his last name). He was an old communist from Laibach. He had fled Yugoslavia in the late twenties. In 1937, he was arrested in Kharkov and was sentenced to ten years for "counterrevolutionary activities." Later I spent some time with him in Norilsk. He was a quiet, courageous human being, I don't know what eventually happened to him.

After Dragic's tragic end, a new prisoner came into our cell, an American named Laitala. He had worked as a specialist in a large metallurgical installation in Petrozavodsk, the capital of Karelia. One day, after working there for two years, he was arrested by the Soviet border police near the Russo–Finnish border. He was accused of being a spy. During his pre-trial detention he demanded, and was promised, that the American embassy in Moscow would be informed of his situation. But his request was not honored. The Troika's judgment: five years.

Laitala was taken to the Solovetsk Islands. After two years there, he attempted to escape, with two other prisoners. The three men hid in a boat, waited until nightfall, and rowed to the mainland, about a hundred kilometers away. The sea was very stormy that night; they didn't reach the shore until dawn. For a short while, they thought they were free, but hardly had they crouched down in the bushes to rest and plan their next move when they heard dogs barking and had to run off into the woods. One of them wasn't able to run fast enough and was caught. Laitala and the third man got away and eventually reached the border. About two kilometers from the crossing, they decided to wait for nightfall and then slip over unnoticed.

When it got dark, they crept to the border, crawling on their stomachs for the last two hundred meters. They could hear the brook that marked the frontier. Then, to their horror, they saw two Russian soldiers with a dog, just a hundred meters away and coming closer. The soldiers had flashlights. As fast as they could, the fugitives ran toward the brook; the soldiers saw them and released the dogs. The animals caught up with them on the other side of the brook, on Finnish territory. The other fugitive succeeded in getting away, but Laitala was caught by the dog and couldn't get loose. The soldiers took him to the nearest border patrol station.

The border police had already been informed of the three men's escape. Laitala was taken to the frontier headquarters, where he was brutally treated by the border guards. Among other injuries, he lost four front teeth. That same day, he was taken to the prison at Kem; from there, he was brought back to the island by steamship.

The two fugitives were tried and sentenced to death in front of all the other prisoners. The sentences were later commuted to ten years. But an announcement was made in the camp that the two convicts had been shot.

THE SHOOTING OF THE NUNS

Laitala had experienced a lot and knew a great deal. He told me about the Ukrainian peasant Hnitetsky, a communist who had spent ten years in a Polish jail, sought refuge in the Soviet Union, was arrested as a "Polish spy," and was sentenced to ten years in a camp. He had worked in Karelia as a woodcutter. Like many another Karelian slave, Hnitetsky chopped three of his fingers off with an ax, hid them among the beams destined for export to England, and added a note: "Greetings to the English proletariat from a liberated Soviet worker."

"I was witness to a terrible thing that happened in the early months of 1935 on Muksulma," Laitala told me. "There were about three hundred nuns and followers of various religious sects in the kremlin at that time. Most of them stubbornly refused to perform any kind of work for what they called the Antichrist. The nuns were willing to work in the camp hospital, but the camp authorities wouldn't agree to that. Those women sat in the punishment cell for months, with three hundred grams of bread and a pot of hot water a day and a dish of soup every five days. Every ten days, they'd be let out and told to go to work; they would refuse, and back they went to the punishment cell. It just went on and on."

One day, these women were transferred from the kremlin to Muksulma, where they were supposed to work on the cattle farm. "We don't work for the Antichrist," they said.

The women were led into the yard and made to line up in one long row. All the other prisoners were herded to the opposite side of the yard. A detachment of NKVD soldiers stood guard with rifles in their hands. The camp commander pulled his revolver out of his pocket, stepped up to the first nun, and asked: "Will you work?"

"I don't work for the Antichrist."

A shot rang out, and the sister sank to the ground. The nuns fell to their knees and began to pray.

The commander asked the second nun the same question and was given the same answer. Another shot, a second corpse.

This continued until the commander's bullets ran out. Then he shouted: "You damned whores, I'll send every last one of you to your God in heaven!"

The nuns just continued praying aloud. The commander ordered the NKVD soldiers to hold their rifles at the ready. Once again, he put his question to the praying women; they didn't reply but continued to pray.

Then came his command: "Fire!" Several salvos followed. When none of the women showed any sign of life, the commander turned to the assembled prisoners and told them there was no room for parasites in the Soviet Union. Anyone who refused to work would be treated exactly as those women were.

A group of prisoners was selected to dig several trenches, drop the corpses in, and cover them with earth.

After he told this story, we weren't able to sleep for a long time. That episode had occurred very close to where we were at that moment.

We had to make room for two more prisoners in our little cell. They were Finns; both of them were being brought to us from a hospital. As members of the illegal communist youth movement of Finland, they had decided, with the backing of their leaders, to flee to Russia. They succeeded in crossing the border unnoticed by the Finnish soldiers but fell into the hands of the Russian border guards. They were taken to the border patrol station and were accused of being spies and saboteurs. It didn't help them that they had with them a letter confirming that they had come to the Soviet Union on assignment from the Finnish Communist Youth. They were beaten day and night until they "confessed" to being Finnish agents planning to commit acts of sabotage in the Soviet Union.

They were taken from the border station to the NKVD in Petrozavodsk, where they were asked to give more precise information as to the orders they had been given by the Finnish General Staff. The boys declared that they weren't agents at all, that their confessions had been forced by beatings. Whereupon they were again beaten until they "admitted" that their original confession at the border had been true.

The verdict was six years. Both became so ill that they had to be taken directly to the hospital by steamship. Their treatment there was so inhuman that they asked to be released several times, claiming to have recovered their health. But that wasn't so easy; the doctors refused. During the three weeks the Finns spent in the hospital, eighty-four people died in a room containing thirty beds. Rarely did a prisoner return to his cell in a healthy condition; anyone entering the hospital was given up for dead. No medicine was administered there, only tranquilizers, to prevent the patients from screaming. Two of the doctors were particularly brutal, whereas most of the nurses were more humane.

They were very likable boys, and we did our best to comfort them. If one of us had a piece of sugar, he would give it to them. When we suggested calling for a doctor, they refused, out of fear of being taken back to the hospital.

The younger boy got sicker and sicker. Finally, the doctor came; he listened to what the boy told him in broken Russian, but he didn't examine him. All he said was: "You will be given some powder."

The next day, when the nurse came to administer the powder, the Finnish boy, who was extremely weak, had to crawl to the door on all fours, lie down on his back, and open his mouth; the nurse stuck her hand through the hatch and poured some powder into his mouth. She wasn't allowed to come into the cell.

After a week, the boy had to be taken back to the hospital. He never returned.

There were a great many gulls on the island. Their loud cries penetrated into the cells and brought some distraction into the prisoners' sad life. It was like a sign of freedom for us.

One day, we heard a volley of rifle fire and thought the soldiers must be practicing. Soon after, we noticed the absence of gulls' cries. Later we learned what had happened: a commission from Moscow had come up with the notion that the prisoners might send out messages by attaching them to a gull, and had ordered the birds shot.

In the spring of 1939, I was transferred to a new cell. There I met the former secretary of the Western Ukrainian Communist Party, Joseph Krylyk. In 1930, Krylyk had been forced to escape from the western Ukraine, which at that time was part of Poland, and settled down in Kharkov and later in Kiev. From there, he directed the work of his party. In 1934, the leader of the Ukrainian communists, Skrypnyk, was threatened with arrest for "nationalist deviations." He committed suicide; after that, a wave of mass arrests swept through the Ukraine, especially among the refugees from the Polish part of the western Ukraine. Krylyk, too, was locked up.

He suffered a stroke in prison, which left him paralyzed on his left side. Krylyk's illness caused him a great deal of pain. He was also extremely nervous, which brought him into frequent conflict with the prison administration. One day, we were given maggoty bread to eat. Krylyk protested angrily. Two days later, he was removed from the cell, and we never saw him again. His toothbrush and some cigarettes of his remained in the cell and were never picked up. From this, we concluded that he had been shot.

In May 1939, all prisoners were thoroughly examined by a medical commission. The doctors asked each of us about any physical complaints. It was very striking to see doctors behaving like doctors instead of like hangmen. From that day on, we noticed a change in the attitude of the prison authorities as well as the guards. There was virtually none of the usual harassment. Our walks became longer, and we were even permitted to have quiet conversations while walking. And the most important change— Bardin was no longer there.

Something unusual was happening, that was obvious, but we didn't know what. Every morning we heard large groups marching across the yard, and in the evenings we could hear similar movements. One day, when I heard the sound of marching again, I climbed up to the window and saw a group of about a hundred prisoners being led out of the prison yard. In the evening, I watched them returning. There was no doubt about it, the prisoners were being taken out to work. Why not us? We didn't find out until later: the presence of foreigners was not desired where those men were working.

On August 2 our cell doors were opened; we were told that we could go out into the yard. We couldn't believe our ears. In the yard, we met many old comrades we had gotten to know in other prisons. I saw my friends Chuprakov, Weber, Morozov, Mareyev, and others; but many were no longer there to experience this moment. I was very surprised to meet an Austrian communist here, Rudolf Ondratschek; and also Josef Berger, a leading member of the Communist International, whom I had met in 1926.

I learned that all prisoners who had been declared fit by the medical commission had to work. In the course of three months, a barracks, an airport, an electrical plant, a hospital, and several other structures were built. These constructions, and the elimination of the prisons as soon as they were completed, are evidence that the Soviet Union's war against Finland was carefully prepared.

A lively atmosphere pervaded the kremlin now. We were almost at liberty to move about as we pleased. All day long, we could enjoy the fresh air. At night, we were locked in again.

During the next days, more prisoners came to the kremlin from the smaller islands—from Saichiki, Muksulma, Lisino. Not from Sekirnaya Gora—nobody ever came back from there. More than four thousand prisoners were assembled now. Our clothes were brought out from storage; some carried suitcases, others bundles. Many had already gotten rid of the hated prison uniform. The prisoners stood about in groups and told one another what they had suffered in the past several years. Everyone was glad to have at least this small moment of relaxation, but at the same time we were asking ourselves: What does this mean? Where are we going next? To a prison or a labor camp?

THE EVACUATION OF THE ISLAND

On August 3, 1939, we were awakened at 3 a.m. All the prisoners were assembled in the compound inside the kremlin. All the NKVD officers, including the prison commander, Korchkov, were there.

Korchkov shouted: "Attention!"

Everyone was listening.

"Prisoners, you are now being removed from this island. I advise you to keep the strictest discipline during the march to the harbor and during the transport. You are to obey the commands of your guards without argument. The guards are instructed to shoot without warning if anyone tries to escape. Is that understood?"

It was so quiet in the yard that you could hear the sound of birds flying overhead. The commander of the guard shouted: "Attention, take up your belongings and assemble in rows of five! Forward, march!"

Four thousand eight hundred men set themselves in motion, accompanied by heavily armed soldiers. All you could hear was the stamping of feet and the barking of the watchdogs. Some prisoners turned their heads to cast a last glance at the island where they had spent so many hard years. The soldiers ordered them to look straight ahead.

After we arrived at the harbor, we were told to sit down without breaking ranks. Two officers approached us. One of them was carrying a weighty dossier; the other called out our names one by one. We had to step forward, answer questions, and step to one side. When two hundred men had been processed, they were led to a barge. A little tugboat pulled the barge out to sea, toward a large freighter. It took several hours for all the prisoners to be loaded on board. The last group consisted of six or seven hundred women who had also been imprisoned on the Solovetsk Islands.

The *Budyonny*, a freighter ordinarily used to transport wood from northern Russia to Western Europe, would now be carrying more than four thousand prisoners to the extreme northern regions of the country. For this purpose, a six-story structure had been built into the belly of the ship, with a wooden stairway connecting each story to the others. There were bunks on each level; you had to crawl onto them because the ceilings were so low. Barrels were lined up in a narrow row between the bunks—those were the toilets.

The soldiers were lodged in cabins. In the middle of the top deck, on top of a large tower, guards kept watch with machine guns.

I had arrived on the ship with the seventh group. As I began to climb down, I heard my name called from several directions—these were my old friends. I found a place next to Rudolf Ondratschek.

At first, the ship impressed us as very large; there seemed to be a lot of room. But more bodies kept piling in, and by the end, it turned out that there wasn't enough room for everybody. The last groups had to stand around for hours while the others moved closer together. The place was like a beehive, a huge humming of voices: one person would be looking for a friend; another, for a more comfortable spot. It was a long time before relative calm set in.

The colossus didn't start moving until the next day. Where were we going?

Until now, no one had thought of eating. We unpacked our bundles: zwieback, herring, some lumps of sugar which we had been given before our departure; there would be warm food by the next day, we'd been told. I, too, ate a little of my provisions.

After eating, we sat down together, Josef Berger, Rudolf Ondratschek, Vasily Chuprakov, Glazanov (a well-known physicist today), and others. We exchanged reminiscences and discussed our prospects for the immediate future, which unfortunately did not look promising. It was evident that we were on a long journey and that we would be spending a good deal of time together. Old friendships were renewed. The two years we had spent separately in various prisons had changed us. Most of us looked emaciated and aged. But even greater than the outward changes was the change in our way of thinking. During the pre-trial detention in Moscow, most of the prisoners hadn't had any objections to the Stalin regime. Many believed that the arrests of countless innocent people were due to intrigues on the part of enemies of the Soviet government. They believed it was a temporary measure, a kind of security screening in the interests of the people; and almost all were convinced that they would be back home in a few months. Only a few understood at the time that all hope was illusory, that Stalin and his clique were waging a war of extermination, with the aim of strengthening their rule over Russia. Years had passed since then, and there was no sign of an imminent amnesty; on the contrary, we were being taken farther and farther away from the civilized world, toward the arctic ice desert. Only now were the prisoners beginning to recognize the implications of the nightmarish investigation and trial they had undergone.

I shall never forget a conversation with Sergei Yegorov, the former mayor of Stalingrad. I knew him from Lefortovo; at that time, he was still one of those who considered all the government's measures necessary. He had told me his story. A man named Kusnetsov, president of the regional Executive Committee of Stalingrad, had previously been the general director of the Manchurian Railway. After the railway was sold to Japan, Kusnetsov was transferred to Stalingrad. Yegorov worked with him. Kusnetsov was later sentenced to death as a spy for the Japanese. Yegorov thought it was absolutely proper that he, Yegorov, should fall under suspicion and be arrested, since he was Kusnetsov's closest associate. He was convinced that his innocence would quickly be established and that he would be released and rehabilitated.

When we met on the ship, Yegorov greeted me happily, as if we were old friends. Yet, in Lefortovo, he had avoided me, saying he wouldn't have anything to do with an "enemy of the people."

"You're still here?" I said.

"Evidently."

"You were convinced that the innocent would soon be released."

"It seems you were right, Karl, and I was wrong."

"How did you come to this conclusion?"

"My impression is that all of us have been arrested by the counter-revolution, under Stalin's leadership."

"You're making brilliant progress," I said with delight.

"I know. The two years I spent in Vladimir and on the Solovetsk Islands opened my eyes."

"I hope you can see now that Stalin's socialism and Hitler's socialism have an awful lot in common."

"Well, I agree that this isn't socialism. But we don't have private capital. So what is it?"

"The same question was once asked of Dan, the leader of the Russian Mensheviks, who lived in Berlin after the October Revolution. His answer: 'Only the devil knows what it is.'"

I got to know one man on the ship who distinguished himself from the others by openly declaring that he was an anti-communist. There were very few such people among us. His name was Shevchenko, a former captain in the old Imperial Army. He had been in jails and camps since 1927. In 1937 he had completed his last five-year sentence. On the way back to his home in the Ukraine, he had been arrested on the train and had been sentenced to another ten years. Shevchenko was always in good spirits; he couldn't repeat often enough what a pleasure it was for him to be in prison with so many communists.

The ocean voyage became more unbearable with each day. A cattle transport would have been organized more humanely. The most elementary necessities, things to which every human being, even a captive, has a right, were lacking; only monsters could have planned something like this. We couldn't even stretch out on the damp, naked boards. There wasn't enough to eat. Barrels in place of toilets. There were two latrines on the upper deck, but you had to stand on line for hours to get to the top deck. One day, I succeeded in getting to the top after several hours. I didn't have to go to the toilet; I only wanted to see where we were. I saw boundless gray water, and on the towers, soldiers with machine guns pointed at the only exit.

There was a scarcity of water, which was particularly painful. The ship was, of course, not built to supply that many people with water. Part of the available water was used at least once a day to cook hot meals; part was used by the guards. Only very little was left for the prisoners to drink. Every time a large pailful of water was let down from above by a rope, fights would erupt and part of the water would be spilled. It was only the strongest who succeeded in getting a little extra water. That was the diet prepared for us by the NKVD: salt fish, zwieback, and very little water.

When hot food was served on the second day—a soup containing sauerkraut and beans—there were more disturbances. One large bowl made of rusty black tin was supposed to serve ten people. Everyone ate in a hurry; those who were too timid or too feeble got very little. Many prisoners started getting sick almost immediately. The first corpses were thrown overboard after three days. Many were seasick and couldn't eat.

The barrels, which hadn't been emptied for three days, began to overflow. The stench was overwhelming. We shouted and banged in protest until we were allowed to empty the barrels into the sea.

A new plague descended on us: in Murmansk, three hundred criminal convicts were put aboard the already overcrowded ship. They immediately began to pillage the political prisoners. Few of us thought of defending ourselves: some were too sick, others too apathetic. Nevertheless, fights did erupt here and there. Some of the criminals had knives. People were injured. The guards pretended not to notice.

The criminals soon stopped attacking us—partly because they were beginning to meet with lively resistance, and partly because we weren't carrying very much that was worth stealing. The newcomers couldn't content themselves with the meager meals, however, and some experienced burglars among them discovered a storage room underneath the wooden floor. They broke through the floor with iron bars, climbed down, and returned with concentrated milk, cookies, and even chocolate. How great was our astonishment when we saw the bandits sitting around in groups, eating delicacies instead of salt fish and zwieback!

The situation became more and more critical; seasickness spread; few could still stand on their feet.

On the fifth day, a huge storm broke. We thought the waves were going to swamp us. Water penetrated the ship, and those who sat near the opening had to move. The storm lasted two days, during which the ship hardly made any progress. No food was cooked during the storm, so there was no hot food; but no one felt like eating. At times, the storm was so violent that the barrels full of excrement and urine were tossed through the air and spilled their disgusting contents over us.

After a week's voyage through the White Sea, the Barents Sea, and the Kara Sea, more than a hundred and fifty dead were counted.

On August 16, the ship got stuck in drift ice. On August 18, the icebreakers _Lenin_ and _Malygin_ came to clear a path for us.

The ship dropped anchor at the island of Novaya Zemlya to replenish its supply of water and fresh bread. Now we finally had enough water and bread; there was also a noticeable increase in hot food. On some days, we were even given two servings of hot soup. Many believed that these improvements had come about because the man in charge of the transport had become frightened after so many prisoners died.

On August 21, we entered the mouth of the Yenisei, the great Siberian river which flows from Mongolia all the way to the Kara Sea. On August 22, 1939, the ship dropped anchor in the harbor of Dudinka.

IN THE
FAR NORTH

Dudinka did not look inviting. Everything was gray—the river, the sky, the land. A desolate expanse of snow and ice stretched before us. There were no trees, just a few shrubs here and there. Our ship laid anchor far from the town; all we could see were a few wooden houses. One of them was the central station of a narrow-gauge railroad. I doubt that there was a man or woman among us whose heart did not sink at the sight of this landscape, who did not secretly think: I'll never get out of here.

The disembarkation began. It was August, and everything was covered with snow! It was cold. We had to kneel in the wet snow and wait to be called by name before we could climb into the small open cars of the narrow-gauge train.

The first people we met were convicted criminals who were working on the railroad. One of them, with a shovel in his hand, asked us: "Hey, brothers, where are you coming from?"

"From the Solovetsk."

"In that case, you've traded a mule for a donkey."

"What's it like here?" one of us asked.

"You'll find out soon enough."

"What about the food?"

"You'll get by, but you won't feel any desire for a woman." (He used a crude expression which I cannot repeat.)

"Why are you here?" I asked.

"Because we didn't honor our fathers and our mothers," replied an adolescent boy.

"You all got twenty-five years, am I right?" asked a young criminal.

"Why do you say that?"

"They're giving fascists twenty-five now."

"We're not fascists, most of us are former party members."

"I guess you didn't like Stalin's mustache," one of the criminals said ironically.

Laden with five hundred men, the little locomotive carried us up to milestone 105 of the Dudinka–Norilsk railroad line. We had to get out there and walk the remaining ten kilometers to the coal mine called Nadezhda—Hope. The trek began with a steep climb. Then we were led over a swamp; occasionally, the ice would break and you'd be up to your knees in the freezing muck until your companions helped you climb out.

There were many sick people in our group who were unable to walk unassisted. Many threw away their bundles and suitcases because they no longer had the strength to carry them. The guards allowed us only rare and brief stops, for they were afraid we would not reach our destination before nightfall.

WE BUILD A RAILROAD

When we arrived at Nadezhda, it was still light outside. The camp consisted of five barracks and as many tents. Each of the barracks—which were built of plywood—housed a hundred and fifty men. I stayed with my friends Rudolf Ondratschek, Josef Berger, and Yefim Morozov. The bunks were arranged in three tiers. Josef Berger found a place on the bottom; Ondratschek, Morozov, and I slept on the third level. In the middle of the barracks stood an iron stove which was heated with coal and was always red-hot.

We made ourselves as comfortable as we could and tried to analyze our new situation. We were extremely dispirited. There no longer seemed to be any hope.

Soon the first camp administrators arrived. These were criminals who had been entrusted with the task of "reeducating" us "counterrevolutionaries" to the ways of useful Soviet citizens. They told us we had to go to work early the next morning and should get to bed early. They also inquired whether we had any decent clothes to sell. "Better you sell your clothes than have them stolen," one of the criminals advised us.

I was very tired and slept soundly. At 6 a.m., a gong rang out—time to get up. Fifteen minutes later, the camp police came storming into our barracks, shouting and brandishing sticks.

Those camp policemen were specially selected criminals whose job it was to make sure all the prisoners went to work. Whoever didn't get up in time was yanked off his bunk. Breakfast had to be finished a half hour after reveille. We went to breakfast in the kitchen, which was thirty meters from the barracks, a shack made of wood, tin, and tar paper. An ancient bald man looked at us through a window; next to him stood a young man in front of a steaming wooden pot, holding a ladle in his hand. A heap of salt fish lay on the table.

I was holding a coupon I had received earlier, along with six hundred grams of bread.

"Where's your bowl?"

"I don't have one."

"Do you want me to pour the soup in your hat?"

I took the salt fish and went searching for a bowl.

In the other barracks, there was no lack of "bowls"—which turned out to be empty tin cans—but no one wanted to lend me one. These were prisoners who had been at Nadezhda for a while. Then I heard the signal for departure. At that moment, the kitchen window closed. Thus, many of the newcomers went to their first day of work without food. Some of us were sent to the mines, the others to the Dudinka–Norilsk railroad line, which was still being built. I went with the second group.

Our small camp was not yet surrounded by barbed wire, as all camps eventually were. Instead, watchtowers had been set up, fifty yards apart; on each tower was a soldier armed with a rifle or submachine gun, ready to shoot anyone who tried to leave the camp grounds.

At a quarter to seven, we assembled in rows of five at a spot that had been designated the "exit." Then we were divided into brigades of fifty men, headed by a foreman, called a "brigadier," who was selected by the commander of our section. Each brigadier then stepped up to the commander and reported: "Brigade number 5, fifty men strong, ready to work!" The commander then counted the brigades: "First, second, third . . ."

After we passed through the "exit," a detail of armed guards took charge of us and counted us again. Then the commander of the guard called out: "Attention, prisoners! You are forbidden to talk during the march, to move from one row to another, to step out to the right or left. Offenders will be shot without warning. Understood?"

"Yes!" we shouted in chorus.

"Guards—weapons at the ready!—forward, march!" Several hundred people stepped into motion. The soldiers pointed their guns at the prisoners. Police dogs followed, flanking our column on either side and barking continuously.

Our place of work was just fifteen minutes away from the camp. A construction engineer explained to our brigadier what we had to do. Our job was to cart gravel with a wheelbarrow from a gravel pit to the railway embankment. Three men were assigned to one wheelbarrow: two to fill it with gravel, and the third man to push it. While he carted away his load, his two partners would be filling another wheelbarrow. The quota, which had to be met after eleven hours of work, was twelve cubic meters for each three-man group—or, by a different calculation, a twenty-five-kilometer hike with a loaded wheelbarrow. Those who met the quota would get seven hundred grams of bread a day, a liter of soup, and two hundred fifty grams of millet gruel or some other kind of kasha in the morning and evening, as well as two hundred grams of salt fish three times a week and, once a month, seven hundred grams of sugar and fifty grams of soap. Those who surpassed the quota by twenty percent would receive a "bonus" consisting of two hundred additional grams of salt fish. Whoever failed to meet the quota received that much less bread and kasha. Those who achieved less than sixty percent of the quota would get a "corrective fare" of three hundred grams of bread and half a liter of soup a day. Only those who met the quota would be given sugar and soap. Since most of us were very weak, hardly anyone ever met the quota.

When we got back to the camp at 8 p.m., I was so tired that I had no appetite, even though I hadn't eaten all day. I crawled onto my bunk and fell asleep. Two hours later, I woke up with hunger pains. Ondratschek had picked up my food: behind my head was a large tin can filled with soup and gruel, and next to it a piece of bread. I ate the cold food, and only after finishing it did I notice how dirty my hands were. There was no water in the barracks, so I got up to wash my hands in the yard. But the minute I stepped out the door a guard shouted down from one of the towers: "Get back in there!" We weren't allowed to leave the barracks after ten.

It was quiet inside; almost everyone was asleep. Only one man was on his feet—the prisoner in charge of heating the stove. He was doing a good job: the room was very warm. My bunk neighbors had taken up most of my narrow space during the few minutes I had left. I squeezed in between them; they were sleeping so soundly they didn't even notice.

The next morning, everything started the way it had the day before. Again I searched in vain for a tin can, and again I was unable to get any warm food. My breakfast consisted of one salt fish and six hundred grams of bread. After that, eleven hours of hard work.

My friends and I discussed the problem of finding a bowl. I decided to sell my suit and buy a three-liter can of beans and use the can as a bowl, which we could all share. After returning from work, we looked up the criminal who had asked us on the day we arrived if we wanted to sell any clothes. He offered me eighty rubles for my suit, but only if I would add my tie. I didn't mind parting with the tie.

There was a small shop in the camp where another criminal sold food, soap, toothpaste, and toothbrushes. That's where I bought my can of beans. Rudolf, Josef, Yefim, and others sat down with me to empty the can and fill our bellies, using wooden spoons we had carved ourselves. Now we could look forward to having a warm meal twice a day.

But when we got up the next morning, Rudolf Ondratschek told me he was ill and couldn't go to work. I hurried to the adjacent barracks to ask one of the old-timers what the procedure was in cases like this. He said there was an infirmary next to the administration building, but the sick man's temperature would have to be thirty-eight degrees Celsius— otherwise, he'd have to go to work, no matter how sick he was. Unless he had a broken bone or some other severe injury.

I took Rudolf to the infirmary. About twenty sick men were in the waiting room. Every two or three minutes, a prisoner would come out of the doctor's room and another one would be called in. Most of the ones who came out were grumbling and cursing; only a few looked sat- isfied—they were the ones who didn't have to go to work.

The doctor asked us why the two of us had come together. I said my friend was so weak he couldn't walk by himself. "We'll see about that," said the doctor, and put a thermometer under Rudolf's arm. I looked around the room: a table put together out of boards; a small medicine cabinet on the wall; in the corner a cot covered with a sack and a blanket. The room wasn't noticeably clean, but not very dirty either. The doctor checked the thermometer, nodded, went to the medicine cabinet, took out three small envelopes, and gave them to Rudolf. "Take this powder three times a day. Come back in the evening. You don't have to go to work."

I was very glad for Rudolf; I hadn't expected things to go so smoothly. I brought him back to the barracks, helped him onto the bunk, and ran to the kitchen, since there were only a few minutes left for breakfast. When we came back in the evening, I asked Rudolf how he was feeling. Instead of answering my question, he said in Viennese dialect: *"Korl, heit hob i a echt's Weana Gobelfrühstuck gess'n!"* (Karl, I had a real Viennese breakfast today!)

"A *Schmoizbrot?*" (A schmaltz sandwich?)

"You guessed it!"

His good mood delighted me; he was obviously feeling better. I asked him where he had gotten such a delicacy. He said that one of the old-timers, a man who was working in the coal mine, had come to see whether there were any compatriots in our barracks. When he found Rudolf and learned that he was Austrian and that he was sick, he brought him a schmaltz sandwich—a typical Viennese working-class breakfast. Rudolf kept a piece for me; I accepted it only so as not to hurt his feelings.

Unfortunately, my joy was premature. Rudolf's condition did not improve; it got worse. He couldn't go to work on the following days either. In addition to a high temperature, he was suffering from diarrhea. The doctor (who, as I later learned, hadn't had any medical training, only some experience as a nurse) didn't know what to do; the powders he was giving Rudolf seemed to be hurting rather than helping him. I finally asked him to send Rudolf to the hospital.

"I'm sorry, but there's no hospital here. The nearest one is ten kilometers away and overcrowded besides. I simply can't risk sending him to the hospital; if he's not very seriously ill, they'll just send him back."

More than a week passed; Rudolf got sicker every day. Then Josef thought up a plan: we would run to the infirmary every evening and scream and shout that Ondratschek was dying. This tactic proved effective. The doctor would hurry into the barracks to examine Rudolf. As we expected, he soon got tired of this; and besides, he was afraid that Rudolf might really die in the barracks, which could have unpleasant consequences for the doctor. The NKVD did not approve of irregularities; a prisoner could die, but woe to the doctor who let him die in his barracks. Deaths were only permitted in the hospital.

So the doctor tried to find a way to get Rudolf into the hospital. But the only means of transportation was dog- or horse-drawn sled. When I stormed into his office again with my cries of alarm, the doctor asked me whether Rudolf would be able to ride to the hospital, adding that it was actually just eight, not ten kilometers away. Stunned, I asked him how a sick man who could barely walk could be expected to ride eight kilometers. The doctor shrugged.

The next morning, before going to work, I took leave of Rudolf and gave him fifteen rubles which I still had left from the sale of my suit. The separation was hard for both of us, but we hoped to see each other again. Later, from our work site, we could see Rudolf passing by on his way to the hospital: he was sitting in a box, with his head and legs dangling out. The box was being pulled by a horse. It left a broad track in the snow. We waved goodbye to him. He was so weak he could hardly respond. We lost track of Rudolf for a long time. Two months passed before I heard from him again.

The camp administration pushed for increased production in the building of the railroad. We had to work longer hours. Most of the prisoners had been in detention for several years; their bodies were weakened by the rigors of camp life, by undernourishment and lack of fresh air. Also, many of them were completely unused to physical labor. The population of the Solovetsk Islands had mainly consisted of former party functionaries, industrial managers, diplomats, doctors, professors, etc. It was no wonder the terrible conditions of life in this camp proved too much for them.

When a prisoner returned to the camp after work, he was not able to wash; water had to be fetched in barrels, and there was barely enough for the kitchen. You could wash with snow, but since the camp was near a coal mine, the snow was always black; no matter how thoroughly you rubbed yourself with it, you didn't get clean.

We slept without blankets or pillows. We didn't even have the straw-filled sacks that served as mattresses in other prisons. You had to use the clothes you worked in as bedding—either to pad the surface you lay on, in which case you had nothing to cover yourself with, or else you could cover yourself with them, and then you slept on the naked board.

The barracks swarmed with bedbugs. On our days off, we were taken to a bath about eight kilometers away. It was a torment to get there because you had to go through a swamp. The bath had a capacity of seventy people; the rest had to wait outside in the cold until their turn came. Having a bath, therefore, took the entire day. Many prisoners were so weak that they would try to avoid these obligatory expeditions. They would hide in another barracks on bath days. Consequently, we were all infested with vermin.

It was useless to complain. The camp commander was a criminal who had surrounded himself with people like himself. They were not susceptible to reason or compassion.

There were no storage bins; the food was kept in barrels outside, next to the kitchen. We often observed the criminals breaking open these barrels right under the guards' noses and pulling out large chunks of meat, which they then cooked in their barracks. Only rarely were the political prisoners given any meat.

The prisoners were entitled to seven hundred grams of sugar a month. I was in the camp for more than two months and was given sugar only once. When I asked the camp commander why there was no sugar, he replied: "To get sugar, you have to work harder!"

Days of rest were rare. We worked through the week, including Sundays. Only the purga could interrupt this backbreaking routine. These snowstorms were so violent that sometimes you couldn't see two meters ahead of you. The purga was always welcomed with pleasure: we would lie on our bunks, sleeping or telling each other stories. Since there were no books, storytellers were in great demand. Some people had a good memory and could virtually recite a book as if they were reading it aloud.

We were allowed to write home. At first, I was convinced that no letter could possibly reach its destination from this godforsaken place; but then I heard from the old-timers that they had received answers to their letters, so I plucked up my courage and wrote. I hadn't heard from my wife in two years. I no longer dared to hope for an answer. But a month later I experienced an enormously happy day: a telegram arrived with a money order. I wasn't given the money. Only prisoners who regularly met the quotas set for their work and who had an unblemished record of good conduct had the right to receive money—up to fifty rubles a month. I did not fulfill these requirements.

One day, during one of the work stoppages caused by the purga, a camp official came to our barracks and read a hundred names off a list, mine among them. We were to pack our belongings and get ready for transfer to another camp in Norilsk as soon as the weather improved. We were glad; we had heard virtual fairy tales about Norilsk. Of course, I didn't believe everything I heard, but just the fact that there was supposed to be a bath there—or even just water—was reason enough to yearn for Norilsk.

The snowstorm didn't stop that day. Usually, we were glad when the purga raged, but now we were highly impatient. We wanted to see that miraculous place, Norilsk. When the weather improved, the prisoners elected for transfer were not sent out to work. Finally, the commander of the guard came and led us to the camp exit, where a detachment of soldiers took charge of us.

We climbed through a gorge and reached the road to Norilsk. After marching for two kilometers, we passed a women's camp. We hadn't seen any women for several years, so this was a great event. Each of us tried to look for as long as possible. They, too, noticed us and smiled as we passed.

Traffic became more and more lively on the wide road. We saw horse-drawn sleds, trucks, and even a team of reindeer in front of a house. We were approaching Norilsk.

HOW NORILSK WAS BUILT

Norilsk, a Soviet city in the region of Krasnoyarsk, is connected by railway to the port of Dudinka at the mouth of the Yenisei. The town of Norilsk was

*raised to the status of a city in 1953. A large state farm is situated near it
. . . By 1954, Norilsk had seven high schools, four secondary schools, five
primary schools, a Young Pioneer clubhouse, a theater, a movie house, and
three libraries. That year, a cultural palace, a public swimming pool, a
second movie house, and a conservatory were built.*

—*Great Soviet Encyclopedia*, 2nd ed., vol. 30

We reached a few primitive wooden barracks that served as storage sheds;
next to them was a workshop. Railroad tracks and other building material
lay scattered about in a disorderly tangle; they would eventually be used
in the construction of the railroad line connecting Norilsk to the Nadezhda
coal mine. I was reminded of a conversation I had had in the Nadezhda
camp one day.

Situated seventy-five miles from Dudinka, the center of the Taimyr
Peninsula, Norilsk had attracted public attention as far back as the sev-
enteen-sixties. The merchant Morozov had tried to exploit the great
natural resources of the surrounding wilderness, but had failed to find
workers willing to endure the forbidding cold and the isolation. Morozov
turned to the governor of Yeniseisk for help. The governor sent a report
to the tsar, pointing out that there were great quantities of precious ore
near Norilsk. Several years later, an imperial commission arrived in Norilsk, accompanied by the vice governor and the merchant Morozov. Another report was sent to the tsar; it confirmed the existence of huge
quantities of precious metals, but concluded that it would be impossible
to exploit them since the region had only two months of summer. During
the rest of the year, the extreme cold and the violent blizzards rendered
the area unfit for human habitation. The tsar concluded from this that
Morozov's scheme was impracticable.

The great "humanist" Stalin did not agree with the tsar. In 1935, he
instructed the NKVD to find the necessary specialists and laborers to set
up a camp in Norilsk by the following year. In the winter of 1935–36,
several hundred mining engineers were arrested; a few dozen doctors
were rounded up as well. All of them were charged with sabotage and
sentenced to ten years by the Troika. At the same time, five thousand
imprisoned workers, peasants, and intellectuals were waiting for the Yenisei to open for navigation. During the first days of the summer of 1936,
ships arrived in Norilsk bearing men, tools, food, and tents. And so, in
the summer of 1936, Norillag NKVD U.S.S.R., the NKVD camp of Norilsk, was set up.

The first prisoners to arrive in Norilsk were young and healthy. The
NKVD had selected them carefully, knowing that only the most hardy
would be able to survive the murderous climate and backbreaking work.
A medical commission examined each man carefully, paying special attention to the teeth, in view of the danger of scurvy.

The arrival of the first transport of prisoners caused great alarm among the Samoyed nomads, who grazed their reindeer and caught silver fox there during the summer. The reindeer became shy of their keepers, and few foxes ventured into the traps. So the nomads withdrew to the northeast.

From the Yenisei to Lake Pyasino, along a stretch roughly one hundred forty kilometers, tents were pitched six kilometers apart. A metal stove and several wooden bunks were installed in each tent. Two tents were used as a kitchen. The food provisions were stored in the open air. The food was good and sufficient. The prisoners even had condensed milk, lemons, and various supplements to protect them against scurvy.

For a year, the work consisted solely of building barracks. There was no wood in the area; it had to be shipped in. But first the snow and ice had to be cleared with pickaxes, crowbars, and spades—enormously arduous labor. During that first year, more than half of those young, hardy prisoners died of exhaustion, exposure, and disease. While the barracks were being built, geologists searched for natural treasures. They were able to send samples of nickel, copper, cobalt, and other nonferrous metals to Moscow. They also found large coal reserves.

In 1937, when twenty thousand new prisoners came to Norilsk, not all of them could be housed in barracks; many had to sleep in tents. More than half of these prisoners were now employed in the construction of the Norilsk–Dudinka narrow-gauge railroad. In 1938, thirty-five thousand prisoners arrived in Norilsk. Although new transports arrived constantly, the total number of inmates rose only slightly, for the death rate was extremely high; and many of those who survived were sick and incapable of working.

After three years of labor and countless deaths, the results were negligible. Stalin needed the nonferrous metals quickly, since he was preparing for war. The price of nonferrous metals rose daily, and the Soviet Union did not have enough hard currency to buy them on the world market. Matveyev, director of construction in Norilsk, was summoned to the Kremlin. Stalin gave him a deadline, in a fairly literal sense of the word: supply nickel and copper by 1939, or you'll be shot. Matveyev promised. 1939 came, and Norilsk had not yet delivered any metal. Matveyev and four of his assistants were shackled, taken to the Kolyma, and shot.

Abram Savenyagin took over the management of Norilsk: eighty barracks and a huge cemetery. Norilsk was only three years old, but its cemetery could compare with that of a hundred-year-old city. Savenyagin asked for qualified workers—engineers, technicians, economists. Four thousand prisoners from the Solovetsk Islands arrived. Those were the men Savenyagin and his assistant Volokhov needed.

Savenyagin and Volokhov distinguished themselves from their predecessors by recognizing that an enterprise of these proportions could not be pushed to completion by simple terror. They provided incentives to the engineers and technicians by granting them small privileges: better living quarters, better food, and other advantages. The general practice of the NKVD was to give the political prisoners the hardest physical labor and give the easier work to the criminals. Savenyagin and Volokhov broke with this principle; they engaged in a constant battle with the so-called third section of the NKVD, which was irritated by the sight of political prisoners—engineers and technicians—making drawings and calculations in heated rooms, instead of chipping away at the frozen wasteland outside. Curiously, however, Savenyagin and Volokhov were not removed from their posts; the NKVD contented itself with forcing Savenyagin to accept a second assistant, a certain Yeremeyev, whose function it was to prevent the political prisoners from enjoying too much comfort.

The first results weren't long in coming. After a year, chimneys were smoking in Norilsk, and the first shipment of nickel left the port of Dudinka.

RUDOLF ONDRATSCHEK'S DEATH

When I arrived in Norilsk, my companions and I were put in the camp's second section. It was already dark when the head of the section, Lehmann, gave us his instructions. We were glad to be sent to the bathhouse, where we not only showered but slept.

The next day, we were lodged in a stone barracks. There were eight thousand prisoners, both politicals and criminals, in the second section at that time. There were also eight hundred women; they were kept in separate barracks surrounded by barbed wire.

The next day, we went to work. It was very cold, about minus forty-five degrees Celsius. As we approached the gate, I thought for a moment I must be having a bad dream: a naked corpse was suspended from the gatepost. Its hands and feet were bound with wire, its head was sunk to one side, the rigid eyes were half open. Above the head was a board with the inscription: "This is the fate of all who try to escape from Norilsk."

The features looked familiar. I looked closer, but couldn't remember where I had seen that face before. On the way to work, I had the horrible thought: Wasn't that Rudolf? It couldn't be! How could Rudolf have planned an escape without telling me about it?

Several days passed. I didn't have friends yet in whom I could confide. I needed to talk to someone. One day, at the bath, I got into a conversation with the doctor who was on duty there. It turned out that he came from Leipzig. His name was Georg Biletzki, and we soon became friends. I asked him whether he had seen the corpse strung up on the main gate.

"Don't be surprised. You haven't seen anything yet," he said.

I told him why I was so interested. Georg advised me not to discuss the matter even with my closest friends. He promised to make some inquiries among his colleagues.

One Sunday, when we had a day off, Georg came into our barracks and asked me to come to his house with him. There he introduced me to Rayvycher, a doctor from Leningrad. Rayvycher worked as a surgeon in the hospital in section 1. He told me he had a very clear memory of the day Rudolf Ondratschek was brought to the hospital from the coal-mining camp. He was in serious condition, in an advanced stage of dysentery. There wasn't much hope for recovery. But after two months his health began to improve, and the doctors considered releasing him from the hospital.

"One evening," Rayvycher continued, "I was on duty when Ondratschek came and asked for some sleeping powder. I gave him some, he walked out, then we heard something fall. The nurse ran out. Ondratschek was lying in front of the door. I examined him, and he was dead. It was heart failure."

I asked Rayvycher why Ondratschek had been dubbed a fugitive. He said he did not know and it wasn't any of his business. Georg wanted to know who Ondratschek had been. I told him what I knew. Rudolf was born in Znaim, which is now part of Czechoslovakia. He was a functionary of the Czech Communist Party. In 1933, when Hitler came to power in Germany, Ondratschek happened to be in Berlin. He was thrown into a concentration camp, and there he experienced the cruelty of the Nazis. He was there for a year. After his release, he testified before an international forum in Geneva, telling about his experiences in the camp.

Later he emigrated to the Soviet Union with his wife and child. He worked for the Profintern, the international communist union, for several years. Then, when Stalin began to liquidate the old guard of the communist movement, Ondratschek was arrested as one of the first foreign communists, together with Franz Koritschoner, one of the founders of the Austrian Communist Party. The Troika sentenced Koritschoner to three years in prison. That was in 1936. He made an appeal, and was given a ten-year sentence in reply. In 1940, the NKVD delivered him into the hands of the Gestapo, who eventually murdered him.

After Ondratschek's arrest, friends advised his wife to return to Austria with her child.

"Ondratschek was a wonderful human being," I concluded my story. "I don't know where his wife and child are now or if they will ever learn the circumstances of his death."

I was put to work in an ore-processing plant. My job was to unload the copper and nickel ore as it was driven up in trucks or lorries. We worked from 8 a.m. to 8 p.m. In the course of those twelve hours, each prisoner had to unload sixteen tons of ore. In exchange, he would receive six hundred grams of bread and two warm meals a day consisting of half a liter of soup, two hundred grams of gruel, and a herring. If you produced less, you ate less. Very many prisoners were unable to meet the high quota. They were called up in the evening before the brigades returned to the camp and had to work until they had produced the required amount. Every two hours, those who had met the quota were taken back. Some had to work all night and continue through the day when the rest of the brigade arrived.

Many prisoners broke down. Some were so exhausted that they lost consciousness and had to be driven directly from the work site to the hospital. When the doctors examined them, the thermometers didn't register the body temperature because it was so far below normal. To revive these people, the doctors would put them in a tub of cold water. Many never woke up at all.

As more and more people died of overexertion, the camp administration set a limit of two hours' overtime for prisoners who couldn't meet the quota.

Despite the hard work, life was better here than in Nadezhda. There was enough to eat, the barracks were roomier, and while there were bedbugs, there were no lice. We were allowed a bath every ten days, and you didn't have to trek ten kilometers through difficult terrain to get there. The medical help here was better, too; we had qualified doctors who made an effort to ease the prisoners' lot.

I remember especially Drs. Nikishin, Bayev, and Rosenblum of the Leningrad Military Academy, as well as Dr. Sukhorukov of Moscow, who did their best to help the prisoners. They worked under the sharp supervision of the heads of medical services, and if they were *too* helpful, they could be forced to trade their white smock for a pickax. But they would rather risk such punishment than send a sick man to work. Sukhorukov had once been the doctor of an athletic club in Moscow. In the summer of 1936, the club's soccer team went to Sweden. It was the athletes' first trip abroad. When they returned and started telling people that the capitalist world wasn't as miserable a place as they'd heard, the entire team was arrested, along with the doctor, and sent to labor camps for ten years.

The head of medical services in section 2 was Alexandra Ivanovna Sleptsova. She had come to Norilsk with her husband, who was the director of the mines. He had been instructed by the party to keep a watchful eye on the prisoners and prevent them from committing acts of sabotage. In reality, it was the prisoners who had to keep an eye on the engineers, most of whom were young and inexperienced, and prevent them from making stupid mistakes. The prisoners, in effect, did the work for which their free supervisors were being paid. Most of the free engineers and technicians had their minds more on drink than on work, as they knew that they could depend on their captive colleagues to do a very conscientious job.

Dr. Sleptsova was young and pretty; she didn't have much medical experience, but she had a kind heart. Her principle was: "I distinguish only between the healthy and the sick." She was noticeably respectful and even friendly toward the doctors among the prisoners; and she wasn't above learning from them. Of course, she had to watch out for the NKVD. Alexandra Sleptsova successfully lobbied for the establishment of a separate hospital kitchen, so that the sick might be given special diets under her supervision. The patients were never made to feel that they were prisoners. Dr. Sleptsova saw to it that men released from the hospital weren't sent back immediately to hard labor. You would often see this young doctor standing in front of the gate in the early morning to prevent convalescing patients from being sent out to work. Naturally, this brought her into frequent conflict with the camp administration. Woe to the camp policeman whom Dr. Sleptsova saw beating a prisoner! She would see to it that such brutes—who were themselves prisoners—were demoted to a hard-labor brigade.

The NKVD agents disliked her attitude, but they were unable to take measures against her because her husband was a leading functionary of the Norilsk party organization. Many prisoners owe their lives to this courageous woman.

I worked in the ore-processing plant for several months. I was unaccustomed to such hard labor; and perhaps the food was insufficiently nourishing to support the constant exertion. I was beginning to feel too tired to go on very much longer. I turned to Georg Biletzki for help. He discussed my case with his colleagues, and Dr. Nikishin requested that I be assigned less strenuous work, in view of my debilitated physical condition. I was summoned before a medical commission, and those doctors ordered that I be given a light work load, despite the protest of the NKVD representative, who kept stressing that I was a "hardened criminal." I was employed as a first-aid man in the hospital.

When a typhus epidemic broke out in the camp, an auxiliary hospital had to be built, and I was made head of that hospital. I worked in this capacity for four months, to the satisfaction of the sick and of Dr. Sleptsova, the head of medical services. After the epidemic passed, the auxiliary hospital was dismantled and I had to return to hard labor; but I had recovered my strength.

There were many foreigners in the camp, among them several striking personalities. Josef Berger, whom I already knew, was the most extraordinary of all. He had been a communist since early youth and was highly educated and exceptionally intelligent. What distinguished him in the eyes of his fellow prisoners was his helpfulness, his kindness, his inexhaustible willingness to subordinate his needs to the needs of others. Although he was physically weak, he exerted himself to ease the heavy work loads of other prisoners. He always took newcomers under his wing; they did not know the ropes yet and were particularly exposed to the caprice of the camp administrators and the terror of the criminal convicts.

Berger procured bread for them, gave them tobacco and warm clothes.

Before he was arrested, Berger had been a leading functionary of the Executive Committee of the Communist International in Moscow; for several years, he had been the head of the Comintern's Executive Committee for the Near East. In 1935, he was arrested as a Trotskyite and sentenced to five years; five years later, he was sentenced again.

THE TRAGEDY OF GORNAYA SHORIYA

It was Josef Berger who told me about the tragedy of the camp called Gornaya Shoriya. He was one of the few survivors.

In the summer of 1935, Berger was driven from the Butyrki to the Moscow–North train station, along with four hundred other prisoners. They were loaded into freight cars and taken across the Volga, across the Ural, to a transit prison in Stalinsk (formerly Novokuznetsk). There they were deloused and permitted to rest for twenty-four hours. Then they were given provisions for three days and sent off—on foot—into the taiga, the primeval forest of Siberia. They were walking on a trail, the only one in that region. Once in a rare while, they would see the tents of Kirghiz nomads, whose narrowly slanted eyes followed the strange procession curiously as it passed by. Some of the guards were Kirghiz as well; they exchanged words with their countrymen which no one else could understand.

The path became steeper. Often, the prisoners had to struggle single file through the wildly tangled bush. Suddenly they reached the end of the forest: all you could see was naked rock and cliffs; each step sent stones rolling down. They walked through this stone desert for several miles. Then they reentered the dense forest. They marched from dawn to dusk, with a rest at midday. Forty small Siberian horses carried the provisions. In the evening, the prisoners set up tents. They slept on the bare ground. A circle of bonfires had to be kept burning around the campsite, to frighten off the wild animals. You could hear wolves and jackals howling all night; the horses reacted with frightened whinnies.

After a three-week march, they reached their destination, a vast high plateau where they were to build their prison. Twenty prisoners had fallen ill and been left behind; when soldiers returned several days later with horses to pick up the sick, they found only bones and rags.

Tents were set up for both prisoners and guards. One large tent served as a kitchen; another, as an infirmary. Then the camp commander declared a three-day rest period. Meals consisted of preserves and dried vegetables, but there was enough to eat and the prisoners regained their strength quickly. The work wasn't hard, because no quotas had been set yet.

Every week and eventually every day, new groups of prisoners arrived. The camp's prison population numbered twelve thousand when the snow began to fall. Eventually, two meters of snow covered the camp, and Gornaya Shoriya was cut off from the rest of the world. The NKVD had forgotten one minor detail: people and horses have to be fed. They had brought enough provisions for two months. The camp commander decided to cut the prisoners' rations in half. He told the prisoners this was a temporary measure; the Gulag (the central administration of labor camps, located in Moscow) had been notified by radio and had promised to send help by plane. Despite their diminished rations, the prisoners did not experience any hunger yet, and waited patiently for the planes.

One day, the entire camp was mobilized to clear a landing site in the snow for the planes. Everyone worked with an enthusiasm that had never been seen in the camp before. Wood fires were lit on the edges of the runway, in case the planes had to land by night. But the planes did not come. It kept snowing; the runway had to be cleared again and again. A month passed without any news. Again, the rations had to be cut in half. The prisoners were still patient. Only the hungry horses began to neigh day and night. Every day, horses were slaughtered to feed the prisoners and save on oats, which were needed to feed the remaining horses.

Finally, the airplanes arrived. At the sound of their approaching motors, everyone rushed outside, shouting with joy and waving hats and scarves. The planes circled the camp for a long time but made no attempt to land. After several hours, you could see boxes and sacks being dropped out of one of the planes and drifting down on parachutes. Most of them dropped into the surrounding woods; a few sank into the deep snow on the edge of the camp. The second airplane tried to aim better but had little success.

The soldiers and prisoners gathered up as many of the provisions as they could find—warm clothes and zwieback, mainly. It wasn't anywhere near enough, but spirits were higher than they had been for a long time. There was hope.

Two weeks later, another airplane came; it landed and brought bread and preserves. The prisoners' rations were raised by a few grams. But by now many prisoners were dying of starvation. The camp commander released most of the guards from duty so they could hunt in the forest. They came back with a great many beasts, including a few bears. It still wasn't enough. Most of the fresh meat was used to feed the guards and officers.

Deaths began to multiply. The corpses couldn't be buried; they were stacked up and covered with snow. When spring came and the snow melted, the stench of rotting corpses pervaded the camp. The few survivors were scarcely able to summon the strength to dig trenches and bury their dead comrades.

A typhus epidemic broke out. The doctors were unable to help, since they had no medication.

When the trail finally became passable, food was brought in on horseback. Only three hundred of the original twelve hundred prisoners were still alive. Then the NKVD brought thousands of new convicts from various transit prisons to Gornaya Shoriya.

THE HUNGARIAN LAWYER KEROSI-MOLNÁR

Many still remember the trials of the Hungarian communists Salaj and Fürst, who were sentenced to death and hanged by the Horthy regime. In Norilsk, in 1939, I met the lawyer who defended Salaj and Fürst. His name was Kerosi-Molnár.

Barracks 14 had a day off for bathing. Two hundred men came into the bath, while their clothes were being disinfected in another room. After the bath, one of the prisoners discovered that his underwear was missing. The thief had to be one of the service personnel, who were all criminals. To lose your underwear was a very serious matter. It was unthinkable to go out into the terrible cold without it. Moreover, the victim of the theft would be severely punished and would have to pay the camp administration five times what the garments were worth.

In desperation, the prisoner turned to the man in charge of the bathhouse, also a criminal. He got a beating in return. An athletically built man rushed up and seized the criminal's arms from behind. Now all the service personnel came running to their boss's aid. There was a brawl, and the politicals gained the upper hand. Thereupon the camp police came and dragged several politicals to the punishment cell, among them the athlete—who was Kerosi-Molnár—and me. We became more closely acquainted in the punishment cell. I learned that after his clients' execution he had had to seek refuge in Russia. He was arrested during the great purge, and a military court sentenced him to ten years for being an "agent of the Horthy police."

After our release from the punishment cell, Kerosi and I were put in the same work brigade. We were helping to build a large metallurgical factory. It was terribly hard work; we had to hack the foundation out of the ground with pickaxes and crowbars. The frozen earth was harder than granite. Despite the great cold, we had to take off our coats; our bodies were steaming.

Kerosi was very strong; the work wasn't as hard for him as it was for the others. He was always in good spirits. In the evening, he sat on the top bunk translating Pushkin into Hungarian. I never heard Kerosi complain of hunger, although he surely was as hungry as everyone else; he was full of hope and confidence; he often dreamed of the day when he would return to Budapest and work as a lawyer again.

THE FATE OF THE SCHUTZBUND MILITANTS

After the Austrian workers' uprising of 1934 was crushed by the fascists, most of the members of the Schutzbund* fled to Czechoslovakia. The Czech Social Democrats and Syndicalists provided them with food and lodging in camps outside Brünn and other cities.

Agitators were sent among the members of the Schutzbund, with the aim of severing their ties to the Social Democrats and recruiting them into the communist movement. Those efforts were fruitful. Demonstrations were organized in the camps against the socialist leadership. Many Schutzbund members pinned the Soviet star to their shirts, and the red flag with the hammer and sickle was hoisted on many barracks roofs. Individual Schutzbund members were expelled from the camps. Those homeless people sought and found refuge with communist organizations. The Austrian Communist Party turned to the Soviet leadership for help, and the Soviets agreed to invite the Schutzbund members to become permanent residents in the Soviet Union.

The first transport which arrived at the Belorussky Station in Moscow was welcomed by a band. A demonstration was organized on the square outside the station. The Austrian communists Koplenig and Grossmann made speeches, and several members of the Soviet Communist Party lauded the immigrants as heroes and revolutionaries. The Schutzbund members marched in closed formation through the streets of Moscow toward the Europa Hotel in the center of town. A banquet had been prepared for them. An orchestra was playing. Delicious food was served, and the newcomers made toasts and sang revolutionary songs.

For several weeks, you could see Schutzbund people walking through the streets of Moscow, either singly or in groups. You could recognize them by their voluminous trousers—*Pumphosen*—and their berets. Gradually they disappeared from the inner city. You could still see them in the industrial quarters of Moscow, Kharkov, Leningrad, Rostov, and other cities.

At that time, bread coupons were being eliminated in Russia. The Russian workers were glad to be able to buy bread and other staples in the industrial centers without the restriction of rationing, but the Austrians were beginning to grumble. They complained that there was only black bread in the stores, and that sugar was in short supply. The Austrian communist leaders in Moscow rushed to the factories where the Schutzbund people were working, hoping to pacify them. They had to listen to some unpleasant words:

---

* Republican Schutzbund—League for the Protection of the Austrian Socialist Party, founded in 1924 and dissolved in 1933 by Dollfuss. The author is referring to conflicts that erupted a year later.—*Trans.*

"You deceived us!"

"Let us go back to Austria!"

Schutzbund members started going to the Austrian embassy in Moscow, individually at first and then in groups, asking to be returned to their country. But the Austrian embassy was in no hurry to accede to their demands. While the Austrian authorities debated the matter, the NKVD arrested the Schutzbund members as they left the Austrian embassy, tried them as counterrevolutionaries, and deported them to the extreme north. As a rule, they were given sentences of eight to ten years.

I met several Schutzbund men in Norilsk in 1939; unfortunately, I don't remember their names. I made friends with one of them, Fritz Koppensteiner. He had lived in the tenth district of Vienna with his parents. Koppensteiner was a very strong fellow. To assuage his hunger, he regularly donated blood. The medical services of Norilsk rewarded every blood donation with ten eggs, a kilogram of sugar, half a kilogram of butter, a kilogram of dried fruit, and two kilograms of fresh vegetables. Koppensteiner gave blood every two months; when I warned him against such frequent loss of blood, he assured me that it wasn't hurting him, that he was feeling quite well. One day, he got sick. He complained of pains in his chest and his kidneys. His condition grew more and more serious, until he had to be hospitalized. After a few weeks, he was released from the hospital; he seemed to be in better health.

Shortly before the outbreak of the war, Koppensteiner was taken to Krasnoyarsk. Whenever prisoners came to Norilsk from Krasnoyarsk, I asked if they knew anything about Koppensteiner, but no one had met him or heard anything about him.

A THOUSAND DEVILS

The construction of the metallurgical factory of Norilsk was assuming larger and larger proportions. Droves of new prisoners were brought in every day; we worked day and night in every kind of weather. We had very few days of rest. It was so cold I sometimes feared my brain would freeze solid inside my skull. But our worst enemy wasn't the temperature—it was the purga, the subarctic blizzard. When the purga broke loose, you couldn't see farther than two meters. We would go to work in groups of five, arm in arm. Even that didn't always help; sometimes the storm was so violent it would throw you to the ground.

Each time the purga erupted, it felt as if the world was coming to an end, no matter how many times you'd been through it. Darkness fell and all you could hear was the shrieking of the storm: "*Sheee . . . sheee . . . sheee,*" as if a thousand devils were screaming around you. This could last as long as four weeks. Sometimes the barracks got completely snowed in, and it was impossible to get in or out. On such days, you couldn't even walk the fifty or sixty meters to fetch your food from the kitchen.

And if anyone succeeded in getting there, he could be sure of losing his food, along with his precious tin bowl.

There was little opportunity to warm up at one's work, especially during the first years, before solid structures were built where you could get out of the purga's way. During periods of extreme cold, the prisoners were allowed to light fires, and people would huddle around them to warm their hands and feet.

The purga was especially destructive if it surprised you on the way to or from work. Everything would go topsy-turvy: the guards would lose sight of the prisoners, and we would come straggling along, unguarded, in small groups. Occasionally, individual guards or prisoners would lose their way and be found frozen to death just twenty or thirty meters from the camp.

For four months in the year, the sun doesn't rise in Norilsk. As if to make up for that, there are four summer months when the sun doesn't set. I think the four months of solar day were harder to endure than the polar night. The long night at least had the advantage of reducing your work hours.

Needless to say, adequate clothing was very important under these conditions: padded pants, a padded jacket (*telogreika*), a short padded coat (*bushlat*), and felt boots (*valenki*). As a rule, political prisoners were not given new clothes; these were reserved for the camp officials, who presumably needed them most, since they didn't work outdoors. To protect themselves from the cold, the prisoners wrapped themselves in all kinds of rags. The face was usually protected by a mask. In full "uniform," we looked like bears. Often, we couldn't recognize each another.

There were brigades in the camps that consisted of completely emaciated, exhausted people. They were called Indians because they were so skinny that they resembled Gandhi. They were only employed for auxiliary tasks like clearing snow, fetching tools, etc. Those unfortunate men suffered more from the cold than any of us. Their garments were stitched together out of rags, and in place of felt boots they were given *burki,* shoes made of old clothes, with soles made of automobile tires. Many a frozen foot or hand had to be amputated. Every year, hundreds of cripples were transported from Norilsk to other camps, where they were put to work making clothes and shoes. If they had been given clothes and shoes in the first place, they would not have become cripples.

Anyone who was sick but was not admitted to the hospital was treated with particular cruelty. Generally, a prisoner had to have a high fever or be seriously wounded or crippled to be excused from work. There were many exhausted men who were forced to work until they broke down. On the way home to the barracks, it was a common sight to see the stronger men helping or carrying others who were too exhausted to walk.

Each camp section had a medical station that was headed by a non-convict. The doctors and their aides were prisoners. As a rule, the medical station represented a prisoner's only refuge. Despite the strict controls imposed on them, the doctors were able, to some degree, to subvert the NKVD's murderous regime. The NKVD's policy was obvious: a prisoner should be kept alive as long as he could be put to work. Once he ceased to be productive, he was to be sent to a mass grave—without any breach of "legality," of course. Thanks to the doctors, though, the NKVD did not always succeed in their plans. I would like to mention a few of those who did their utmost to keep the prisoners healthy and alive: Nikishin, Mardna, Bayev, Rosenblum, Sukhorukov, Brilyant, Biletzki, and Baltes; their achievement was great. There were very good people among the noncaptive doctors as well, such as Sleptsova, the head of the central hospital, and Sorokin, and others.

But there were also some who were worthy instruments of the NKVD— like Shevchuk, Kharchenko, and their like.

SPANISH REPUBLICANS IN THE U.S.S.R.

After Franco's victory, the remnants of the Republican Army fled to France, where they were interned in refugee camps. The non-Spaniards returned to their respective countries—those which weren't under fascist rule. Some of the Spanish Republicans emigrated to Latin America; others were able to settle in France. The rest led a pitiful existence in the camps. Not a country in the world wanted to take in these revolutionaries. They weren't welcome in Stalin's Russia, either—even though many of them were members of the Spanish Communist Party.

Finding adequate employment and housing for all those people was becoming a very difficult problem for the French government. The bourgeois newspapers took up the issue and asked why the Soviet Union was turning a deaf ear to the plight of the Spanish refugees. Finally, Stalin declared himself willing to grant asylum to the children of Spanish Republicans.

About five thousand Spanish children came to the Soviet Union in several transports. They were received by the International Red Aid (MOPR) and taken to child-care centers, where they were well treated. Adult Spanish refugees were still not allowed into the country, except for Dolores Ibarruri and other leading officials of the Spanish Communist Party—they were given asylum. They expressed their thanks by applauding Stalin when he put Lenin's old comrades before a firing squad.

On some occasion or other, Manuilsky asked Stalin to allow a few thousand members of the Spanish Republican Army into the Soviet Union. Stalin was capable of generosity: he gave his consent, and he is supposed to have said to Manuilsky, by way of conclusion: "Take care that these Spaniards don't give us the same problems we had with the Schutzbund people."

In Paris, the Spaniards received new clothes at the expense of the

Soviet government. Then they were taken to Odessa, where they were given a festive reception rather like the one that welcomed the Schutz-bund members. They were put up in hotels for several weeks, a period of rest and relaxation. Then they were sent to various Russian and Ukrain-ian cities. Those who had skills found work in factories; the others were apprenticed.

The Central Committee of the Soviet Communist Party gave instruc-tions to pay the Spaniards the maximum monthly salary allowed a Soviet worker. No quotas were to be set for them. The Spaniards enjoyed those privileges for three months. Then they were told that from then on they would have to meet a quota just like the Russian workers. They didn't take this seriously and continued working at their accustomed pace. When they received their salary at the end of the month, they discovered that it amounted to only a few hundred rubles, scarcely enough for eight days. They made some noise. Attempts were made to calm them down, but their indignation only grew. In order to avoid a scandal, the unions vol-unteered to pay the Spaniards out of their own funds. For a month, everything was quiet.

The Spanish workers who were qualified found that if they made an effort they could earn just enough money to support a modest existence. But the unskilled workers were earning so little that they couldn't afford the necessities of life. The agitation among the Spaniards mounted. Many abandoned their work and went to Moscow, where they laid siege to the Spanish section of the Comintern. They were given temporary financial support and were instructed to return to their places of work. But the forty Spaniards employed in the locomotive factory of Kharkov went on strike after receiving their paychecks. That was the signal for the NKVD to step in. Spaniards in all Soviet cities were arrested, tried for counter-revolutionary activities, and sentenced to eight to ten years.

In 1940, a group of two hundred and fifty Spaniards arrived in Norilsk. These children of the south had to serve their long sentences in northern Siberia! Many had fallen ill on the way from Moscow. I was told there were three hundred on the day they left the capital; more than fifty had to be hospitalized on the way. Of the two hundred and fifty Spaniards who came to Norilsk, a hundred eighty found their graves there. The rest were transported to Karaganda in 1941.

KOLARGON—A DISCIPLINARY CAMP

There were several disciplinary camps in Norilsk. They were reserved for prisoners who were guilty of a breach of discipline or some other infraction. Internment in these places was limited to a maximum of six months, but there were some prisoners who never came back.

One of the worst disciplinary camps was Kolargon. Whoever entered its gates was very quickly persuaded to abandon all hope. Kolargon had two regimes: the camp regime and the prison regime, according to the nature of one's transgression. Everyone had to work; the only difference was that some were locked into cells after working, while the others could move around the camp freely after a certain hour.

Kolargon was mainly populated with prisoners who had refused to work. Many of them were criminals who tried to avoid work as a matter of pride. They stuck to this principle with remarkable firmness, which wasn't difficult for them, since the camp administration treated them with leniency. But woe to the political prisoner who refused to work, for whatever reason! Mostly the reasons had to do with religious conviction. There were members of various religious sects in the camp; a great number of them were Adventists, who had refused to work for the Antichrist, Stalin. When the usual measures—disciplinary rations, punishment cells, etc.—failed to work, those people were sent to Kolargon, where they had to live and work alongside the worst criminals.

There were various methods of avoiding work in the camps. Some prisoners dug holes in the ground and crawled under the barracks; others hid in the toilet after inspection; some would lie down among the corpses in the morgue and hope that the inspectors, who searched there too, wouldn't see them. Others didn't hide but looked for excuses, like sickness or lack of warm clothes. These cases were usually reported by the brigadier to the head of the work division or his assistant; he would call for the camp police, who would storm into the barracks with heavy sticks in their hands. The matter usually ended with the prisoner being dragged to the punishment cell and being beaten up there. Then the commander of the military guards would report to the camp commanders, who would sentence the prisoner to five days in the punishment cell. After that, the delinquent would have to work all the harder and would be given less food into the bargain.

It often happened that a prisoner could not be cajoled or forced to go to work. He'd strip naked, hide all his clothes, and climb into the top bunk; the camp police would come, but they couldn't bring themselves to chase a stark-naked man into the terrible cold. This problem was eventually solved by keeping some clothes on hand. If a man refused to get dressed, they would carry him out naked, throw him on a horse-drawn sled, cover him with a sheepskin, tie him to the sled, and drive him to work; there they would untie him, after which he was forced to get dressed. By this time, his hands and feet would be so frozen that he was unable to work. This technique served the camp administration well: the number of work refusals decreased. Recidivists were sent to Kolargon.

The majority of the prisoners at Kolargon worked in a stone quarry; others did construction work. The work wasn't harder there than in the other camps, but the conditions were so terrible, the regime so capricious in its constant violence and injustice, that no normal human being could endure it for long.

The camp's food stock was constantly stolen, and whatever was left went to those who had done the least to earn it.

There was a perpetual war among the criminals. For there were two kinds, the so-called decent criminals and the "whores." The "decent" criminals were those who refused to compromise with the camp administrators; that is, they refused to work, refused to serve as camp policemen, and lived like parasites. Even though it was practically impossible to escape from Norilsk, many criminals dreamed of escaping. Some of them did manage to run away and disappear for a while among the small free population of Norilsk, stealing and often murdering, until they were caught again and given new sentences. "Whore" was the name given those criminals who were on good terms with the camp authorities, held relatively cushy positions as camp officials or policemen, and denounced others to the authorities.

The war among the criminals sometimes took a brutal turn—murders and severe injuries were the order of the day. Regular battles sometimes broke out, with tools being used as weapons. Usually, these fights ended with several deaths and serious injuries.

Needless to say, living in this kind of environment was torture for any decent person. It wasn't much fun for the criminals either, which is why they tried hard to get out of Kolargon. One favorite method of shortening one's stay there was to inflict a serious wound on oneself. There were carefully staged accidents: a heavy stone would drop on a man's foot with such force that he would have to be taken to the hospital. Others would freeze their toes or fingers. Self-mutilation with an ax was very popular. Many didn't have the courage to do it themselves and would ask someone else for assistance. The operation would usually be performed as follows: one of the men would set up a wooden block and position himself, ax in hand; the others stood in line, stepping forward one by one to have two or three fingers chopped off. No more hard labor after that!

When self-mutilation started to take on epidemic proportions, the camp officials decreed that self-mutilators were not to be taken to the hospital; a doctor would bandage them on the spot, and they would have to stay at their place of work. Many died as a result—not because their wounds were fatal, but because they became infected due to the lack of medical care.

The criminals kept searching for and finding new ways of getting out of Kolargon. They would commit terrible crimes in order to be transferred to the central prison—a murder was what it took. You might be sitting peacefully by an open fire, trying to get some warmth, when one of the criminals would suddenly raise an ax or some other instrument of death and cleave the next best skull in half. In the winter of 1939–40 alone, more than four hundred murders of this sort were committed. The investigation would last three or four months; during this time, the murderer didn't have to work and lay back comfortably on his prison bunk.

Eventually, the director of the NKVD ruled that in such cases the investigation should be conducted in Kolargon, so that the crime would not be "rewarded" with a transfer to another place.

PROVOCATEURS

The NKVD submitted its prisoners and deportees to constant spying. Individual prisoners were recruited by means of promises—easier work, perhaps even an early release—to report on the conversations of their fellow convicts. As the years passed, a regular network of informants was organized in this manner. It wasn't hard to find critics of the NKVD or Stalin among people convicted for crimes they hadn't committed.

Particular attention was given to certain prisoners who were considered especially dangerous by the NKVD. One day, a prisoner named Roshankovsky came up to me and asked where I came from. When I told him I came from Vienna, he seemed happily surprised and said he had studied in Vienna and was extremely fond of the Viennese. I, too, was glad to have found a compatriot of sorts. Roshankovsky was very interested in knowing whether I was finding my work too hard or my meals insufficient. He promised to talk about me to his friend, the kitchen supervisor, to see if he could arrange for me to get bigger rations, maybe even a job in the kitchen. I was very grateful to Roshankovsky.

After some time, he came back to me and said the kitchen supervisor, Larionov, had said he was willing to help me out. I went to speak to Larionov. He asked me whether I had ever worked in a kitchen. I told him I didn't know the slightest thing about cooking. "Well, I'll see what I can do for you," Larionov said, and began to ask me about my past. I briefly told him my story: that I was an Austrian, a functionary of the Austrian Communist Party, that I had worked for years in the Yugoslavian Communist Party, had lived in Paris for a while, and then came to the Soviet Union. Larionov listened with intense interest and wanted to hear more and more. To encourage me, he told the cook to give me "something good" to eat. The cook served me a bowl of soup with meat and noodles and a large piece of bread.

"Eat first. We can talk later," Larionov said.

The food was good; it was nice and warm in the room; my face was sweating. When I finished eating, Larionov asked me if I wanted anything else. I said thank you, I'd had enough. I had left a piece of bread uneaten; Larionov advised me to take it with me. He put it in a paper bag and added a large lump of sugar. "Honestly, Steiner," he said with a smile, "when you were walking around those Western cities, did you ever imagine that socialism would be like this?"

"No, I never imagined it," I said.

He wasn't satisfied with that. He kept asking questions and was terribly eager to hear my opinion.

"It's not just I who had a different idea of socialism. Millions of people believe that a better world is being born in Russia and that this Soviet socialism will bring freedom and prosperity not only to the Russian people but eventually to the whole world. Instead, what do we have here? Millions of prisoners and slaves. Doesn't this prove that what we have here is not the power of the people but the power of an incomparable tyranny *against* the people? Where do all these enemies of the regime come from? Haven't we always heard that, under capitalism, a tiny minority holds power, and all you need is to smash that minority's power and the masses will be free to finally govern themselves? But what do we see in Russia? The old evil has been replaced by a new one, an even greater evil."

Larionov was thrilled. "Just come here any time you're hungry! People like you shouldn't go without food. I'll talk to the commander and ask him to let me hire you."

GENRIKH YAGODA'S SISTER

That same day, a man from the kitchen came and said Larionov wanted to talk to me. Larionov told me with obvious satisfaction that he had succeeded in convincing the camp commander, Lieutenant Lehmann, to let me work in the kitchen; he had found some easy work for me.

There was a small grain mill, built by prisoners, in a little room next to the kitchen. Under Larionov's tutelage, I learned how to operate it. I was overjoyed. Now I had an easy job, didn't have to go out into the terrible cold, and could eat my fill.

The mill had to be operated around the clock, and the person working the second shift was a woman named Taissa Grigorevna Yagoda, sister of the former head of the NKVD, Genrikh Yagoda. A former druggist, Genrikh Yagoda had worked for the GPU for sixteen years. In 1933, Stalin had awarded him the Lenin Prize. In 1935, he was appointed General Commissar for State Security. In 1938, he was a defendant in one of the great show trials. Accused of being a foreign agent, he was sentenced to death and was shot.

Taissa Yagoda was thirty-two years old, tall, slender, with black, slightly graying hair. She had been arrested for the sole reason that she was Yagoda's sister, and had been given ten years. Because of her relationship to Yagoda, she had a particularly hard time in camp. I could see in the kitchen that the cooks deprived her of food.

Taissa was very happy to have me for a friend, as the criminal who had preceded me had tormented her constantly. I would go to the kitchen and pick up enough food for the two of us. But when the cooks learned that I was sharing my meals with the hated Taissa, they didn't want to give me anything either. I tried to explain that the poor woman wasn't responsible for her brother's crimes; but the only result was that they began to hate me, too. In the beginning, Taissa was taciturn; later she began to trust me and confided certain details of her and her brother's life.

One Sunday, we were sitting in the room where the fish was prepared for cooking; we were alone. Taissa told me that she liked me a lot and that she had long yearned for a friend. She leaned her head on my shoulder. I hadn't been this close to a woman in years; I had recovered my health and occasionally felt the stirring of desire; but for some inexplicable reason I did not feel attracted to Taissa. I disengaged myself as gently as I could.

I was working the night shift that day, and Taissa stayed till eleven o'clock. There was enough flour in the bin, so we had time to rest and talk. I asked her why she thought her brother, one of Stalin's close associates, had been shot. At first, she didn't want to talk about it. Then she said her brother wasn't as bad as some people believed. "Otherwise," she said, "he'd still be alive and in office. He had to die. During the last years, Stalin was demanding such inhuman things that Genrikh just wanted to quit. He had to do many things that went against his conscience. Secretly, he was living in deep conflict with himself. Then, after Stalin murdered his wife, Alliluyeva, a dramatic struggle developed. Stalin told my brother to find a reliable doctor to certify that Alliluyeva had committed suicide. My brother summoned Levin, a well-known heart specialist, and told him what Stalin wanted. Levin was indignant. My brother said he would not let Levin leave his office unless he did what he was told, but Levin firmly refused.

"Several days later, the newspapers reported that Levin had been arrested, that he had committed horrible crimes, such as deliberately making false diagnoses in the treatment of leading party officials, molesting little girls, etc. Levin was interrogated day and night for several weeks, and his whole family was arrested. Finally, he gave in and signed a certificate stating that Alliluyeva had committed suicide.

"A rumor was already circulating in Moscow that there was something suspicious about Alliluyeva's death. Levin was a highly respected medical authority; his signature was supposed to silence these suspicions. Levin was released, and the newspapers published a short announcement that the charges against Levin had been based on slanderous reports and that the individuals responsible for these attacks would be severely punished. Later, Levin was arrested again; he died in prison.

"My brother's fate was sealed when Stalin decided to get rid of Maxim Gorky. Gorky was, to all appearances, on good terms with Stalin. He had publicly condoned his crimes through the years; in exchange, he seemed to have gained the right to criticize him—at least, he thought so. Stalin went along with this for a while, but eventually he got sick of Gorky and decided to liquidate him. So he turned to my brother—knowing that he was a friend of Gorky's daughter-in-law and a frequent visitor in Gorky's house.

"My brother was simply unable to act. He procrastinated. One day, Stalin asked him how long Gorky was going to go on 'stinking up the atmosphere.' My brother hurried home and took steps to get his closest relatives out of the country. He confided in his friend Besedovsky, the head of the NKVD's foreign division. Besedovsky promised to help him but instead went to Stalin and told him about my brother's plans. My brother was arrested and locked up, along with Bukharin, Rykov, Pyatakov, and the other old Bolsheviks whose liquidation he himself had helped prepare."

I worked only a few more weeks in the kitchen. It wasn't until later that I learned why.

AFTER THE STALIN–HITLER PACT

On August 29, 1939, Molotov and Ribbentrop signed the German–Soviet non-aggression pact. After several dozen bottles of champagne had been emptied, Ribbentrop turned to Stalin and asked for the repatriation of German nationals living in the Soviet Union. Stalin agreed; the technical details were left to Molotov. No one asked the German expatriates whether they wanted to return to their country. Most of them were communists, and the majority were locked up in prisons and camps.

In late January 1940, in Norilsk, all German and Austrian prisoners were rounded up and herded into barracks 0 of section 2. None of the prisoners had any idea why, since no one knew of the Stalin–Hitler pact. Many presumed that the end was near; but the general mood was so apathetic that only a few lamented at the thought of imminent death. The atmosphere changed radically when a truck laden with packages pulled up in front of the barracks. We were told to unload the packages and bring them into the barracks. Then an officer came in, called up the Germans one by one, and told us to take off our ragged clothes and boots and put on the brand-new garments that had come in the packages. In addition to clothes, everyone got a knapsack filled with lard, bread, and sugar. We were speechless with astonishment. The NKVD officers were being unusually friendly; but they answered our questions evasively. Finally, the head of the Norilsk NKVD came to tell us that we were being taken to Moscow.

It turned out that we couldn't leave right away: the purga was in full fury, and the airplanes couldn't land. After a few days, a plane succeeded in landing in Norilsk; eighteen Germans were taken aboard. But after two hours, the plane had to turn back and the eighteen men returned to the barracks. We had to wait for the weather to improve. In the meantime, the new provisions were being greedily devoured; many of us got sick because we were unaccustomed to such rich food. Then more provisions were brought to replenish the empty knapsacks. The camp officials were being awfully generous. We sat around in groups, discussing our situation.

My friend Roshankovsky, who had lots of free time, took a great interest in these discussions.

Finally, the weather improved, and after waiting for two weeks, the same eighteen men who had been aboard the plane earlier were flown off. Another forty were supposed to be picked up the next day. But the weather got worse again, and the airplanes stayed away. Another ten days passed. Then we were all taken back to our former barracks. No explanation was given.

It wasn't until 1941, after the outbreak of the Russo–German War, that the secret of all those comings and goings was clarified. In the summer of 1941, a new group of prisoners arrived in Norilsk, among them one of the eighteen who had been taken off by plane. His name was Otto Raabe.

"We flew to Krasnoyarsk," Raabe said. "There we met up with a group of about a hundred and eighty Germans, all from various camps in the Krasnoyarsk area. From there, we went on to Moscow by train. Our treatment throughout the trip was superb. When we stopped at the major stations, we were taken to the station restaurant, and there'd be tables set just for us, and we could order beer and wine. The food was fine. In Moscow, we were taken to the Butyrki, but to a special ward where the cells were locked only at night; during the day, we could walk around in the yard. There was plenty to eat, and the food was pretty good, with real variety. Everyone had his own bed, with a straw sack, white linen, and a down blanket. The first time we were there, years ago, at least two hundred men would have been crammed into a cell the size of ours; now there were just twenty-four men. They had a tailor's and a shoemaker's workshop in the prison, so we had clothes and shoes made to order. We were obviously being prepared for transport to Germany. But we couldn't get the prison officials to tell us anything.

"Most of us were communists who'd escaped from Germany. So being handed over to the Nazis would have meant certain death. We were very worried. A lot of us still hoped we'd at least be asked whether we wanted to go.

"Finally, a high NKVD officer summoned us individually to his office and told each of us that he'd been pardoned by the Supreme Soviet of the U.S.S.R. and that his sentence was being commuted to expulsion from the Soviet Union. We had to sign a statement confirming that we had been informed of this decision. Some of us refused and tried to explain to the officers that, as communists, we did not wish to return to Nazi Germany. It was no use, the officers said we'd have to go whether we wanted to or not.

"There were a few who actually looked forward to going back to Germany. They went so far as to sing Nazi songs in the Butyrki, and they abused anyone who doubted that going back to Germany would lead to Nirvana.

"Every week, there was a new transport of prisoners to Germany.

"One day, we stopped getting hot chocolate, white bread, and butter for breakfast. Instead, we got the usual *kipyatok* (hot water) and a piece of black bread. We were upset; many of us refused to accept the food. Two days later, all the Germans who hadn't been shipped off were taken back to their various camps."

AFTER THE RUSSO–FINNISH WAR: A CAMP EPISODE

In December 1939, Soviet troops attacked Finland. Tass reported that Finnish border troops had attacked a Red Army patrol with artillery: this was the official pretext for a giant nation's invasion of its tiny neighbor. For us who had been on the Solovetsk Islands, this war came as no surprise; we had seen the preparations for it a year and a half before. Soon the first victims began to arrive. This was after outraged world opinion forced the Soviet Union to put a halt to its war against Finland.

Six thousand Red Army soldiers who had been captured by the Finns and repatriated after the armistice were brought to Norilsk. They thought they were being put under temporary quarantine; they had no idea that they were facing five to ten years of hard labor. In the beginning, they went to work unguarded, and they were divided into battalions and companies instead of brigades.

Our attempts to communicate with the "Finns," as we called them, were rejected: they didn't want anything to do with "counterrevolutionaries." Several weeks passed. Then one day the soldiers were herded into the large empty area in front of the kitchen. They were in high spirits; they believed they were about to be taken home. An NKVD officer stepped in front of them; some guards pulled up a table. The officer laid a stack of papers on the table and announced loudly: "Attention! All those called, step forward and give your first name and patronymic."

As the soldiers' names were checked off, they were told to line up in three groups: one on the right, one on the left, and one in the middle. After everyone was lined up, the NKVD officer stepped in front of the first group and recited a resolution by the NKVD Special Commission: they were to be punished with a five-year sentence "for dishonorable deportment in the face of the enemy." The second group was given eight years, and the third group ten years.

The soldiers were in despair. Most of them had fought bravely, had suffered injuries; some had been severely wounded. Many of them rued the fact that they hadn't stayed in Finland. Now it was too late.

The winter of 1940–41 brought additional suffering. Food provisions stored in Dudinka were supposed to be transported to Norilsk on the narrow-gauge railroad, but there were such violent blizzards that the tracks were buried deep in snow. Thousands of prisoners were put to work clearing the tracks every day, but they couldn't make any headway.

The three snowplows that were being used were constantly getting stuck and snowed under.

For four months, we lived in tents alongside those tracks. This was an almost unendurable period. The bunks were set up in a circle; in the middle stood an iron stove—that was the only warm place. All around the bunks, inside the tents, there was snow. The ground was frozen. When we came back from work, our clothes were frozen stiff. We huddled around the stove to thaw out the clothes, for we had to use them as bedding. But there wasn't enough room for everyone around the stove; there were frequent fights.

The criminals were completely out of control here. Since the camp police consisted of criminals, there was no one you could turn to. These people felt they were the lords and masters and could do as they pleased. You couldn't eat your bread in peace; someone was likely to snatch it out of your hand.

For four months, the Dudinka–Norilsk line was impassable. Food was running out. The only flour in Norilsk was white flour for the officials. To prevent a famine, the prisoners had to be given white bread; we were also fed dumplings made of white flour—nothing but dumplings for weeks.

Several serious accidents occurred. The clean-up brigades were in constant danger of being run over by a train. Once, several hundred meters from the Norilsk II station, a women's brigade that was working at night was run over; of fifty women, forty-six were either killed or seriously injured.

Finally, spring came. The snowstorms abated, the railroad line was cleared, and I returned to Norilsk to my old friends.

In the middle of June 1941, a week before war broke out, a prisoners' transport arrived: officers from the Baltic countries—Latvians, Lithuanians, Estonians—2,600 altogether. Like the Russian prisoners of war, these officers were at first given better treatment than the other prisoners. They all wore their full uniform. You could see various ranks, all the way to general. At first, they didn't have to work and were given better food. The camp officials addressed them as *tovarishchi*.

The officers were completely unaware of their impending fate. The only chance we had to talk to them was when they came to the kitchen to pick up their food. They wouldn't tell us much, but we learned that early in 1941 they had been taken to a place near Gorky, by the Volga, to be "reeducated," and were then suddenly shipped to Norilsk.

DURING THE RUSSO-GERMAN WAR: A PRECARIOUS EXISTENCE

IN THE NKVD PRISON OF NORILSK

On Sunday, June 22, 1941, I went to the bathhouse. It wasn't our brigade's normal bath day, but my friend Vasily Chuprakov knew the man in charge of the baths, and he allowed me occasionally to bathe with Vasily. After the bath, I accompanied Vasily to his barracks.

Vasily was a good engineer; his work was appreciated by the administration, and that brought certain advantages. He lived in a clean barracks where everyone had a straw sack, a blanket, and a pillow. There was a loudspeaker there, too. The speaker was connected to the camp's cultural services, which occasionally broadcast recorded music; sometimes they played radio music as well. When we stepped into the barracks, some radio music was playing. Suddenly the music was interrupted, and we heard Molotov's voice speaking of the Nazis' "treacherous attack" on the Soviet Union. After a few words, the program went off the air. There were about a hundred people in the barracks, but you could have heard a pin drop; we were all staring at one another. Vasily's neighbor said: "It's all over for us now."

Little by little, the barracks came back to life—but no one talked about the war. Vasily brought hot water, and we drank tea. There was some bread, but no one touched it.

"Karl, what do you think, what will happen to us now?" Vasily asked quietly.

"I don't care. Maybe a horrible end's better than horror without end," I replied.

A camp policeman came in and ordered everyone who didn't live in the barracks to return to his brigade. The yard was completely empty. Usually, on a free day at this time of the year, groups of prisoners would be standing around or sunning themselves. When I returned to my barracks, the same picture presented itself: a deep silence, with only a few people quietly talking. Everyone knew from experience that a major political event always had unpleasant consequences for the prisoners.

On Monday morning, when the gong sounded for work and the prisoners assembled on the *lineika*—the road leading out through the camp gate—we immediately noticed a change. Usually, only the camp police were there to supervise our getting in line before going off to work; this time, soldiers were there to guard us as well. There was more pushing and shouting than usual. There were more than the normal number of soldiers at the gate; more officers, too. On the way to work, we were stopped and counted several times.

On the second day of the war, our rations were cut; sugar was eliminated completely, and even our soap ration was cut in half. On June 25, all foreigners were rounded up and put into the ninth section. Only two foreigners were left in the second section—my friend Josef Berger and I.

"I wonder why they're not taking us to the brick factory," I said to Josef the next morning.

"They've probably got something better in store for us," he replied.

In the evening, I returned home late from work. As usual, I went to the kitchen to pick up my supper. Larionov, the cook, spotted me, beckoned to me with his hand, and pointed at his door. I went to his room.

"You probably want to eat?" He took a piece of bread and some cold meat from a shelf and put them before me on the table. "I can't offer you any tea," he continued. "I don't want to go to the kitchen. People would notice someone's in here with me."

While I ate, Larionov said mysteriously: "The German Army's advancing with giant steps. They say Kiev's been bombarded several times already."

"If Hitler were to win, we former party members would be dead," I said.

"If Hitler were to win, you, an Austrian, would be free."

"That's out of the question. Hitler has put German and Austrian communists into prisons and concentration camps."

The signal for bed was sounded. I was glad to be able to break off my conversation with Larionov. When I returned to my barracks, I gave my neighbor my soup; he wondered why I wasn't eating it myself. I told him how Larionov had fed me. "Watch out for Larionov," he warned me. Only then did I realize why Larionov had tried to involve me in a conversation about the war.

While my neighbor was still eating his soup, the door opened, and in came two NKVD officers, a man in civilian clothes, and three camp policemen. Everyone froze. Given the tension that had set in since the beginning of the war, the sudden appearance of the officers was ominous. Everyone scurried off to hide under blankets and coats; only I remained seated.

"They're coming to take my soul," I said to my frightened neighbor.

One of the two officers asked the man on duty: "Is there anyone here from the Matveyev brigade?"

I was sitting at the opposite end of the room, but I could hear him clearly.

"Yes, sir," said the prisoner on duty.

"What's his name?"

"Steiner."

"That's the one we're looking for."

They all walked up to me. Without asking me what my name was, one of them shouted: "Hands up!" I raised my hands. "Search everything thoroughly!"

The three camp policemen ransacked my bunk and threw my few belongings in a pile. I was ordered to come along. It was still light outside, even though it was after 11 p.m.—these were the white nights. With my hands on my back, I slowly crossed the compound in the direction of the gate. And there was Josef Berger, who was also being led away. He greeted me with a nod, and I responded in like fashion.

The soldiers at the gate let us pass without a word. We walked slowly down the street that led to the NKVD building. I tried to talk to Josef, but as soon as I opened my mouth, one of the officers thundered at me to be quiet. We walked on in silence. I breathed the fresh air. I knew it would be a while before I would walk outside again.

In the NKVD building, I was separated from Berger. One of the officers disappeared with him behind a door, while the man in civilian clothes took me to another room. He sat down behind a desk and told me to sit down on a chair. He lit a cigarette and pulled out a printed form.

"What is your name?"

"Karl Steiner."

"What was the date of your arrest?"

"November 4, 1936."

"What were the charges?"

"I was accused of being a Gestapo agent and of belonging to a counterrevolutionary organization."

"Did you confess?"

"I had nothing to confess, since I was not a Gestapo agent and had not committed any crimes against the Soviet Union."

"Did you file an appeal?"

"I did. It was turned down."

"Listen, Steiner, you committed grave offenses against the Soviet Union, you were punished very mildly, all you got was ten years, you really should have been shot. You ought to be grateful to the Soviet government instead of continuing with your counterrevolutionary agitation."

"I did not commit any crimes in the past. Neither have I been agitating in the camp."

"So you persist in your old tactic of denying everything?"

"It's not a tactic, it's the truth. I am not an agitator."

"I can promise you one thing: this time, you won't get off cheaply. Sign this." He handed me the minutes of the brief hearing.

I refused to sign. The NKVD officer looked at me with surprise. "Why won't you sign?"

"I refuse to sign any more NKVD documents."

"Why?"

"I'll tell you why. In 1936, when I was arrested in Moscow on fantastic, completely false charges and was sentenced to ten years in prison, I was convinced that I would eventually be rehabilitated. And I believed this to this day. Now I'm being investigated all over again. Experience has taught me that neither the investigation nor the NKVD nor the judgment of the court has any legal basis. For this reason, I will from now on refuse to make any deposition or sign any document."

"I see," said the interrogator, and pressed a button.

A soldier came into the room. The official left and returned after a few minutes with the chief of the Norilsk NKVD, Polikarpov.

I stood up.

"Playing games?" shouted Polikarpov.

"It's not a game, I'm quite serious. I'm not playing your game any more."

"What!" he roared, grabbing me by the neck with both hands. He pressed me against the wall, choking me. I didn't defend myself. I almost would have preferred him to strangle me. But he let go. I remained standing immobile by the wall.

"Scared?" Polikarpov asked, and straddled the chair. "Listen," he went on. "You know the times we're living in. I have the right to put you up against a wall without any trial. We are not doing that; we want to make a regular investigation. You ought to be grateful instead of carrying on like this. I ask you: Will you behave properly or not?!"

"Do with me what you will, I'm not signing anything."

Polikarpov stood up and turned to the interrogator. "Throw him in the cellar; let him croak there."

A soldier led me to a dark hallway and shoved me into a corner, snarling: "You fascist scum, I'll beat your guts out!"

I tried to protect myself with my hands. This enraged him even more, and he started beating me more violently. "I'm not the fascist. You are!" I shouted.

He finally left me alone. A second soldier came, and together they led me across the yard to the central prison of the Norilsk NKVD. One of the soldiers rang a bell. A huge guard with a key ring came to the metal gate, saying: "Another fascist. Come on in. We'll teach you to respect Soviet power."

Several steps led down to the cellar. A long hallway with cells to the right and left. I was taken to a room where I had to strip. My clothes were searched, the contents of my bread bag—a piece of bread and a wooden spoon—were dropped on a table, and the bread was cut into small pieces. After the guard had examined everything thoroughly, he ordered me to get dressed again.

I was led back to the hallway. I could hear many voices as I passed the cells. We stopped. The guard opened a door and shoved me in. The men in the cell surrounded me, plying me with questions: what camp section was I from, what was happening out there. Most of them wanted to know whether I had any tobacco and were very disappointed to learn that I was a nonsmoker.

Someone called down from one of the top bunks: "Leave him in peace, give him a chance to rest, you can ask him later."

Most of them withdrew. Someone took me by the hand and led me to one of the bunks. Then another man came up to me, held out his hand, and introduced himself: "Engineer Brilov."

A pair of sharp and cunning eyes peered out from a round face framed by a salt-and-pepper beard. He leaned toward me and whispered in my ear: "There are many *urkas*, criminals, here—watch out! Do you have any food on you?"

I turned around and was going to take the bread out of my bag. The bag was gone. I didn't make a fuss about it; I knew it was useless to ask for the bread. I just told my new acquaintance that the bag was gone. He looked up at the top bunk but didn't say a word.

The cell wasn't crowded; there was enough room for the eighteen men who were there. The middle bunks were for the *blatnye* (major criminals), the lower ones for the *fraery* (the politicals), and the four topmost bunks, right below the ceiling, were reserved for *kusochniki* (petty thieves).

The man next to me on the bunk was the engineer Semsky of Tver (Kalinin today), a city seventy kilometers northwest of Moscow. Semsky had been arrested on the first day of the war for praising German technology in a conversation with a colleague. He was given ten years for "defeatism." In the two weeks I spent with Semsky, I got to like him a lot. Two months later, he was sentenced to death and shot.

A rather motley crew lived in that cell. Ivanov, the *pakhan* (boss) of the criminals, lounged on his bunk all day long, feeling like a tsar, while the *kusochniki* danced around him like courtiers. Even the other *urkas* respected him. He was constantly issuing curt little commands:

"Bely, bring me some water!"

"Korsuby, hand me the towel!"

"Belaya *ruchka*, give me a light!"

None of Ivanov's "subordinates" dared contradict him, for the other *blatnye* would have beat him to a pulp.

Ivanov always had food; the other *urkas* saw to that. The only way to get additional food was when a newcomer arrived in the cell; he'd be immediately deprived of whatever food he had with him. I was.

The criminals spent all their time playing cards. These cards were made of little cut-out pieces of newspaper pasted together with a glue made of soft bread, and then marked with an indelible pencil they had hidden away. The stakes were bread, soup, even clothes. Often a criminal would gamble away several days' rations and have to go hungry unless he managed to clip a newcomer or was given some food by the winner. Such gifts had to be repaid with a good deal of subservience.

The *urkas* didn't just gamble for their own clothes but for the clothes of the other men in the cell. It was an honor to steal from a political. A criminal would step up to his unsuspecting victim, point at the desired article of clothing, and say: "Take it off!" Only rarely did anyone refuse.

Once in a while, the object of the game would be a human life. A victim would be designated—either because no other stake was available or because a conflict had erupted among the criminals—and the loser had to carry out the murder. If the victim was present, the murderer would pick up a suitable instrument and take immediate action. But if the victim was in another cell or in another section of the camp, the killer had to find a way to reach him. Sometimes the victim would be warned in time; then a regular manhunt would ensue. In some cases, it was years before a killer caught up with his victim. But if the elected killer refused to carry out his assignment, he would be killed himself. Among criminals, treason was punishable by death.

There was a strict ordinance against card games, but that didn't bother the criminals. Usually, the players would sit on a bunk and the others would form a "wall" around them to prevent the guard's seeing anything through the peephole. The criminals would get so excited about these games that they would lose all sense of their surroundings.

Two days after the first hearing, I was called back by the interrogator, who wanted to know if I was ready to be "reasonable." I repeated that I was not going to sign anything.

I was taken back to the prison—not to my regular cell, but to the punishment cell, a windowless box with a concrete floor, about one by two meters in size. A small lamp shed its light night and day. I squatted on the floor but wasn't able to hold this position for very long because my legs kept falling asleep. I walked back and forth but soon became tired and had to sit down again—until that became uncomfortable again; and so it went.

In the morning, the guard brought me two hundred grams of bread sprinkled with salt, and a pot of hot water. I refused the two hundred grams of bread. Thereupon, I was taken to the prison warden, who asked me why I was going on a hunger strike.

"I'm not going on a hunger strike. I'm not accepting the two hundred grams of bread and I'm demanding the normal ration of four hundred grams. That's a hunger diet to begin with, but on two hundred grams I would starve."

The warden replied that the ration in the punishment cell was two hundred grams and that he couldn't give me four hundred.

The next day, a young man was shoved into the box with me. His name was Viktor; he said he was twenty-one years old, but his soft, girlish face made him look no older than seventeen. He said he came from Minsk and that he had committed several burglaries there, together with eight other students. They received five- to eight-year sentences. Viktor was given five years. He was brought directly from the ship to the punishment cell because he had tried to run away with two of the others in the port of Igarka. One of his friends had been severely in-

jured during the flight attempt. Now Viktor was going to be tried for
the attempt.

During our five days together, Viktor told me the story of his life.
His mother was a teacher. She had visited him every day in prison and
had done everything she could to save him. When I asked him why he
had become a criminal, he said it was out of boredom, and because his
friends had persuaded him. Viktor's father had abandoned the mother,
and she'd had to work hard to support herself and her three children,
and hadn't been able to give Viktor enough attention.

I got sick. On the sixth day, I was taken to the doctor, who ordered
that I be removed from the punishment cell immediately. I was put on
a special diet, since I hadn't eaten anything for five days and had had
only water. I was worn out. I was also suffering sharp pains from an
inflammation in one of my ears, probably from lying on the cold stone
floor. I asked to see the doctor. He promised to send me to an ear
specialist.

The only ear, nose, and throat specialist in Norilsk was an old acquaintance, Nikolai Ivanovich Sukhorukov. He treated both prisoners
and nonprisoners. In order to be treated by him, I had to be taken to
the "free" infirmary, right across from the NKVD building. A soldier took
me there. Not knowing that Sukhorukov was a prisoner too, he addressed
him as *tovarishch*. Then he closed the door and left me alone with the
doctor. This meeting was extraordinary for me as well as for Sukhorukov.
Both of us were burning with curiosity—he, to learn what was happening
in the prison, and I, to find out any news about the outside world. I
quickly told him about my experiences, and he informed me of the war
situation and told me about the latest events in the camp. I described
the symptoms in my ear; he gave me an injection and promised to have
me transferred to the central hospital.

Now that the most important things had been discussed, Sukhorukov
called in the soldier and said: "Bring him back in two days." When I was
brought back to Sukhorukov, however, we weren't able to talk so inti-
mately. The soldier had evidently been given orders not to leave us alone.
Sukhorukov said to me in an officious tone of voice: "I have written a
report to the chief of the NKVD, requesting that you be taken to the
hospital immediately. You are seriously ill."

That was clear enough; I understood. I kept myself awake in my cell,
pacing all night, and when the guard told me to lie down I complained
of sharp pain in my ears. The next morning, I was summoned by
the officer on duty, who threatened to punish me for violating prison
rules. When I complained of the terrible pain in my ear, he sent
me to the doctor. Again, I wasn't able to exchange more than a few
words with Sukhorukov. He told me he had written a second report
stressing that my life was in danger and that I must be sent to the hospital immediately.

IN THE CENTRAL HOSPITAL

Five days later, two soldiers came to pick me up. I thought I was being taken to the doctor again, since they were leading me in the direction of the infirmary. But, to my surprise, the soldier walking in front of me made a right instead of a left turn. Now I thought I was being led to a medical commission to determine if my condition was really so serious that I had to be hospitalized.

The central hospital was situated in the fifth camp section. To get there, you had to cross the yard of the second section. Prisoners emerged from all the barracks to look at me. Many knew me; some waved.

I was taken to the hospital's reception office. One of the soldiers who had brought me handed the official a piece of paper; the official read it and said to the soldier: "It's all right, you can leave now. The sick man stays here."

I hardly dared believe my ears—I could stay in the hospital! I could visualize the white bed and the good food. The soldier conferred with the prison officials by telephone. I was burning with impatience. I heard the soldier answering: "All right, all right . . ." He put down the receiver and left.

The official who had received me was drinking tea and eating bread. When he saw me staring at the bread, he divided it and gave me half. I was embarrassed and wanted to refuse it, but my hunger was stronger. I took the bread and bit off a piece. The official said: "You won't go hungry here."

Soon a nurse came and led me to the bath.

My bed neighbors in the sickroom came from various camps. Almost all of them had broken bones. One of them had fallen off a chimney from a height of a hundred five meters and, miraculously, had suffered only slight internal injuries; he was released after only four days.

That same afternoon, I was summoned to Sukhorukov's office. To my surprise, he led me to the toilet and locked the door behind us. Instead of discussing my sickness, we talked about the most recent reports from the front. Sukhorukov told me the alarming news about the extraordinarily swift advance of the Germans; he also told me about some very severe measures that were being taken in the camps. I told him about conditions in the prison. Sukhorukov wanted to know what I was accused of. He approved of my tactic; the most important thing, he felt, was to gain time. He would do everything he could to keep me in the hospital for as long as possible. If I agreed, he could perform an operation on my ear; that could keep me in the hospital for as long as two months. "A lot can happen in two months," he said.

I agreed to the operation, even though it wasn't necessary. My life was at stake, and it wasn't threatened by illness but by the NKVD. During my brief stay in the prison, there had been four executions.

The hospital was directed by Alexandra Ivanovna Sleptsova. I received every kind of attention: solicitous care, nutritious and individually prescribed meals—despite the war—and, best of all, a white, clean bed. Only someone who for years has slept on hard, vermin-infested bunks can imagine the luxury of being able to lie on a real bed.

Of the six men in my room, only two could walk: a man who had undergone an eye operation, and a man with a broken arm. The latter's name was Sasha Brovkin. He was a criminal of the vilest sort, with several murders on his conscience. In order to prolong his stay in the hospital, he would secretly take off his bandage at night, when the other patients were sleeping, and move his arm to reopen the fracture.

One day, the doctor who was treating Brovkin asked me if I hadn't noticed something unusual in his behavior; I told her I hadn't. One morning, the nurse Olga Mykhalchuk came into the room and noticed Brovkin's bandage wasn't properly tied. She took a needle and sewed up the bandage. As she did this, she said, half jokingly: "Don't you dare open up the bandage!" Brovkin abused the nurse in the foulest language.

Olga was very attentive and solicitous toward all the patients. Everyone liked her. She had once lived in Odessa. Shortly after her wedding, her husband was arrested for some crime. Olga, too, was put on trial, and even though she hadn't known anything about her husband's crime, she was sentenced to five years in a work camp for being his "accomplice." Olga made an appeal and was acquitted by a higher court. But it took nearly five years for the good news to travel from Odessa to Norilsk. She had decided to continue working here as a free employee.

It wasn't the first time Brovkin had abused Olga. He had once tried to court her and found her unresponsive; when he became impertinent, she had kindly but firmly reproved him. Now he was taking revenge.

The treatment of my middle-ear infection consisted at first of a daily injection in the inflamed ear. The doctor said I would have to convalesce a little before subjecting my body to the stress of the operation. Sukhorukov told me that the NKVD chief frequently inquired about my condition and was pressing for my release. After fourteen days in the hospital and a fairly complete recovery of my strength and normal body weight, the day for the operation was set. It was on a Saturday that Sukhorukov told me to prepare myself for Monday. All Sunday I was restless, not because I was afraid of the operation, but because I kept thinking of having to go back to prison soon.

On Monday morning, Olga led me to a room where she gave me an injection in my left arm. Very soon after that, I began to feel a sense of relief—I walked into the operating room proud as a bullfighter. Sukhorukov, Director Sleptsova, and a nurse were waiting for me. Sukhorukov put on an official air, addressing me as if I were a stranger: "How are you feeling?"

"Good."

"In that case, everything's as it should be. Did you sign the statement?"

I didn't understand.

"It's a formality. Every patient has to sign a statement certifying that he is submitting to the operation of his own volition and at his own risk."

"Yes, I signed that on Saturday," I said.

"Nikolai Ivanovich, perhaps we could do without the operation, why take unnecessary risks?" asked Sleptsova.

"Ask the patient. It's his affair," replied Sukhorukov.

"How do you feel about it?" asked Sleptsova.

"I've made up my mind."

"Then let's do it," said Sukhorukov. "Lie down on the table."

The nurse covered my eyes with a cloth and tied my hands to the operating table. Some liquid was rubbed into the area where they would make the incision, and then I felt an injection which was very disagreeable. After just a few minutes, I could feel my skull being prized open. It was unpleasant, but it didn't hurt; it seemed to be happening far away. I could distinctly feel the blood running down my neck.

Occasionally, Sukhorukov would ask me something or other, nothing important, and intermittently I would hear him say: "Wait, pincers . . . A little more cotton . . . All right, there now, we're almost done."

Finally, the hammering stopped. Something was still being done in there, but it wasn't so unpleasant. While the doctors completed their life-saving task of making sure I'd be ill for a while, I asked myself whether this would really be of any use. I might be gaining time but still be unable to save my life.

The news that had reached the hospital from the prison in the past few days had been very alarming. The camp tribunal, consisting of the hangman Gorokhov and two other NKVD officials, was pronouncing several death penalties a day. I knew that if I was brought before Gorokhov, I would be shot. No, I told myself, I must stay alive and I will; they won't get me this easily; if need be, I'll have a second operation.

My hands were unfastened, and the cloth was removed from my eyes.

"Can you walk, or should we get a stretcher?" asked Sukhorukov.

"I'll walk," I said.

Supported by two nurses, I returned to my bed and lay down. Now I really felt sick. My temperature rose, I had no appetite. Sleptsova and Sukhorukov devoted a lot of time to me; Sukhorukov often came to visit me at night. Olga brought me various kinds of food, which I barely touched. Brovkin took advantage of that. No sooner had the nurse brought my food than Brovkin would arrive at my bedside. "You're not going to eat anyway, and I'm so damned hungry." And without waiting for my reply, he'd empty the plate.

Finally, I began to feel better, my fever went down, I even tried to get up. When Olga saw this, she scolded me, which prompted Brovkin to remark: "She's sure taking care of that fascist!"

Every day, Sukhorukov changed my bandage. A week after the operation, he said: "Why, you're doing splendidly. The wound is healing very nicely."

Several days later, my condition deteriorated again and I had a high fever. Sukhorukov and Sleptsova were very worried, for the wound was festering. I had to go back to the operating table, where the wound was cleaned, but my condition did not improve. When we were alone in the operating room, Sukhorukov asked me whether I had done anything to the wound. I assured him that I hadn't touched it. He said I needn't worry; he'd keep me in the hospital for a long time, even though the NKVD chief had asked about me several times.

I was getting worse every day. I was scarcely conscious; there was a darkness in front of my eyes. Sleptsova was very worried and called a medical council. The doctors felt that I wouldn't survive a third operation. Sleptsova requisitioned the most expensive medicines, which were ordinarily reserved for the NKVD people.

Once, to stimulate my appetite, she brought me a glass of wine. Olga, too, was extraordinarily solicitous. One day, she brought me a delicacy from the kitchen, put it on my night table, and left the room. As usual, Brovkin immediately sidled up to me and, without saying a word, took the plate. At that moment, Olga came in. "Aren't you ashamed of yourself, stealing food from a sick man? You have plenty to eat yourself!"

Brovkin threw the plate in her face, screaming: "There, feed your face and stuff your little fascist!"

Olga ran out of the room. I was enraged, and frustrated that I hadn't the strength to get up and demolish him. As a result of that incident, Brovkin was banished from the hospital. He was allowed to return three days later, after he had promised Olga to behave decently.

Finally, my condition improved again. My temperature went down. The doctor allowed me to get out of bed and visit other patients. One of them was Gustav Schöller, who had come directly from the prison. Schöller was German, born in Rostov-on-Don, a party member since 1917. He had been director of the agricultural department of the local government of Rostov. He had been arrested in 1937, sentenced to fifteen years in a camp for "sabotage," and sent to Norilsk. His agronomic skills were of no use to him there; he had to do hard labor. Several months before our encounter, he had succeeded in getting a position as assistant bookkeeper in the administrative office. Two weeks after the war broke out, Gustav was put in prison; he was accused of having praised Hitler and the German

Army in conversation with other prisoners. Gustav vehemently denied this, and when he refused to sign the interrogator's report, he was so brutally beaten that he could no longer stand and had to be brought to the hospital. The doctors were treating him for severe internal injuries.

"Karl, I am so happy to see you"—those were Gustav's first words when I came to his bed. He was in despair. Before being put in prison, he had learned that his wife and two children had been deported to Kazakhstan. "I don't care what they do to me. I can't stand it any more. As soon as they take me back to prison, I'll sign whatever they want."

"That doesn't make any sense, Gustav! You have to fight for your life, as hard as you can, just as you fought in 1917 and later."

"That was a different time. I still believed in socialism; I was willing to give up my life for it. Now I don't believe in anything."

I talked to Gustav several times but found it impossible to restore his courage.

There was another patient who had been brought in from the prison, an Air Force captain named Simakov. He had been arrested in Vladivostok as one of a group of forty officers; they were charged with having planned the secession of the Far Eastern republics from the Soviet Union. Why Simakov, a native of Orel in central Russia, should have wanted to cut off the Far East from his native land will remain a secret of the NKVD. Simakov made a full confession and was sentenced to twenty years in a camp, along with six of his colleagues. All the others were given twenty-five years. His squadron commander had jumped out of a window during his interrogation and had remained stretched out on the ground with his limbs broken.

Simakov was taken to Dudinka, where, with several friends, he discussed the possibility of seizing one of the planes that were parked near the port of Dudinka and flying to another country. Someone denounced them to the NKVD. Simakov, Brilov, Bespalov, Ignatiev, and several others were arrested and sentenced to death. In protest, Simakov went on a hunger strike. After a week, he was brought to the hospital, where he had been refusing to eat for four months. He was so weak that he could scarcely move or even talk.

I tried to convince him to break off his hunger strike. Such means were ineffectual, I said, in this kind of situation. Simakov moved his eyes, from which I concluded that he had understood what I said. But he wouldn't give up his desperate battle. The only nourishment he permitted to pass his lips was pickles, which he would chew with evident pleasure and then spit out.

One day after lunch, the interrogator Sakulin came into Simakov's room with the hospital's manager and two soldiers. The nurse on duty pointed to Simakov's bed.

"Take him!" Sakulin said to the soldiers.

"Wait," said the nurse. "I'll get his clothes."

"He won't need clothes any more," replied Sakulin.

The nurse burst into loud sobs.

One of the soldiers took Simakov by the head; the other seized his feet. They carried him out to the courtyard, where a horse-drawn cart was waiting. Simakov was dropped onto the cart and driven to the camp cemetery. There the death sentence was carried out.

That evening, only a few of the patients touched their supper.

My condition was improving daily. My temperature was normal. The doctors and the chief doctor were being besieged by the NKVD, who wanted me released right away. The doctors held them at bay, explaining that I was still too weak to leave the hospital.

Prisoners were usually informed of their release in the morning and were then sent off after lunch. If you hadn't heard anything by lunchtime, you knew you could stay at least another day. But one day at five in the afternoon Sleptsova came to my bed and said: "I can do no more for you. I have received an order to release you immediately. The soldiers are downstairs waiting for you."

A few minutes later, I was given my clothes. When I was dressed, Sleptsova returned. "Come to the room of the doctor on duty." There was no one there, only she and I. She gave me a little pouch full of zwieback and some sugar in a paper bag. "Take this. You'll need it."

I seized her hand and tried to kiss it. Sleptsova pulled back in alarm. I turned around and walked out.

BACK IN PRISON

We walked slowly to the prison. Two months had passed. I was taken back to my old cell.

I met many old acquaintances there, but some were missing; and there were some new faces. The cell was overcrowded; many were lying on the concrete floor. The oldest man in the cell ordered a young fellow to give up his place on the bunk. I protested, but the boy said he was glad to do it. I distributed my zwieback among my cellmates. The next morning, when we were given our *kipyatok* I gave everyone a piece of sugar.

Just two hours after my return, I was taken before the interrogator. I couldn't believe my eyes: there, on a chair in the corner, sat Brovkin. His arm was still in a cast. I had a sense of what was coming and gave Brovkin a questioning look. His long, pockmarked face twitched contemptuously.

The interrogator tore off a small piece of newspaper, poured some makhorka on it, and rolled himself a cigarette. Brovkin asked: "May I smoke one, too?"

The interrogator handed him a piece of paper and some makhorka.

Then he turned to me. "You have continued spreading your counterre-volutionary propaganda and anti-Soviet agitation in the hospital. You and the nurse Olga Mykhalchuk praised Hitler and predicted the defeat of Soviet power."

I said nothing.

"Very well, we will proceed with the confrontation. Accused Steiner, do you know this man?"

"I already told you that I refuse to cooperate with any proceeding against me and will refuse to make any deposition—especially now that you are bringing in a criminal as a witness."

"So you are determined to sabotage this investigation? That can only count against you in the end. I advise you to give up this tactic. Do not force us to take measures which we prefer to avoid."

"I can only repeat: I categorically refuse to take part in this inves-tigation."

Konyev—that was the man's name—pressed a button, and a soldier came in. "Stay here for a moment," Konyev said to the soldier.

Then he went out and returned after a few moments with two NKVD officers, Sakulin and Soldatov. He sat down on his seat, while the other two officers remained standing in the middle of the room. "The confron-tation continues. Witness Brovkin, do you know this man?" Konyev pointed at me.

"Yes, I know him well. We spent two months together in the same hospital room," Brovkin replied glibly, as if reciting a lesson.

"Who is he?"

"His name is Karl Steiner."

"What was your relationship with Steiner? I mean, did you have any quarrels or disagreements?"

"No, we got along well; he often shared his food with me."

"So you never quarreled."

Konyev turned to me. "Accused Steiner, do you confirm these state-ments?"

I didn't reply.

He said to the two officers: "The accused is using the tactic of silence. He is not answering any questions and states that he refuses to take part in the investigation."

"You are behaving exactly like some criminals. They refuse to testify, too," Sakulin said in a challenging tone of voice.

"The criminals who refuse to testify want you to give them bread and tobacco before they'll agree to talk. I'm not making any such stipu-lations. Therefore, you have no right to compare my behavior with that of a criminal. Besides, I can see that you and the criminals are on pretty good terms," I said.

"We are at war," Sakulin said menacingly. "We don't have time to fool around with you forever. Stop making a fuss, do what you're told; otherwise, you're in very deep trouble."

"Save your precious time. I'm not going through this investigation comedy again. This farce of a confrontation is perfect proof that I'm right."

Konyev turned to Brovkin. "Tell us what you know about Steiner."

Brovkin spoke: "The free nurse Olga Mykhalchuk often came into our room. She would sit next to Steiner and tell him about the great German advances at the front. I heard Steiner say to Olga: Soon it'll be all over with Stalin; the Germans will come and liberate us all."

"Do you confirm this, Steiner?" Konyev asked.

I remained silent.

Konyev asked Brovkin several more questions, which he answered at length. Everything he said had only one purpose: to compromise me and Olga—especially Olga. After each of his statements, the interrogator asked for my confirmation, and I remained silent. Then Konyev wrote a report stating that I refused to answer questions and repudiated the confrontation with Brovkin. Brovkin was the first to sign the document; next came the two officers, and finally the interrogator. I didn't sign.

When I came back to the cell, it was late. Most people were asleep. I lay down on the hard bunk, but I couldn't sleep. I compulsively reviewed what had happened, wondering what the future would bring. It was October 1941. The situation at the front was critical. The Germans had reached the gates of Moscow. I could only expect a death sentence, under these conditions. But mine wasn't the only life at stake. There was Olga.

I tried to think of a way to warn her. There was only one solution: Sukhorukov. I had to try to reach him in the infirmary to tell him about the danger Olga was in. But what if the soldier didn't leave us alone together? The best thing would be to write a message and slip it into Sukhorukov's hand at the right moment. I had in my pocket a receipt for the clothing that had been taken from me. I borrowed a pencil and wrote my message on the back of the receipt: Brovkin's accusations and the fact that I had refused to confirm any of them.

The next morning, I asked the warden to take me to the doctor because I had a bad earache. The following day, I was taken to Sukhorukov's office. The soldier stayed outside in the hall; we could talk freely. But, to be doubly careful, I kept silent and gave Sukhorukov my note. Before I said anything, he told me that Olga had already been summoned by the NKVD. She had been told that I had confirmed Brovkin's accusations. I told Sukhorukov what had actually happened and asked him to tell Olga categorically to deny everything.

Josef Berger had gone on a hunger strike. On the fifth day, the prison doctors started to force-feed him. After a month, Josef's physical condition was so critical that he had to be admitted to the camp hospital. There he continued his hunger strike. He broke his fast after sixty-two days, when the chief of the NKVD promised him that he and I would not be brought before the camp tribunal but would be tried by a higher court. Two other factors contributed to Josef's decision to call a halt to his fast: the pact between the U.S.S.R. and the Western powers, which brought about a reduction in the number of death sentences; and the influence of Dr. Mardna of the central hospital, who warned Josef that if he continued fasting, he might die. I, too, had advised Josef to give up his fast; while we were in prison, we communicated through knocks on the wall, the usual secret language of prisoners.

ATTEMPTED UPRISING

On the night of October 20, 1941, the entire prison was roused from sleep by a loud commotion in the hall and the sound of cell doors being opened and closed. We thought it might be a "meat day"—the prison term for mass shootings. Eventually, our cell door was opened, and in came four prisoners from the first camp section. They told us that a hundred forty prisoners from their section had been transferred to the prison under heavy guard. Most of them had worked in the central repair workshop, and some of them in the electric plant. The majority had no idea why they were being put in prison; there were both politicals and criminals among them.

That same night, two of our new cellmates were summoned to a hearing. One of them, a criminal named Misha, came back the next morning; the other, a political named Hryshnyak, returned after twenty-four hours. Now we learned the reason for the mass arrests. A former army colonel, Kordubailo, who had been sentenced to twenty years in a camp, had worked as warehouse manager in the central repair workshop. He had been given this important position (after working in the mine for several years) because of his good relations with the NKVD. After the declaration of war, Kordubailo conceived the idea of organizing an insurrection. He started telling his fellow convicts that he had excellent contacts in the outside world and had secured the aid of some of the guards and some members of the fire department, and that he had obtained reliable intelligence about the strength of the guard and other armed personnel. He then organized a "staff" of eight men, elected himself commander in chief, and picked another prisoner as his deputy and Misha as his "staff major."

Naturally, all of this came to the attention of the NKVD. Kordubailo and his co-conspirators were observed for a while, and once the NKVD had put together a large enough list, everyone was arrested. Kordubailo made a full confession on his first hearing. Thereupon, the number of arrests rose to two hundred. Some of the arrested men confessed everything, but the majority refused to confess, since in fact they had been ignorant of Kordubailo's plans.

Staff Major Misha—about forty, tall, thin, black-eyed, bald, with an English-style mustache—told me how he got involved in the conspiracy. He had never concerned himself with politics. He had been the leader of a band of criminals in Odessa who had made headlines in 1934 after a sensational holdup that brought Misha and his two accomplices into possession of four million rubles and nearly one and a half million in foreign currency. For two years they eluded the detectives, but eventually one of Misha's accomplices was denounced by his girlfriend in connection with some minor crime—she hadn't known anything about the bank robbery—and soon after that, Misha was arrested.

Misha exercised great authority among the criminals in Norilsk. When he came into the cell, all the criminals jumped up and tried to bring themselves to his attention, demonstrating their devotion. He didn't have to say a word; a simple gesture was enough to get someone to do his bidding. His gaunt figure and bald head gave him an intellectual appearance; it was surprising to learn that he was the son of a wealthy peasant.

Misha gave me a brief account of his life. His father had owned a farm not far from Odessa. He specialized in vegetables and competed with the Bulgarians who grew their crops in the same region. He also sold produce to almost all the foreign ships that laid anchor in Odessa. He even owned a truck. In 1929, agriculture was collectivized. Misha's father was expropriated as one of the first kulaks. The entire family of nine was squeezed into a freight car, together with fourteen other peasant families, and deported to Siberia. On the way, Misha and four other adolescent boys escaped; they returned to Odessa and drifted around the city for a while. The little money they had was soon used up. In order to survive, they resorted to holdups, usually of single people walking alone at night. Then they moved on to burglaries. After the great bank robbery of 1934, Odessa became too hot for them, and they moved to another region. When Misha was arrested, his only thought was finding a way to avenge his family's unhappy fate.

Like most common criminals, Misha was given an easy job as controller in the electric plant. He had the time and opportunity to make contact with the outside world, and with the help of accomplices, he managed to acquire everything he needed for a comfortable life in the camp, including liquor. He also had a lover, a cleaning woman in the electric plant. The only thing he lacked was freedom, but he was planning an escape. Then the war came, and Kordubailo approached Misha with his plan.

Many prisoners wrote petitions to Stalin when the war situation began to worsen, hoping that they might be permitted to serve in the army instead of in a camp or behind bars. Kordubailo was one of them. After swearing that he was innocent, he begged to be allowed to prove his loyalty to Stalin and to Soviet power by risking his life in battle. He received no answer. Then he began to search for another way to get out.

Misha, too, wrote to Stalin; his chances were better than Kordubailo's, since he wasn't a political prisoner. Immediately after the outbreak of the war, tens of thousands of criminal convicts were let out of the camps and sent to the front. But Misha's family background made him ineligible, and he was struck from the list.

It was around this time that Kordubailo approached Misha. Further discussions followed, and eventually a staff for the uprising was put together. The staff was to recruit as many prisoners as possible and to establish liaison with the outside, especially with former camp inmates. The plan was to occupy all the important NKVD buildings—the power plant's management building, the camp administration building, the prison guard building. Then all NKVD officers were to be shot. The conspirators succeeded in attracting a number of prisoners and outside sympathizers. Most of the recruits had no idea what it was all about, since their leaders had contented themselves with inquiring after their followers' mood and morale and then entered them on the list without their knowledge.

Hryshnyak had been "recruited" in this manner. Kordubailo had implicated him in the planning of the uprising, but Hryshnyak had known nothing about it. He was over fifty, a strong, stocky man with a long gray beard. He was an old party functionary; after the Revolution, he had been the manager of several factories in Belorussia. In 1937, in Minsk, he was sentenced to ten years for "sabotage."

The case of little Misha, a peasant boy from Belorussia, was similar. This pale boy with chestnut-brown hair was twenty-four years old and not as stupid as he pretended to be. He had worked as a turner in the prison factory. In order to earn some additional bread, he also made scissors, knives, and other metal objects unavailable in Norilsk and sold them to people on the outside. Little Misha was put on the list of insurgents without his knowledge. During the hearing, the interrogator asked him whether he had manufactured any "cold weapons" in the factory. Misha denied this but admitted to having made scissors and knives. This was enough to establish his guilt.

The investigation of the conspirators went on for two weeks, after which there was a lull. Exactly two months after the mass arrests, at four o'clock in the afternoon, we heard the sound of rapid footsteps in the hall and of doors opening and closing. Of the four prisoners in our cell who had been embroiled in the Kordubailo case, only little Misha stayed behind. The next day, he, too, was called. He had to sign a document to confirm that he was being sentenced to ten years for being a member of a counterrevolutionary organization and helping to plan an armed insurrection. Of the two hundred men arrested in the Kordubailo case, a hundred sixty-four were sentenced to death and shot. The rest were given ten-year sentences. The verdict was pronounced by the Special Tribunal, the OSO.

On the morning of the day he was shot, Hryshnyak told me he had had a terrible dream. Then he added: "I can feel it. I'm not going to be around this evening."

Big Misha, too, was taken away. Now Ivanov, who had played a subordinate role while Misha was there, took command in the cell. But he didn't have Misha's authority or stature. With Misha, no one ever got out of hand in the cell, and the politicals were left in peace.

A few days after the liquidation of the Kordubailo "band," a large number of criminals were shot, among them Ivanov. It happened on a Sunday afternoon. The criminals did not submit to fate as philosophically as the politicals, who usually left the cell with a quiet *"Proshchaite, tovarishchi*—Farewell, comrades."* The criminals struggled and kicked and screamed, and the guards had to tie them and stuff so-called pears, hard rubber gags, into their mouths. The guards beat them and dragged their bleeding, struggling bodies down the hall and across the yard, threw them into a truck like blocks of wood, and drove them to the other NKVD prison, where they were shot.

That Sunday, forty-eight criminals were shot—for "sabotage"; i.e., because they didn't want to work. During the war, three days of unexcused absence from work were punishable by death, according to Article 58, paragraph 14. Before the war, it was rare for a criminal even to be brought to trial for refusing to work; usually, mild disciplinary measures were applied.

After the mass shootings, there was peace and quiet for a few days, and no one was called to a hearing. Maybe the NKVD needed a little rest.

THE INVESTIGATION CONTINUES

The next time I was called to a hearing, I experienced a new surprise: a second witness was waiting for me in the interrogator's room, a man who had been in the hospital at the same time I was. Ironically, his name happened to be Brovkin. He was not related to the other Brovkin. The only thing they had in common was that they were criminals. This second Brovkin's testimony against me was virtually identical with the first's. The only difference was that, since he had not slept in my room, he claimed to have overheard my conversations with Olga while visiting the other Brovkin. I remained silent, as I had the first time; again, two officers were brought in to sign a written statement that I had refused to take part in the confrontation.

I received news from the adjacent cell that my friend Georg Biletzki was there and that he was implicated in my case even though he was in a different section of the camp—but that was no obstacle for the NKVD.

Georg was being indicted for the third time. The first time, in Moscow, he had been given five years in a camp. On the evening before his term expired—the date was October 19, 1939—Vasily Chuprakov, Josef Berger, and I went to Georg's barracks to say goodbye. This was, of course, a very special event: one of our friends was being released—what better cause for celebration? Vasily had managed to get hold of a large bottle of liqueur; for the first time since my arrest, I was going to have alcohol. Josef had procured some real coffee. I remember the man who prepared it: he was the former party secretary of the Saratov district. Soon the aroma of coffee spread through the barracks; the bottle was taken from its hiding place; and each of us poured some liqueur in his coffee.

But we had scarcely begun to drink when two camp policemen came in. My first thought was that someone had denounced us for having alcohol. I quickly hid the bottle in my padded trousers.

"Where is Biletzki?" asked one of the policemen.

Georg stepped out of the dark corner.

"Ah, good," said the policeman. "There you are." And they left.

What could it mean? At any rate, our good mood was spoiled. We were about to leave the barracks when the two policemen came back in, accompanied by a man in civilian clothes. The man said to Georg: "Pack your stuff and follow me. You're under arrest."

Georg silently gathered up his possessions and left with the three men. That was the end of our farewell party.

Georg was taken to the prison and indicted for "counterrevolutionary agitation," as defined by Article 58, paragraph 10. Two witnesses testified against him. One of them, a prisoner, declared that he had been listening through a wall when Georg had made anti-Soviet statements. The other witness was the head of the medical services where Georg had worked. His reply to the interrogator, when asked what he knew about Georg, was: "Nothing concrete, but I know that Biletzki is a counterrevolutionary element."

Because of these two statements, Georg was sentenced to another five years in camp. And now he was facing a new trial.

CHRISTMAS 1941

It was Christmas. The temperature outside was minus forty-five degrees Celsius. We chose to forgo our ten-minute walk in the prison yard. It wasn't cold in the cell. We sat on our bunks and exchanged memories. Many dreamed of someday being able to celebrate Christmas with their families. Some wept. Others expressed the hope that they wouldn't be called to a hearing on this day.

As we were conversing in this manner, the door opened, and in came a man with his whole body wrapped in rags. Only his head was bare. He was holding something resembling a hat in his hand. He said softly: "Good day."

My first thought was: This is not a Russian. He could hardly stand up and was searching for a place to sit down.

I went up to him. "Where are you from?" I asked.

He just looked at me, without answering. I offered him my place on the bunk and asked him who he was and what language he spoke. He replied, very quietly: "Magyar."

"Do you speak German?"

"A little."

After a few minutes, he removed a few rags, and said: "It's warm here."

He continued to peel off rags. Then we saw with a shock that he looked like a skeleton, nothing but skin and bones. If he hadn't been moving, you couldn't have believed he was still alive.

Several criminals began to make fun of him. "You've been on a long trip, haven't you? Where's your suitcase?"

But everyone else protected him. One of the criminals even gave him a makhorka cigarette.

That day, all I learned about the newcomer was that his name was Magyaros. The next day, after he had rested a little, he told us that he had fled from his place of work but had soon been captured. I asked him where he had wanted to flee to. He replied: "Home. To Rumania."

"Don't you know how far away that is?"

He shrugged.

After breakfast, he told me his story. He was a Hungarian from Transylvania, born in Kübet. In 1939, he enlisted in the Rumanian Army. His garrison was in Bessarabia. After the Hitler–Stalin pact, when Bessarabia was occupied by the Russians, the Rumanian soldiers stationed there were sent home. The Russians gave them passes that had to be stamped in every town where Soviet troops were stationed. Magyaros and five other soldiers arrived at the Hungarian border and went to an inn to eat. An NKVD officer approached them and asked what they were doing in the town. The Rumanian soldiers showed him their passes and told him they were on their way home. The NKVD man asked them to follow him to his headquarters for "clarification." At headquarters, their names were recorded. Then they were left waiting. Several hours later, they were taken to prison in Kosov. After spending eight days there, they were transported to Stanislavsk by truck, and from there in a mass transport to Krasnoyarsk and eventually to Norilsk, where they were told that they had been condemned to five years in a camp for attempting an unauthorized border crossing.

The hard work and fierce climate had made a skeleton of what had once been a hardworking peasant boy. When he felt he had reached the end of his endurance, he contemplated suicide, but didn't have the courage; so he decided to escape. A few days later, Magyaros told me he could see clearly now that it was impossible to escape from Norilsk. It hadn't been a rational decision but an act of desperation.

Magyaros was called to a hearing. The interrogator couldn't communicate with him, since Magyaros spoke very little Russian. Magyaros asked to have me as an interpreter. I tried to explain to the interrogator that the attempted escape could not be taken seriously, and that, in any case, the completely emaciated prisoner had been apprehended not far from the camp. The interrogator was reasonable enough to recognize the truth of what I was saying and brought charges against Magyaros according to Article 82, which called for a maximum penalty of five years, instead of the usual indictment according to Article 58, paragraph 14, which called for the death penalty. Magyaros was given three years, so his total sentence was raised to eight.

Magyaros spent several weeks in our cell. He felt comfortable there; it wasn't cold, and he didn't have to perform hard labor. He dreaded the day when he would have to return to the camp. Sometimes you could see him silently weeping. When I tried to console him by telling him that the war would eventually end and that then he would be able to go back to Transylvania and wouldn't have to suffer any more hunger or cold, he said: "It's not myself I'm concerned about, it's my mother. I'm afraid the Russians will come to my village and chase my mother out of her house and maybe deport her to the Far North, like me."

I laughed at that.

That was January 1942. The Germans were penetrating more and more deeply into Russia, and this peasant believed that the Russians might reach Transylvania! Later I came to realize that he was right.

I lost sight of Magyaros when he was sent back to the camp after being sentenced.

KOLYA TELLS HOW A COLLECTIVE FARM WAS FOUNDED

Half a year passed. My old cellmates had gone; new ones had arrived; and I was still in the same cell. I often fell into despair; how long could this go on?

The new prisoners brought conflicting reports. The advance of the German Army was making the officials more and more nervous, and incidents like Kordubailo's conspiracy only made matters worse. The NKVD tyranny was taking on unimagined proportions. Large batches of new prisoners were coming in every day from other camp sections and also from the town. A prisoner only had to say a few words about the hard work and the bad food and the NKVD could sentence him to death or to ten years for "anti-Soviet propaganda." The criminals, who knew that their days were numbered, harassed the politicals, mocked and abused them, told them Hitler was coming to hang all the communists. Most of the criminals were sons of peasants, and they considered the politicals responsible for the persecution and deportation of their parents to Siberia.

One of the most vindictive criminals was a young fellow named Kolya. He had assumed command of the criminals in the cell after Ivanov's death. I got along well with him. He didn't know I was a communist, and he liked me for being a foreigner. He repeatedly asked me to tell him about life abroad. No matter what country I was talking about—Austria, Yugoslavia, France, or Italy—he always asked: "Do they have collective farms?"

When I told him they didn't, he was thrilled.

One day, when he was pressing me again to tell him about life outside Russia, I asked him why he hated collective farms so much. Instead of answering directly, he told me the following story.

His parents had lived in a village sixty kilometers from Krasnodar, in the region of Kuban. His father owned twelve hectares of good soil, enough to feed the family of fourteen. In 1929, the rumor spread that everything was going to be collectivized. The peasants talked about it, but no one could imagine what this collectivization would be like. Some people thought the women would belong to all the men; others believed the children would be taken from their parents. Almost no one discussed what would happen to the land and the animals. Most of the peasants in the village owned between eight and thirty hectares. Some were able to hire a few laborers, but most of the peasants worked their own land. At harvest time, everyone worked, from six-year-old children to old men and women. There were few really poor people among the two thousand villagers.

In the fall of 1930, a commission from the district capital came and called a meeting of all the peasants. The entire village was present, even the sick and the very young children. A poor peasant from the village, a man who owned little land and had a lot of children, was chairman of the meeting. He announced that the district party secretary was going to talk about collectivization. A young man stepped up to the podium and talked for two hours about the kolkhoz, the collective farm. At the end of his speech, he asked all peasants who were in favor of Soviet power to join the kolkhoz.

Then the chairman asked if anyone wanted to speak. No hands were raised. Finally, a young Cossack woman wanted to know: "How is it with this kolkhoz—is it just for a while or forever?" The secretary said that from now on there would only be collective farms, so it was forever.

Everyone in the room protested. The secretary stood up again and began to list the great advantages of collectivization: the wonderful machinery the state would provide, the abundant crops, etc. Suddenly stones started flying in the direction of the stage. The tumult was so great that the members of the commission barely succeeded in pushing their way out of the room.

Two weeks later, some men came from the city. Certain peasants were summoned to the community meeting room and told that they were kulaks because they employed laborers on their farms. Twenty-two rich families were de-kulakized. Their land, their animals, their houses—all this was taken from them and declared to be collective property. The next day, a detachment of NKVD soldiers surrounded the village. No one was allowed to leave. Accompanied by several villagers, the commission went to the houses of the wealthy peasants and forced the families out of their houses. They were allowed to keep only a few possessions and some food. Some went along without resistance, but most of them had to be literally torn from their land—they lay down with their children and refused to move. The soldiers broke down the doors and dragged the people out. The whole village could hear the screams of the children, the crying of the women, the cursing of the men.

Only half of the de-kulakization was accomplished that day. Four peasants were led away in shackles because they had attacked the commissioners with pitchforks and sickles. At night, you could hear the cries of the hungry and unmilked animals in the abandoned farms. The next day, when the commission wanted to continue their work, the entire village had banded together with sickles and pitchforks in their hands. The commission had to withdraw.

Then the peasants stormed the houses of those who had cooperated with the commission, dragged them out on the street, and kicked them. Four villagers were killed by the crowd; four others were able to run away. The rich peasants returned to their houses. The next day, no one came to the village. No one came on the following days, either. Three weeks passed in this manner.

One night, the villagers were awakened by the barking of their dogs. When they looked outside, they saw that the village was surrounded by trucks equipped with searchlights. No one dared leave his house. At 6 a.m., soldiers knocked on the doors and told all the peasants to assemble in the community house. Hesitantly, the peasants did as they were told. The district party secretary and an NKVD officer sat down behind a table. The officer read a communiqué from the regional Executive Committee according to which those kulaks who had offered armed resistance to the de-kulakization and participated in the brutal murders of four peasants would be relocated to Siberia with their families; in addition, the guilty parties would have to stand trial for the murders. Their houses, land, and livestock would be placed in the hands of farm workers for the purpose of organizing a kolkhoz. Before the eyes of the assembled villagers, twenty-two families were forced to climb into trucks and were driven off, heavily guarded, toward the unknown.

Eighty farm workers' families were instructed to move into the houses of the deported peasants. The next morning, a new meeting was held, to which only the farm workers were invited. A decision was passed to establish a kolkhoz. A party delegate, a worker from the Kharkov locomotive factory, was chosen as the chairman of the kolkhoz. One of the large kulak homesteads was made the seat of "The Road to Socialism"—that was the name of the new kolkhoz.

Thereupon, the village was seized by panic. The peasants began to slaughter all their cattle, for fear that they would have to give it all up to the kolkhoz. By the next spring, there were only a few cows left. More than three thousand cows, oxen, and horses had been slaughtered in the course of the winter. The number of slaughtered pigs, sheep, and goats was even greater. The kolkhoz began its work by herding all the cattle as well as horses, pigs, chickens, and geese into a single stable. Certain people were entrusted with the care of the animals; they did such a good job that more than half of the livestock died in the course of three months.

Spring came. The peasants were very hesitant to go about their fieldwork, and produced just enough to take care of their own needs. The new collective farmers, on the other hand, did not have enough manpower to cultivate the large fields they had inherited from the deported rich peasants. When the harvest was collected that fall, another commission came to the village and informed each peasant how much grain, meat, milk, and butter had to be delivered to the state. So much was asked of the peasants, and so little had been produced, that not enough was left for their families. Many had to buy produce to be able to meet the quotas. Whoever didn't deliver on time was punished. Then, after everything had been delivered and the peasants thought they would be left in peace, they were told that they had not delivered enough and that each farm would have to supply a portion of the missing amount. Now the peasants refused.

Armed NKVD troops and party activists came from the city, went from house to house, and prodded each family to deliver the extra grain. Everything was searched—barns, stables, living quarters; even the floors were torn apart. Dogs were used to search the fields, where some peasants had hidden a little grain.

After dark, the party activists and kolkhoz farmers didn't dare walk around the village; their lives were in danger. There were mornings when party workers were found with their bellies slit and a few grains of corn in the wound, with a note by their side: "Here's your grain!"

That winter, hunger set in. The remaining animals were slaughtered and eaten. In the spring of 1931, most of the villagers were so weak that only a few were capable of working in the fields. Many died of starvation. Those who had the strength fled to the cities to beg.

Summer came, and most of the fields remained uncultivated. The NKVD paid the village another visit. The majority of the villagers were called together in the community house and were told they would be deported to Siberia for "sabotage." They had three hours to get ready. Each family member was allowed sixteen kilos of luggage. The peasants were taken to a train station, loaded on freight cars, which were locked from the outside, and shipped off to Siberia under NKVD supervision. Once a day, the cars were opened up. Each person was given hot water and every three days one kilo of bread.

After a four-week trip, they arrived in Verkhni Udinsk. Many had died on the way; many others were sick and had to be taken to the hospital. The rest were put in a barracks camp, where they were allowed to rest for fourteen days and were given three meals a day.

After the two-week quarantine, the peasants were divided into three groups and shipped to different locations. The group with Kolya's relatives took off toward an unknown destination, guarded by NKVD soldiers. Children and old people were allowed to sit on the carts where the luggage was loaded; everyone else had to walk. They were led through a forest. Frequently, they would pass groups of prisoners who were chopping wood under the supervision of guards. Every twenty-five kilometers, they would stop to rest. They slept in tents or barracks, together with the prisoners who were working in the woods. When it rained, the peasants stayed in the tents and waited for the weather to change. Sometimes it was several days before the forest trails were passable again.

The group penetrated 350 kilometers into the forest, and there the trek came to an end. More than two hundred men, women, and children assembled on a meadow near a brook. An NKVD officer read a government decree according to which the peasants here assembled were entitled to inhabit and cultivate two hundred and fifty square kilometers of this land and raise animals on it "for all eternity." Unauthorized departure from this territory would be punishable with ten years in prison. Having read this proclamation, the NKVD officer made a speech in which he explained that the peasants had committed serious crimes against Soviet power and deserved to be shot; but the government was humane and was giving them an opportunity to begin a new life in this fertile region. They would be given tools to begin building their houses immediately—one house per family. They would also be given seed. He advised them to cut as much grass as possible so they would have enough fodder for the animals. Each family would receive one cow, for which they could pay in installments.

Field kitchens were set up; tents were pitched. Twenty horse-drawn carts that had been used to transport the luggage were left with the peasants. A week later, a field bakery was brought in, and six cows to provide milk for the children. The peasants immediately set to work. Thirty wooden houses were built in three months.

An officer of the NKVD escort troop stayed in the settlement as its commander. He was a thoroughly decent man and did everything he could to help the peasants begin their new life. Often, he would ride 350 kilometers to the neighboring city to get medicine from a pharmacy or buy nails. When a doctor was needed, he would bring him from the nearby prison camp; after a while, he brought in a medical aide as a permanent resident in the village. He also brought twenty hunting rifles from the city and distributed them among the peasants, so they could hunt the abundant wildlife in the forest.

In the fall, the commander assembled the peasants and said: "Now we have an almost finished village. It needs a name. What shall we call it? Let's have some suggestions!"

No one said anything. Finally, an old peasant suggested that they should name the village after the beloved leader of the Communist Party of the Soviet Union: Stalin. The commander did not indicate that he had understood the irony of this suggestion; he simply objected that a more neutral name might be better. They settled on Beryozovka, Birchtown— the surrounding trees were, in fact, mainly birches.

Several years passed. The new village was beginning to look like all Russian villages—a street in the middle, flanked by houses made of shaved logs, with just a few shingled roofs. Tens of thousands of trees had been cut down. The fertile earth produced rich crops. Some of the peasants cultivated bees. Most families had two or three cows and several pigs. In the winter, they would go hunting and come home laden with the rich catch. Some peasants trapped silver foxes; buyers paid a great deal of money for them in the city. The old people had adjusted to their new circumstances and tried not to think of the past. The young were happy.

The kindhearted commander was recalled and replaced by a young, brutal officer who soon began to harass the peasants. Anyone who wanted to drive to the city had to get his permission; the person making the request would be submitted to a regular interrogation—why, for what purpose, for how long?

One day, it occurred to him that the peasants were gradually getting rich and therefore represented a threat to the Soviet state. He drove to the city, came back with a stranger after a week, and called a general meeting. The commander made a short speech, from which the peasants gathered that it was now time to organize a collective farm. They did not resist, since they knew from experience where resistance would lead. The kolkhoz was established. The stranger was appointed as its chairman.

That winter, Kolya ran away from the village with four other young men. On the way, they attacked two men who were coming from the city; they stole their papers and some money. When they attempted their second robbery, the victim defended himself and people came running out of a nearby house, overpowered Kolya and his friends, and turned them over to the police. All of them were sentenced to ten years in a camp.

At Norilsk, Kolya killed a chief guard who refused to transfer him to an easier job. For this, Kolya was given an additional ten years. Now he was in prison for the third time. He was accused of "sabotage." Since he had already received two major sentences, he could expect the death penalty next.

ASSEMBLY-LINE EXECUTIONS

After twice refusing categorically to sign any document, I wasn't called to another hearing. The NKVD prison was overcrowded, and some inmates were transferred to the other prison. The first building had been made of wood; this was a stone building with just a ground floor, about forty meters long. On either side of the corridor were twenty cells of varying size. The smallest had four bunk spaces; the largest, forty. But at this time there were three or four times that many prisoners in the cells. About half the cells were reserved for men who were under sentence of death: these were separated from the other cells by a heavy iron grill. At the end of the corridor were four punishment cells. To the left of the main entrance was the office of the prison administration. Next to it was a room about forty meters square, insulated with lead sheeting, where the executions were carried out.

I was put in cell 14. As I stepped in, I was immediately reminded of the Butyrki in Moscow. The eighty prisoners who were squeezed in there were squatting half naked on their bunks. The cell was very warm, due to the overcrowding. I met several acquaintances from the camp here. There were others I knew from the first Norilsk prison. Among my cellmates were many officers from the Baltic countries. They had spent time in a special camp some forty kilometers from Norilsk, near Lake Pyasino. They had been imprisoned two months after the beginning of the Russo–German War.

I found some room between the Estonian General Brödis and his adjutant, Captain Rüberg. I also remember the Estonian Captain Lujk and two Latvian officers, Lieutenant Grünberg and Captain Lidaks. I have forgotten the other officers' names.

The most impressive personality among the officers was, without a doubt, General Brödis. We became good friends. Brödis was a highly cultivated man with a great fund of military expertise and a fluent knowledge of German, Russian, English, French, and Italian. He was very well versed in French and German literature. He had lived several years in France and in Germany and had attended the General Staff Academy in Paris. Brödis had been arrested together with the Estonian Minister of War, General Lajdoner. Lajdoner was put in a different camp; he was shot at the beginning of the war.

Most of the inmates in the second prison were people whose pre-trial investigation had been concluded and who were now awaiting their trial by the regular camp court or the Special Tribunal, the OSO. The OSO passed judgment in the absence of the accused; many prisoners who were already sentenced to death did not know it. Often, a prisoner who was being summoned to his execution left the cell believing that he was being taken to trial. Perhaps it was better that way. Death itself was not the greatest ordeal prisoners had to go through. Many longed for death;

what was worse was the endless waiting for the decision, which could take months, even years.

I met a young Tatonian in this jail. The Tatonians are a small ethnic group, followers of the Moslem religion, who live in the Caucasus. The camp court had sentenced him to death for making pro-Turkish remarks. He appealed the sentence and waited six months for a decision. The district court rescinded the verdict for lack of evidence; the camp court sentenced him to death again. This was repeated three times, and after nearly two years in death row, the poor fellow was half mad. In the end, he was shot, after all.

As in the first prison, politicals and criminals were locked up together; but here they kept their distance. Here, too, hunger plagued us constantly, and there were fights when the bread was distributed in the morning.

The *starosta*, the prison elder, would receive the bread from the guard and pass the pieces around one by one. There was always someone who thought that someone else had gotten a larger portion; the corner pieces were considered particularly desirable. In order to avoid fights, we agreed to take turns eating the corner pieces. Some prisoners would remind the elder before going to sleep: "*Starosta*, tomorrow it's my turn to get the corner piece." And if there was no corner piece the next day, how great his disappointment!

The warm meals were distributed by the guard instead of the elder. The large food container stood in front of the cell door. The prisoners would line up, and the guard would hand each in turn his tin bowl full of soup. He would count the portions as he dealt them out, and when he had reached the number of prisoners in the cell, he would close the door. It would happen sometimes that one or two prisoners, the last in line, would miss out on their portions because others had picked up two portions, or else because the guard had made a counting error.

There were prisoners who particularly looked forward to "meat days," which were very frequent here. As I've said, "meat days" were days when mass executions were carried out. There were extra portions on those days. The politicals rarely took advantage of this sort of supplementation, no matter how hungry they were.

Life in the second prison was much more hectic than in the first. Hardly a day passed without some event that profoundly affected us. With the many executions and the many condemned men waiting to be killed, the guards had their day's work cut out for them. You could frequently hear screams and shouts coming from the death cells. The condemned demanded more food, but the guards would usually answer with: "What do you need food for, your hours are numbered." This would set off a desperate torrent of abuse. It would usually end with one or another of the death candidates being dragged out to the hall and beaten up by the guards.

For a while, the executions were carried out at night. This caused tremendous agitation throughout the prison. Many of the condemned refused to leave their cells, and the guards had to use force. Often, the whole cell would unite against the hangmen, with the result that the victims were beaten bloody before they were shot. On such days, the guards were given a lot of vodka to drink; some of them were so drunk they could hardly stand up. Fired up by alcohol, they would rage and riot to their heart's content, and the racket would be audible for some distance outside the prison. For this reason, the NKVD decided to carry out the executions during the day.

The shooting would usually start at four in the afternoon. You could usually sense its coming at lunchtime, when the vodka-reddened faces of the guards presaged another "meat day." The corpses would be loaded on trucks at night, driven to the prison cemetery, and thrown into a mass grave. This atmosphere had a highly stressful effect on the prisoners' nerves. This was no longer the normal routine of Russian prison life, with its predictable phases: interrogation, beatings, hunger, judgment. Here everyone waited for death. The only question was when it would be your turn.

In the first NKVD prison, I had observed many prisoners dividing the four hundred grams of bread they were given in the morning into several pieces, so as to have some left over at noon and in the evening; a Russian does not enjoy his meal unless it includes a piece of bread. But here most people ate up their bread in the morning: every prisoner was afraid he might not be around to enjoy a next meal.

One morning, as we woke up, General Brödis turned to me and said: "Let's treat ourselves to a good breakfast this morning." I didn't understand what he meant, and looked at him, surprised.

The general pulled out a little pouch which he had hidden under his pillow. "I've kept a few lumps of sugar so that I could celebrate the Estonian national holiday with a sumptuous breakfast. But it looks as if I won't live that long; so let's have the breakfast today."

"I'm sure we'll be able to celebrate many holidays; keep the sugar," I said.

The general shook his head. "I am not as optimistic as you are." And turning to Rüberg, he said: "Captain, please see to it that we have enough *kipyatok*, and invite the two comrades." He was referring to two other Estonian officers in our cell.

When the *kipyatok* came, the two Estonian officers sat down on our bunk. We formed a circle, using a dirty towel as a tablecloth. The hot water was steaming from a tin pot. Brödis gave each of us a lump of sugar, and then we drank the sweetened water and munched the bread we had just been given.

At the end of this festive repast, the two guests thanked their host and withdrew. Then Brödis said: "Now there's only one thing left for me to do—make out my will."

"Let's not spoil our good mood after such a lovely breakfast," I said.
"I'm used to looking truth in the eye."

"Do you really think we're going to be shot?"

"I don't just believe it, I'm sure it'll happen within a few days," he said quietly.

"I don't want to lose hope."

The general was silent for moment, and then went on: "I remember when I graduated from the military academy and was stationed as a young officer in the border town of Suvalki. What a beautiful life we had in that little city! Many young girls, the promenade in front of the train station, oh, what a time that was . . ." His gaze was lost in the distance. When he continued, his voice was quivering. "And later, Paris, London, Rome, Petersburg. That was all so beautiful. Now it's gone."

"Tell me, why did you wait until the Russians deported you to Siberia?" I asked.

"Ah, that's a long story."

"I would like to hear it."

"I'll tell you how it happened. Our tragedy began on the day we allowed the Russians to establish bases in our ports. At that time, many of us believed that we were threatened by Germany. The occupation of the Sudetenland, the annexation of Austria—these things made us afraid of losing our independence. I personally was against making concessions to Stalin, but Lajdoner, our Minister of War at the time, believed, as all our bourgeois politicians believed, that it would be best to come to an understanding with the Russians. Of all the parties in our republic, only the Social Democrats were against a pact with the Russians that would allow them to set up bases in our country. I agreed with the Social Democrats. Lajdoner, who was my superior, lived in the same house as I. We got together often, and during the days of the crisis we were in constant contact. A week before the pact with the Russians, I woke up in the middle of the night and couldn't go back to sleep, I was so worried about the fate of our country. I rang Lajdoner's bell; when I explained to the maid that I had some urgent business to discuss with the Minister, she said he had company, some gentlemen were visiting. I insisted. Lajdoner came to the foyer, trembling with agitation. I begged him to let me speak with him. Lajdoner asked if it could wait an hour. I went back to my apartment, which was one floor below his.

"Half an hour later, the maid came to call me. The Minister led me to his room, locked the door, and looked at me questioningly.

" 'I want to speak to you as a friend,' I said.

" 'So speak, speak, what's going on?'

" 'Do we really want to let the Russians occupy our country?'

" 'It's not the whole country; we're just giving them a few bases.'

" 'That's just the beginning. You're an officer; you must realize that once they're here, we can't get them out again.'

" 'What are you suggesting? War with the Russians?'

" 'I'm in favor of resisting the Russians if they try to march in against our will.'

" 'How long could we hold out? Three days, a week at the most. And then they wouldn't be satisfied with a few bases; they'd want the whole country.'

" 'We wouldn't stand alone. The whole world would fight along with us.'

"It was morning already. I was not able to persuade Lajdoner of the necessity of resistance. I realized that all was lost.

"I returned to my apartment, called the office to say I wasn't coming in, and drove off to see my old father. He was a forester just outside Tallinn. I told him the news. At first, he refused to believe me. Then we talked about what we should do. I advised him to emigrate to Germany. But although my father was born in Germany, he rejected the idea of asking Hitler for refuge from Stalin. He would rather stay. He said his life was nearly over, so why uproot himself?

"I returned to Tallinn in the hope that I would find others who would be willing to defend our country against the Russians. But it was too late.

"It wasn't until the Russians set foot in our country and then ended up occupying all of it that people woke up and realized that all was lost. For a while, the Russians allowed us to keep our own administration. Then they began to arrest and deport people—first the bourgeoisie, then the rich peasants, the intelligentsia, and finally it was our turn. At first, we were told we were going to be sent to a military academy for reeducation; then we were lured into a forest outside Tallinn, supposedly for a military exercise. Several hundred officers of the old Estonian Army were there. The NKVD had surrounded the forest before we arrived; now they showed themselves and told us to lay down our arms. It would have been senseless to offer resistance to the cannons and machine guns pointed at us. We had to raise our hands and submit to a body search. Then we had to take off all our clothes and line up in formation. The clothes were lying in front of us, and several hours passed before we were allowed to put them on again. We were taken by truck to the train station in Tallinn. There they loaded us on freight cars with tin sheeting over the windows. The cars were divided in half by a metal grill, and there were wooden bunks in each of the compartments. Eighty men went into each car.

"During the trip, we were closely watched by an NKVD man. We were told to keep our voices low. At every station, the strength of the walls was tested from outside with a wooden sledgehammer (this was particularly unpleasant at night). Apparently, prisoners occasionally managed to jump off the train while it was moving. And so it went, the usual prisoner's odyssey, via the various transit stations along the Trans-Siberian Railroad, until we reached Krasnoyarsk. There we were put into a big covered barge. There were three other barges like ours, probably filled with nonhuman freight. A little steamship pulled those four barges downstream to the mouth of the Yenisei. At Dudinka, our barge was tethered to a tiny steamer that pulled us up the Valyek to Lake Pyasino. There we lived in tents until we had constructed barracks. Everyone had to work hard. Three generals and I were given 'light labor' because of our advanced age—we had to clean the latrines and dispose of the garbage.

"Things went on like that until the war broke out. We didn't even know about the war until we were transferred to the prison in Norilsk on August 5, 1941. I was interrogated. I was accused of the very worst crimes: high treason, liaison with the enemy, serving the army of an enemy, terrorism, counterrevolutionary agitation—there were only a few points in Article 58 that weren't applied to my case. I gave them a complete confession; I didn't care what excuse they used to shoot me."

We were so engrossed in our conversation that we hadn't noticed the time passing; it was already noon. As the first men were being given their soup, they saw that the guards were drunk. One of the criminals proclaimed loudly: "Brothers, it's another meat day!"

Some people protested: "You're always raising a panic!"

Another man said: "Spare us your stupid jokes—that's nothing to laugh about!"

I was the last to be fed, and I, too, noticed that the guard could hardly stand up straight. I thought: That criminal is right, something's going to happen, maybe it's my turn today . . . However, this thought did not spoil my appetite.

After lunch, I lay down. My neighbors, General Brödis and Captain Rüberg, were also lying on their backs, each of them lost in thought. Some prisoners were standing by the door, listening. It was quiet in the cell, and you couldn't hear anything outside. The excitement that had been caused by the drunken guard subsided, and the listeners returned to their places on the bunks.

Suddenly we heard a scream in the hallway. Everyone jumped up; a few men put their ears to the door. There were no more screams, but instead we heard something heavy being dragged along the hall. Ten minutes later, we heard the cell opposite ours being opened and a man walking out without resistance. Now the sounds grew livelier: doors were opened and closed; you could hear many steps. Suddenly the listeners leaped back from the door. We could hear the guard's bundle of keys jangling in front of our cell, and everyone hurried back to his place. The door opened, the guard came in, stopped in the middle of the cell, and scrutinized the prisoners, scanning the lower bunks first, then the upper ones.

When he had nearly come to the end of the bunks, he made a summoning gesture with a crooked forefinger, indicating a criminal who was known as Sedoi, Grayhead, because of his whitish-blond hair. "Come on, Sedoi."

"Where to?"

"The *nachalnik,* the commander, wants to see you."

"Fuck your *nachalnik!*"

"He just wants to tell you something, you can come back after that."

"Leave me alone, I'm not going."

The guard left without a word. After a few minutes, he came back with three other guards. "Sedoi, get moving!"

"I'm not going."

"You *are* going, and it's better if you don't make us force you."

Sedoi responded with a curse.

The guard grabbed his foot; the other guards moved in to help him. But Sedoi tore himself loose and tried to climb on the shelf above the second bunk. The four guards seized his legs and pulled at him, but he was hanging on to the shelf. After a while, the bolts gave way. The shelf fell, along with Sedoi, on top of the people sitting underneath; and Sedoi was dragged to the ground over the heads of the others. He began to scream horribly. The whole cell became very agitated, and there were shouts: "Let him go! Butchers! Bloodsuckers!"

A fifth guard came storming into the cell and tried to gag Sedoi with a pear. Sedoi defended himself desperately. The guard boxed him in the mouth until he bled, and after several powerful blows the guard succeeded in stuffing the pear into Sedoi's mouth. Now all you could hear was Sedoi's muffled gagging. The guards dragged him out of the cell by his feet and slammed the door, leaving behind a long trail of blood. We all crept back to our places, terrified, and stayed there in a funereal silence for a long time. That day, no one else was taken from our cell.

When the evening soup was served, the cell revived. Most of us ate as if nothing had happened.

It was a great surprise for us when the one-armed marine captain Menshikov came into our cell. We knew very little about the war. Now we had a cellmate who had been at the front and who had many interesting things to tell us. Menshikov had been the commander of Novaya Zemlya. This island was a relay point for goods arriving under strong escort from the United States and England. The ships would move on from there to Dudinka and Igarka. Some of the goods stayed in Dudinka to supply the metal-ore processing plants of Norilsk. The rest was reloaded in Dudinka and Igarka and transported up the Yenisei to Krasnoyarsk.

In August 1942, another such transport arrived in Novaya Zemlya. The escort ships turned around and went back. Just a few hours later, the watchman in the tower announced that a ship was in sight. Everyone assumed it was one of the Allied warships and didn't give the matter any importance. Shortly after, the watchman announced that the ship was nearing the bay.

"I went outside," Menshikov told us, "to see for myself. As soon as I had climbed the tower, I realized to my horror that this was a German warship. I gave the alarm, but it was too late. Our ships were lying at anchor in the bay, the crews resting from their long, exhausting voyage. It would take several hours to steam up the engines. Meanwhile, the German cruiser was coming closer. One of the Allied freighters—the first ship we managed to get moving—steered its way out of the bay. That's all the Germans were waiting for. At the moment when the ship reached the narrowest part of the bay, the German guns sent off their first salvo— a direct hit. The ship sank and blocked the other ships in. We were trapped.

"Our coastal batteries opened fire on the Germans, but the guns didn't reach far enough. The Germans came closer and destroyed all the ships in the bay, as well as a large part of the harbor. They left a hundred dead and wounded. I got hit, too"—Menshikov pointed at his stump. For three weeks, Captain Menshikov lay in the hospital of Dudinka. Then he was arrested and imprisoned. He was accused of being a German agent and of deliberately having failed to secure the island against enemy attack.

One day, when a new *starosta* was to be elected, I was surprised to find myself recommended by the physician Olenchik, who scarcely knew me and with whom I had quarreled. Olenchik was of Polish parentage, but born in Russia. As he told me later, he had served in the NKVD as a doctor. After Soviet troops marched into eastern and southern Poland in 1939, several thousand captured Polish officers were shot in a forest near Lublin. When Olenchik learned about this, he asked to be relieved of his duties. Instead, he was arrested. In Norilsk, he was tried for a second time for allegedly fomenting an armed insurrection.

Olenchik and I became friends, but this friendship did not last long. One day, we were given herring for supper. I watched Olenchik take some grain sugar from a small pouch and sprinkle it over the herring. I asked him how one could eat herring with sugar. Olenchik asked me what was so unusual about that. I replied that I didn't think it was normal. That made him angry. We quarreled and stopped talking to each other.

The incident with Sedoi brought us back together. The renewal of the friendship began with my giving Olenchik a firm handshake after he had loudly protested the brutal treatment of Sedoi. It took a lot of courage to do that: he had risked at least twenty days in the punishment cell and possibly a formal charge of incitement to riot.

Olenchik was sentenced to death by the camp court and was shot in September 1942.

The German cruiser's surprise attack on Novaya Zemlya and the sinking of the food transports had catastrophic consequences for the population of Norilsk. Stalinist propaganda had been stressing the need for patience: wait till the end of the next Five-Year Plan and you will have plenty of everything. Before the war, the Russian people had also been told that large quantities of food had to be stored up in case there was a war between the Soviet Union and one or all of the surrounding capitalist countries. When the war broke out, it turned out that there were almost no food supplies. Severe rationing was imposed on the population on the very first day of the war. Minimal food supplies were made available for the large cities; the rest had to provide for themselves. The situation was particularly bad in Norilsk, where nothing grows except some inedible weeds.

It was the Americans who eventually supplied Norilsk with food and other wares, in exchange for nickel, copper, cobalt, and other nonferrous metals. No Soviet food supplies had been set aside for Norilsk in 1942–43. After the sinking of the ships at Novaya Zemlya, the population was left without provisions. There were supplies in the warehouses of Norilsk, but they would run out in two or three months. What there was, was distributed among the NKVD, the guards, and the few free civilians that lived in the town. Almost nothing was left for the prisoners. The usual prison ration of four hundred grams of bread was reduced to three hundred grams. The rations in the camp were also reduced. Our warm meals consisted of nearly inedible local weeds and salt fish. Meat, fat, and sugar disappeared completely. To forestall a total catastrophe, food was flown in to Norilsk: still, there was nowhere near enough.

People were growing more agitated every day, not only the prisoners but the free population as well. The prisoners were promised that they would retroactively receive the food they were entitled to, but that didn't fill any stomachs. Weeks and months passed, and the food problem got worse. Now we weren't getting salt fish anymore. The situation was more and more threatening.

The NKVD knew how to deal with such problems: terror replaced food. The head of food provisioning, Krichevsky, was arrested, with his two aides. Then the NKVD had its agents spread a rumor in the camp: the authorities had discovered a counterrevolutionary organization led by the Polish agent Krichevsky (Krichevsky was of Polish origin). These conspirators had deliberately been spoiling food to sabotage the administration's efforts to feed the free population as well as the prisoners under the strained economic conditions imposed by the war.

Krichevsky and his aides confessed to everything they were accused of and were sentenced to death. However, they weren't shot. After a year in prison, they were released and returned to their former positions. No explanation was given, but the reasons were obvious—food supplies were again available, and scapegoats were no longer needed.

FROM MOTHER VOLGA TO THE GRAY YENISEI

In the beginning of September 1941, four Germans were brought into our cell. I later learned that they had been among twelve hundred men, women, and children who were deported from the Volga–German Republic to a spot about eighty kilometers from Ust-Port, on the left bank of the Yenisei. The soil was infertile there, and neither work nor bread could be found in the surrounding area. Like all deportees, the Volga Germans were given tools and materials to build their new homes. The NKVD ordered them to establish a fishing kolkhoz.

For one month, each person received, free of charge, six hundred grams of bread a day, along with other food. By the end of this period, they were supposed to have built their barracks and begun to feed themselves. The German peasants, who had lived hundreds of kilometers away from the nearest river, were now supposed to catch fish in the mouth of the Yenisei. It is almost misleading to call the Yenisei a river in this area; it is so wide that one cannot see from one bank to the other. The peasants sank to their knees and begged the commander to give them other work to do. The women and children came to him in a group and pleaded to be taken someplace else. The commander granted them another month of free rations and ordered the peasants to start fishing the banks of the river. They could keep the catch for their own consumption.

Reassured, the peasants returned to their barracks. What they managed to catch from the shore was not much, but it helped to supplement the rations. The second month passed quickly, and now it was time to climb into the boats and venture far out onto the river to cast the large nets. They went out in groups of four to six. Most of the boats returned after two hours. Terrified, the novice fishermen—most of them were women—swore they would never set foot in a boat again. The bravest stayed out on the river longer, but their catch was barely enough for dinner.

One Sunday, the fishermen were surprised by a storm. Of thirty boats that set out, six sank. The rest reached the shore with great effort. Thirty people drowned on that day. Of the eighteen women who died in the accident, five were mothers. Sixteen children were orphaned. After this disaster, the commander had trouble persuading the deportees to set out in their boats again. But when NKVD headquarters withheld their rations for a few days, the peasants were forced to fish. Not long after the accident, the commander set a minimum quota of fish that had to be brought in by each person. They were rarely able to meet the norm: the fish "wouldn't go into the net," as the peasants put it. Failure to meet the norm was punishable with cuts in the food rations.

Winter came, and the Yenisei froze over. The peasants were glad that they couldn't be forced to go out on the dangerous river now. But their rejoicing was premature; they were ordered to make holes in the ice and fish with small nets. Since in the arctic the beginning of winter coincides with the beginning of the polar night, the peasants had to set out by torchlight. The ice was almost a yard thick in places; it took hours to break it up with pickaxes and crowbars. Against all expectations, the catch was bountiful.

Often, the frost was so severe that the holes would freeze over within four hours. So as not to have to keep making new holes, the peasants went out in twelve-hour shifts. To protect themselves against the enormous cold, the deportees set up tents and covered the ice with reindeer furs they had bought from nomads. But then the great arctic blizzard, the purga, came sweeping across the vast plain of ice and tore the tents from their fastenings. It didn't seem worth setting them up again, since the next purga would blast them away once more.

On New Year's Eve, there was such a violent storm that you couldn't see a step ahead of you; torches were completely useless. It was only through a tremendous effort that the settlement was saved from destruction. That day, five women froze to death, and most of the others suffered severe frostbite on their hands and feet. Two women and a man had to have their legs amputated.

The storm raged for more than two weeks. During that time, it was impossible to fish. After the purga subsided, the settlers went out on the river. There wasn't a trace left of the holes, and all their tools and implements had disappeared. Now began the hard work of breaking up the ice once again, and it had grown thicker. There were spots where the settlers were unable to reach the water even after hours of labor. Since their nets were gone, they had to resort to angling, and their catch was meager, scarcely enough to satisfy the most severe hunger.

Spring came. Now they had to go far out on the swollen, turbulent river. On the very first day, there was a bad accident: six people were swallowed up by the waves. No one saw it happen. When the six failed to return the next day, the others surmised that they had drowned. Very few people were able to meet the quota during those first days of spring. When the commander reduced the daily bread ration to three hundred grams, some of the fishermen refused to set out in their boats. Two days later, a detachment of NKVD soldiers came and arrested almost all the men; they were accused of sabotage. Two of them, the "instigators," were sentenced to death. All the others were given six years in camp.

On days that weren't marked by big events such as "meat days," we passed the time in storytelling, doing puzzles, and even telling jokes. The jokes were mainly political; this wasn't without its danger, but we did it anyway. Among the eighty people in our cell, almost all the nations of Europe were represented. There was a constant coming and going. When someone was taken from the cell, no one knew where he was going: that was the NKVD's secret. Many people we believed had been taken back to the camp had in fact been shot; others whom we had presumed long dead turned out to be still among the living. Some people disappeared without a trace, and it was impossible to learn anything about their fate.

I often talked with General Brödis about the international situation. We learned very little about what was going on outside. During the war, the Russian people had access only to the official news, ninety-nine percent of which consisted of lies. Nowhere in the world were people lied to as much as in the Soviet Union under Stalin. Any Russian who gave serious thought to political events understood that the truth was usually the diametrical opposite of the official proclamations. Since no one was allowed to own a radio during the war, it was impossible to listen to foreign radio reports. People tried to arrive at some reliable conclusion from the scanty and distorted information they were given. Many believed that the pact between Russia, America, and England would lead to a democratization of the Soviet Union after the war. Postwar history shows how badly mistaken they were.

THE EXECUTION OF GENERAL BRÖDIS

Early in the morning of September 20, 1942, as we were coming back from the toilet, we noticed an unusual number of soldiers in the hall. We recognized most of them: they were regulars around the prison. Like every event, this change was the subject of lively discussion in the cell, and as usual the most fantastic suppositions were voiced. There was only one thing no one assumed: that this would be a "meat day." When someone suggested the possibility, others pointed out that none of the guards were drunk.

Breakfast and lunch went by in a normal fashion. While the food was being distributed, some people tried to involve the guards in casual conversation to see if they were drunk. They didn't seem to be. After lunch, eight prisoners were called into the prison office, among them General Brödis and Captain Rüberg. We waited for their return in great tension. They came back after just fifteen minutes and said they had been photographed in groups of twos and threes. That reassured us; it was something that had happened before—not often, but occasionally.

Most of the inmates of cell 14 had already been through their pretrial investigation. We decided that the photographed men would probably be tried soon, since the dossiers presented in court were usually accompanied by a photograph of the accused. The only one who didn't concur with this optimistic interpretation was General Brödis. He had withdrawn to his corner, as he usually did when he wanted to think, and emerged after one or two hours to ask me a question. "Mr. Steiner, do you believe that we were photographed in preparation for an imminent trial?"

"I'm almost certain of it. There is a second possibility: that you're going to be transferred to another prison. But it seems very unlikely that they would do that while the war's going on."

"No, you're mistaken. It means something else."

"Surely not something bad," I said.

"Something very bad. That was probably the last picture that will ever be taken of me."

I continued trying to reassure the general, but inwardly I was convinced that he was right. I remembered that on the day before that Sunday when so many criminals were shot, several of the condemned men in our cell had been photographed. They hadn't suspected anything.

Two hours after this conversation, the chief guard came and called the names of two of the men who had been photographed. They answered, and the guard said: "*S veshchami*—Get your stuff!"

I heard several people mutter: "They're going back to the camp."

After the two had left, we heard other cell doors being opened, and then the steps of people being led away. Most of the men in our cell were convinced that a large group was being taken back to the camp. Some gave the other photographed men messages to deliver and errands to run if they got back to the camp. Nothing special seemed to be happening. It was a common occurrence in prison: people went and people came.

But there was a flaw in the NKVD's performance: our door was opened, and in came several soldiers, one of them with a pear in his hand. The soldiers looked around, and then one of them said: "Hell, this isn't number 15." They cursed the guard who had opened the wrong door and walked on.

We sat in a dead silence. Then one of the criminals said: "This is a rest stop on the way to eternity."

Of the six prisoners who had been photographed and were still with us, only two remained calm: General Brödis and Captain Rüberg. One of the Latvian officers started to lament so loudly that some people called him a coward; the other three weren't exactly heroic, either.

At midnight, more people were taken from the cells. The usual heartrending sounds echoed through the prison: screams, sobs, the jangling of bunches of keys that were being used to strike those who resisted. That night, no one in our cell got any sleep, and we could sense the great agitation in the other cells. We could hear the victims bidding their comrades farewell: "*Proshchaite*," and the many voices answering: "*Proshchaite!*" After midnight, we heard the noise of trucks driving into the prison and leaving it again after a short time. By about 5 a.m., there was complete silence.

I was glad the terrible night was over. When we were led to the toilet, I didn't notice anything unusual. The guards were walking back and forth in the prison corridor as usual. One of them stood in front of the toilet door watching the prisoners relieve themselves. From time to time, you would hear the usual cries of "*Skorei, skorei*—Faster, faster!*"

We ate our four hundred grams of bread and drank our *kipyatok*. After breakfast, I saw General Brödis putting his possessions into a bundle. He took off his slippers (which I had always envied, since it was hard to walk around the cell wearing shoes all the time), placed them on top of the bundle, and then handed me everything, saying: "You have been a friend to me. Please keep this as a souvenir; I won't need it anymore."

I didn't want to accept the gift and tried to convince the general that he would live a long time.

"Dear friend," he said, "you can see what is happening here. I know that my time is up. You can make good use of these trifles; if you don't take them, the butchers will get them. I have one request: if you should be fortunate enough to survive all this and return to Europe, try to find my father and tell him everything. If my father is dead, tell my people how dearly we paid for our credulity. And warn Europe."

I promised. My heart was heavy, but I tried not to show it.

Unfortunately, I have not been able to carry out my promise yet, as Estonia is still under Soviet rule and the old man, if he is still alive, might get into trouble for receiving a letter from abroad. As for the world at large, I hope that this book will redeem my pledge to General Brödis and the other victims.

I didn't accept the general's bundle; I wanted to leave that brave man a shimmer of hope, even though I myself did not believe that either of us would leave the prison alive. All morning I sat with Brödis, trying to distract him, but he kept turning the conversation back to the subject of his imminent death. He spoke about it in such a calm and relaxed way that it sounded as if he were talking about some trivial, everyday matter.

There was a violent incident at lunchtime. Brödis, Rüberg, and I were the last in line. Brödis got his soup, but when Rüberg stretched out his hand, the guard said, "That's it!" and slammed the door. Rüberg and I were left without food. After we did a lot of knocking, the guard came back. We explained that we hadn't been given our meal; he shut the door without a word and left. Again we knocked; after a very long time, the guard came back. Rüberg, who was standing in front of me, asked him to please give us our soup. Several men shouted from the bunks: "Give them their food; they didn't get anything!"

Then the guard kicked Rüberg in the shin and roared: "You fascists, just wait, we'll feed you all right!"

Bleeding and limping, Rüberg retreated from the door, and I, too, sat down. My cellmates urged me to fight for my rights and demand my food: "Today it's two who don't get fed; tomorrow it'll be ten of us—just because those bastards don't know how to count!"

Under this pressure, I went back to the door and knocked for a long time. Finally, the guard opened the door, grabbed me, and dragged me out into the hallway, pummeling my head with his fists and shouting: "There's your soup, there's your gruel!"

I began to scream. Then the chief guard rushed up to us and had me locked in the punishment cell. The punishment cell was a long, dark room on the other end of the corridor, where the death cells were. The iron gate was opened, and the guard shoved me in. There was a small red lamp above the door, but it shed so little light that I couldn't see the other side of the cell. When my eyes had become accustomed to the dark, I noticed someone lying on the concrete floor in the corner. I moved closer. A weak voice addressed me; it sounded familiar, but I didn't recognize it. The man held out his hand and said: "Help me get up."

Now I saw who it was, and he, too, recognized me. It was Pechatnikov, a worker from Leningrad who had gotten to know Trotsky during the Civil War. When Trotsky left Russia, Pechatnikov was deported. In 1935, he was arrested and sentenced to ten years in camp. He was sent to Norilsk. When the war broke out, he was jailed and tried again, this time for "spreading false rumors" (he was supposed to have told some prisoners that Hitler's army had occupied Kharkov), and was sentenced to death.

Pechatnikov's first words to me were: "You, too?" He meant, was I also sentenced to death.

I told him why I had been put in the punishment cell.

"Strange," he said.

When I asked him why he was here, he said: "Probably to be shot." "Didn't you appeal?" I asked.

"It's pointless," he said.

He told me that he had been brought here with four others the day before. The others had been shot; he had no idea why his turn hadn't come yet.

We had been talking only a few minutes when the door opened and the NKVD officer Sakulin came in, accompanied by two soldiers. When Sakulin saw me, he yelled: "What's your name?"

"Steiner."

"How the hell did he get in here?" Sakulin shouted at the guard. Then he turned to me: "Up! Out!"

Walking behind me along the corridor, with two soldiers holding him by the arms, was Pechatnikov. I was glad to get back to my cell. I didn't tell my cellmates about my encounter with Pechatnikov. It wouldn't have served any purpose.

As soon as I was back in my cell, I began knocking on the door again. It took the guard a long time to come—a different guard this time. I told him that I hadn't had any lunch and asked him to bring me some food. To my amazement, he said: "I'll see if there's any left."

After a few minutes, he brought an aluminum bowl with fish soup. I devoured the soup without even tasting it. I only noticed that it was cold.

Suddenly the door opened and the deputy prison warden stepped in and read off the name of a prisoner. No one replied. Then he asked loudly whether there was anyone by that name in the cell, and received a barely audible response from a man on the lower bunk.

"Take your things and follow me."

The man did not move.

"Hurry up, move, I don't have all day," the official shouted.

"I don't have any things," the victim said.

Crying and quivering from head to toe, he walked out, saying over and over: "*Za chto? Za chto?*"—What for?"

Ten minutes later, the official came back and called Rüberg's name. Rüberg stood up without a word, and walking unsteadily, his long, gaunt figure slightly bent, he left the cell. General Brödis was called next. As we heard the keys jangling near our door, he embraced me tightly. "Farewell, farewell . . ." he repeated several times.

"Brödis!"

Calmly, as if taking a walk, Brödis strode out of the cell. This brave man was murdered in the casemates of Norilsk on September 21, 1942, around four o'clock in the afternoon.

That day, no one else was removed from our cell, but all afternoon we heard prisoners being led out of the other cells, especially the death cells. Around midnight, we heard the trucks driving into the prison yard to take the corpses to the cemetery. The next day, the news was relayed from one cell to another by the usual prison telegraph. More than four hundred people were shot on those two days. Most of them had been sentenced by the Special Tribunal, the OSO; the rest by the camp court.

I was now prepared for the worst. The only question remaining was whether the OSO had already sentenced me, as they had most of the others, or whether I had yet to be tried by the camp court. I pictured myself walking out of the cell and told myself that I would carry my head high like General Brödis and many others before him. If I was put on trial, I would spit the truth in the hangman's face. I would ask the judges whether this program of extermination was compatible with the ideas of Marx, Engels, and Lenin. I would ask them whether the Revolution had driven out the Romanovs to put an even worse tyrant on the throne. But I knew all this was useless; the trials weren't public. For whose ears was this speech intended?

My thoughts turned back to my youth. In 1919, when I was a poor printer's apprentice in Vienna, I attended a meeting of the Communist Youth. The speaker's words went straight to my heart. Everything he said was true; I had experienced it. I was a fatherless boy when I was apprenticed in a trade school. I was fed twice a day and earned five kronen a week, which I shared with my sister, who was still going to school.

I joined the Communist Youth to fight against this misery. I received my baptism of fire two months later. On June 15, 1919, I was marching at the head of a procession of young people in the Hörlgasse. The police blocked our way, and we marched toward them. Shots were fired, and I was left lying on the pavement with a serious injury. As soon as I was out of the hospital, I resumed my political activity.

In 1921, when Willi Münzberg, the secretary of the Communist Youth International, suggested I go to Yugoslavia to work in the illegal Communist Party there, I enthusiastically accepted. I was looking for danger and was prepared to take any risk. For almost ten years, I worked in Yugoslavia under the most difficult conditions, until in 1931 the police discovered the illegal print shop I ran. I went to Paris to work with the Yugoslavian immigrants. I wandered from one suburb to another, making contact with Yugoslavian workers and organizing them. Saint-Denis, Villejuif, Ivry, Vitry were soon as familiar to me as Favoriten, Ottakring, Floridsdorf, and Hernals in Vienna.

I couldn't stay in Paris, either. On the instigation of the Yugoslavian ambassador in Paris, Spalajkovic, I was expelled from France. So I returned to Vienna, where I established a print shop which supplied the Communist Parties of the Balkan countries with literature. Eventually, I was jailed.

Nothing was more precious to me than the Communist Party. In 1932, when I came to the Soviet Union, I was the happiest man on earth. At long last, I was in the land of my dreams. But how great was my disillusionment! Instead of the affluence I had expected, I found deprivation and misery. As I stepped off the train at the Belorussky Station, ragged, destitute children besieged me with cries of *"Dai, dai—*Give, give!" How was this possible—children begging in Moscow, the capital of the world revolution? I was ashamed—ashamed of myself. I was glad when the car took off and brought me to the Lux Hotel, where the Comintern bureaucracy lived.

I left my bags in the hotel and took a walk in the city. Many stores were half empty; the shelves displayed shabby packs of ersatz coffee; people were standing on line to buy a few hundred grams of black bread, and old women stood begging outside the stores, thanking the occasional giver with a "God bless you!" as they dropped the piece of bread into their pouch.

When I went into the dining room of the Lux that evening, things looked a little different. For these people, communism was becoming a reality. The menu was comparable to that of any international hotel in Vienna, Berlin, or Paris. Caviar, lox, fowl, every sort of dessert—this was the menu of the communist functionaries.

Hitler wasn't in power in Germany yet, but already you could see Comrades Pieck, Hörnle, and others having a much better time in the Lux than Thälmann was having in Berlin. There were other German communists in Moscow, but they lived in the rear of the Lux, behind the back yard. Those were the people who took the fight against Hitler seriously and were summoned to Moscow for that very reason: Heinz Neumann, Hermann Remele, Werner Hirsch, Max Hölz. They were all eventually murdered by the NKVD.

I was even more amazed when I continued my excursion through Moscow the next morning. Suddenly I was standing in front of a store filled with food and clothes, and here the people weren't standing on line as they did in the bread shops, where all you could buy was a fixed ration of black bread. What sort of miracle was this? I found out that this was one of the so-called Torgsin shops, where you could buy all sorts of things for foreign currency or gold. This was where diplomats and foreign businessmen went shopping. You could see poorly dressed Russians there too, selling their wedding rings or other jewelry to buy a little bread for themselves and milk for their children.

In the Metropol, Savoy, and National hotels, foreigners could buy anything they wanted for foreign currency, from caviar and authentic champagne to pretty Russian girls (who supplied the NKVD with information about their unsuspecting clients). That was the face of "communist" Moscow. There were large banners suspended over the streets at that time with the slogan: "The foreign proletariat regards us with envy!"

When I was eventually appointed director of the MAI publishing house, I discovered that in Moscow, too, there were people working illegally to help communists in the capitalist countries. The publishing house produced not only propaganda material but false foreign passports and financial papers.

It was with these thoughts and memories that I lay awake on my hard bunk all night. I also thought of my old mother, of my wife, of my brothers and sisters; what would they say if they knew where I was? Fortunately, they had no idea.

When day broke, we had another surprise—soup for breakfast instead of bread and *kipyatok*. What was going on? Later we realized it was left over from the day before. It had originally been cooked to feed the men who had been shot. That was why the soup was cold. After having the soup, I began to feel sharp abdominal pains which became so intense that I had to knock on the door and ask for a doctor. The guard promised to get the doctor, but he never came. I couldn't get the guard to take me to the toilet either; I had to use the *parasha*. I excreted a stream of blood. The pain decreased, but I suddenly felt so weak that I was almost unable to get back to my spot on the bunk.

Lunch was served. I was unable to stand up. My cellmates brought me my meal, and I gave it to them. They felt sorry for me, but they were also glad to have a little more to eat.

CAMP WITH SEVERE REGIME

That afternoon, we heard more commotion in the corridor. I lay motionless on my bunk and was glad I was no longer feeling any pain. Nothing else mattered. For the first time, I hoped the end would come soon. But something completely unexpected happened. Twenty-five men from our cell—I was one of them—were taken to the prison yard. A large number of prisoners were already there. To my surprise, there were no guards other than the ones in the watchtowers. The prisoners stood about in groups, trying to guess what would be done with us. I saw my friend

Georg and walked up to him. Georg threw his arms around me. He was appalled by my appearance. I told him I was sick and could hardly stand up. Georg solicitously spread his padded coat on the ground, and I sat down on it.

More and more groups of prisoners were being led out into the yard. One of the men in the last group was Josef Berger; he hurried up to me to ask what had happened to me. Everyone was saying I looked very bad, but I found that the others, too, looked colorless and emaciated, especially Josef, who looked like a living corpse. The general opinion among the prisoners was that we were being transferred to another prison, since none of us had been tried yet. Several people expressed the suspicion that we were about to be driven to the cemetery to be "liquidated."

Finally, the large prison gate opened. We could see a detachment of heavily armed NKVD soldiers outside. Some of them had dogs on leashes. The moment the dogs saw us, they started to bark and gnash their teeth; some of them were straining so hard in our direction that the soldiers had trouble holding them back. The prison director handed an officer a stack of documents.

We marched out of the gate in rows of five. When the officer noticed that I was being supported by two comrades, he asked what was wrong with me. Georg explained that I was very sick. The officer told me to step out of line. One of the watchdogs jumped at me, but the soldier pulled him back before it was able to bite. I heard the officer telling the prison warden that he couldn't take me, I wouldn't be able to walk that far. I asked the officer to please take me along anyway. "It's a long walk. I don't want to hold everyone up for three hours just because of you," he replied.

My friends, who were supporting me again, promised to get me to our destination without delay, and the officer agreed to take me. Then he made the usual proclamation: "Attention, prisoners! It is forbidden to speak or to switch rows during the march. A single step to the right or left will be taken as an attempt to escape. The guards are instructed to shoot without warning."

Then he gave a command to the soldiers: "Guard, ready for action!" The soldiers released the safety on their submachine guns and rifles. "Forward, march!"

There were sighs of relief as we set off in the opposite direction to the cemetery. Despite my sickness, I, too, felt relieved, but not for long. Soon I was again in the throes of sharp abdominal pain; I couldn't go on; I collapsed. My helpers had trouble holding me up. The officer saw this, ordered a halt, and came up to us. My companions told him I had gotten sick again. The officer allowed me to sit down and rest a little.

After fifteen minutes, he came back to me and said: "How are you feeling?"

"Better."

"You can rest a while longer."

He actually waited until I told him I was ready to go on. But just a hundred meters later I felt very sick again, and my knees buckled. When the officer came up to me again, I asked for permission to relieve myself. My friends helped me walk a few steps away. Again, I excreted a jet of blood. I heard murmurs among the prisoners: "He's done for."

It was all the same to me. I would have been glad to be left behind to die. But I had to go on. The column was moving very slowly. The officer came up to me several times to ask whether I could still walk. It was getting dark when we reached some barracks—these were the camp guards' quarters. Another eternity passed before we finally reached a large area surrounded by watchtowers with searchlights that cast their beams on a fence consisting of several rows of barbed wire.

At last, we reached a large wooden gate with a sign: "*Norillag NKVD USSR, VII. Camp Section.*" We stopped in front of the gate. The officer went to the guard post by the gate and returned after a short time to tell me to step out of the row. Supported by two comrades, I went into the house, where a doctor was waiting. He asked what was wrong with me. I told him I had abdominal pains and diarrhea. He felt my pulse and said to the officer: "He has to go to the hospital immediately."

The officer replied that that wasn't his responsibility. He would report my presence to the camp authorities, and whatever happened to me after that was up to them. When the doctor asked if he couldn't just take me with him and leave me at the infirmary, the officer replied that that was impossible. I had to leave the room. I curled up in the hall. I don't know how long I lay there. I was only half conscious when I was finally put on a stretcher and taken to the infirmary, where a doctor gave me some powder.

I stayed in the infirmary until the middle of the night, when a camp official came and informed the doctor that I was not to be taken to the hospital but was immediately to be put in the prison barracks. The doctor was in no hurry to carry out the order, however, but kept me in the infirmary until morning. He came several times to ask how I was feeling. A nurse brought me some hot tea.

When the director of medical services came in the morning, the doctor reported my condition, using Latin terms which I didn't understand. The director said I had to be taken to the hospital immediately. The doctor replied that he had intended to do that the night before, but the camp administration hadn't allowed it. Whereupon the director left; he returned after a short while and said to me: "You must have done something terrible. I wasn't able to convince the commander to let you go to the hospital."

Then a camp policeman came to pick me up; the doctor came along. On the way, I saw rows of whitewashed wooden barracks. The whole camp gave a ghostly impression. The first sign of human life was smoke rising from the chimneys of a large wooden building. That, I learned later, was the kitchen. Opposite the kitchen, surrounded by a double row of barbed wire, was a low building with low, barred windows—the punishment cells.

We reached our destination: a large wooden barracks in the middle of a narrow, very long courtyard, its windows boarded up and equipped with iron bars. A barbed-wire fence enclosed the yard. There was a watchtower at each corner. The camp policeman rang a bell at the door of the tiny watchman's hut. A man came out, examined a piece of paper the camp policeman handed him, and let us in. The doctor explained to the watchman that I had an infectious disease and had to be isolated from the other prisoners.

"Isolation?" The watchman laughed aloud and said there were only two large rooms, each built to hold fifty men, and there were a hundred and fifty in each right now. "He'll be lucky if I find him some space," he said.

The doctor left after promising to make another effort to get me into the hospital. The watchman led me to the prison barracks. He unlocked two huge padlocks and led me into a kind of anteroom with two doors; apparently, the barracks was divided in half. He opened the left door and told me to go in. Standing in the door, he called out: "Brothers, make room for a sick man, but don't get too close to him, he's got an infectious disease!"

Several of my friends—one of them was Georg—came up and led me to the opposite end of the room. People were lying very close together; it took some doing to make room for me. I was so glad to be with my friends that I felt better for a moment. But as the hours passed, I got sicker and sicker, and when lunch was brought in, my friends asked the guard to tell the doctor the condition I was in.

BACK IN THE CENTRAL HOSPITAL

In the afternoon, an ambulance stopped in front of the barracks. My comrades, who could see the car through a crack in the boards covering the window, came to me with expressions of joy and told me I was being taken to the hospital. Sure enough, two hospital orderlies entered the room, accompanied by the doctor, who was visibly pleased that he had been able to get me into the hospital. After a speedy ride, the ambulance stopped in front of the central hospital's infectious diseases ward. I already knew the place somewhat, having spent two months of the previous year in the surgical ward.

A doctor examined me thoroughly and had me taken to room 2. The infectious diseases ward was a large barracks divided into four sections. Three of these were equipped with ordinary bunks in two tiers, just like all the barracks in the camp. On each bunk was a large and a small straw sack that served as pillow and mattress. Each prisoner had a blanket. Everything in the room was meticulously clean.

I was given a new set of clothes—a clean pair of blue pants and a light coat of the same color. Since there was no space on any of the bottom bunks, the head nurse told one of the less seriously ill patients to climb to the top tier and leave his bunk to me. I was overjoyed to be able to lie on a sack and cover myself with a blanket. The nurse brought me some powder to swallow, and soon after that, I fell asleep.

That evening, when the night shift arrived, I had an amazing encounter with an old acquaintance: one of the nurses was a Viennese woman named Else Kämp whom I had known when we were both members of the Communist Youth in Vienna. Else had gone to Moscow with her sister in 1920. At first, we had received letters from them describing their life in Russia; then the correspondence broke off. In 1932, when I returned to Vienna from Paris, I inquired after the Kämp sisters. My friends told me they had died in an accident while mountain climbing in the Caucasus.

I had heard from several people that there was a Viennese woman in Norilsk; I had even been told her name, but I had assumed she had to be someone other than the Else Kämp I had known so long ago.

As soon as she had a free moment, she came to my bedside.

"Else, what are you doing here?"

She asked me the same question.

"People in Vienna said you died in an accident in the Caucasus."

"Me, in the Caucasus? I've never been there in my life."

She listened to my account with great interest. Then she told me her story. She had married a Russian named Olenikov, who had been one of Trotsky's secretaries. When Trotsky was sent off to Turkey, Olenikov stayed in Moscow to pack Trotsky's archive; he intended to follow Trotsky into exile. Just as Olenikov and his wife were about to depart, officials of the NKVD arrived and ordered Olenikov to open the crates containing the archive. Olenikov protested that Stalin had promised to allow Trotsky to take his archive out of the country without having to submit it to police investigation. The officials left and returned after a few hours. Olenikov was arrested, and Else never heard from him again. She herself was deported to central Asia, where one of her children died very painfully of malaria. In 1937, Else was arrested as a "Trotskyite" and was sentenced to ten years in a camp. Her sister suffered the same fate. Else's youngest daughter, who was studying medicine, had to interrupt her studies after her mother's arrest and was now working in a cotton factory near Leninakan.

Else was particularly eager to hear anything I had to say about Vienna; she had been out of touch with her city since 1930. The next day, Else came to work early; she was burning with curiosity, as she put it, to hear more news from me. That day, I learned from her that my friend Kerosi, about whom I have written earlier, was dying in the next room. I went with Else to see Kerosi. The head nurse said it was strictly forbidden to enter that room, but after a good deal of pleading and arguing, Else succeeded in obtaining permission.

The prisoners lay in beds that were stacked side by side without any space in between. I walked around the room twice, scrutinizing each face, and was unable to find Kerosi. I asked the nurse to point him out to me, and she led me to his bed. I thought at first that she was mistaken, but when I looked closer, I thought I recognized him. Could this be the athletic Kerosi? His head looked as small as that of a child.

I stood looking at him for a long time. Finally, he opened his eyes and returned my gaze. He tried to smile. He had recognized me and moved his lips as if to speak; and then, almost inaudibly, I heard him say my name. I bent over, trying to make out his whispers, but he was emitting no sound, only moving his lips. I was glad when the nurse told me it was time to leave. I wanted to give Kerosi my hand, but his hands under the blanket were immobile. He nodded almost imperceptibly.

I asked Else what was wrong with Kerosi. She said he had been brought in with dysentery. At first, he had lain in the bunk I was lying in. He spoke good German, and Else had enjoyed talking with him. He recovered quickly. Then something happened that was fairly common: shortly after the doctor told him that he would soon be released from the hospital, he had a relapse, and his condition deteriorated daily. The doctors tried in vain to help him. Now he was in the room for the dying.

I asked Else whether there was any hope at all. She said only a miracle could save Kerosi. Anyone who ended up in that room had been given up for lost. Kerosi's sad condition made me resolve to cooperate with the doctors in every way I could.

On the third day, an official of the hospital administration came with an order to have me transferred immediately to the main building. The doctors had no explanation for this decision.

In the main building, I was locked in a room with bars on the windows. If I needed something, I had to knock and wait for the head nurse to arrive. She was the only person who had a key to my door and the only one authorized to open it. The other nurses and even the doctors could come in only if accompanied by this woman. Occasionally, an NKVD officer would come to check whether this rule was being observed.

There were four beds in the room. One of them was empty. My two roommates had also been brought in from the prison. One of them was Gustav Schöller, who had repeatedly fallen ill in prison; this was his second stay in the hospital. He had signed his "confession." The camp court had sentenced him to death, and while awaiting the decision on his appeal, he had fallen ill again. Gustav realized that he had made a grave mistake. Now that his days were numbered, he clung to life. He was not a little surprised to learn that my case was not yet closed and that I had been transferred to the seventh camp section.

"Karl," he said, "you are a hero."

The other patient was a criminal who had gone on a hunger strike in jail; he was being fed intravenously. He had begun his fast two months before; at night, you could hear him secretly chewing on the pieces of sugar and bread we gave him. He was sure that we politicals wouldn't betray him.

The doctor treating me was the head of the department of internal medicine, Dr. Mardna. He was Estonian and was serving a ten-year sentence. Mardna took great care in his treatment of the sick prisoners; he was a worthy assistant to the chief doctor, Alexandra Ivanovna Sleptsova. The patients were always glad when Dr. Mardna appeared by their bedside with his long gray beard and smiling eyes. When he learned of my experiences in prison, he was full of pity for me. As long as I was still seriously ill, Dr. Mardna came to visit me two or three times a day.

One day, Sleptsova came into the room. She was very surprised to see me. She consoled me, as she had always done, and wished me a rapid convalescence. I was genuinely glad to meet this noble woman again.

On September 30, 1942, at three in the afternoon, the prison warden came into our room, accompanied by two soldiers. They went directly to Gustav Schöller's bed. "What is your name?" asked the warden.

Schöller stared at him without answering.

Instead of repeating his first question, the warden asked a second one: "Do you have any possessions with you?"

"My clothes are here. The rest is in the prison," Gustav replied.

After a while, a hospital attendant brought his clothes. Gustav was so disturbed that he put on his pants without putting on his underwear first. He wanted to take his pants off again, but the warden said: "Don't bother with that, we're not going far. You can change your clothes in the prison."

I noted with gratitude the absence of cynicism in the warden's behavior; he was allowing Schöller a glimmer of hope.

Schöller didn't dare come to my bed. He nodded in my direction as he left. As Gustav was being led away, Dr. Mardna came to my bed and remained standing there for a few minutes without saying a word. Then he left.

Now I was alone with the criminal. He said to me: "They were taking him off to be shot, weren't they?"

"I don't think so. Probably he got a reprieve."

"What are you talking about! Did you ever see soldiers coming directly into the hospital? They do that only when somebody's going to be shot."

I didn't answer.

Two days later, Dr. Mardna fell ill. He was replaced by Dr. Müller, a German from Leningrad. He had visited me often during my first stay in the hospital and had talked to me in German. Now he pretended not to know me and spoke to me in Russian; when I addressed him in German, he would still answer in Russian. I once told Dr. Sukhorukov about Müller's behavior, and Sukhorukov said: "As long as the Germans were advancing, Müller took every opportunity to stress his German origins, especially when he was talking to Jewish doctors. Now that the Germans are retreating, he's rediscovered his Russian heart. He's getting friendly with his Jewish colleagues and expresses outrage at the Nazi atrocities." Müller called the criminal an "enemy of the people" for going on a hunger strike.

One day, Sukhorukov brought me a small linen pouch filled with sugar: "It's from Olga." Olga did not dare visit me. The NKVD had ordered a hospital attendant named Morozov to keep an eye on her and report any attempts at reestablishing contact with me. He himself had told her, in spite of having promised to tell no one.

The central hospital was part of the fifth camp section. Looking out through the bars on the window, I often saw friends and acquaintances walk past. Many of them came to visit me at that window: the doctors had given out the word that I was in the hospital. I obtained a string from one of the orderlies; I attached a little bag to the string and let it out the window, and my friends would put notes and little presents into it— sometimes a piece of bread or a little sugar. Everyone wanted to know how I was doing.

One day, Dr. Müller came into the room just as I was pulling the bag into the room. "What are you doing? You are under pre-trial investigation. Don't you know that you're not allowed to have any contact with the outside world?"

"I thought you were a doctor, not an NKVD man," I said calmly.

"I am a Soviet patriot and I will not tolerate any counterrevolutionary activities in this hospital!"

I put my hand in the bag, took out the lump of sugar I had just been given, and handed it to Dr. Müller. "Here is the evidence of my counterrevolutionary activity."

Müller yanked the bag from my hand and threw it out the window. The next day, I was declared "healthy" and released from the hospital. I weighed forty-seven kilos; my normal weight was seventy kilos.

Two noncommissioned NKVD officers armed with submachine guns accompanied me from the central hospital to the seventh camp section, which was about three kilometers away, just outside Norilsk. It took us five hours to get there. One of the NKVD men was a sensitive young man; he didn't say a word, but I could tell he felt sorry for me. The other man was a trained NKVD dog in human guise. When I asked him to let me rest a little, he showered me with obscene abuse. I asked him why he was being so rough. His answer: "Why didn't you just crap out?"

"People are brought to the hospital to get well, not to die," I said.

"The lot of you should be exterminated with rat poison."

I said no more.

PANOV

The watchman of the prisoners' barracks was surprised to see me. "You're back? I thought you were dead." He said the people in the infirmary had told him I had died. I later learned that an inquiry to the central hospital had been answered to this effect.

I was joyfully welcomed in the barracks. My friends told me I looked much better. After briefly recounting my experiences in the central hospital, I learned some terrible things about the prisoners' life in this section of the camp. At 5 a.m., everyone, even the sick, had to line up outside. Laggards were driven out of the barracks with sticks. Then the commander would read off the names of those who had been given sick leave by the doctor. They went back inside; everyone else went to work. I couldn't imagine working in my condition, but I was told I would have to be prepared to do so. Breakfast consisted of soup made of herring heads, and a hundred grams of oatmeal. At first, I was unable to eat this food; I was spoiled by the hospital fare. I ate zwieback which I had saved up and drank *kipyatok*.

When the doctor, a young Lithuanian, came to see whether anyone was sick, I raised my hand. He took one look at me and told the commander of the camp police to relieve me from work and send me to the infirmary later. Three other sick men stayed behind in the barracks with me. After the others left, two of the sick men carried the *parasha* out to the yard and emptied it. After that, we were locked in. Our job was to clean up the barracks and heat up the stove.

Later in the morning, I was taken to the infirmary, where I was examined by a medical commission. After tapping and listening to my body for a while, they asked me some questions. They were very surprised that I had been released from the hospital so soon. The Lithuanian led me back to the barracks and told the guard that the medical commission had determined that I should have sick leave for the time being and that he would inform the camp commander. He promised that I would have a special diet to help me recuperate.

I lay down on my bunk and examined my surroundings. The barracks looked uninhabited, for the prisoners had taken all their "bedding" to work: their trousers, which they used as a mattress, and the padded jacket and coat that served as pillow and blanket. If somebody owned a towel, he would usually wrap it around his neck as a scarf.

Darkness had long fallen when my friends returned from work. They stampeded into the barracks like a horde of wild animals, each man rushing to his bunk, eager for a little warmth. They were all wrapped in padded clothes from head to toe; ice had formed on their mouths, noses, and eyes—it was hard to recognize them. Their hands were frozen stiff, so that it was a while before they were able to unbutton their coats and untie the strings they had used to tighten some of their protective wrappings.

I helped my comrades take off their clothes. Only after the prisoners had thawed out a little would you dare ask a question; if you didn't wait, you could be sure of receiving a rude answer.

Dinner was brought into the barracks and distributed by the brigadier and his assistants. Supper usually consisted of half a liter of herb soup and a piece of salt fish; sometimes some cereal was added. The bread ration varied between three hundred and eight hundred grams. I was given the same food as the others on that day; I wasn't put on my special diet until the third day. After the meal, the prisoners would liven up a little; you could even hear someone laugh here and there. My friends would tell me about their workday. There was always some story to tell. Sometimes the guards had beaten one or several prisoners nearly to death, or else someone had been severely injured or shot in an "attempted escape."

I spent two weeks in the barracks without being sent to work; all I had to do was heat up the stove, together with another sick prisoner. My friends gave me some of their clothes to mend, and I lent them my own. As a result, my clothes were torn in those two weeks.

The good food I was getting and the rest were effective: I got better. One day, the doctor told me I was ready for work now. So I prepared myself. I mended my padded trousers; there was only one button left on my padded jacket; the only whole garment I had was my coat. Many envied me for owning this long and well-padded coat. My felt boots were very large, too, so I could wrap innumerable rags around my feet (oversized boots were highly prized possessions). My fur hat was in good shape, too. My gloves presented a problem, though; there were many holes in them and they needed quite a lot of mending.

The next morning, I stood with my comrades in line. Camp policemen escorted us as we marched from the barracks to the main gate; there the guards took charge. My comrades had already told me that we would have to walk more than two kilometers to work. We marched up a steep incline, through a mining region where other prisoners interrupted their work as we passed, watching us with great interest. Though we were almost unrecognizably masked with hats, upturned collars, and makeshift scarves, one of the miners would occasionally manage to make out a familiar face and raise a hand in greeting, whereupon our guards would point their guns at the miners and drive them away.

We had to stay in strict formation during the march. There were many times when we had to stop and listen to the guard commander's tirades. Often he would threaten to make use of the weapons. If someone slipped and fell on the ice, we were all made to kneel in the snow for fifteen minutes and submit to the usual barrage of coarse insults. I was glad when we finally arrived at our place of work, a large gravel pit. We stopped in front of a wooden shack. The guard commander went in and returned after a while with the manager of the gravel pit. The two of them went off with the brigadier to show him what had to be done that day. Our workplace was circled with signs with a death's-head and the inscription: *Zapretnaya zona*—Forbidden area. The soldiers took up positions behind them. Our job consisted of removing the snow and digging up the frozen gravel with pickaxes and crowbars, loading it on lorries, and pushing the lorries to a bunker. Work parties of six men were formed. Four had to dig up the gravel and load it; the other two had to push the lorry to the bunker and unload the gravel. Despite the extreme cold, our bodies warmed up quickly. The quotas were high, and the guards watched closely to make sure everyone was working hard. If in the opinion of the guards someone was shirking, he had to take off his coat; that would force him to exert himself more, so as not to freeze. If the soldiers still weren't satisfied, the victim would have to take off his padded jacket as well. Prisoners were frequently made to work in their shirtsleeves, with the result that many developed pneumonia and died.

We worked from eight in the morning until eight in the evening without a stop, without a moment to warm up by a fire. The guards and their dogs were relieved every two hours. After the day's work, the manager would give the guard commander a form indicating how well the quota was met. If we exceeded it, the guards would receive a bonus for each percentage point above a hundred. If we failed to meet the quota, the soldiers would vent their rage at us on the way home. A favorite technique was to drive us into the deep snow, requiring us to stay in strict formation. This would be repeated every five minutes, and the commander would shout: "Well, how do you like that? I'll teach you to work!" Only rarely did we succeed in meeting the quota; but the manager of the gravel pit was a compassionate man—he would usually state that we had met or exceeded the norm.

It was pleasant to come back to the barracks in the evening and take off one's heavy, ice-caked clothes. After the hard work and the great cold, the herb soup tasted better than caviar or roast calf. Nothing was left in the pot; we wiped it clean with fingers and tongues until it looked freshly washed.

Bloody brawls broke out when the bread was distributed. The brigadier, a political prisoner, tried to be fair: he gave those who had worked harder the larger portions. This did not please the criminals, who generally worked less than the politicals. They constantly threatened the brigadier and occasionally beat him. One day, the brigadier tried to prevent a criminal from taking a large piece of bread from the bread box. The criminal pulled a knife and stabbed the brigadier about fifteen times. We yelled for help, but no one came. I picked up a piece of wood and smashed a window; and one of the guards in the watchtowers fired a shot in the air. A few moments later, camp policemen came rushing into the barracks. The brigadier died on the way to the hospital.

After this murder, a *pakhan* (boss) of the criminals was made brigadier. He saw to it that the politicals got the watery portion of the soup and the criminals the more substantial portion, and that criminals always received more bread than the politicals. As a result, those who worked hardest were given the least to eat and soon were incapable of prolonged exertion. Meanwhile, the criminals continued to slow down the work as much as possible. We were no longer able to meet the quotas. The manager of the gravel pit said productivity had fallen so low that he couldn't afford to give our day's work a satisfactory mark. The guard commander had been reprimanded by his superior.

One night, we were awakened by a terrifying noise. Several soldiers were standing in the middle of the barracks, shouting and threatening us with their fists: "Fascists, counterrevolutionaries, Trotskyites!" and the usual Russian invectives against our mothers.

They started dragging prisoners off their bunks, throwing them to the ground, and trampling them with their heavy boots. "We'll teach you to work!"

One took a prisoner by the throat. "Are you going to work? Are you going to meet the quota?" The poor fellow was unable to answer, and that enraged the drunken soldiers even more; they started to beat the prisoner over the head while the guard went on choking him. It was at least a half hour before a sober soldier came in and persuaded the drunken guards to leave the barracks.

The next day at work, the soldiers continued to torment us. As soon as they felt a prisoner wasn't working hard enough, they would take him to their commander, Panov, a consumptive-looking man who would beat the prisoner with a short rifle, shouting: "This is what will happen to everyone who doesn't work!" That day, at least twenty prisoners were brutally beaten by Panov.

Everyone made the utmost effort to avoid these beatings. In the evening, before we marched home, Panov made a short speech. He would now go to the office to pick up the report. If we still hadn't made a hundred percent, he would shoot us all. Fortunately, the report was satisfactory.

But we weren't able to keep up the enormous effort for very long. Even the strongest, who usually met their quota, were soon exhausted. The guards intensified their attacks. There wasn't a day when Panov or one of his assistants didn't beat up several prisoners. They would pound their victim with a rifle butt until he fell to the ground, then force him with further blows to get up again. Anyone who had undergone this treatment was unable to return to the camp unassisted; he had to be supported by his friends.

Once the head of the labor section came into our barracks and asked the brigadier why we were working so poorly. The brigadier replied that he couldn't think of any way to force the "fascists" to work. One of us stepped forward and said: "Citizen director, it is not true that we don't want to work. We are all overworked. Just look at these people. How do you expect them to meet the quotas?"

Those words encouraged some of the others. They took off their dirty shirts and showed the head of the division their emaciated, black-and-blue bodies. The official asked where they had gotten their bruises, and several men told him: "They beat us, on top of the hard work." The head of the labor division left without another word.

When we arrived at the gravel pit the next day, we noticed immediately that Panov was in a rage. First he took the brigadier aside, and after talking to him for several minutes, he singled out those who had complained the day before and assigned them to a separate work site. "Very well," Panov told them. "If you want to get back to your barracks alive, you're going to have to exceed your quota. I'll teach you to complain about me!"

At the day's end, Panov discovered that this group had scarcely met fifty percent of the quota. "What am I going to do with you? What do you think is going on here? Do you think you fascists can take a vacation at the expense of the Soviet government? What the hell are you doing on Soviet soil if you don't want to work?" Panov turned around, picked up a spade, and handed it to a prisoner. "I want you to give each of these parasites a thrashing—but the way I do it. Is that understood?"

The man didn't move.

"Well, what's up? What are you waiting for?"

The prisoner said nothing.

"So you refuse?"

"I can't" was his reply.

Panov grabbed the shovel out of the prisoner's hands and started beating him with it. The prisoner tried to ward off the blows with his hand, and that fueled Panov's rage. "What, you dare strike back?"

Panov handed his rifle to a soldier and went back to beating the prisoner with all his strength, until his victim collapsed in the snow. "*Vstavai!* Get up!" Panov shouted.

The man didn't move.

"*Vstavai!*"

The prisoner didn't move. Panov went into the wooden shack, returned with a pailful of water, and poured it over the prisoner. "That'll make you move!"

The prisoner didn't move.

Panov called the brigadier. "Get him on his feet!"

When the brigadier picked the man up, we saw blood pouring from his mouth, ears, and nose. The brigadier was unable to hold him up for long and dropped him. He was dead.

The corpse was taken to the infirmary.

When we had returned to the barracks, no one thought of dinner. A man began to scream: "How long do we have to put up with this! As if starving us and working us to death isn't enough! Now they beat the life out of us!"

When the brigadier heard this, he hurled himself at the screaming man. "What are you trying to do, start a riot? Who do you think you're shouting at, anyway? Soviet power?" He was about to strike, but other prisoners grabbed him and twisted his arms behind his back. Two of his assistants tried to intervene, but they, too, were quickly subdued.

When the guard brought us our dinner, we demanded to speak to someone from the camp administration. The guard conveyed our request to the officer on duty. It happened to be my turn to receive my portion of cereal when the officer came in.

"Attention!" shouted the guard.

"Who asked for me?" asked the officer.

A prisoner stepped forward and said: "Look what's going on here! We're being worked to death, the soldiers beat us, and the brigadier continues to beat us here in the barracks!"

"Where is the brigadier?"

The brigadier stepped forward. The officer shouted at him: "*Banditskaya rozha*—bandit face—what's going on here?"

As usual, the brigadier started to denounce the political prisoners: "The fascists refuse to work . . ."

The officer interrupted him: "I know you're the only one who works, everybody else is lazy. Forward, march! You can have a rest from all your hard work—in the punishment cell!"

Early next morning, the same officer returned to the barracks with the inspector of the labor division. After many prisoners had voiced their complaints, a new brigadier was appointed: a man named Sabakar, who was serving a five-year sentence for fraud. He was awaiting trial on charges of "counterrevolutionary agitation" that had been brought against him in the camp, after the war broke out: he was accused of having told other prisoners that he believed the reports of the Soviet Information Agency were nothing but lies. The very next day, Sabakar ingratiated himself with the commander of the guards by telling him what had happened in the barracks and reporting which of the prisoners had complained to the labor division.

That day, the guards left us in peace. There was no intimidation on the way home, no bullying. It was the first time we had walked home without incident.

A medical commission was waiting for us in the barracks. We had to strip. The doctors, who were surely no strangers to the sight of starved and mistreated bodies, were shocked. When we tried to state our complaints to the commission, the chief doctor said: "You don't have to tell us anything. We can see with our own eyes what's been going on."

Three days after the examination, our quota was lowered by forty percent. Many were happy about this, but others felt that even this quota was beyond our capacity. Panov disappeared, and the new guard commander didn't care whether we met the quota or not. The new brigadier, too, was less abusive than the old one, but he invented a new method of spurring us on. At mealtimes, there was always a little food left over, and he promised an extra portion to those who exceeded the quota. At other times, he would announce that the guard commander had a package of makhorka as a premium for anyone who exceeded the norm. These tactics were of course harmless in comparison with Panov's, but they drove many prisoners to overexert themselves in the hope of getting an extra dipperful of soup or gruel.

After a while, the regime was loosened up somewhat. Our meals were no longer delivered by camp policemen but were brought by prisoners under the supervision of a camp policeman. You would often have a chance to talk to old acquaintances through the kitchen window and perhaps get a piece of bread from them. All sorts of ruses were devised to ease the pangs of hunger. Once, when it was my turn to get the food, I ran into a barracks to exchange a few words with Sasha, a student from Leningrad and a former cellmate of mine in the Solovetsk Islands. Sasha back then had not yet received any money from his relatives, and I had helped him out with food and tobacco.

He was sitting at a table reading a book. I told him I didn't have much time and described my situation in a few words. He interrupted me coldly. "You're locked up in prison; you should know better than to bother other people. Besides, this barracks is out of bounds for you." I hurried out. That exchange was a blow for me; I lost my appetite.

A second medical commission came to examine us: in addition to undernourishment, almost all of us were suffering from scurvy. The sickest among us were removed from our prison barracks and returned to the regular barracks. Among those released was Josef Berger; I had to stay. From then on, my situation began to improve; Josef did everything he could to help me and found all sorts of clever ways to send or bring me food. It wasn't easy to do that, for all contacts with us were forbidden and were punishable with incarceration.

One day, I received a piece of bread with a note from Josef: Kerosi had died in the hospital. Although the news did not surprise me, I was deeply shaken. I passed on the note to others who could read German. Some of them had known Kerosi and were saddened by the death of that courageous man.

The next day at work, I noticed a fellow inmate named Kruk approaching Panov, the guard commander (he was back again), and telling him something. That wasn't unusual; prisoners often asked questions of the guard commander.

Half an hour later, I was summoned by Panov. "What's that leaflet you passed around yesterday?"

I couldn't believe my ears. "I don't know what you're talking about."

"Hand me that leaflet, or you've had it."

I knew I was standing in front of a killer who was perfectly capable of shooting me for "attempted escape" or beating me to death with his rifle butt for "assaulting a guard." I searched for words to convince him that I had not passed around a leaflet, but found none. I had no idea what he was referring to. Maybe the terrible cold had paralyzed my brain, or else it was fear.

"Are you going to hand it over, yes or no?"

"I don't have a leaflet," I said quietly. Then I realized that Kruk must have denounced me.

Panov plunged the bayonet end of his rifle into the snow, so as to free his hands. "I'm going to strip off your clothes and search for that leaflet. Either I'll find it, or you'll freeze to death. Off with your coat!"

He searched my coat thoroughly, found nothing, and threw it on the snow. "Your jacket!"

He searched the jacket—again, he found nothing. His hands were freezing, and he was working himself into a rage, cursing me. Next were my pants. I stood in my underwear, shivering with cold and fear.

Finally, he found the note I had received the day before. Only then did I understand what he had meant by "leaflet." He was unable to read it, turned it upside down and sideways, and finally asked me what it said. I replied it was nothing political, just the news that a friend had died.

"Very well, I'll show the note to your interrogator. God have mercy on you if you've lied to me." He let me get dressed.

I didn't hear from Josef for a long time after that. I tried to reestablish contact with him but didn't succeed.

Once, on the way back from work, I noticed that the barbed-wire fence was almost completely snowed under. Before we carried the *parasha* into the yard, I asked my partner to carry the bucket back in by himself and leave me outside. The watchman let us out and immediately withdrew, to get out of the icy wind. That's what we had counted on. I crept on my belly to the mound of snow that covered the fence. There was such a blizzard that the man in the watchtower couldn't see me; if he had, I would have been shot.

When I stepped into Josef s barracks, he couldn't believe his eyes. "How did you get here?"

"Very simply, across the fence."

He looked dumbfounded for a moment. "You're playing with your life," he said then.

I told him I couldn't possibly be seen from the tower, and that reassured him. He quickly moved through the barracks, begging for me, and filled a pillowcase with bread. He also told me all sorts of news. The question now was how to get back to the barracks and what to tell the guard. An old popular song came to mind:

Was macht der Mayer am Himalaja,
Wie kommt er runter vom Himalaja . . .

What's Mayer doing on the Himalaya,
How does he get down from the Himalaya . . .

If I crept back across the fence, I would run the risk of being seen by the watchman on the tower, and even if I got across unnoticed, I would find the barracks shut. I decided simply to go to the watchman's hut and ring the bell, come what may.

I rang. The watchman stepped out into the storm, shouting: "Who's there?"

"Let me in!" I called out.

The blizzard drowned out my words. "Why the hell don't you answer?"

"Open up, I'm from the barracks!" I yelled louder.

The watchman still couldn't hear me. He stepped up very close and shouted again: "Who's out there? Do you want to get shot by the watchman?"

Finally, he realized that I wanted to get into the prison barracks. He stepped in and I followed him.

"What do you want?"

"I'm from this barracks."

"You? From the prison barracks?"

"Yes."

"How did you get here?"

I told him the truth. He stared at me and noticed the sack in my hand. "What's that?"

"Bread."

"All right, you just wait till my assistant comes. He'll have a word or two to say to you . . ."

I sat down on a bench and waited. I knew what would happen: they would take my bread, beat me up, and throw me in the punishment cell. The room was very warm. I opened my coat, made myself comfortable, took a piece of bread from my bundle (it was frozen solid) and held it near the stove to thaw it. I wanted at least to fill my stomach before they took my bread away.

The assistant didn't come. The fire in the stove had nearly gone out. The watchman grumbled: he was mad at his assistant for being so late; now he had to get the coal himself. He picked up a pail and moved toward the door. I offered to get the coal. The watchman looked at me sideways and said: "You're not going to run away?"

"Where am I going to go in this storm? I'll be glad when I can get back to my bunk."

I took the pail and a small shovel and went out into the yard. It took me a long time to clear the snow from the box where the coal was stored.

The watchman came out twice to check up on me. Finally, I reached the coal. When I came back in with a full pail, the watchman looked pleased. I stoked up the stove. Now the watchman began taking an interest in me. He wanted to know who I was and why I was in pre-trial detention for the second time. "It's really very foolish of you to risk your life for a few pieces of bread."

"I was thinking more of food than of my life," I said.

"I like you. Come, I'll take you back to the barracks. But don't pull any more stunts like that in the future."

My friends welcomed me with a big hue and cry. When I told them my adventure, some of them criticized me for taking such a risk, while others praised me for my courage. I emptied out the pillowcase and gave each of my friends a piece of bread. One of the criminals came and asked me to "lend" him some bread till the next day. I had to give him a piece too.

After the sick were released from our barracks, about a hundred new inmates moved in, most of them criminals. Their arrival marked the beginning of a very hard time for all of us. Theft, robbery, even murder were a daily occurrence. Whoever didn't immediately consume his bread ration could be sure of having it stolen. All you had to do was put a piece of bread down for a few minutes, and it would be gone.

One day, an *urka* (criminal) left a piece of bread on his bunk and went to the stove to get some water. When he came back, the bread was gone. "Stop fooling around, give me back my bread!" he said. No one budged. Then he realized it wasn't a joke. He went to the stove, picked up the poker, and walked directly up to a group of adolescent boys, also criminals, and accused them of having stolen his bread. They swore by all the saints that they hadn't touched his bread.

"I'll give you ten minutes. If you don't come up with the bread by then . . . you know the law." He paced back and forth with the poker in his hand like a tiger in a cage.

No more than five minutes had passed when the boys called him. One of them whispered something in his ear. The *urka* turned around and walked up to a boy who was sitting on the top bunk. "Hey you, Lyosha, give me the bread!"

"Leave me alone," the boy said.

The *urka* crept onto the bunk, searched under the pillow, and produced a large tin can containing a partially eaten piece of bread. "Brothers, have a look at this! He's got so much bread he can't even finish it."

The criminals shouted from all sides: "Go ahead, kill him, make mincemeat out of him!"

The *urka* started beating the boy with the poker, aiming at his head. The boy buried his head in the clothes on his bunk. Then he was holding his head with both hands. "I didn't take anything, I didn't take anything," he cried.

Blood was streaming down onto the lower bunk. The boy fell silent. The *urka* went to the window and knocked. After a while, the watchman came. "We've got a stiff here. Take him out so he doesn't stink up the place."

The watchman looked at the dead boy, shook his head, and muttered: "Some goings-on here." He left, locking the door.

The *urka* sat down on his bunk and ate the piece of bread he had found in the tin can. Laughing, he said: "That'll teach them who to steal bread from!"

Late that night, the NKVD agent, the camp commander, and a doctor came into the barracks. We all woke up. A report was written up; the corpse was removed, and the killer arrested. There followed a discussion about the incident. Opinions were divided. Some said the boy was innocent; others believed he had taken the bread and that the bread in his tin can proved it. The boy's neighbors claimed that he never saved up his bread but always ate it right away. A friend of his, on the other hand, reported that the boy had been feeling sick and hadn't been able to eat anything. Two days later, it turned out that the murdered prisoner had been innocent, that the real thieves were those who had accused him.

Brigadier Sabakar made Kruk his assistant. Now Sabakar, Kruk, and two other prisoners went to get the food every day. The two prisoners carried the soup container, and Sabakar and Kruk carried the fish and any other food. In order to supplement his own and his assistant's portions, Sabakar deprived the prisoners of theirs. Occasionally, for example, there would be soup, gruel, and fish for dinner, but the prisoners would get only soup and gruel; Sabakar and Kruk would have eaten the fish. After a while, the prisoners caught them at their game, and the criminals nearly beat them to death. Sabakar had to be hospitalized for several weeks.

After this incident, I was chosen as the new brigadier. When the head of the labor section informed me of this decision, I refused. Thereupon, he said: "I suppose tomorrow you'll tell me you don't want to be in prison. You do the work I tell you to do."

I had no choice but to accept. The very next day, I had a clash with Panov. Whenever we were assigned to a new work area, the first job was to clear away the frozen moss beneath the deep layer of snow. It was relatively easy work: chipping square chunks of moss loose with pickax and shovel and piling them up. This job had so far been reserved for the friends of the brigadier or the favorites of Guard Commander Panov. I assigned the weakest prisoners to it. Those who had previously cut moss complained so loudly that the guards were alerted. Panov arrived immediately. The criminals shouted that the new "fascist" brigadier had given all the easy work to other "fascists."

Panov gave me a curt order: "Divide up the work the way it's always been. Right away."

I tried to explain that I wasn't concerned with who was political or criminal but with the most efficient way of getting the job done. Panov, deaf to my arguments, repeated his order, threatening: "If you don't do it immediately, I'll take care of it."

I asked Panov what a brigadier was there for if the guard commander was going to divide up the work. He was speechless at first; then he took his rifle from his shoulder, saying: "I guess you haven't made the acquaintance of this fellow yet. I'll introduce you!"

The soldiers shouted: "Don't fool around with him. Just break his head!"

One of them, a Mongolian with a dog that was straining at his leash in his eagerness to attack, said: "Let Minus deal with him; he'll make him human!"

But Panov suddenly changed his mind. "Very well, we'll do it your way. But if you don't all meet the quota a hundred percent, you'll have to be carried home tonight."

When the manager of the gravel pit gave me his instructions, I told him: "I've been made brigadier against my will, and I've gotten into trouble with Panov . . ." I told him of my decision and of Panov's threats. The manager of the gravel pit, a former prisoner who had served a ten-year sentence for "sabotage," reassured me. "Make sure everyone works. We'll take care of the rest."

That evening, Panov emerged from the manager's shed with the record of the day's work in his hand. He waved the sheet in the air and said to his subordinates: "What do you know, a hundred and thirty percent!"

The soldiers were amazed, and the Mongolian said: "Too bad, I was looking forward to letting Minus drag him back to the barracks."

There is an old proverb: Where there's hunger, there are mice. Indeed, there were very many mice in our barracks, even though they found nothing to eat there, since anyone who dropped a crumb would carefully pick it up and eat it. One day, we noticed two prisoners getting up at night and rummaging around the stove. After observing them for a while, we discovered that they were catching mice and cooking them in a tin can. Many prisoners strongly objected, but others defended the mice eaters.

Half a year passed and our situation had not improved. Panov and his men seemed to find pleasure in tormenting us in every way. One day, when Panov was applying one of his favorite punishments, forcing a young fellow to strip to his underwear for not working hard enough, the prisoner shouted at the soldiers: "While real heroes are bleeding at the front, you're trying to prove your courage against us."

Panov wasn't used to that kind of talk. "Come a little closer!"

The prisoner hesitantly obeyed.

"Hurry up! Face down in the snow!"

The boy did as he was told.

Panov took his rifle off his shoulder and began beating the prisoner. When his rage was spent, he ordered the prisoner to stand. The boy could hardly move. Panov began to beat him again. After every blow, he shouted: "Get up!"

Finally, the boy gathered up his last resources and stood up.

That evening, when he took his shirt off in the barracks, we saw that his entire body was bruised. It seemed incredible that he had survived such a beating.

As such abuses multiplied, the prisoners began fleeing from their place of work. Of course, the fugitives knew they wouldn't get very far, but they hoped at least to spend a day without enduring the cold, the hard work, and especially the rifle butts of Panov and his assistants. They would wait for the "black" purga, when you couldn't see more than an arm's length away from your face. On such occasions, we were herded together, and if it didn't stop soon, we were led back to the barracks. We'd often have to stand for three or four hours without moving; every half hour, the guard commander would count us, and if someone was missing, he'd call for the emergency squad. They would come hurrying out of their barracks with dogs, and the manhunt would begin. A favorite hiding place was the big metal foundry. It wasn't hard to get there, for the soldiers on duty in the watchtowers didn't dare stick out their noses during the purga.

In the big foundry, there were many warm nooks where a prisoner could hide. A particularly attractive place was near the great caldrons into which the molten metal from the smelting furnaces was poured, and which were put out to cool in a large shed. The exhausted prisoner would curl up behind these caldrons and, very often, fall asleep. Soon he would be roused, taken back to the guards, and beaten until he found eternal rest.

Sometimes a captured fugitive would be brought into our barracks to be beaten with rifle butts as an object lesson to the others. The soldiers would accompany the blows with statements like: "There, that's your reward for shirking. Now you don't have to work anymore!"

Sometimes several days passed before a fugitive was caught. One man hid for two days in the free workers' kitchen. During the day he would work in the kitchen to earn his meals, then go to sleep in the loft next to the chimney.

Some prisoners killed themselves to avoid falling into the hands of the soldiers. One of my bunk neighbors was Podolsky, a Polish Jew. When the Germans occupied Poland, he tried to flee across the Soviet border. He was arrested right at the border by the NKVD and was brought to Kiev, where a special tribunal sentenced him to five years for crossing the border illegally. He was brought to Norilsk, tried to escape, was captured near Igarka, and was waiting to be tried and sentenced by the camp court. Podolsky was singled out for particularly brutal attacks by the guards because he was a Jew. He was a good worker; Panov had nothing to reproach him for on this account. But the commander found other pretexts to test his mettle against the Pole. One day, Podolsky confided to me that he was planning to escape from the gravel pit. I urged him not to, pointing out that almost all such attempts ended tragically. He said they would not catch him alive again.

One evening, we assembled in rows of five, as usual, for the return march to the barracks; the guard commander counted us; everything was in order. When we arrived at the camp gate and were taken over by the camp guards, someone was missing. The count was repeated twice, with the same result. The guard commander pulled the list from his pocket and called each of us by name. Podolsky was missing. No one had seen when, where, or how he had disappeared. Since we were in the camp, in the presence of the camp administration, the guards couldn't vent their rage on us, but Panov threatened to "settle this account" with us the next day.

We got ready for work the next morning as usual, but the moment of departure passed and we were not led out of the gate. For three days, we stayed in the barracks; we were informed that for the time being we would not have to work. All the guards of the seventh camp section had gone out hunting for Podolsky—without success. Then one day we were taken to work again. We assumed Podolsky had been captured. To our surprise, the guards were silent; we didn't hear a rough word all day. Not until the evening, during the final count, did Panov speak up: "Everyone's here today, no one ran away. Why would you, anyway? Where would you go? We'll get that Podolsky too, just wait."

So they were still searching for him. We were all happy about that. We hadn't experienced such a pleasant day in a long time.

A week later, some prisoners from our barracks were taken to the doctor. They came back with the news that Podolsky had been seen near factory number 25. Three days later, there was another major alarm and many brigades, including ours, were not sent to work because the guards had been mobilized for a new manhunt. They found Podolsky at the place where the red-hot liquid dross from the foundry was deposited. When he saw himself surrounded, without any chance of escape, he jumped into the boiling mass, leaving only a puff of smoke.

After that, the camp administration began to show some concern for our situation. The commander of the seventh camp section came to the barracks; some of us dared to complain about the guards and the criminals. From then on, there was an improvement. Criminals found guilty of theft were now strictly punished by the camp police. Once, a criminal, Paklin, stole another prisoner's fur hat. Two policemen came into the barracks and ordered Paklin to return the hat. He denied having stolen it. The policemen searched his bunk and found nothing. But then they discovered the hat under the bunk. Paklin was stripped naked and beaten with nightsticks. He endured this stoically for a while and then broke down and pleaded for mercy, promising that he would never steal again. After that incident, there were no more cases of theft in our barracks.

Despite certain ameliorations, conditions were still unendurable. Some tried to save themselves by hopeless attempts to escape; others by self-induced sickness. One method was to drink unboiled water or eat soap on an empty stomach. In many instances, the weakened prisoners never recovered from these artificially induced sicknesses. Hardly a day passed when someone did not deliberately subject his hands or feet to frostbite. All you had to do was hold an iron tool with your naked hands for a few minutes, or wrap fewer rags around your feet, and you'd have a case of second- or third-degree frostbite. In the former case, you could count on recovering your health after two or three months; in the latter, you'd lose some fingers or toes, maybe even lose an arm or a leg by amputation. In either case, it meant a respite from hard work, especially from hard work outdoors.

Eventually, only about half the prisoners were still capable of working. Those who stayed in the barracks were given even smaller rations than the others. The constant hunger was becoming unbearable. A bowl of soup was worth a human life.

Once, as dinner was being served, a young fellow was shoved and spilled his soup. At first, he stood there, perplexed; then he threw himself to the ground and lapped up the spilled soup like a dog. He cried and was unable to calm down for a long time. Some of my friends gave him pieces of bread, which caused a great deal of comment. All around the room, you could hear voices saying: "They gave him bread, they gave him bread . . ."

Panov had not forgotten our clash on the day I was appointed brigadier. He was waiting for an opportunity to punish me. In order to meet the quota, the prisoners made use of little tricks and deceits. The group that dug out and piled up the frozen moss sometimes heaped up earth and garbage and surrounded and topped it with moss. Panov noticed that.

"Brigadier, get over here!" he shouted.

When I was standing about five meters away from him, he asked me: "What are these people doing?"

I gave him a questioning look.

"Don't play the fool with me!"

"What do you mean?"

"I'll tell you what I mean in a moment!"

"What's wrong?"

"Go to that group up there on the right and have a look at what they're doing."

I turned around, wondering how I could get myself out of this mess.

Of course I had immediately known what Panov meant. I walked up to the moss diggers and reproached them in a loud voice, with feigned indignation, for making *tufta*, as cheating was called in the camp. Then I returned to Panov, but very slowly, so as to hold off as long as possible the ordeal that was in store for me. Again, I stopped about five meters away from him.

"Come closer and tell me what you saw."

I mumbled something.

"Who do you fascists think you're hurting with your sabotage, anyway?"

"It's not sabotage. Those people are weak and are trying to make things a little easier for themselves."

"What? You defend them? You dare protect people who try to sabotage Soviet power?"

"I'm not defending them, I'm just trying to explain it to you."

"*You* want to explain something to *me?*"

I didn't know what to say. Then Panov took his rifle off his shoulder and slapped my face with the flat side of his bayonet. "Get moving, beat it!" Hardly had I turned around when he struck me in the back with the butt of his rifle, knocking the wind out of me. Gagging for breath, I managed to move out of Panov's reach and threw myself in the snow.

When we returned to the camp, I asked the watchman to take me to the head of the labor division. I told him what had happened and asked him to relieve me of my duties as brigadier. He didn't want to. Only when I told him that from then on I did not regard myself as brigadier did he relent; but he said I would have to wait three or four days until he appointed a new brigadier.

The next day, something happened that caused me to give up my brigadier's position without further delay. A twenty-year-old fellow sat down in the snow during work time. This was not allowed; we could rest only during the five-minute breaks we were allowed every two hours. One of Panov's assistants, who was taking Panov's place that day, ordered the boy to stand up and get back to work. The boy remained seated as if he hadn't heard.

"Are you going to get up or not?" asked the soldier, who was about a hundred meters away. The boy shouted back that he was sick and could not work. The soldier ordered the boy to come to where he was. We couldn't hear the soldier's questions or the boy's answers; all we could see was the soldier pointing out a direction to the boy. The boy turned around and started walking. Then the soldier aimed his gun and fired. The boy fell, dead.

Alarmed by the shot, soldiers rushed out of their nearby barracks. Shortly after, a commission arrived and took down the killer's report. Two days later, a communiqué by the guard commander of Norilsk was read out to us: the soldier was praised for his vigilance, thanks to which an attempted escape had been foiled; in addition, he was given a bonus of five hundred rubles.

After that incident, my only thought was to escape the certain death that awaited me here. There was only one possibility—self-mutilation. I decided to freeze off the toes of my left foot. The next morning, when I put on my felt boots, I wrapped so many rags around my left foot that I could hardly get the boot on. The fit was so tight that the blood circulation was blocked. It was enormously cold that day; I had no doubt that I would succeed. To be doubly sure, I stepped aside to urinate and aimed at the point of my left boot; the moistened area froze over quickly. I moved as little as possible, to make sure the foot really froze. I pictured myself lying in a warm hospital bed that same evening. It would probably take months for the foot to heal. Of course, I would suffer a great deal of pain later on, but that seemed a small price to pay for months of rest and recuperation. It didn't even occur to me that I would be a cripple for the rest of my life.

The day dragged on endlessly. I was burning with impatience for the moment when I would walk into the infirmary. I could already hear the doctor's voice giving the order to have me sent to the hospital immediately.

On the way back to the camp, I was surprised at the complete lack of pain in my foot. I told myself that frostbite did not make itself felt for several hours. In the barracks, I pulled off my boot with the help of a comrade. To my great disappointment, I had only first-degree frostbite; gone was the dream of luxurious peace in a warm bed. I went to the infirmary anyway. After three hours' wait, my turn came. The doctor laconically said to the nurse: "A cold footbath." I returned to the barracks with my head hanging low.

My friendship with the watchman whose acquaintance I made on the day I climbed over the barbed-wire fence proved advantageous in various small ways. He would often summon me to his little hut, where I would stoke the stove, fetch coal, or wash the floor in exchange for some food. Sometimes, when he knew that the section commander was absent, he would let me make a quick visit to another barracks where I knew I could get some bread. He would frequently send me to the kitchen, and the cook would give me an extra portion.

On the evening after my unsuccessful attempt at self-mutilation, I complained to the watchman about the unbearable conditions at the gravel pit, about the maniacal tyranny of Panov and his men. The watchman promised to get me a job as cleanup man in the barracks. Usually it was the sick who cleaned up, but thanks to my friend, I actually got this job for a few days. Then the section commander learned of it and ordered a return to the previous system of using the sick prisoners for cleaning up.

Fortunately, I fell ill again and was taken to the hospital with a high fever. The doctor suspected typhus, so I was put in the ward for infectious diseases. During my brief stay there, many patients died of enteric fever. Prisoners would often eat virtually anything that promised to ease the pangs of hunger. They would rummage about in the trash cans, collect fish heads and other pieces of refuse, and eat them without washing them. Diarrhea was the most frequent reaction, but some men developed serious intestinal and stomach diseases, and eventually typhus.

Quite a few died of the effects of sudden overeating. Occasionally, a prisoner would get his hands on a large amount of food, which his intestines, weakened by years of starvation, were unable to absorb, and the man would die of a volvulus.

You could observe patients in the hospital who were unable to eat but would anxiously guard their zwieback. Every hour, they would count their supply. What a crisis if one piece was missing! The dying man would scream at the top of his voice: someone had stolen his zwieback. That was usually a sign that he had only a few more hours to live.

There were actual disputes over the "estate" of a dying man. It might just consist of a few pieces of zwieback or sugar. Whoever was first to lay his hand on the treasure had the right to claim it. It wasn't just the prisoners who waited for the last breath of the dying, but the attendants as well. You could see them suddenly showing a solicitude that had been completely absent when the patient was comparatively well and called for water. Suddenly everyone wanted to help.

Some very good news reached me in the hospital: the prison barracks was no longer in use. Its inmates had been transferred to the regular barracks. But when I was released from the hospital, I was locked up in a punishment cell, and a solitary one at that. Once again, my hope of returning to "normal" camp life had proved an illusion. What were their plans? Why was I singled out among all the others? I knew that the NKVD was not prone to release its victims so easily, but I couldn't believe that I was supposedly the most "dangerous" of the more than a hundred thousand prisoners in Norilsk. The charges against me had been fabricated out of thin air. Naturally, I had every reason to hate Stalin's regime and the NKVD, which embodied that regime, but I wasn't a fascist, and the NKVD knew that very well. What made me so special?

The mass executions had been carried out eight thousand kilometers behind the front, where the prisoners could not represent any possible danger to the regime. Stalin had ordered a halt to the killing, as a concession to his Western allies. But this did not prevent the chief of the Norilsk NKVD, Polikarpov, from executing individual prisoners who had incurred his personal hatred. He had focused on me and my friends during the first days of the war, and did not want to see us slip through his fingers. He considered himself omnipotent in Norilsk—no prisoner could prevail against him. Now he was preparing his final attack; and no doubt he hoped that my terrible experiences had weakened my will.

I spent two weeks in the stone barracks with its barred windows.

SENTENCED TO DEATH

In May 1943, I was transferred from the punishment cell back to the prison. There were the same bunks and, you might say, the same people, just with different names, and of course the same accusations. Only one thing had changed. There were numerous concurring reports that the camp court was only rarely pronouncing death sentences. Our fight to gain time had been successful. We had, in effect, been fighting for our lives, not for freedom; we knew only too well that there could be no freedom in the Soviet Union so long as Stalin was in power.

My new interrogator, Captain Gisayev, told me right at the outset that I did not have to worry about being shot. He was a native Caucasian who had been evacuated from Nalchik when the Germans occupied the northern Caucasus. He began the hearing with the following words: "I would like to close your case, which has dragged on for such a long time."

"If you want to close the case, you will have to withdraw your accusations against me and my comrades," I said.

"I cannot do that. There are several very damaging witness accounts against you."

"Do you mean the criminals who were used by the previous interrogator?"

"No, even if we disregard the testimony of the criminals, we have enough other witnesses."

"That's news to me. More witnesses?"

"Yes. And you'll be even more surprised when you hear their names."

"I am very curious to find out."

Before Gisayev told me the names of the new witnesses, he stressed that he was completely uninterested in this whole affair and only wanted to finish what the others had begun. He promised to be objective and not allow any illegalities to mar the proceedings. Almost incidentally, he informed me that the three of us had been sentenced to death by the Special Tribunal but that the Supreme Court had overturned the decision and ordered a new investigation. Even though I had considered this possibility, I was surprised. Gisayev added that he would allow me to examine the dossier.

"Will you tell me the names of the witnesses?"

"Certainly. But before I tell you their names, you must tell me if you are now willing to testify and to sign the records of the proceedings."

After I had given my consent, Gisayev said: "Our crown witnesses against you are Roshankovsky and Larionov."

I was truly surprised. Now I understood why Larionov and especially Roshankovsky had been so concerned for my well-being. I had never imagined that they were secret agents—*seksoty*, as they were called in the camp. What moved people like Roshankovsky and Larionov to serve the NKVD? Did they sympathize with Stalin's regime, whose victims they were? Surely not. Larionov, a Komsomol functionary from Leningrad, had been arrested, after the murder of Kirov, as a member of the former opposition, and was then sent to Norilsk. Roshankovsky was a functionary of the Western Ukrainian Communist Party and had exchanged a Polish for a Soviet prison, like so many others. Why did such people help the regime wage its war of extermination against others like them?

The answer is not hard to find: Soviet camps were fundamentally different from Western penal institutions. In the latter, the prisoner lives in comparatively humane conditions. After he has served his sentence, he is released; he can return to his profession and his family, and time heals the wounds inflicted on him during his incarceration. But a Soviet prisoner becomes fair game at the very moment of his arrest. It is not the law that determines his fate, but "expedience," and it is always some NKVD officer who determines what is expedient. He does not have to fear censure for sending an innocent person to a prison camp; on the contrary, he will be reproached for not being severe enough.

Every prisoner, even one serving a light sentence, knew that he could survive only with a great deal of luck, and even then he might very well leave the camp a cripple. Once released, he could expect to be banished to a Siberian village where life was often so miserable that you wished you were back in the camp. People like Roshankovsky and Larionov tried to evade the ruthless clutches of the NKVD by delivering their comrades to the knife.

The NKVD did its best to conceal the identity of its spies, but in this they rarely succeeded, for the prisoners were very suspicious. Often, a man would attract undeserved suspicion to himself simply because he had been given easier work to do. Agents in privileged positions like those of Larionov and Roshankovsky were usually unmasked fairly soon. In my case, the NKVD had to reveal the identity of their spies because they could find no other witnesses.

The next day, at my hearing, I found Roshankovsky sitting to the left of the door. I was seated across from him, and between us sat Gisayev at his desk. When Roshankovsky saw me, he lowered his head. He looked miserable—emaciated, his body twisted as he turned his cap between his hands, his head pulled in between his shoulders, deep grooves in his forehead.

The interrogator opened the session with the customary preliminary remarks. Then he began the hearing proper and recorded each of our exchanges. He asked Roshankovsky: "Do you know this man?"

"That is Karl Steiner."

The interrogator turned to me. "Do you know this man?"

"Yes, that is Lev Roshankovsky."

"Witness Roshankovsky, did you have any quarrels or other disagreements with the accused?"

"No. On the contrary, my relations with the accused were excellent."

"Accused, do you confirm this?"

"My relations with Roshankovsky were normal," I replied.

"Witness, what do you have to say about the accused?"

"I got to know Steiner when we lived together in a barracks. We had many conversations. I could tell by his remarks that he hated Soviet power and especially the leader of the people, Stalin."

"Accused, do you confirm these allegations?"

"I never discussed politics with Roshankovsky. What he's saying is pure invention."

"Witness, what else do you know about the accused?"

"In February 1940, when a group of Germans and Austrians were about to be repatriated, Steiner told me that if he had the good fortune of getting back to Europe, he would do everything he could to inform the whole world of what is going on in Russia. By this he meant that he would tell lies about the Soviet Union."

"Accused, do you confirm this?"

"I deny it absolutely. I never discussed such matters with Roshankovsky."

In the course of our confrontation, Roshankovsky told several other fairy tales that were designed to "unmask" me as a counterrevolutionary. This lasted more than an hour. I denied everything he said. Contrary to the previous interrogators, who had tried to force me to confess, Gisayev contented himself with verbal suggestions and prods. He said it would be in my interest to admit everything—the matter would be settled quickly. But I refused to confirm the lies of the provocateur Roshankovsky.

That evening, I was confronted with Larionov. Gisayev's procedure was the same as it had been in the morning. "Please tell me what you know about Steiner."

"One day, the accused came to the kitchen—I was the supervisor—and asked me to give him a job there. I asked him who he was. Steiner told me he had been a communist as a very young man. He had adored the Soviet Union, but when he came here he experienced the greatest disappointment of his life. He said he'd expected to find a land of justice and had found even greater injustice than he had experienced in the capitalist countries. He said that while the rich people had disappeared, the poor had just gotten poorer. He said that instead of a dictatorship of the proletariat, we had a dictatorship over the proletariat, and that the party members were like a herd of sheep."

"Accused, do you confirm Larionov's statements?"

"It is a very long time since I have talked to Larionov. I can no longer remember the content of our conversations and cannot therefore confirm any of what he is saying."

Once again, there was no pressure whatsoever. The interrogator took down everything exactly as it was spoken, after which the three of us signed it. When the confrontation was over, I asked to speak to the Public

Prosecutor. The interrogator wanted to know why—did I have any objections to the way he was conducting the investigation? I replied that I had no complaints about him and that I wished to speak to the Public Prosecutor only to ask him why I had been kept in pre-trial detention for nearly two years just to be confronted with agents provocateurs like Larionov and Roshankovsky. Gisayev promised to convey my query to the Public Prosecutor. That was the end of the hearing. I was led back to my cell.

When I stepped into the interrogator's office the next day, a man was standing in the middle of the room, dressed in a raincoat and a cap, with his hands in his pockets. "I am the Public Prosecutor. What do you want?"

"I want to ask you why I've been kept in prison for so long."

"The interrogator could have told you that, and probably you know the answer by now."

"The investigation is arbitrary, and the manner in which I have been treated is inhuman."

"It's fairly obvious that you are a counterrevolutionary element. That's why you're in prison."

"I was put in the camp for being a so-called counterrevolutionary element. I've never heard of anyone being accused of the same crime twice."

"It's not for you to tell us how often we can bring charges against you. We hold to the law."

"I would also like to know what law allows for criminals like the two Brovkins to be used as witnesses. In addition, two of your agents are being used as witnesses against me."

"What proof do you have that Roshankovsky and Larionov are agents of the NKVD?"

"It is obvious from their behavior that they are agents provocateurs. The mere fact that both of them work in the camp administration proves that. You as a Public Prosecutor know very well that people who have been sentenced according to Article 58 don't ever work in the camp administration."

The Public Prosecutor did not answer me and turned to the interrogator. "Enough of this."

Back in the cell, I was joined by Degtyarov, who had been imprisoned together with two others from the ninth camp section. They had worked in the brick factory. Someone had told the NKVD that they had formed a counterrevolutionary group, had engaged in anti-Soviet conversations, and had predicted the victory of the Nazis. Degtyarov had denied everything at his first hearing. But now, learning that I had been in jail for almost two years as a result of my refusal to confess, he said: "No, I don't want to sit here that long. I'm going to ask for an immediate hearing and confess everything. They'll give me another ten years, that's not so bad. The war will be over soon and we'll be amnestied."

He was, in fact, called to a hearing that very evening. He came back at midnight and told me with joy in his eyes that his case would be closed in three or four days, after which he would return to light labor in the camp. Several days later, after another hearing, he reported happily that his case was closed now. The interrogator had assured him that he was accused according to Article 58, paragraph 12; that is, for failing to report a counterrevolutionary organization. He added that one of his friends had confessed everything too, and that only the third had stood firm. Soon after, they were brought before the camp court. Degtyarov and the friend who had confessed everything were sentenced to death; the third man, who had denied everything, was given ten years.

A young secondary-school teacher from Norilsk was in our cell for two months without knowing what he was accused of. He had been sent from the teachers' academy to the front, where he had lost an arm. After his release from the military hospital, he was given a teaching position in Norilsk, and was soon chosen to be head of the communist teachers' group. Everyone in the cell liked Kulikov for his sense of humor, his helpfulness, and especially because he was very well read. To pass the time, we would tell each other the plots of novels and stories we had read, and experiences we had had. Kulikov was a very good storyteller; he could recite written texts, especially short stories, almost word for word. Nearly every day, he would tell us a story.

We tried to figure out why he had been arrested. I asked him if he remembered any conversations he'd had at the front. He couldn't remember. Nor could he imagine having said anything at the school that would get him into trouble.

"Kulikov, to your hearing!" the guard called through the *kormushka,* the opening in the door through which food is passed into the cell. Kulikov, who was usually very calm, suddenly lost all the color in his face. I helped him put on his jacket, for the guard was waiting impatiently at the door.

After several hours, Kulikov returned from his hearing and told us what he was accused of. After Savenyagin was recalled, General Panyukov was appointed director of the Norilsk industries. Panyukov lived in a luxurious villa with his son and daughter-in-law. When the son was drafted into the army, Panyukov remained in Norilsk with his daughter-in-law. And while the son was fighting at the front, his father and wife were having an affair. The wife became pregnant and gave birth to a child. The son heard of this, returned from the front, and raised a scandal. His father appeased him with a large sum of money. The son returned to the front, and the matter seemed settled.

Young people in the Soviet Union were not particularly preoccupied with questions of sexual morality. Nevertheless, there were some people in Norilsk who were upset when they learned this story. Kulikov was among the most indignant. He raised the issue at a meeting of the Komsomol, without ever suspecting that this would lead to an accusation of "anti-Soviet activities." Since the NKVD couldn't very well condemn him for discussing the Panyukov affair at a meeting, they collected various pieces of gossip during Kulikov's two months of preventive detention, and the result was: "Spreading false rumors about high officers of the Soviet Army." The court took Kulikov's war injury into consideration as an extenuating circumstance and gave him only five years in camp.

My new interrogator was in a hurry. He wanted to close my case in ten to fifteen days and deliver the results to the court. I, too, wanted to get it over with.

Gisayev wrote two or three more brief affidavits without any significant content; I signed them. I could feel Gisayev's satisfaction at being able to bring this protracted case to a close. As he had promised, he kept strictly to the letter of the law. When the investigation was concluded, he had me summoned to his office and told me to sit at the little table opposite his desk, where he could watch me closely. He handed me a fat dossier and asked me to read it. The pages were bound and numbered consecutively. The first page indicated the total number of pages and stated that the interrogator had eliminated four pages.

I began to read attentively. I was especially interested in the witnesses' statements. In addition to Roshankovsky and Larionov, the NKVD had questioned some of my friends and acquaintances. The first one to be questioned was my close friend Vasily Chuprakov. As I learned from Chuprakov later, he refused to testify against me, even though the interrogator threatened to put him on trial if he didn't. A second witness was Batlan; his statements were trivial and could not therefore be used against me. The third witness was Yefim Morozov. He indicated that he had heard of critical remarks I had made about certain measures of the Soviet government, but said he didn't know any details. I didn't bother reading the testimony of the two Brovkins, since I already knew what they had said.

Included in the dossier were the records of the proceedings involving my two friends Josef and Georg as well as the witnesses against them. They were virtually indistinguishable from the documents in my case; the only difference was that several NKVD officials and doctors testified that Josef had gone on a hunger strike and had to be force-fed after the fifth day. There were also accusations against the Bulgarian communist Blagoye Popov and against the Hungarian communist Jaquert. Some witnesses had claimed that these two men had belonged to our "counter-revolutionary organization." But Popov and Jaquert had been taken out of Norilsk before the beginning of the war (because they had both become invalids); consequently, they could not be tried.

The document ended with the verdict of the NKVD:

After a thorough examination of the material presented in accusation of Karl Steiner, Josef Berger, and Georg Biletzki, all serving sentences in the Norilsk camp for counterrevolutionary activity, the above-mentioned authority has arrived at the conclusion that these three men must be regarded as incorrigible counterrevolutionary elements. Therefore, the NKVD of Norilsk recommends the death penalty for Karl Steiner, Josef Berger, and Georg Biletzki.

Commander of the Norilsk NKVD
Major Polikarpov

On the next page was the decision of the Norilsk Public Prosecutor:

After an examination of the dossier furnished by the inquest commission of the Norilsk NKVD, the Public Prosecutor of Norilsk concurs that the three accused, Karl Steiner, Josef Berger, and Georg Biletzki, are incorrigible individuals. I call for the death penalty.

Public Prosecutor of Norilsk
Mikhailov

Next was the verdict of the Special Tribunal in Krasnoyarsk:

After examining the material produced by the inquest commission of the Norilsk NKVD and the verdict of the Norilsk Public Prosecutor, the Special Tribunal of the Krasnoyarsk region supports the recommendation of the inquest commission of the Norilsk NKVD to apply the death penalty against Karl Steiner, Josef Berger, and Georg Biletzki.

Karl Steiner, Josef Berger, and Georg Biletzki, all serving sentences in the Norilsk camp for counterrevolutionary activities, terrorism, espionage, and diversionary maneuvers, have continued to practice their misdeeds in the camp. The accused have spread intensive counterrevolutionary propaganda among the prisoners, attempting to create a defeatist spirit and predicting a victory of the Hitler army against the Soviet Union.

For the above reasons, the Special Tribunal of the Krasnoyarsk region is passing the following verdict:

Steiner, Berger, and Biletzki, currently in preventive detention, are to be executed by firing squad.

Chairman of the Special Tribunal of the Krasnoyarsk District
General [signature illegible]

The final document was the verdict of the Supreme Court of the Soviet Union, dated September 1, 1942:

After examining the material furnished by the inquest commission of the Norilsk NKVD, the Supreme Court of the Soviet Union has determined that the death sentence against Karl Steiner, Josef Berger, and Georg Biletzki, all serving sentences in Norilsk for counterrevolutionary activities, cannot be executed, for the following reasons:

1. Among the many documents of the Norilsk NKVD, there is

not a single one bearing the signature of one of the accused, Karl Steiner. It is impossible to determine whether this man even exists.

2. Every dossier compiled by the inquest commission must contain an accurate record of the interrogation of the accused. This was not done in the case of Karl Steiner. Instead of a verbatim record, explanations are given to the effect that the accused refused to make a deposition. These statements have not been signed by the accused Karl Steiner.

3. According to the documents submitted, the accused, Josef Berger, went on a protest hunger strike for sixty-three days. The prisoner was kept alive by force-feeding. In his case, as in Karl Steiner's, a regular inquest could not be conducted.

For the above reasons, the verdict of the Special Tribunal of the Krasnoyarsk region cannot be ratified. The dossier on the cases of Karl Steiner, Josef Berger, and Georg Biletzki is being returned for a renewed inquest by the inquest commission of the NKVD of Norilsk.

> Chairman of the Supreme Court of the U.S.S.R.
> [signature illegible]

After perusing the dossier, I sat immobile in my chair, amazed that I was still alive. Three powerful agencies—the NKVD of Norilsk, the Public Prosecutor's office, and the Special Tribunal—had tried to murder me and my friends, and they had not succeeded. How could this have happened? The Supreme Court had overturned their verdicts. Was it conceivable that a sense of justice had swayed them at the last moment?

The Supreme Court of the U.S.S.R. was nothing other than a branch of the NKVD, as were the Public Prosecutors and Special Tribunals. So why had they gone against the first three verdicts? I could think of only one plausible explanation: among the thousands of death sentences that were pronounced every day by the various "judiciary" agencies and sent to Moscow for approval, some verdicts had to be annulled. It was technically impossible for the Supreme Court to subject this vast flood of dossiers to more than the most cursory examination. They had to content themselves, therefore, with skimming off the most blatantly mismanaged cases. My refusal to testify and Berger's hunger strike had earned us the status of special cases requiring closer examination. By ordering a new inquest, the Supreme Court gave the NKVD leeway to keep us locked up in the camp for a long time.

The interrogator did not disturb me while I read; he seemed to be engrossed in his work. I was able to think. He didn't look in my direction until I told him I was finished. "Have you read it all?" he asked.

"I read everything I was interested in," I said.

"Do you have any comment?"

"Yes. Please tell me one thing: how is it possible for high Soviet officials to pronounce the death penalty at the drop of a hat against people who haven't committed any crimes?"

"We're in the middle of a war, we can't afford to fool around. Even minor crimes have to punished severely."

"Even in wartime, you can't just arrest anyone you please and pass out death sentences at random."

"Well, at any rate, your case is settled; you don't have to fear getting shot. You'll get ten years, and once the war's over and we've beaten Hitler, maybe you'll be amnestied." Gisayev handed me a sheet of paper with a printed statement that the inquest into my case was closed. I signed it.

I was in prison for another week. On a Monday morning in July 1943, the guard came into my cell and, without calling me by name, told me to gather up my stuff and come along. My "stuff" consisted of a towel, a toothbrush, and a bread bag. I bade my comrades farewell and left.

The guard led me into the prison office, where the prison warden Sukhardin greeted me. "So you've finally succeeded in slipping away! I was looking forward to the day when I could put you up against the wall."

"I guess you like to kill people."

"I can assure you, with a fascist such as you, my hand wouldn't shake. It would give me the greatest pleasure to shoot you in the neck right now."

"As a former communist, I cannot understand how a member of the party can be so bloodthirsty."

"Yes, it gives me pleasure to kill the likes of you."

In the meantime, other prisoners had been brought into the office. Then we had to line up in the yard. Each prisoner had to answer when his name was called; then we marched off. A detachment of soldiers took charge of us at the gate. Five minutes later, we arrived at the office of the second camp section. Each of us was given a meal ticket for lunch. The official told us we could move around freely and would have to be back at the office by five o'clock.

I knew the second camp section well, having lived there for two years. I decided to visit the barracks one by one to see if I could find any old friends and acquaintances. Most of my foreign friends were in the ninth section, but perhaps I would find some of my Russian friends. The camp was almost empty, since everyone was at work. Only the sick and those who had worked the night shift were home.

One of the old acquaintances I found was Batlan, who worked the night shift in the shoemaker's shop. It was pitch-dark in the barracks; the windows were covered with a thick layer of ice. A single candle burned at one end of the long room. After a few steps, I bumped into an iron stove; the noise awakened the man on barracks duty, who had been sleeping next to the stove. He demanded to know what I was looking for. I asked if Batlan lived here.

"Up there, the second from the left."

My eyes had gotten used to the dark by now, and I found my friend. He was sleeping. I pondered for a while whether to wake him. I was reluctant to do so, but I was afraid I would not have another opportunity to see him. I quietly called his name; he kept snoring. I decided to let him sleep, returned to the man on duty, and asked him when Batlan usually woke up. The man was very irritated by my questions, but I did find out that Batlan would get up around noon to pick up his meal in the kitchen. So I decided to come back later.

I went to all the other barracks, but found no familiar faces.

I had a meal ticket, but no bowl. I went to the kitchen window and asked the cook to lend me a bowl. He gave me a rude answer. I went to the nearest barracks to ask the man on duty there for a bowl. He was busy scrubbing the floor. I waited a few minutes until he was done, and then made my request.

"You look familiar," he said. "Where have I seen you before?"

"I used to be in this section. We probably ran into each other back then," I said.

"What's your name?"

I told him.

"So you're Steiner?"

"Yes."

"It's impossible. Weren't you arrested shortly after the beginning of the war?"

"Yes, I just got out of prison."

"They sure know how to change a person! I wouldn't have recognized you if you hadn't told me your name."

He gazed at me, full of curiosity. It turned out that we had spent a long time in the same barracks. He was a railroad worker from Leningrad. He had joined a revolutionary group in 1912 and actively participated in the Revolution; then he became the stationmaster of the October Station of the Leningrad railroad. In 1937, he was arrested for "planning the assassination of Stalin." He was crippled by his interrogators and was unable to work when he arrived in the camp. That's why he was working as a barracks janitor. The old man took my coupon, went to the kitchen, and brought me soup and gruel. He also gave me a piece of his own bread. I ate my meal quickly to make sure I didn't miss Batlan.

I found him washing himself with water out of a tin can. Batlan, too, was shaken by my appearance. I realized then how badly my health had been affected by the two years behind bars. Batlan went to get his food and insisted on sharing it with me. It was the first day in a long time that I had had enough to eat. After my friend returned, he led me into another barracks, where I found another acquaintance, Plotnikov, the former party secretary of Dnepropetrovsk. The secretary of the Dnepropetrovsk regional section, Hatayevich, had been shot as the alleged leader of a Trotskyite organization; after that, Plotnikov was arrested on charges of having belonged to Hatayevich's organization, and had been given a fifteen-year sentence. He had been my brigadier in the camp for a while. Once again, I was offered food; Plotnikov had recently received a package from his aged mother in Alma-Ata. The package contained lard and American canned meat. Plotnikov gave me two portions of bread and a piece of lard to take with me.

The moment I stepped out of Plotnikov's barracks, I felt ill. I had cramps and nausea. I had eaten too much after a long period of undernourishment. I sat down; after a while, I felt better.

It was time to report to the office. Even though no one told me where I was going, I knew I would be put in the ninth section.

IN THE NINTH CAMP SECTION

By six o'clock, all the prisoners who were going to be transferred to the ninth section—i.e., the sixty-odd people who had been released from the prison with me, and about twenty others—had assembled in front of the camp office. We had to walk almost four kilometers, past the camp administration building and the barracks and staff quarters of the camp guards, past the central garage (a large stone building with room for about eight hundred vehicles), and past Dolgoe Ozero (Long Lake). Now we could see the buildings of the ninth section and the large brick factory. We were walking slowly, for the commander of the escort troops, realizing that many of us were incapable of walking faster, didn't spur us on, as he might have. We made two rest stops on the way.

It was ten in the evening when we arrived in the ninth camp section, but it was still light outside; it was the time of year when the sun didn't set. We had to wait a long time for the gate to open. Inside, the camp officials were expecting us. The chief overseer checked our names and birth dates against a list and told each prisoner the number of his new brigade. The first ones to be called were all put in the same brigade. When my turn came, the chief overseer at first gave me the same number as the others. Then he changed his mind and said: "No, you'll go to a different brigade. You're too weak to work in the gravel pit."

After conferring with his assistant, he said to me: "You'll work with the twenty-first brigade, barracks 9."

Barracks 9 was made of wood, as most of the barracks here were. I opened the creaking door. Everyone was asleep. I looked for a place to lie down; there was none. As I stood there holding my little bundle, I heard a voice behind me: "Pst, pst!" I turned around. A man was gesturing to me from one of the lower bunks. When I stood before him, he asked me what I wanted. I told him the chief overseer had sent me here.

"I'm on barracks duty, but where am I supposed to put you? You can see for yourself—there's no room." He thought about it a little more; then he stood up and went searching along the row of bunks. Finally, he shook several men awake and told them to move closer together. They grumbled and cursed under their breath. Only one of them moved up a little; the others went on sleeping.

"Squeeze in there," the man said.

I took off my coat and my shoes and crept onto the bunk. I was virtually lying on top of my neighbors. Little by little, they made room; I could feel the hard boards. I placed my shoes and bread bag under my head, covered myself with my coat, and tried to think of sleeping, for it was late and we would be sent to work early in the morning. Suddenly I felt something falling on my face. I looked up at the boards of the upper bunk—they were swarming with bedbugs! I had slept in vermin-infested rooms before, but I had never seen anything like this. I squashed the one that had fallen on me, but others quickly followed. I soon had to give up trying to get rid of them. I saw the other prisoners wiping them off their faces in their sleep. I didn't sleep a wink that night.

Those who weren't awakened by the gong were shaken out of sleep by their neighbors. The men next to me were surprised by my presence. Most of the prisoners went into the front room, where there was a washbasin; others went directly to the kitchen with their tin cans. I had to rush to the office to get my food coupons. With difficulty, I managed to find the guard in charge of these matters; he gave me the food coupons and told me I wouldn't get bread until the evening. When I returned to the barracks, I discovered that my little bread bag had been stolen.

The second gong sounded: *Na razvod*—To work. The prisoners came out from all the barracks onto the *lineika*, the yard, and lined up in rows of five. Each brigade formed its own group. I reported to the brigadier of the twenty-first brigade and stepped into line.

Then the chief overseer, who had told me to join this brigade, came along. "Where is Steiner?" I heard him ask.

"That must be the new one," the brigadier said.

I stepped out of line.

"Go to the ninth brigade," the overseer said.

I asked him to please let me stay with the twenty-first. He said he could see I wasn't fit to do hard labor, but he couldn't do anything about it, he'd gotten orders "from above" to use me only for hard labor. This made me despondent, but I didn't have time to think. The gate was opening and the brigades were beginning to march out. I hurried to join up with the ninth brigade; a detachment of armed guards took charge of us outside the gate.

The walk to work seemed endless. Lack of sleep and the exertion of running around to get my coupons and then my breakfast made it difficult for me to keep up. Several times, I was rudely scolded by a soldier for walking too slowly. When we finally arrived, the commander of the guard made a careful inspection of the workplace. Sometimes people who sympathized with the prisoners' plight would leave bread for them, and this was not allowed.

The guards surrounded the work site. The commander checked to see if the signs saying *Zapretnaya zona*—Forbidden area—were in order. Then he gave the order to start work. The foreman came out of the shack that served as an office and gave the brigadier his instructions. They were always the same orders: the prisoners performed the same work every day.

Our job was to level a hill. The prisoners dug holes and filled them with explosives, after which specialists would set up the detonators. During the noon break, we were removed some three hundred meters away from the site while the charges went off. After that, we had to apply pickaxes and crowbars to the chunks of frozen earth that had been torn loose by the explosions, load the earth onto wheelbarrows, and drop it into a landfill some two hundred meters away. Every wheelbarrow had a number; a prisoner stood by the landfill recording the number of times each wheelbarrow was emptied. At the end of the day, a tally was made, and the result determined the amount of bread and warm food each prisoner was entitled to.

All the others had gone to their customary place of work; I was still waiting for my instructions. The foreman looked at me. "How old are you?" he asked.

"Thirty-five."

"Thirty-five? I thought you were seventy. Are you sick?"

I told him where I came from.

"What are we going to do with him?" he asked the brigadier.

"I've been wondering myself. He was almost unable to walk up here."

"Can you write?" asked the foreman.

"Yes."

"You'll do the tallying."

I sat down on a broken wheelbarrow, holding a blackboard on which the wheelbarrow numbers were recorded. Every time a wheelbarrow passed by, I made a mark under the corresponding number. On the way home, I was no longer as desperate as I had been in the morning. I thanked God for leading me to good people who had given me easy work to do.

Ninety percent of the brigade were Germans; there were only a few Russians. Some of the Germans came from Germany; others were members of the German minority in Russia. On the very first evening, several acquaintances from the brigade asked me to give them a few extra points. I promised some of them to do so.

My first concern after work was finding a food bowl. I found one fairly quickly. A member of my brigade had an extra bowl which he was willing to sell me for two portions of bread, which I could pay off in four installments.

Just two days later, the foreman asked me how come everyone was meeting the quota and even exceeding it when the landfill was still half empty. I assured him that I was keeping exact records. After that, I reduced the number of extra marks I was willing to give anyone. The prisoners accused me of being heartless. After a while, I began to feel personally responsible for the small food rations people were getting. I started counting more "generously." Once again, the foreman approached me, saying: "Dear friend, I can see that you have more pity for others than you have for yourself. If this goes on, I'll have to replace you and you'll be pushing a wheelbarrow. I'll give you one more chance."

I promised to mend my ways. Realizing that my days as a record-keeper were numbered, I went to the office that same evening and asked the chief overseer to transfer me to an easier job. He repeated that he was very sorry not to be able to help me. He suggested I turn to medical services and ask them to request a less taxing job for me on account of my weakened condition.

I went to the infirmary and spoke to Dr. Maier, a portly Volga German with a wreath of gray hair on the sides of his large balding head. He had been arrested in 1934 and had been sentenced to ten years as a "German spy." He had performed hard physical work for a long time and was now employed in the infirmary because there was a lack of doctors. I started to take off my clothes to show him my emaciated condition, but he waved his hand, saying: "Don't bother. I can see you're in bad shape."

Dr. Maier promised to send a report to the camp commander requesting my transfer to another brigade. I thanked him. As I was leaving, he held me back. "You'll be getting *tsyngotnoe pitanie* as of the first of next month." That was a special diet to ward off scurvy, consisting of sauerkraut and carrots with a few drops of oil, and a quarter of a liter of kvass, a fermented beverage which was produced in the camp kitchen out of bread flour and hops.

I kept my record-keeper's job for another two days. On the third day, as I sat down on the broken wheelbarrow with my blackboard, the brigadier came along with another prisoner. I had to push a wheelbarrow now. I managed to get the first five loads to the landfill without any mishap, but by the sixth trip I was so exhausted that I was no longer able to hold up the wheelbarrow. It tipped over, spilling half its contents, and only with a great effort was I able to push the rest all the way to the landfill. Another man took over the wheelbarrow now. My job was to unload it. My friends repaid the favors I had done them as record-keeper by tolerating my incompetence and sparing me the usual reproaches.

I was glad when the day was over. I returned to the camp supported by two comrades. I went immediately to the infirmary. A doctor put a thermometer under my arm. My temperature was normal, so I had to go to work the next day! I considered refusing, but that would only have landed me in the punishment cell, after which I would have to work even harder and be given less bread into the bargain. No, that wasn't the right approach. I went to the camp commander to ask him for lighter labor. The commander was not there. When I opened the door, his deputy shouted at me: "What do you want this time?"

"This is my first time here."

"There was another rattlebones here yesterday; he looked just like you."

I complained that the work was too hard for me.

"What's your name, what's your paragraph?"

I told him my name and the law under which I was sentenced.

"For your ilk, all we've got is *tachka* and *kirka*—wheelbarrow and pickax."

I realized it was senseless to argue with him. *"Do svidaniya,"* I said, and left.

It was ten o'clock, and the gong was being sounded for bedtime. I went to the barracks, not to sleep, but to feed the bedbugs, which attacked me before I had settled down on the bunk. As I lay there hunting bedbugs, I thought about what was in store for me in the morning. Perhaps I should work as hard as I could and exhaust myself so thoroughly that I would finally break down and depart these miseries forever. But no, that was too simple. I had to survive. At long last, I fell asleep. I slept past the morning gong and had to be awakened by the man on duty.

I hurried to the kitchen to get my breakfast. I felt weak and wondered if I would be able to work at all. I was standing on line just before the gate opened when Dr. Maier passed by. I greeted him. He was surprised to see me there. He came closer and asked whether I hadn't been given easier work to do. He told me to come and see him after work. That encouraged me. The march to work didn't seem quite as long and tiring as usual. I worked as hard as I could, to avoid angering my comrades. During the noon break, I told them I would be seeing Dr. Maier that evening and that he might help me get into another brigade.

"I hope that happens soon," one of my comrades said. "Otherwise, we'll be living on reduced rations forever. This is the third day we've failed to meet the quota because of you."

Right after we returned to the camp, I went to see Dr. Maier. He told me he had put in a request with the labor section and had been told I would be given easier work in a few days. I felt like crying. I had hoped not to have to go through another day like this one, and now . . . The doctor tried to console me, but I couldn't hear what he was saying. All I could think of was the next day.

As I was leaving, I ran into the nurse who worked with Dr. Maier. She knew me from my first visit.

"How are you?" she asked.

"Excellent. If I felt any better, I wouldn't be able to stand it."

"Are you still doing that hard work?"

"Unfortunately, yes."

"What does Dr. Maier say?"

"He's trying to help me, but the people in the office aren't exactly rushing things."

"I'm sure Dr. Maier will help you. He said he would the last time you were here to see him."

"I know, Dr. Maier is a good man, but when I think of tomorrow, I just want to die."

"Wait a minute, let me talk to the doctor."

After a few minutes, she came back and asked me to follow her back into the doctor's office. "You won't have to work for the next three days. In the meantime, I'll do everything I can to have you transferred to an easier job," Dr. Maier said.

I didn't know how to thank him and the nurse. Three days of rest! Now I had time to get to know the ninth section a little better; usually I was so tired I wouldn't even think of visiting another barracks. The first man I visited was Sasha Weber, who was working as an assistant book-keeper in the brick factory. As I've mentioned, our relations hadn't been the most cordial, because of our very different views concerning Stalin's regime. Sasha greeted me very warmly, which led me to suspect that he had changed his opinion. I wasn't mistaken; Sasha almost immediately let me know how he felt about the "beloved leaders"—he called them bandits. He was especially outraged at the Russian leadership's chauvinistic treatment of the German emigrants and the Volga Germans.

He brought us some *kipyatok*. We sat down on the bunk, drank and talked until the gong sounded for bedtime. Before my three days were over, the chief overseer told me that I was being transferred to a brigade that worked in the brick factory. I would be moving to another barracks as well. I noticed the difference between the two barracks immediately: there were far fewer bedbugs here; you could sleep undisturbed.

The brick factory was near the barracks, so we could go to work without escort. Surrounding the factory were several watchtowers. My job was to wheel a cart full of unfired bricks fresh from the press, unload them in the drying room, and pile them up. It was strenuous work, since the quota was very high, but it was bearable, especially since I was spared the long march to and from work. I asked those who had been working here for a while what the *paika* was, the bread ration; they assured me that it was pretty good in most instances. Most of the prisoners here were women.

The brick factory divided the ninth section in half. The women's barracks were on one side of the factory; the men's on the other.

LOVE IN THE CAMP

The women who worked alongside men were more attentive to their appearance. They wore makeup and kept their garments clean; some of them wore clothes sent to them by relatives. Men from other sections often visited ours on account of the women. These encounters usually led to little more than harmless flirtations, but there were also more intimate relationships. The warmth and darkness of the drying rooms were ideally suited for this purpose, even though you had to lie on a stone floor.

Despite frequent checks and severe punishment, sexual activity was a daily occurrence. The extensive factory rooms provided many hiding places for women who had been imprisoned as prostitutes and continued practicing their profession in camp. The payment usually consisted of a piece of bread, more rarely a piece of lard, or sugar. The prostitutes' clients were cooks, shoemakers, tailors, and other *lagernye pridurki*, as the privileged prisoners were called. The majority of the prisoners did not have the means to afford themselves a prostitute; nor were they plagued by sexual desire, despite the fact that there were many young men among them. Once in a while, you would hear about a tragic love affair, no different from those that occur under ordinary conditions; some of them ended in suicide or murder.

After a month in the brick factory, I felt much better, though I was still weak. Most of the male workers here were physically weak prisoners of the third category.

A considerable proportion of the many millions of Soviet prisoners were women. There were several women's camps in Norilsk, and several camps containing both male and female prisoners. Usually the women's barracks were separated from the men's by barbed wire, and men were not permitted to enter. As in the men's camps, politicals and criminals were interned together, and by all accounts, the female politicals suffered much more than the men did from constant contact with the criminals—prostitutes, thieves, robbers, and murderers.

Despite the strict prohibitions, certain men visited the women's barracks every day, joined the women in their bunks, and slept with them in plain view of all the other prisoners. These were criminals who were in good standing with the camp administration. Some of the camp policemen kept a regular harem. A few prisoners enjoyed ongoing relationships, and these were not only tolerated but welcomed by the camp administrators, for it gave them an additional means of control: the least transgression could be punished by an enforced separation.

Certain workplaces also provided an opportunity for contact between the men and the women—especially projects that brought men and women together in an open space fenced in with barbed wire. The brick factory was one such site.

The commander of the ninth section had devised a special punishment for couples who were discovered: they had to clean the latrines after the day's work, load the frozen excrement on a cart, and get it out of the camp. Every evening, curious onlookers would gather to watch this spectacle. Usually the punished prisoners bravely pulled their cart or sled, without any tears.

Occasionally, a couple would form such a deep attachment that the inevitable separation came with all the force of tragedy.

Needless to say, the political prisoners, men as well as women, rarely involved themselves in love affairs—for moral reasons, but also because they were subject to more stress and suffering, and because they had to fear for the fate of their relatives. Most of the men had left wives and children behind and knew how difficult their lives were—since the wives and children of political convicts were regarded as "enemies of the people" and were treated accordingly. This term can have little meaning for someone who has not felt its harsh impact on his own life. The women were dismissed from their jobs; the children thrown out of school. They had to leave the big cities even when they weren't exiled, since usually their apartments were taken away and their possessions confiscated. Relatives rarely dared offer them refuge, as that would expose them to the risk of arrest. Thousands of women divorced their jailed husbands. Every day, the newspapers carried notices by women disowning their husbands, children disowning their parents, because they had been branded "enemies of the people." For these reasons, political prisoners were less inclined to engage in amorous adventures; this was as true of the women as it was of the men. Of course, there were exceptions, due mainly to the physical hardships prisoners were subjected to.

Male prisoners who had privileged positions and could afford to give away food presented a great temptation for some female prisoners. Prostitution, too, was widespread. At the time I was in Norilsk, there were always women who were willing to sell themselves for a little food. The price of their services usually consisted of one day's bread ration, about seven hundred grams. Often, these women were cheated of their wages: they would be shown a piece of bread or some other morsel of food, which would later be withheld. Once I met a young teenage girl in front of the camp's fire station. She was crying bitterly. I asked her what was wrong; she said the cleanup man, Vasyka, had cheated her of her payment.

My friend Sasha Weber, who was also employed in the brick factory, met a lab technician named Ida there, a Volga German. Her husband was shot as an "enemy of the people" and she was given six years in camp. She and Sasha fell in love. In 1947, Sasha was released and continued working in the brick factory as a free laborer, so as not to abandon Ida, who had to serve another five years. In 1949, Sasha was arrested again and given another ten-year sentence. Ida was released in 1952. Now it was she who waited for Sasha to be released. But Sasha died in 1953.

The women had to work as hard as the men. In this respect, the Soviet government applied the principle of sexual equality in a perfectly literal way. Most of the women in Norilsk were employed in the brick factory, and their labor included digging out and loading clay (this was extremely hard work) and transporting sand and gravel. Unloading fifty-kilo sacks of cement was considered light labor for women.

It made no difference whether these prisoners had been peasants or office workers, doctors or university professors before their arrest. The quotas were the same for all. The hard work and miserable conditions destroyed some women both morally and physically. There were women who at first always dressed neatly and made an effort to look attractive, then gradually stopped taking care of their appearance; eventually, they could be seen disappearing into various hiding places along with a male prisoner.

Many, of course, became pregnant and gave birth. Some women deliberately sought out men with the express purpose of becoming pregnant, to get relief from their hard work. The children were taken away from their mothers several weeks after they were born. Only rarely did a mother recover a child she lost in this manner.

BEFORE THE CAMP COURT

Every three months, a medical commission examined the prisoners and divided them into "categories," according to their physical condition. Everyone feared these examinations, because they could mean one's transfer to a category involving harder work. Many tried to prevent their health from improving. The fear of being put to work in the clay pit or loading heavy materials was so great that many prisoners fasted during the two or three days before the examination or smoked large amounts of makhorka until they started to tremble and lost all the color in their faces. But usually these ruses didn't help.

My period of relative rest was of short duration. One evening when I returned to my barracks from work, the man on duty told me I was to go to the office immediately. Habitual questions assailed me: What were they up to now? Was I being given new work, or did I have to account for my mediocre work performance of a few days ago? I was about to go directly to the office, but then I changed my mind and decided to eat first. Nothing pleasant could be waiting for me in the office, and I would learn the bad news soon enough. I took my bowl and went to the kitchen. They were serving pea soup, a rare treat. I asked the cook to give me a double portion of soup instead of gruel. He gave me the double portion of soup and the gruel as well; I saw this as a good omen.

I hurried back to the barracks, ate my plentiful dinner, and went to the office. The chief overseer told me that I was not to report to work the next day; instead, I should come to the office, from where I would be taken to court. I knew what awaited me there: I would be read my sentence, which had been passed long ago by the NKVD. Nevertheless, I was excited. The war situation had radically changed, with the German Army retreating on all fronts. I speculated. When my friends and I were jailed, Russia was in a desperate situation. When the war broke out, Stalin's "inspired" policies had deprived the Red Army of virtually all its generals: the most experienced military leaders—Tukhachevsky, Yakir, Blücher, and many others—had been shot in 1937. The men who commanded the Red Army, with only a few exceptions, were creatures who knew how to lick their master's boots but were ignorant of warfare. It was mainly thanks to the large supplies of war materials, food, medicine, and other aid from the United States that the situation had improved.

Now I might hope that the regime could afford to do without scapegoats for all the unhappiness Stalin's policies had brought the Russian people. But once again I came to realize that Russia cannot be measured by the same criteria that apply to normal European circumstances. The trial took place.

I slept very little that night, spending most of it in thoughts of the next day. I got up at five, as usual, washed, and regretted not being able to shave. My trousers were a patchwork; I went to the barracks next door and borrowed a better pair of pants from a friend. I wanted to make a neat appearance in court. I arrived at the prison office a few minutes before eight. An overseer took me to the guardhouse, and from there I was taken to court by two armed guards.

It was an unusually beautiful fall day, and we were walking at a leisurely pace. The soldiers were smoking, and I had time to think and prepare my answers to the judge's questions. I looked forward to seeing Josef and Georg. I was also curious to observe the witnesses' behavior. I toyed with the hope that one of the witnesses would feel a twinge of conscience and take back his mendacious statements. But then I told myself that such things could not happen in the U.S.S.R., that the NKVD only employed witnesses they were very sure of.

We arrived at a one-story wooden building. One of the soldiers went in and returned after a few minutes. I was led into the hallway. Josef was there. The soldiers stayed outside. Roshankovsky was standing by a corner and didn't dare look in our direction. Josef and I greeted each other with a handshake. A few minutes later, Georg was brought in; his escort stayed outside, too. The three of us could talk freely. A second witness was also brought in, the engineer Yerus, who was to testify against Josef. Unlike Roshankovsky, Yerus approached and greeted us, took some salt fish and bread from a little pouch, and offered it to us. We sat down on the bench and had breakfast.

The court secretary appeared in the hallway several times to see if everyone had arrived. We waited until twelve; then the secretary told the escort that the trial was being postponed until the day after next because some of the witnesses hadn't shown up. When we came two days later, Yerus was the only witness present; Roshankovsky was absent. Once again, the trial was postponed, this time for a week.

When we came to the court barracks the following week, we knew that this time the trial would take place regardless of how many witnesses were there. We were led into the courtroom and had to sit down in front. The witnesses remained in another room. Two soldiers stood at attention to the right and left of our bench, with their fingers on the triggers of their submachine guns. Soldiers also guarded the door.

A side door opened, and one of the soldiers called out: "Stand up!" We stood up. The members of the court came in, led by the notorious Gorokhov and followed by a civilian, a man in NKVD uniform, and a young girl, the stenographer. The trial was held without a prosecutor or defense attorney. Even if we had been entitled to a defense, no Soviet lawyer would have dared defend a criminal accused under Article 58.

We sat down. The members of the court took their seats on the podium behind a table that was covered with a red cloth. While Gorokhov leafed through his dossiers, I observed him with interest: this was the man who was so rightly hated by the prisoners in Norilsk. I had noticed his limp when he came in. Now I saw a large hump on the back of his small, thin body. His face was covered with pockmarks, and his left eye had been ineptly replaced by a prosthesis. This was how I had imagined Quasimodo when I was a boy.

Gorokhov mumbled something, presumably the routine phrase that opens a trial. Josef was the first to be questioned. When asked whether he pleaded guilty, he answered "No." I was next.

"Do you plead guilty to having engaged in counterrevolutionary fascist agitation among the prisoners of the Norilsk camp?"

"That is an invention of the NKVD. Neither I nor my friends are fascists or counterrevolutionaries," I replied quietly.

The last one to be questioned was Georg. When Gorokhov asked if he had any objections to the composition of the court, he replied: "I refuse to recognize the validity of a court made up of NKVD officers."

Gorokhov turned to the right, then to the left. We could see the other judges' mouths moving. Then he turned to us and announced: "The court rejects the objection against its composition."

Next, the witnesses were questioned. Gorokhov read off the contents of eight small sheets of paper. Each one explained why a particular witness had not come to court: one man was sick; the other dead; the third had been transferred to another camp. Only two witnesses were present. One of them was Larionov, who repeated word for word what he had said about me during our confrontation.

I put a question to Larionov: "How is it that you were released after serving your sentence, while thousands of others did not have this privilege?" Gorokhov interrupted and said that my question was out of order.

The second witness testified that he had been in a cell with Berger and had heard him engage in counterrevolutionary talk with other prisoners. Then Yerus came in as a third witness—he had arrived late. Gorokhov asked him several quick questions, but Yerus confirmed only one accusation: that, according to Josef, most prisoners condemned for counterrevolutionary activity were innocent.

Josef had the final word. He characterized the witnesses as NKVD agents and pointed out that they had appeared five to six times before this same court during the past two years. Gorokhov interrupted Josef and forbade him to "insult" the witnesses. Josef went on to point out the absurdity of accusing him, a Jew, of anxiously looking forward to Hitler's victory. Surely the NKVD was well aware of the fate that would await him if the Germans won.

I was the next to speak. I concentrated mainly on Larionov and

Roshankovsky, the chief witnesses against me. Gorokhov let me talk for a while, and interrupted me only by impatiently tapping the table with his pencil. But finally, when I argued that not every criticism of the regime was fascist, that there were other political movements in the world besides communism and fascism—for instance, in the Western countries presently allied with Russia—Gorokhov shouted: "That is enough!" He stood up. So did the attendant judges and the stenographer; and together they left the room.

They returned after a half hour and Gorokhov stated the judgment. All three of us were found equally guilty of having organized a counter-revolutionary group in the camp and of spreading a defeatist atmosphere among the prisoners. We were each sentenced to ten years in camp and to a five-year suspension of our civil rights, according to Article 58, paragraphs 10 and 11. Finally, Gorokhov informed us of our right to appeal the sentences.

I took leave of Josef and Georg and returned to the ninth camp section.

THE STATE THAT CAN'T BE FOUND ON ANY MAP

Back in the barracks, the man on duty told me that Sasha Weber had been looking for me and wanted to see me right away. It was still too early to get my dinner, so I went to visit Sasha in his barracks. He rushed up to me. "How did it go?"

"As you see, I didn't get a death sentence."

"That's the main thing; you'll be absolved in due time."

"I'm sure I'll have to serve those ten years, every one of them."

We sat down on the bunk. Sasha had saved my lunch for me. After I had eaten, he asked: "Do you still think nothing will change after Germany loses the war?"

"As long as Stalin's in power, the camps and prisons are going to be full of millions of people, and we'll be among them."

"I wonder why they're doing this. Why is it necessary to deprive so many people of their freedom? I can't help thinking that this is a childhood disease of the new society."

"This is not a childhood disease; it's the society itself."

"In a socialist state, this can only be a transitional phase," he said.

"Sasha, do you still refuse to understand that after Lenin's death and after Stalin's accession to power everything socialist in this country has been stamped out? It began with the dissolution of the Society of Old Bolsheviks and ended with the deliberate wiping out of every trace of genuine socialism."

"But why? It would be so much better to let people work in freedom. That's the way to make use of them, not grinding them down till they're wrecks."

"A lot of people get to be wrecks here, but you can be sure they bring in a handsome profit."

"Do you really think the whole idea is to get cheap labor into this wasteland?"

"It's certainly not the only reason. Another motive is social control, keeping the whole population in check by terror. Under ordinary conditions, terror has a damaging effect on the economy, but Stalin has come up with a totally new economic system. There has never been anything like it in the history of man."

"You mean a kind of serfdom?"

"No, I don't. Serfdom was about as different from this system as the first steam engine from a locomotive. It was primitive and comparatively humane, while the Stalinist system represents barbarity in its most modern and technically perfect form."

"Most people believe that forced labor is not profitable. You don't think so?"

"Whoever says that the labor of Soviet prisoners is not profitable does not understand the significance of these camps. They are the very basis of Soviet economy. Not only are the camps profitable; they're practically the only enterprises that bring in any gain. Most of the so-called free industrial plants are producing at a loss, and let's not even talk about the farms. Billions of rubles are spent every year in subsidies to industry and agriculture. Where does this money come from? It's very simple: it's the clean profit from the camps."

"You can claim that, but how can you prove it?" Sasha said, shaking his head.

"Let's start with Norilsk. To house and feed a hundred thousand prisoners, the Soviet government spends two hundred and forty rubles a month per prisoner: that includes the cost of administration, supervision, etc. The prisoners' food is supplied by the labor of prisoners in agricultural camps. The fish we get here is caught by prisoners in Murmansk. The coal we heat our barracks with was mined by prisoners. The railroad that transports coal and food to our camp was built and is operated by prisoners. The clothes we wear were sewn by prisoners. Even the material they're made of and the thread they're sewn with were produced in the women's camps of Potyma and Yaya. For the little bit of food we get, we produce thousands of tons of nickel, copper, hundreds of tons of cobalt, not to mention uranium. Most of these products are sold on the foreign market for millions of dollars. And still there are people who compare this system with serfdom and claim that Soviet prison labor is not profitable!"

"All right, Karl, you've convinced me as far as Norilsk is concerned. But what about the hundreds of camps in other parts of the Soviet Union?"

"Do you mean to suggest that Norilsk is an exception and that the other camps don't produce any gain?"

"Yes, that's what I'm saying."

"Very well, I'll give you other examples. Let's start with Kolyma. You remember Gundarov, who was in Kolyma for six years. You remember what he told us. Kolyma is in the extreme northeast of the Soviet Union. A few years ago, there were no Europeans there, just like here in Norilsk. The only people there were nomads who raised reindeer. Now there's a gigantic camp there with one and a half million prisoners. Most of them work in gold mines. Do you really think running this camp is not profitable? Do you want some other examples? Very well. In Vorkuta, the prisoners work in a coal mine. This coal is of better quality than the coal from the Donets Basin. It's loaded on freight cars that travel two thousand kilometers. That railroad was built by prisoners. Another camp, Embaneft—where they drill for oil: the installations were built by prisoners, and most of the workers in the refineries are prisoners. Or take forestry—everyone knows that raw lumber and boards and especially railroad ties are among the most important Soviet exports. Wood brings in huge amounts of dollars, pounds sterling, and other currencies. And who are the woodcutters? Surely you know that ninety-five percent of all the wood is cut and processed by prisoners. Most of the sawmills in Siberia, in the Urals, and in northern Russia are manned by prisoners. Every one of those countless laborers costs the state two hundred and forty rubles a month, and the labor's even cheaper in European Russia."

"You're talking about industries that are already established and capable of bringing their product to market. I can see they're very profitable. But what about the cost of developing the great construction sites—the big railroads like the BAM (Lake Baikal–Amur) line or the southern Siberian line that reaches all the way from Chelyabinsk via Abakan to the Mongolian border; or the great northern line along the coast of the Arctic Sea from Vorkuta to Igarka, which is supposed to be extended all the way to Yakutia; or the Tayshet–Bratsk–Lena–Komsomolsk line; and lots of others. And add to these a dozen hydroelectric plants that are being built along the banks of Siberian rivers."

"That is another matter. Now we're not talking about profitability but about financing."

"That's right."

"Well, you might say that the prisoners finance their own constructions."

"What? That's ridiculous. You must be joking!"

"No, I'm serious. The prisoners finance these constructions—not totally, but in part. I'll show you how it works. Take the building of the BAM line: a million and a half prisoners were put to work there. Now, as soon as a prisoner arrives, the camp administration hands him a postcard with the following printed message: 'Dear ———, I am in good health and am sending you my new address: BAM, P.O. Box ———. Please send a little money every month to this address, so that I can buy food and tobacco at the store. With best wishes, ———.' All the prisoner has to do is fill in the blanks and add the date and his relatives' address. Now, you can be sure that most relatives will do whatever they can to send their unfortunate family member a little something once a month, even if they themselves are very poor. After little more than a week, sums of fifty to a thousand rubles come pouring in. But only a maximum of fifty rubles a month is ever given out to the prisoners, and even that only rarely, because the conditions are so impossibly hard: you have to meet the quota a hundred percent, no less, for three months in a row. If once in a while a prisoner succeeds in earning his fifty rubles, he'll write to his relatives, asking for more. Most relatives don't wait for a receipt verifying that the money they sent got into the right hands. Since the prisoners are only rarely allowed to write letters home, the only sign of life the relatives get is, more often than not, the postal receipt, which is usually signed by the camp accountant, not the prisoner. That is how hundreds of millions of rubles are collected by the camp administration.

"That's just one way of doing it. I'll show you another way in which the prisoners help finance giant constructions like railroads. Every year, as you know, the workers and employees of one or several industrial or agricultural centers will 'request' from the Soviet government the opportunity to increase their contribution to the building of socialism. Of course, the Soviet government cannot resist such an appeal and hastens to accept the workers' sacrifice: 'voluntary' forfeit of one month's salary. The sum is subtracted from the regular salary in ten installments. Now, Sasha, you know that prisoners also 'voluntarily' sign these gift certificates over to the state. Since they don't have a regular income, they sign away the money that is sent them by their relatives. This amounts to millions of rubles a year."

"I'm almost ready to concede, but . . ."

"Wait, that's not all. You know the standard final phrase every time someone's sentenced to prison or camp: forfeit of his entire estate. The people condemned by Soviet courts of law are not millionaires, but almost everyone owns something—furniture, clothes, a clock, a picture, jewelry. And you know how thoroughly the NKVD proceeds in these matters: they're not ashamed to cart away a pair of old felt boots. Some of these objects 'disappear,' of course, but hundreds of millions flow into the state treasury."

"I think you're exaggerating," Sasha said.

"I'll prove it to you. In all major cities, and especially in Moscow, there are stores where you can buy diamonds, gold broaches, rings and chains, paintings, porcelain, rugs, even old icons. The Soviet Union makes millions of rubles a year in dollars, pounds, and francs from the sale of these treasures. Where do you think all this stuff comes from? Most of it is confiscated property. And that's not counting the nice sums of money in cash that are confiscated at every arrest."

"It's a very clever system."

"System? That's putting it too simply. It's an actual political state, but one that can't be found on any map. The name of this state is Gulag— *Glavnoe upravlenie lagerei*—central administration of camps. Its inhabitants—twenty-one million, according to a 1938 census—are all prisoners. They are supervised and guarded by eight hundred thousand 'free' employees."

"What's the structure of Gulag?"

"You don't know that? You, a former Minister of State!"

"Don't be surprised. Only three or four Ministers knew about this besides Stalin. And no one dared ask any questions."

"The structure is very similar to that of the regular government. Only the names are different. Gulag has as many ministerial branches as any normal government: there's a forestry Gulag, a Gulag of roads and bridges, a Gulag of nonferrous metals, a mining Gulag, and so on. Each of these sections has its own boss, and these leaders form a sort of Council of Ministers."

"Nobody in the world would believe this!"

"That's what's so awful about it—most people don't have any idea what's going on here. There are some foreign journalists who hang around Moscow or tour some Soviet cities for a few days, and they're the ones that inform the rest of the world about life in the Soviet Union. Some are full of praise; others are critical—but what does the criticism amount to? That Muscovites don't dress in the latest fashion, that the stores aren't well stocked, that hotels aren't as good as they might be. So what's the impression people get? At worst, that it's not as good as in some other countries, but certainly not bad. It's the same with the diplomats. You can just picture some experienced old diplomat in Moscow who's done the same job in Vienna, Berlin, Tokyo, and Rome, and he sits there writing regular reports, which his government takes at face value. And of course it's all baloney. These people haven't the faintest idea what's going on in a country they've been living in for years."

"Still . . . those kind of people aren't complete idiots," Sasha remarked. "How do you explain their ignorance?"

"They look at Russia from a foreign point of view. To really know what's going on in this country, you have to be in a situation like ours."

"But you're forgetting that some people have managed to escape from a camp and get out of the country and write about it. I remember a Pole who escaped from the Solovetsk Islands and later published a book in his country about his experiences."

"That's true. But most people don't believe it, and those who do believe it say it's an internal affair of the Soviet Union and isn't anyone else's business."

"What about the big politicians? Surely people like Churchill and Roosevelt aren't totally uninformed, even if they don't know everything?"

"I'm sure these politicians have a fundamental understanding of what is happening in Russia, but they place their country's immediate interests above the collective interest. And they don't understand that what's happening to people in Russia today can happen to people in Germany tomorrow, Hungary the day after, Poland next, and so on. In the end, England, France, and Germany could become Russian provinces."

"Do you really think so?"

"It's not inevitable. It really depends on a third force intervening in the world. You can't depend on the so-called bourgeois politicians. Most of them are mainly preoccupied with petty advantages, and the rest are simply greedy."

It was late. I returned to my barracks. The conversation with Sasha had for a short time obliterated the fact that I would be Stalin's prisoner for another ten years. I dropped myself on the bunk and spent the rest of the night with my eyes open. When I got up, I felt like a physical wreck; a headache was added later. By noon, I felt a little better; I consumed the bread I hadn't been able to eat in the morning. Several friends came to console me. They all said the same thing: "The war will be over soon. Then we'll all be let out."

I thought to myself: How good that people don't lose hope.

I had gotten accustomed to work in the brick factory. I was glad to be working inside, for the polar night was beginning, and for four months there would be no sun. Working by lamplight seemed less bleak inside than outside. Besides, the warmth made you feel less hungry.

The November holidays came and we were given two days off. On November 7, everyone had to shovel snow in the yard. On the eighth, the chief overseer came into our barracks and gave the brigadier a surprising assignment: he was to bring the entire brigade to the infirmary for a medical examination. This news affected everyone like a cold shower; I, too, hung my head low. My time of light labor in a warm room was probably coming to an end. I told myself, though, that I was still very weak and that no doctor was likely to assign me to hard labor in my condition.

In the infirmary, we were told to strip to the waist and wait in the hallway till our names were called. I observed the others to see whether they looked more fit than I did. Most of them were just skin and bones. I actually looked healthier than most. My name was called. When I stepped in, the orderly handed the head of the commission my health card.

"Do you have any physical complaints?"

"I feel very weak," I replied.

"*Vtoraya*—Second category!"

My heart sank. This meant a transfer to more strenuous labor.

The next day, the overseer came to the barracks and called out the names of several prisoners; I was one of them. We were being transferred to the railroad brigade, he said. I gathered up my possessions and went to the railroad workers' barracks.

I BECOME A RAILROAD WORKER

Our job was to keep a section of the Dudinka–Norilsk line, from kilometer 105 to the Valek station, in working order. The summer months were used for digging and terracing the earth and replacing ties; in the winter, we had to clear the tracks of snow and ice. The summer work was harder because it involved carrying tracks and ties from one place to another; but though the work itself was easier in winter, the enormous cold and the blizzards were exhausting.

There was no opportunity to warm up on the way from the brick factory to Valek. Every day, we went on this nine-kilometer trek, sometimes without a halt, and marched back the same distance after work. The long hours of exposure to the cold increased your hunger; no matter how much food you managed to get, the feeling of hunger was always there.

I performed odd jobs around the kitchen to get some extra food. After work, I would chop firewood and clear away snow in the courtyard, in exchange for a bowl of gruel or soup. Later I made a deal with the man in charge of heating: every day, I would cart coal into the kitchen from 8 p.m. until 1 a.m. For this, I received three kilos of gruel. I would stand in the shed where the coal was stored and wait for the man to tell me to start working. Once, I was so exhausted I fell asleep and would have frozen to death if my employer hadn't come to see what was keeping me outside so long.

On another occasion, he gave me a pot full of gruel after I finished working. I sat down in a corner. The pleasant warmth of the gruel spread through my body, and I fell asleep. I dreamed that someone was yanking the tin pot from my hand; I woke up and noticed, before opening my eyes, that my hand was empty. Then I saw a man running out of the barracks. I pursued him and caught up and tried to get the pot back, but he wouldn't let go. By chance, someone came out of the barracks and helped me recover this valuable possession.

One evening, as I walked into the yard outside the kitchen, the chief cook, a Chinese named Chan, told me to get him some dry wood. The only place to find wood was by the brick factory. I crept back and forth through the fence, stealing the wood. Then I chopped it into small pieces. I worked until one in the morning. Then I reported to Chan that I had done my job and asked him for the meal he had promised. He replied that he hadn't cooked anything, and only after I told him I was very hungry did he bring me two salt herring. I asked him at least to give me a little soup, and again he replied that he hadn't cooked it yet. He suggested I come back at five in the morning. So I went to my barracks; I was so hungry that I ate both herring before I reached my bunk. At five I went back to the kitchen to get my soup, but Chan told me he had already paid me just the right amount for the little bit of work I had done. I had to go to work hungry and exhausted; I had only slept four hours. When I sat down briefly during the lunch break, I fell asleep. I decided to give up working for the kitchen.

All over Europe, the Chinese are famous as jugglers, but in the camps they were employed in the laundry. I cannot remember seeing any non-Chinese laundry workers in any of the camps I passed through. During the war, the Chinese prisoners endured hunger, as all prisoners in the camp did. Our chief staple, aside from bread, was unground wheat boiled into cereal. Naturally, the grains went undigested and were passed out with excrement, which would freeze to stone-hard consistency after a few minutes. The cesspools were cleaned with pickaxes and crowbars; then the hard lumps of excrement were loaded on sleds and deposited in the tundra.

One day, the Chinese decided to use the undigested wheat for nourishment. They dragged a few lumps of frozen excrement into the laundry and threw them into the caldron that was used to wash the prisoners' laundry. When the mass had thawed out, they fished out the wheat kernels, washed them, and cooked them. After eating, they gave the leftovers to other Chinese prisoners who worked elsewhere.

This went on for several weeks. I no longer remember whether it was the stench or envy over the additional food the Chinese were getting that made someone report them to the camp authorities. The Chinese were threatened with dismissal from the laundry if they did not put a halt to their unappetizing culinary practice.

JUVENILE CRIMINALS

The criminal convicts were better off than the politicals in every respect. Only criminals were employed as administrators, tailors, shoemakers, and barracks janitors. They took it easy and frequently stole from the politicals. If a political prisoner received a package from his relatives, he could expect to have it stolen. Practically every day, you would see a prisoner crossing the yard with a package he'd just picked up, and a criminal holding him up at knife point and taking the package away. It was not only useless to inform the camp police of such crimes (since they were often in league with the criminals), but dangerous; a criminal would murder a fellow prisoner who denounced him to the camp police.

The adolescent criminals were among the worst. There were thousands of boys between ten and fourteen years old who had been brought to Norilsk for having committed various crimes. Most of them were children of peasants who had been arrested by the NKVD for refusing to join the collective farms. Usually the children were put in special NKVD schools; many ran away to escape mistreatment or hunger, banded together, and kept alive by theft, robbery, and murder, hiding in caves or in back yards in the big cities, sleeping by day and hunting for prey during the night. They were called *besprizornye*, derelict children. Efforts were made to bring them back onto the right path, but there were too many of them, and the resources to help them were too limited. Eventually, these children became hardened criminals.

Quite often, they were initiated into a criminal way of life by adults who used them to commit robberies and thefts. Then the child criminal would be arrested and shipped off to the subarctic camps. They lived in separate barracks for juvenile criminals, but they had contact with adults, since they were fed in the same kitchen.

When the first group of these young criminals arrived, we felt sorry for them and shared our bread rations with them. But soon we found out that they didn't deserve to be pitied: they continued robbing and stealing in the camp. Armed with knives or razor blades, they would attack individual prisoners coming out of the kitchen and take their food. Often, a gang of them would come into a barracks when most of the men were out working and only the sick and the old had been left behind, and steal anything they could lay their hands on. If anyone tried to resist them, he would be beaten or stabbed. Sometimes the young criminals would lie in ambush, waiting for a prisoner who was getting bread for his brigade—that way, they could take forty or fifty portions of bread in a single attack. Eventually, we were forced to send only the strongest men to pick up the bread. After a while, we concluded that these youthful bandits could not be reached through reason and friendly persuasion.

However, there were children of arrested parents whose behavior was exemplary despite the bad influences they were exposed to. I got to know one of them, the son of Panas Lyubchenko, the former premier of the Ukrainian Council of People's Commissars. Volodya Lyubchenko was sixteen years old when the NKVD sentenced him to ten years in a camp for being related to an "enemy of the people." When Panas Lyubchenko learned that he was going to be arrested, he shot his wife and three of his children. Volodya, the oldest child, happened to be visiting his grandparents in the country. We took this boy under our wing and tried to find easy work for him. When I saw Volodya again after two years, he was unchanged, which gave me a lot of pleasure; he was in good health as well. There were quite a few brave children like that—usually the offspring of political prisoners.

A RELUCTANT COOK

The winter of 1943–44 had reached its peak. After the great frosts came the purga; no sooner had the blizzards abated than the temperature plummeted again. The thermometer rarely rose above minus forty-five degrees Celsius. On such days, the camp administration found itself forced to put a halt to outside work, since too many prisoners were suffering severe frostbite, not just in their hands and feet, but in their faces, even though they wore masks.

But the railroad workers had to continue working. The only change for us was that the weakest were assigned to the sections of the line that were nearest to the camp, so that they would not have to walk such a great distance. My section extended from the entrance of the brick factory to the first railroad switch, and my work consisted of keeping the tracks clear. Despite the cold and the hunger, I was glad to have this work; I was envied by many. As soon as the workday was over, I was home, just ten minutes away from my barracks. The other members of our brigade often didn't get home before ten, eleven, or even later. Being near the brick factory also gave me the opportunity to warm up, especially on wind-still days when the tracks were clear of snow.

I couldn't always go into the factory (since unauthorized entry was forbidden), but I found other hiding places. One of my favorite shelters was switchman's hut number 3, a shack right in the middle of my section. It had two excellent advantages: it didn't take long to get there; and in case the inspectors came, I'd always be at my place of work. Switch number 3 was operated by a prisoner named Melbardos, a former officer in the Latvian Army. Melbardos was a giant of a man; he could scarcely squeeze past the potbellied iron stove in the middle of his tiny hut. This stove was always well heated: whenever trains loaded with coal stopped by the switch, Melbardos would climb up and help himself to as much coal as he needed.

The first time I came to the switchman's house, Melbardos looked at me quizzically.

"I just want to warm up a little, it's so cold today," I said.

"All right, get yourself warm, but just for five minutes. If the stationmaster comes along, I'll be in trouble." I promised not to stay any longer than that. Ten minutes later, I found myself back in the terrible cold.

That winter was particularly harsh. The biting frost continued for weeks. I chopped ice and shoveled snow off the tracks, working hard to keep warm. When I got very tired, I would look for a warm hiding place. I could rarely rest for more than ten minutes. Supervisors and even some workers liked to entertain themselves by chasing prisoners who were searching for warmth back into the cold. Many times I stood with my shovel and pickax under my arm, wondering where I could go.

On that day, I could see beckoning clouds of smoke curling out of several chimneys, but I knew I couldn't go there: one place had one of the meanest supervisors, a human bulldog who barked at you as soon as you showed your face; the hut on my left would have been available if I hadn't already been there earlier in the day; and the one on my right was too far away. I walked back to switchman's hut number 3.

Just before I reached the hut, Melbardos stepped out and barred the door with his huge body. I stopped and greeted him, even though I had greeted him just recently. He looked away and started fussing with the switch. I remained standing where I was. He looked at me: my frozen face, my pleading eyes must have spoken more eloquently than any words could have.

"Go in, but just for a short time."

I quickly slipped into the hut, as if afraid he would change his mind. I sat down in a corner so as not to get in his way. I took off my fur hat, and then my coat. When Melbardos saw this, he said: "Don't get too comfortable. You know you have to leave soon."

I tried to gain time by getting into a conversation with him. But no matter what subject I broached, he remained unresponsive. Only when I said it would be good to have something to eat did he reply: "What would you like to eat?"

"A piece of black bread," I replied.

"I know, of course, but I mean, if you had a choice?"

"I'd have noodles with sugar and poppy seeds," I said.

"You like that?"

"Yes, I like noodles."

"Did your wife cook that for you?" he asked curiously.

"It's a standard Viennese dish."

"You're Viennese?"

"Yes."

"I see. I didn't know that."

I told him about Vienna and Viennese cooking; the more I talked, the longer I could stay inside. I'm sure I spent more than an hour with Melbardos that day. I came back the next day. The Latvian did not object. I sat down where I had sat the previous day. As soon as I had made myself comfortable, Melbardos started plying me with questions about various sorts of meals. I told him everything I knew. He drew a notebook from his pocket and wrote down the names and recipes of the dishes I had described. Suddenly he interrupted me: he could see the railroad inspector approaching. I had to rush out of the house.

The next day, Melbardos welcomed me as if I were his favorite guest. "Sit down, make yourself comfortable . . ." Now it was time for Parisian cuisine. I had started to tell him about my life in Paris. I talked a little about the Louvre; so long as I told him that the Louvre had once been Napoleon's residence, he listened, but when I started describing the *Mona Lisa* and other famous paintings, he interrupted me, saying: "I'd rather you told me about French cooking." I told him about meals I had eaten in Paris and also about meals I had never eaten in my life. Melbardos took copious notes and I was happy to sit next to his stove.

After exhausting the subject of French cuisine, we turned to Hungarian cooking. I knew only two dishes: Paprikash and Szekely goulash; the rest I invented. As I watched him writing everything down, I imagined some amazed Hungarian learning about his national dishes from Melbardos's notebook. As soon as I stopped reciting recipes to him, he told me it was time to leave. One of his ways to get rid of me was to raise a false alarm by looking out the window and saying: "Quick! The inspector's coming!" Then I'd rush out into the cold and get to work shoveling snow and inventing new recipes for Melbardos.

Melbardos had his own reasons for keeping other prisoners out of his hut: it served as a hideaway for lovers. I often saw couples slipping in there. Those were the cooks and their girlfriends. Melbardos would go outside and clean the switch; the cooks would pay him with food. One day, I was sitting with Melbardos in his hut when one of the cooks came in and sat down on the bench. Melbardos pointed at me and said: "This is the Viennese cook." I was very embarrassed. The cook asked me where I had worked; Melbardos answered for me and listed the restaurants I had mentioned.

One day, as I was lying on my bunk after work, enjoying the warmth of the barracks, a messenger came from the camp office and addressed a question to the brigadier. Whenever a messenger came, everybody paid attention, for usually his message consisted of some new regulation. I saw the brigadier shrugging. Then he shouted: "Attention! Silence!" Everyone fell silent. "Is there a cook in this brigade?" No one responded. "You see, I told you, there's no cook here," the brigadier said to the messenger. The messenger left.

I was glad, for I sensed this had something to do with me and the cook I had met in Melbardos's hut. Fifteen minutes later, the door opened again and that very cook came in, accompanied by the messenger. I wanted to hide, but it was too late; the cook had already seen me and was pointing his finger at me: "There he is!" I didn't move, didn't say anything. But my bunk neighbors spoke out for me: "Yes, he's a good cook, take him!" They prodded me to get off the bunk.

The brigadier stood in front of me. "Why didn't you say you were a cook?"

"Because I'm not a cook."

No one believed me. Everyone wanted me to go to the kitchen; they all hoped I would get them extra food. On the way to the office, I tried to think of a way to get out of this fix. The cook was surprised that I didn't want to work at "my profession," especially since I'd be much better off, with plenty to eat and constant warmth. I answered evasively. The cook led me to the office of the camp commander, Panzerni. The head of the camp kitchen was there, too. As we stepped in, the cook said to the camp commander: "Here he is!"

The commander looked at me from head to toe and asked me how long I had worked as a cook and where I had been employed. I replied that this was a misunderstanding, I wasn't a cook at all.

"I've never come across anything like this in my career!" he exclaimed. "Usually everyone wants to work as a cook." Then, turning to the kitchen supervisor, he said: "This is a decent man. Kick out Kusnetzov and put this one in his place."

On the way, I told the kitchen supervisor that I didn't know anything about cooking.

"If I don't take you now, the commander will accuse me of hiring a bunch of crooks for the kitchen. You're going to have to accept the job. You'll learn it soon; it's not so hard to prepare soup and kasha."

My arrival in the kitchen provoked great agitation among the personnel, which consisted entirely of criminals. I could hear them murmuring all around me: "There's a new cook!"

The cooks plied me with questions, apparently to put me to the test. I told them right away that I didn't know a thing about cooking. My candor seemed to please them; they were glad I wasn't presenting them with any serious competition.

In the beginning, all I did was wash the cooking pots. Cleaning those huge vessels, with a capacity of five hundred to one thousand liters, was harder work than keeping a stretch of railroad tracks clear of snow and ice. I had to crouch down low and scrape and rub away at burned crusts of gruel; sweat poured down my back. I was usually so exhausted after a day's work that I had no appetite.

The cooks secretly prepared special meals for themselves. At first, they tried to hide this from me as well; but later they revealed their secret to me and I was allowed to eat with them. We had frozen meat, all sorts of preserves, dried potatoes and vegetables from the United States, and sugar imported from Cuba. I learned that there hadn't been such good food in Norilsk before the war broke out and foreign aid began to pour into the country.

Naturally, these special meals were strictly forbidden. All the cooks were afraid of the camp commander, Panzerni. He frequently came into the kitchen to search its corners and crevices with a flashlight, and whenever he found evidence that one of the cooks had helped himself to contraband food, the culprit was immediately sent to a punishment cell and was subsequently banished to a hard-labor brigade. The cooks, however, were willing to risk these harsh punishments. The best foods in storage, such as lard, meat, and dehydrated eggs, were stolen in large quantities and distributed among the camp police and the guards. The rest went to the cooks' girlfriends—it was a matter of honor for a cook to have his own woman.

A representative of the camp administration was always present in the kitchen, but these officials were quite indifferent to the illicit cooking and stealing of foodstuffs. There was always a prisoner, too, who had been removed from his brigade to help in the kitchen; the only concern of these men was to pilfer a little food for themselves. Whenever the camp commander came into the kitchen, his first question to the chief cook was whether he was satisfied with my work. The chief cook would praise me, whereupon the camp commander would say: "You see, I told you he was the right man for you!"

I got used to the work. It wasn't long before I was recognized as a cook, even though the only meals I knew how to prepare were soup and cereal.

One evening, shortly before the end of the day's work, I wanted to eat something. One of my colleagues suggested I fry myself a salted fish. I had nearly finished frying it when Panzerni came into the kitchen.

"Who is this fish for?"

"For the cooks, citizen commander," I replied.

"So now you're starting, too?"

"It's the same fish the prisoners get, sir. I'm just frying it a little."

"And you're turning into a smart aleck! If I see this once again, I'll send you off to work in the clay pit."

I took the fish off the stove and put it aside.

When Panzerni came back to the kitchen several days later, he asked me: "You're not frying fish today?"

I didn't reply. Panzerni took his flashlight and started searching. He didn't find anything. As he was leaving, he opened an oven door and looked in. "What's this?"

I looked and saw a frying pan with rolls made of white flour.

"Who's the cook in charge today?"

"I am, citizen commander."

"Take off your apron and get out of here!" He was red with rage.

I walked out with my head drooping. I was very sorry to have lost my job in the kitchen for such a silly reason. I had no idea which of the cooks had baked those rolls. Later I learned it had been a deliberate maneuver by one of the cooks to get me out of the kitchen.

That evening, I went to the chief overseer to find out what brigade I would be working with. He hadn't received any special instructions. I was glad when he told me to rejoin my old brigade, instead of sending me to the clay pit—the hardest work of all. Probably Panzerni wasn't completely convinced of my guilt in the matter.

WORKING AS A SWITCHMAN

The worst three winter months were over. It was March—not the beginning of spring in that region, but the temperatures rarely sank below minus forty degrees, and that was something to be thankful for. My comrades and the brigadier were pleased with me. While I had worked in the kitchen, I had often given the people from my old brigade extra food, and this had raised me in their esteem. Everyone was sorry I hadn't been able to stay in the kitchen longer.

Once again, I was armed with a pickax and a shovel and put in charge of a stretch of tracks. I no longer visited Melbardos, for I had been assigned to the area near the fifth switchman's hut. That was where I now went to warm up. The switchman was bored and didn't mind my offering him a little company.

One morning, I went into the switchman's hut, as usual, to pick up my tools, which were stored there. The switchman working the night shift asked me if I had seen his colleague from the day shift. When I returned after two hours to warm up, the missing switchman still hadn't come to work. His colleague asked me to replace him while he went to the stationmaster to clear up the matter. I stayed in the hut. After half an hour, the switchman returned with an official, who asked me if I wanted to work as a switchman. I said I had never done that kind of work before. He explained what the job consisted of: I would be given instructions, by telephone, to operate the switches, and I would have to report that switch number so-and-so had been set in this or that direction. I would also be given written instructions, which I could study in my free time.

Every evening, I had to go to the station and receive lessons from the stationmaster. Each time I came, he would test my understanding of the previous lessons. My friends couldn't believe their eyes when they passed by and saw me giving signals to the approaching locomotive, with a little flag in my hand. I was now officially a switchman.

At one end of the camp, a new barracks was being constructed. This was nothing unusual, since the camp was constantly being expanded. But the workers building the barracks said that it wasn't designed in the usual way: the rooms were small, the windows barred, and the doors were especially thick and reinforced with iron. The prisoners surmised that they were building a new prison barracks similar to the one that had once been used in section 7. If that was the case, I would have every reason to fear being again subjected to the conditions of "camp with severe regime." But then a new rumor spread: the new barracks was supposed to house captured German officers.

The secret was out as soon as the barracks was ready. A large transport came in from Dudinka under heavily armed escort. No one was allowed to go near while the prisoners got off the train, but you could see from afar that most of them wore civilian clothes and a few were dressed in German Army uniforms.

It was several weeks before we learned the first details about the new prisoners. They had to work in the clay pit, and the prisoners who had worked there before were transferred elsewhere. From a distance, we could see the newcomers being led to work. They were all identically dressed, and each man had a large number on his back and the same number on his hat. They didn't go to work through the gate the other prisoners went through; a special gate had been built for them. Finally, we learned from prisoners who had become ill and had come back from the hospital that these were a new kind of prisoner, the so-called *katorzhniki*.

After the retreat of the German Army and the Soviet counter-offensive, all those who had been found guilty of any form of collaboration with the Germans but who had not been shot immediately were arrested by the NKVD and sentenced to *katorga*, forced labor, by a military court. The prisoners were mainly mayors, village elders, policemen, and teachers. Most of the Germans among the *katorzhniki* had been guards in the extermination camps who had been unable to flee. For the first time, we saw political prisoners who had really committed crimes.

Soon, a second such barracks was built. The next group to arrive consisted of women who been found guilty of some form of collaboration with the Germans. Among them were many teachers who had continued their work in the schools under the conditions set by the occupation forces. Some women had had intimate relations with German officers; others had been arrested because they had washed clothes for German officers or cleaned their rooms.

One day, I managed to exchange a few words with a German officer. A group of *katorzhniki* were unloading wood near my switchman's hut. I overheard a conversation between two of the prisoners and noticed that one of them was German. I took my shovel and pretended to be clearing snow from the escarpment by the side of the switch while I conversed with the German.

"What are you doing here? Are you German?" he asked me.

I explained briefly who I was.

"Do you have anything to smoke?"

"I don't smoke, but I can get you something," I said, and noticing that a soldier was watching me, withdrew.

I went to the nearby concrete-production unit of the brick factory and asked some acquaintances for some makhorka. I stuffed the tobacco into a matchbox, took my shovel, and started clearing snow near the *katorzhniki*, waiting for an opportunity to pass on the tobacco to the German. But as I was about to drop the matchbox (I had wrapped it in a rag), a soldier called out to me: "Hey you, what are you doing? Get back into your hut!" I went back inside. Through the window, I could see the German looking in my direction, making signs which I could not decipher.

The telephone rang; the man in charge of the railroad wanted to know how far the *katorzhniki* had progressed with the unloading of the wood. This gave me a new opportunity to get near the prisoners. At a moment when the soldier had his head turned, I threw the tobacco in the direction of the group. Then, through my window, I watched the German repeatedly trying to approach the matchbox. But as soon as he stepped aside, the soldier would order him to stay away from the tracks. Later, one of the prisoners managed to reach the tobacco.

Now I was afraid the smokers would immediately roll cigarettes and light them up. This could have had dire consequences for me, because the soldier would have quickly guessed why I had been so eager to clear the snow. But they didn't smoke, perhaps because they had no matches, or else out of caution—in any case, I felt relieved.

All subsequent attempts to talk to the *katorzhniki* were frustrated by the vigilance of the guards. Once, when the *katorzhniki* were working near my switch, a soldier came into my hut to warm up. I was about to go outside when he warned me not to go near the *katorzhniki*. I desisted; I didn't want to jeopardize my job.

Nevertheless, my good fortune was not to last long. One day, the NKVD chief of the ninth camp section paid me a visit. Instinctively, I started to withdraw into my hut, but I remembered my instructions, which were to report to my superiors next to the switch.

I stepped forward as he approached me. Then I reported: "Switch number 5, switchman Steiner, everything in order."

When he heard my name, he asked me to repeat it. "What did you say your name is?"

I said it again.

"How did you get this job?" he asked.

I told him truthfully how I had come to be employed as a switchman.

"Very interesting, the kind of people they take for switchmen," he muttered, and went inside to make a telephone call. I heard him saying to the stationmaster: "Send someone immediately to replace switchman number 5."

Once again, I returned to working with pickax and shovel. But now that the NKVD officer had fixed his attention on me, I wasn't allowed to stay in this position long either. Very soon after my dismissal from the switchman's post, I was told to pack my stuff and get ready for transport. I scarcely had time to say goodbye to my friends.

During my stay in the ninth camp section, I had accumulated a small fortune: a set of bedclothes, a tin can, a wooden spoon, even a blanket. I had acquired all these things during my stint as a cook. The tin can, an American product, came from the kitchen. I had bought the wooden spoon for six hundred grams of bread. The bedclothes had cost me four portions of bread; and the blanket was a gift from Sasha Weber. I packed these possessions in an American duffel bag after thoroughly washing it.

As usual, all those who had been selected for transport were taken to the bathhouse and thoroughly searched by the camp police. My bedclothes were confiscated as "state property." I was allowed to keep the tin can and the wooden spoon. I struggled to persuade them to leave me the duffel bag, and fortunately succeeded.

About forty of us stood waiting at the gate, and there were at least forty different opinions as to where we were going. As it turned out, no one had guessed right. It was getting dark when the guards finally came to escort us to the train station. Apparently, the guards wanted to make up for lost time, for they goaded us mercilessly to hurry: *"Skorei, skorei!"*

The dogs said the same thing in their own language. At last, we arrived at the station. We had to squeeze close together in a corner and wait for the train. When it finally came, we were led into the closed freight car, two by two. After everyone had climbed in, the door was shut and locked from outside. As soon as we had settled down on the floor of the car, the guessing started again: Where were we heading?

We traveled for twelve hours. It was eight in the morning when we arrived in Dudinka.

IN DUDINKA |

HOW WAS THE VODKA?

Dudinka had changed a great deal during the five years since I had first been there. Even before getting out of the train, we could see the new *katorga* section through a crack in the side of the car as the train waited for a signal light to change. These barracks were built just like those of the ninth camp section of Norilsk: iron bars on the windows, doors reinforced with iron, several rows of barbed wire instead of an ordinary wire fence, and the watchtowers connected by a telephone cable. A nearby military barracks was under construction and already partly inhabited.

The train came into the station. The door was opened, and we stepped out. On the way to the camp, we could see prisoners erecting a large wooden structure near the train station, with tracks leading inside through a large gate. As we later learned, this was a new locomotive depot. About five hundred meters farther on was the new camp section, which had a capacity of a little over five hundred prisoners. All the convicts housed here worked on the railroad. One of the four barracks was reserved for the engine drivers and other railroad staff, including the switchmen. These were all criminals who went to work without escort. In the second barracks were the workshop laborers, among whom were both politicals and criminals. The third barracks, where we were housed, was reserved for track-maintenance workers. The fourth barracks was divided in two. One half contained the infirmary, with a single sickroom, and the other was divided into two sections: one for twelve women, who also worked for the railroad (this group was composed of both criminals and political prisoners); and the other for the *lagernye pridurki*, the camp officials, who were all criminals, except one.

The difference between this camp and the one in Norilsk was evident from the first moment. This was what prisoners called a "jolly prison." Right after our arrival, we were offered bread and other food for sale. In the evening, many of the old-timers left their soup untouched or gave it to the new arrivals. Some people were sipping tea, which they had sweetened with ample amounts of sugar, and eating flatcakes they had baked themselves. We were amazed at so much prosperity. After a few days, we found out where it all came from: the railroad workers regularly plundered the food transports. Soon we, too, no longer felt hunger.

Every year, in the harbor of Dudinka, the tracks had to be removed in many spots to prevent them from being crushed and washed away by the ice floes from the thawing Yenisei; when the danger had passed, the tracks had to be replaced. There were years when the ice would carve out the land as deep as two hundred meters, crushing everything in its way. Many houses disappeared as tracelessly as if they had never been there.

As we laid the tracks, we often stood knee-deep in water. To encourage us to work harder, each prisoner was given fifty grams of vodka. However, it wasn't the prisoner who drank the liquor, but the brigadiers, the guards, and the stationmasters. Once, someone complained to the head of the railroad division that we never got any vodka, and he promised to be there when it was given out. The next day, the head of the division brought the vodka himself. The brigadier held the bottle in one hand, a little glass in the other. One prisoner after another stepped forward and received his portion of vodka. Everyone drank; some men even gasped with pleasure.

"How was the vodka?"

"First-rate!"

No one dared to say that it had been ordinary Yenisei water. It remained a mystery, too, just *when* the brigadier had managed to fill the bottles with water. That was the last time anyone complained about not getting any vodka.

We often worked in the harbor. That was pleasant because we weren't supervised by guards there. The whole port of Dudinka was surrounded by barbed wire and encircled by watchtowers. The harbor comprised a large area; here were the warehouses where the food was stored before it was transported to Norilsk. A lot of this food was stored outside.

Prisoners from all departments of Dudinka worked in the harbor; only the *katorzhniki* were excluded. More than five thousand prisoners and free workers were employed there. Often, prisoners and free workers labored together in one room, indistinguishable in their appearance.

During the lunch break, we could move around freely in the harbor. From the very first days after our arrival, many in our brigade examined the terrain and found out from the old-timers where you could steal some food. Pretty soon, you saw men coming back to work with their pockets bulging. Sugar, flour, preserves, and other foods were easy to steal, as there was very little supervision. Consequently, no one went hungry here. Some of the stolen food was brought back to the camp. At the exit from the harbor and at the gate leading into the camp, everyone was searched by the guards, but many succeeded in smuggling their loot back home. A lively trade flourished there; you could buy bread, sugar, soap, and even cologne. The camp police searched the barracks often and confiscated whatever they found there; but everything was replaced within days. There was never any scarcity. Theft had become an ordinary part of life; it was just a matter of getting good at it.

Elsewhere, it was every prisoner's ideal to get a job as barracks janitor (*dnevalny*) or at least find work under some roof, to be spared the eternal drudgery, the cold, and the hunger. Not in Dudinka. Hardly anybody wanted to be a *dnevalny*. Almost everyone wanted to work in the harbor, no matter how hard the work—it paid off.

One day, I was appointed *kipyatilshchik*—hot-water boiler. Three times a day, morning, noon, and evening, I had to boil water. The *ki-*

pyatilka, the hot-water kitchen, was in a small barracks where there were two large caldrons in a brick enclosure. I slept on a bunk in a corner of this room. Four camp officials lived next door: the chief overseer, the commander of the camp police, the head of the food warehouse, and the head of the railroad's freight division, Alexander Bozhko. All four of them were *beskonvoinye*, that is, they could come and go without escort. Each had a *propusk*, a special pass. In addition to my duties as *kipyatilshchik*, I had to clean up these officials' room. Now I was as far from hunger as I had ever been.

The *lagernye pridurki* not only had plenty of food, but also vodka and women. Of the twelve women in the camp section, nine had steady lovers. Nothing was done to conceal this. Intimate relationships were strictly forbidden, but no one paid this rule any attention. After a while, the officials moved to the barracks where the infirmary was. They insisted on my moving with them, as they appreciated my discretion. Another prisoner replaced me as *kipyatilshchik*, and I became a *dnevalny* for the officials' room and the room where the twelve female prisoners lived.

Almost all the women were between twenty and thirty years old. The criminals among them had been sentenced for petty fraud or embezzlement and had been given eight to ten years in camp. Their life was not hard. Each of them had a *propusk*. Some of them worked as officials or as cleaning women for the railroad; two of them were maids (one for the camp commander, the other for the stationmaster). The female political prisoners went to work under escort. One of them had been sentenced under Article 59, for "banditry." Her name was Shura—a short, pudgy girl with a pretty face and beautiful black eyes. The women did not like Shura because she was a hypocrite. She was constantly lamenting her separation from her two children, who lived with their grandmother, and swore by all the saints that she didn't want anything to do with any man and thought only of the children—but everyone knew that Shura was the warehouse manager's lover and that he plied her with delicacies. The women wanted me to tell them whether Shura ever went into the officials' room. I did not reveal her secret, even though I knew that she often slipped under Shipitsin's blanket. Shura was very worried that I might betray her to the other women and tried to buy my allegiance with little gifts like white bread and sugar.

The most striking of the twelve women was Olga Srba, a young, slender medical student from Kishinev in Bessarabia. A doctor's daughter, she had been arrested in 1940 for belonging to a "counterrevolutionary" group and distributing leaflets among her fellow students, and was given a ten-year sentence. Olga worked as a nurse in the infirmary. The camp commander, Borisov, a man of liberal temperament, had expected her to become the doctor's mistress, but for some reason that had not happened. Olga washed the doctor's clothes, and that seemed to be the extent of their intimacy. It wasn't because she was prudish; years later, when I saw her again in Norilsk, she was pregnant. Bozhko, the head of the freight division, courted her assiduously, without success. He probably was neither young enough nor handsome enough for her. His gifts, consisting of canned meat, sugar, and other food, were ineffectual, since she was supplied with such things already.

Relations among the established couples were not always harmonious. There were many quarrels, and I frequently had to intervene as peacemaker and mediator.

One day, the liberal camp commander, Borisov, a man with a real understanding of human needs, despite his being an NKVD official, was replaced by a new commander, Putintsev, and everything changed. Putintsev didn't have the resources to do very much about the conditions in the harbor, but he instituted a new regime in the camp. He appointed new guards and instructed them to exercise thorough control. The women's and the officials' rooms were inspected with particular frequency. Once, I happened to be in the infirmary across from their rooms when one of the new guards broke in the door to the officials' room and found the commander of the camp police in bed with his mistress, Marusya. Marusya was dragged off to the punishment cell. One day, the camp commander himself came to inspect the *pridurki*. I happened to be clearing away their vodka bottles when he came in. He asked me where the bottles came from and I replied that they were petroleum bottles.

He sniffed one of the bottles and said: "I see, your bosses like to drink petroleum. Do you like to drink petroleum, too?"

I said nothing.

"And what about the women who come trooping in here every day? I suppose they're actually wooden dolls?"

"I haven't seen any women here," I said.

"In a half hour, after I've made my rounds, I want to see you in the office."

When I came to his office an hour later, he had me sit down on a chair in front of his desk. "All right, now tell me what's going on in the barracks, and don't leave anything out. Who's sleeping with whom, when do they drink vodka, and how much."

"I'm a *dnevalny*, not an informer. It's the job of the camp police to keep you informed about these things, not mine."

"Ah, so you're that sort!" he shouted. "I'll show you—tomorrow you'll get the toughest job we have to offer. Now get out!"

I told the chief overseer what had happened. He consoled me and promised to ask Bozhko to employ me in the shipping office of the freight division. I continued working as *dnevalny* in the camp for a few more days. Then the camp commander issued an order to have me transferred. The chief overseer had kept his word: I was put to work as *dnevalny* in the shipping office of the freight division.

IN THE HARBOR

The shipping office was in the harbor, in the railroad administration building. My new boss was Alexander Bozhko, who was serving ten years for "sabotage." He was one of the few political prisoners with a *propusk* that entitled him to move about freely in Dudinka.

My job was to fetch coal from the shed and to keep two stoves stoked. Some of the employees of the freight division were prisoners; others were free. The free workers were usually women, and most of them were young girls. I immediately noticed that prisoners and free workers had very friendly relations, the exact limits of which I was not able to determine right away. Later I noticed that the free workers not only were glad to eat the preserves the prisoners stole, but they baked flatbread with the flour the prisoners hauled in by the sackful. And that was by no means all. The free girls had a great deal of sympathy for the prisoners' emotional misery, and in return the prisoners offered gifts like silk stockings, powder, and cologne. Some girls prized the linen flour sacks from America— they made clothes out of the material.

There was always a supply of vodka, cookies, and preserves on Bozhko's desk. One of the young free girls had conquered his heart: he had promised to marry her after his release. But nothing came of that: fourteen days after Bozhko's release, his wife and grown daughter arrived in Dudinka. Bozhko was not very happy about this, and Valya, the girl, accused him of deceit. This, however, did not prevent her from continuing her relationship with Bozhko.

I felt as if I had landed in paradise. The camp officials would frequently leave stolen food in my safekeeping, and I could eat as much of these delicacies as I wished. After a month, I, too, became an official. I was put in charge of the loading and unloading of the freight cars. I had to take note of the time spent on this labor and keep the train officials informed of the work's progress. I also had to make sure that everything was done according to regulations. This was the most pleasant work imaginable for a prisoner. It involved very little effort and was rewarded with plentiful food. A few officials had managed to save fairly large sums of money, which they had acquired through the sale of stolen goods. You worked for twelve hours and rested for twenty-four. The night shift was not unpleasant here; there was less work at night than during the day. We had a stove in the shipping office which was used for cooking and baking.

I soon learned how to help myself to the contents of crates that had been broken and sacks that had been ripped open. In the beginning, my heart would race with anxiety, but then I became calmer, and eventually I stole as nonchalantly as if I were taking food from my own pantry. At first, I restricted myself to the parasitical role of partaking of other thieves' loot, but eventually I attained full honor as a thief among thieves.

One day, something unprecedented happened in Dudinka. Far from the harbor, a group of about fifty *katorzhniki* were recovering a shipment of logs from the frozen Yenisei by hacking through the ice. A few of the workers succeeded in overpowering one of the guards and seizing his submachine gun; they killed two soldiers and wounded three others. A sixth soldier escaped and called for reinforcements. Some forty-five prisoners fled; five refused to run away and remained where they were. All the fugitives were captured within a few hours. All were shot on the spot, except for three who were kept alive to be used as witnesses.

To us who had been in prison for so many years, it was incomprehensible how the *katorzhniki* could have expected to escape this way. Even if they had not been captured, they would have perished somewhere in the endless ice desert. We could think of only one explanation: the *katorzhniki*'s situation was so desperate—most of them had been sentenced to twenty to twenty-five years—that they had decided to commit a kind of collective suicide.

The new commander was continuing his purge of the camp. One of his victims was Olga: he chased her out of the infirmary and put her in the fourth camp section. Now she had to unload heavy sacks of flour, cement, and other goods in the harbor. I often saw her at work and could see how hard it was for her, and how proudly intent she was on not showing her weakness. Bozhko's efforts to pull strings on her behalf were unsuccessful for a long time; but finally Olga got a somewhat easier job making charcoal. Later, when I was back in Norilsk, I learned that Olga had been given another ten-year sentence for "counterrevolutionary agitation among the prisoners."

Bozhko was highly satisfied with my work; so was the director of the Dudinka railroad. I was appointed chief administrator, and had to supervise a group of officials and employees. My unit became one of the most efficient, and I received several bonuses from the camp and railroad administrations as a reward for my good work.

There was a young girl in my group, a free worker named Nina Khaban. She was athletically built, had lovely blue eyes and an enchanting laugh—it sounded like a little bell. Nina lived with her parents; her stepfather was the head of the harbor's packing and crating division. On holidays, Nina would always bring a basket full of food and liquor. She was especially nice to me. Since I was much older than she was, it never occurred to me that she might be in love with me; instead, I assumed that she wanted to please me because I was her supervisor. One day, a friend of Nina's told me that Nina was very unhappy because I was not responding to her friendly overtures. I was very surprised and replied that I was a prisoner and Nina a free woman, and that a relationship could only hurt us, especially her.

More and more American and British ships came to the port of Dudinka. They docked at special piers far from where the prisoners worked. Only free workers were used to unload those ships. For this purpose, they were given special shoes and clothes, which had to be returned to the harbor authorities after work. The prisoners paid special attention to the cargo that came on these ships. The harbor officials and the thieves collaborated. The former saw to it that freight cars laden with food were shunted onto a sidetrack where the thieves could plunder at ease. Later, the loot was fraternally divided.

The narrow-gauge train ran day and night. Still, it could transport only a small portion of the freight destined for Norilsk at one time. Most of the goods were stored in Dudinka and could only be moved out gradually in small shipments in the course of the winter. A decision was therefore made to build a standard-gauge railroad from Dudinka to Norilsk. This work was assigned to the *katorzhniki*. The new line was to run a different course from the old one. The *katorzhniki* labored through the winter. Their work had to be interrupted in the summer because there were no rails, and construction was not resumed until several years later. Today, Norilsk and Dudinka are linked by a standard-gauge railroad.

There was a special loading department in the harbor. It was headed by a free man who had once served a sentence in Dudinka for criminal activities. His name was Stamboli. His two deputies were political prisoners. One of them was Zborovsky, once a leading Soviet official, who had been in pre-trial detention in Kharkov together with the Austrian Weissberg–Zibulski and was then sentenced to ten years in the camp. The other deputy's name was Zilzer; he had been deputy to the NKVD chief in Tiflis.

I got to know these men quite well; that was a natural consequence of my work, which required constant contact with the loading department. The railroad administration had set quotas for the loading of the freight cars, and failure to meet these norms was punished with sizable fines. For this reason, the heads of the loading department were eager to be on good terms with the harbor officials and especially with the chief administrator since the efficiency of the loading work depended largely on them. The harbor officials were offered gifts by the loading officials, and in almost all cases these were gladly accepted.

But my relations with Zborovsky, Zilzer, and others had a different basis. We were all former party members, and this constituted a common bond: we conducted our transactions on a party level, so to speak. Most former communists tried to support each other in prison.

THE FIRST STRIKE IN CAMP

On May 9, 1945, I took charge of several freight cars filled with various technical materials. There were just a few weeks left before the regular shipping routine would begin; it was necessary to empty out the warehouses to make room for the new shipments. I asked the workers to hurry, since the cars were needed for the next train to Norilsk. To make sure no time was lost, I called up a railroad official and asked him to send a locomotive to pick up the cars. A few minutes later, the locomotive arrived, and the engineer leaned out of his cab and shouted: "Brothers, the war is over! Peace! The Germans have capitulated!"

These words spread like wildfire through the entire harbor. Everyone stopped working and started walking toward the harbor exit. The word "peace" united all—prisoners, free employees, and soldiers. We called out to the guards: "The war's over, take us to the camp, nobody's working today!"

The guards didn't know how to respond. Some officers said: "We don't have any instructions."

"Instructions for what? The war's over, take us to the camp!"

The gate opened and the great mass of workers streamed out. We marched to the camp without first having been counted by the guards. The soldiers walked by our side, relaxed, with their submachine guns lowered. For the first time, we didn't hear them curse us. They didn't wait, as they usually did, until the last prisoner had entered the camp, but went on to their own barracks. Everyone stayed outside in the courtyard. Friends shook hands; everyone was glad the war and its horrors had come to an end.

"I bet we'll be able to go home soon"—this was said by many people.

"I'm sure there'll be an amnesty; everyone will be able to go back to his family."

"Sure, if you still *have* a family. My people were all killed by the Nazis."

The camp commander appeared and made a brief speech: now that Hitler had been beaten, the Soviet government and Comrade Stalin would not forget that the prisoners had contributed to the victory of the Soviet Army by their hard work throughout the war years. A great amnesty was already being prepared, he said. Everyone would be included. This did not mean that everyone could go home right away, but most people could count on a suspension of their sentences.

Everyone joyfully returned to the barracks. At dinnertime, when we were served the usual herb soup, you could hear, for the first time that day, the voices of prisoners expressing discontent: "Why couldn't the bastards cook something better on a night like this!"

Days and weeks passed without any sign of the promised amnesty.

The prisoners' lives continued as if nothing had changed in the outside world. When I spoke about this later with my friend Josef Berger, he said: "Everything changes. Only the Gulag remains the same."

A LETTER FROM MY WIFE

I hadn't heard from my wife since 1940. Though I had only rarely received any mail before then, I had at least known that Sonya was living in Moscow, and she, too, knew that I was alive. Once in a while, I would get a money order from her, and that was as good as a letter. Of course, I couldn't tell her about my real situation, but we were both glad to receive signs of life from each other. These contacts had come to an end in 1940. I was convinced, after the five-year lapse, that I no longer had a wife. Sonya was twenty years old when we were married. I assumed that our child's death and the persecution Sonya must have suffered because of my arrest—presuming she was still alive—had almost certainly led to her marrying another man.

After the end of the war, I decided to write to her. I did not send the letter by the regular camp mail but gave it to a German woman who had been exiled to Dudinka and worked as an assistant bookkeeper for the railroad administration, asking her to drop it in a mailbox. Many prisoners sent their mail this way. The free employees' mail was frequently inspected as well, but most of the letters sent by this route arrived at their destination. The answer reached me by the same route, via the German woman's address.

Several weeks passed. I no longer dared to hope. Then, one day, the German woman asked me to come to her room during the lunch break. I was literally weak with excitement; never before or after have I felt that way. It was 10 a.m., the lunch break would be at noon, I had to wait for two hours—it seemed impossible. To kill the time, I went down to the ships to watch the men and women unloading the freight. Everything was in order; there wasn't much work for me to do. When I came back to the office, only half an hour had passed. Now I tried to speak to the German woman; but as I approached her desk, she gave me a negative signal with her pen. She had every reason to be cautious, for there was a known NKVD informer working in her office. I left the room.

At long last, the lunch break came, and everyone went to eat. When I stepped into the German woman's office, I found it empty. No one was there, not even the German woman. I was about to leave the room when she came in—she had left with the others so as not to arouse suspicion. She took a newspaper out of her pocketbook. Inside the newspaper was a little envelope, which she held out to me. I recognized Sonya's handwriting immediately. I yanked the letter out of the woman's hand and hurried off. I hid in the coal shed and opened the envelope with quivering fingers, tearing the letter slightly in the process.

"My dear Karli," the letter began. I was so happy I could not go on reading, the words danced before my eyes: "My dear Karli"—everything is all right, I thought to myself; it has to be if she begins her letter like that: she's still mine.

I read on. My letter had reached her via a detour, for I had sent it to our old address; I had no way of knowing that Sonya had moved long ago. Now I learned how she had survived the war years. Both she and her relatives had given me up for dead. The letter ended with the most tender words. That was the first happy day in my years as a prisoner. Now I had the answer to the question: Why go on living? Yes, it was worth going through all those torments to experience even one day like this.

I received several other letters, money, and even newspapers from my wife via the German woman, until one day the NKVD agent somehow caught wind of it. The prisoners in the third camp section knew that the official Zubkov was an NKVD informer. He was serving a ten-year sentence for embezzlement. Zubkov did not content himself with telling the NKVD what the prisoners were eating and where they hid what they had stolen; he also provoked them, to create a basis for his denunciations. He would listen in on the conversations of prisoners and then report them to the NKVD in an exaggerated and distorted form. His reward for this dirty work was a *propusk*. He could stay away from work for days; all he had to do was call in. Zubkov also had a girlfriend, a free woman with whom he often spent the night. He was an official, as I was, and we worked alternating shifts. I often quarreled with him when we changed shifts. He always had some kind of complaint: the number on the freight document wasn't legible enough, the precise location of the freight car wasn't properly indicated, and so on. I tried my best quietly to explain things to him, but I rarely succeeded. Zubkov was fully conscious of his power and let everyone feel it—not only the prisoners but the free employees as well. When Zubkov found out my secret, he ran to his "employers" and informed them of his discovery. Naturally, it wasn't enough to tell them that I had been getting personal letters from my wife; he said he had found evidence of a counterrevolutionary foreign spy ring funded with large sums of money. Zubkov was instructed to keep an eye on me; that was why I wasn't instantly demoted.

The German woman was the first to be interrogated by the NKVD. They told her she would be better off if she confessed everything right away, since they knew all the facts. Then her husband, a railroad worker, was called in. He, too, was made a member of the "spy organization" and told to confess everything right away. The German woman approached me in the harbor one day as I was taking down the numbers of the freight cars. "For God's sake, write to your wife immediately and tell her not to write to my address. The NKVD is making a spy story out of it!" She spoke so rapidly and so softly that I scarcely understood what she said.

And she walked off before I had a chance to reply. I immediately wrote to my wife and told her to address all future letters to the camp.

My clothes were searched in the camp. All written and printed matter was confiscated, including a brief biography of Tchaikovsky. Probably the NKVD realized that the "spy story" was nothing but a stupid fantasy and were content with rousting me out of my comfortable job. The camp commander was instructed to transfer me without delay to a brigade that didn't work in the harbor.

I was sent to work in the sandpit. But not for long; after a few days, I was transferred from the third camp section to the nearby transit station. There was a good deal of animated activity there. That was the time when new prisoners were being brought in to replace those who had died or been crippled during the long winter months. A lively trade was conducted with the newcomers' possessions: for a few kilos of bread and a little tobacco, you could get a new suit, and with two portions of bread you could buy a silk shirt or a good pair of shoes. The buyers were criminals who were looking for anything that could be resold to free workers. The sellers were mainly Germans or Russians freshly released from German captivity. These prisoners were eventually transferred from the Dudinka transit camp to Norilsk. I, too, returned to Norilsk with one of these transports.

BACK
IN NORILSK

IN THE SIXTH CAMP SECTION

When our transport arrived in Norilsk, the camp administration conducted us to the various camp sections. We marched in rows of five from the train station through the city to the extensive tract of the big metallurgical factory, the BMS, where I had worked during my first years at Norilsk. Back then, it had been a huge construction site where tens of thousands of prisoners excavated the rock-hard frozen soil with pickaxes, shovels, and spades. Eventually, a small and not very productive metal foundry had been built. Now there was a huge plant stretching as far as the eye could see, with giant chimneys, workshops, sheds, warehouses. A network of railroad tracks covered the entire area, and smoke was billowing from every chimney. Lorries filled with the hot ore tailings were pulled to the slag heap by locomotives. And there were new construction sites where prisoners were digging the earth with the same kinds of tools my friends and I had once used.

Yes, great things had been achieved in Norilsk. But where were the builders of this vast enterprise? Where were Ondratschek, Kerosi, Feldmann, and thousands of other foreign communists who, together with hundreds of thousands of Russians, Ukrainians, Uzbeks, Georgians, and members of other nations, raised these mighty structures out of the frozen earth? Were they enjoying the fruits of their labor? No, they were rotting in the mass graves of Norilsk, and most of the men I saw working today would eventually join them there.

The sixth camp section, where I was now housed, was situated at one extreme of the plant. Our group of two hundred men was first sent to the infirmary for a medical examination and to be classified in the usual work categories. As I waited my turn, I noticed a man repeatedly walking in and out of the doctor's office. Years of experience told me that this was a *lagerny pridurok*. I was not mistaken: he was the *sankhoz*, the director of medical services.

"Excuse me," I said, "could I please speak to you for two minutes?"

"What do you want?"

"I'll be frank. Of all the people who have just arrived from Dudinka, I am the only one who has been in various prisons and camps since 1936. I know we're all going to be sent out to do hard labor. Please help me avoid that, at least for the time being."

"What is your category?"

"The doctors haven't seen me yet."

"What is your name?"

He took down my data and went into the doctor's office, where the newcomers were being examined. He returned after ten minutes. "You're in category 2A. Are you satisfied?"

"Thank you very much. What's next?"

"You'll be working as an orderly in the convalescence unit."

I sighed with relief.

Section 6 had not only a hospital but a convalescence unit, known as OP. This was a place for prisoners who were not acutely ill but were so weak that they could no longer work. At the sight of these unfortunate men—most of them were young—you wondered how they managed to remain upright at all. Some were so weak that they were unable to walk without holding on to some firm support. The food was better in the OP, and the prisoners were given three meals a day. Frequently, there would be butter or margarine at breakfast, and, every day, meat was served for lunch, which consisted of three courses. Since most of the patients had scurvy, they were also given raw vegetables and half a liter of kvass to drink.

Most patients were in the OP for three weeks. Everyone was exempt from work, but in order to provide some physical exercise, the doctors had those who were not too weak perform light manual labor, such as cleaning up the camp yard, for two hours a day.

Some prisoners fasted, to avoid regaining their strength; they would sell their bread or trade it for tobacco. When the doctors discovered this, they instructed the kitchen personnel to break the bread into small pieces and drop them into the soup. This last activity was my principal occupation, in addition to cleaning the barracks. I did not find it difficult to resist the patients' pleas that I not crumble the bread into the soup. A few times I relented, but this had unpleasant consequences for me, since some of the men I had refused denounced me to the doctor.

There were three other orderlies besides me. We slept on field cots equipped with straw sacks, sheets, and blankets. We had the same food the patients did. I was there for two months. By that time, I looked so fit that my benefactor, the director of medical services, told me the doctors had recommended that he replace me with a weaker prisoner. I had no choice but to thank him for the help he had given me.

I was put to work digging the foundation for the new coke plant. This project, like all construction work in the area, was directed by a firm called Metallurgstroi. Its head was the engineer Epstein, whom I already knew: we had worked together on the construction of the Dudinka–Norilsk railroad line. He had been serving a ten-year sentence for "sabotage" at the time. When the war broke out and the establishment of metallurgical factories became a national priority, Epstein's engineering skills served him in good stead: he was taken out of our brigade and was made the head of a construction unit. He proved so useful that the authorities decided to reduce his sentence; later, when his project was completed before all the others, he was set free and appointed head of the whole enormous enterprise. When I met him again, he was wearing two important medals which he had been awarded for his achievements.

During the noon break, I went to the administration building to see whether Epstein could give me an easy job. I had no idea how he would respond to my request; whether he would be able to see past his glittering decorations or even recognize me. I entered the secretary's room with mixed feelings, even with some anxiety. Maybe I would be thrown out? When I said I wished to speak to "citizen director of construction Epstein," she cast a contemptuous glance at my clay-spattered clothes and said: "The director is busy."

I wanted to ask her to please arrange an interview with the director, but then I changed my mind, turned around, and started walking out of the room. Just as I reached the door, Epstein passed me on his way to see the chief engineer. He seemed not to notice or recognize me. I waited hesitantly in the hall for a while. Then Epstein came back, and we stood facing each other.

"How did you get here?" he asked.

"I was looking for you."

"Come along, come along."

Epstein walked ahead, and I followed him into his office.

"How are you doing?"

"How would a prisoner be doing? You can see for yourself." I pointed at my dirty clothes.

"Where are you working?"

"In one of the brigades, the one building the coke plant."

"Would you like a brigadier's job?"

"I don't like being a brigadier."

"I know, it doesn't suit your character. To be a brigadier, you have to be able to curse—or have you learned that by now?"

"No, not quite."

I told him what kind of work I had done in the meantime—whereupon he said I should see his deputy, and if he couldn't find me a suitable job, I should come back to him. I went to Epstein's deputy. His name was Lyam and he asked me all sorts of questions: he wanted to know who I was, what my sentence was, what sorts of jobs I had performed in the course of my years in the camps. When I mentioned my work as a harbor official, Lyam said Metallurgstroi was looking for someone to head the transport division: would I like that position? I considered it briefly and declared myself willing to try it.

That same day, I handed the commander of section 6 a letter, signed by Epstein, which specified the work I would be performing and requested of the commander that he promptly facilitate my assuming my new responsibilities. In response to this request, the commander moved me to the barracks where the foremen and supervisors lived. This had its advantages: the barracks did not have large dormitories with ordinary bunks, but compartments similar to those in a sleeping car. In each compartment there were four beds with real sheets and pillowcases. In the middle of the barracks was a large table, where you could eat, write, and read. Those who lived here could come and go as they wished, and they were permitted to walk around the plant with impunity. Our food was better than the usual fare.

The next morning, I started my new job as head of the transport division. I was put in charge of a hundred and fifty men who worked around the clock in four brigades, unloading all freight coming in by train or truck. Strict quotas had been set: for example, a twenty-ton freight car had to be emptied in ninety minutes; a three-ton truck in twenty minutes. I knew from my experience with the railroad what challenges I would be facing. There were only a few men in the brigades who were young and strong enough to meet the quotas without great difficulty. Therefore, if I wanted to succeed, I could not count on my workers. I had to find other ways.

A simple but very cruel tactic was used to force the prisoners to work harder. You wouldn't think that tobacco could have such a devilish effect. The Allies, as I've mentioned, were sending thousands of tons of food to Norilsk, thanks to which both prisoners and free employees were saved from starvation; but there was very little tobacco. The camp administration made clever use of this scarcity. Makhorka was now only available as a premium for meeting the quota. The incentive was extraordinarily effective: where previously the quotas had only rarely been met, suddenly they were being exceeded. The construction manager would show up in the early morning, inform the brigadier of the day's job, announce how much makhorka was available for distribution in the evening—and the rush began. The foreman and brigadier no longer had to prod and curse; the workers did it to each other. Their craving for tobacco compelled them to exert themselves far beyond their normal capacity. The hour-long noonday break was now frequently cut short by the workers themselves. Nonsmokers were of course forced to keep up the tempo the smokers set. Friends became enemies, just for the sake of a little tobacco. At the end of the day, the foreman or the manager would come to see if the day's goals had been met; everyone waited tensely for the result. If the norm had been met, he would pronounce the words of blessing and redemption: "Brigadier, here's the voucher, take it to the office and pick up the tobacco."

The workers would wait impatiently for the brigadier to come back. The nonsmokers, too, looked forward to getting their share of tobacco, as they could trade it for bread. The portions of tobacco were measured with a matchbox; the allotment was rarely more than two matchboxes per person.

And the following day would begin with the same furious pace. You could hear the workers shouting at each other: "Hurry up, why aren't you working, we're not going to get any tobacco because of you!" There were even bloody fights in which prisoners attacked each other with shovels.

Frequently, the prisoners were cheated of their reward: they would be promised two packs of tobacco per person and then be told there was only one pack per four. Perhaps the brigadier had stolen the rest and shared it with the foreman. Sometimes the promised tobacco wasn't distributed at all. The foreman would simply say: "The quota wasn't met." Or else that the warehouse manager was absent. On such days, the smokers would beg the construction manager or the foreman to give them at least a small portion of makhorka, or even a single cigarette that could be shared among ten prisoners.

On my first day of work, Lyam gave me fifty packs of makhorka and said: "Use this well. Each of these is worth more than a large meal." I was determined not to employ this tactic, but to put my experience as a railroad official to good use. I used the tobacco to get on good terms with the railroad officials. By the end of the month, it turned out that for the first time Metallurgstroi did not have to pay any fines to the railroad for delays in unloading the cars. My prestige immediately rose. The director of Metallurgstroi was pleased that he had made a good choice. I was satisfied with my success, but there were some who were not—especially the dispatchers. At first, I couldn't divine the reasons for their dissatisfaction; only later did I realize why they were constantly making difficulties for me. The former head of the transport division had made little deals with the dispatchers and even used the trucks for this purpose in broad daylight. Mountains of coal lay around the factory grounds, unguarded. The dispatchers would load the coal onto trucks and sell it to people in the town; the proceeds were shared with the guard at the gate. When I refused to take part in these transactions, the dispatchers began their vilifications of me. Any mistake or failure on my part was immediately exposed, exaggerated, and reported to the director of Metallurgstroi. Epstein wasn't very interested in this gossip. It was more important to him that his company no longer had to pay any fines to the railroad.

After two months, I realized that I had made a mistake in accepting this position. The constant sabotage on the part of the dispatchers and the incompetence of the brigadiers, whose only thought was to find things to steal, were turning my "easy" job into a veritable hell. I was reduced to personally supervising the work day and night. After a while, I could no longer take the strain. I asked Epstein for another job, but he would not hear of it.

The chief engineer in the electrolytic plant (BEZ), Strogonov, was a friend of mine. I had made his acquaintance during the war, in the Norilsk prison, where he was incarcerated for belonging to a religious sect. He was given ten years in camp, but was allowed to return to his job—the administration needed his technical expertise. The director of BEZ was a free man, but everyone knew that Strogonov was the real director of the company. The free man was the so-called party eye; he was given a good salary, while the prisoner Strogonov worked for a bowl of soup and a plateful of gruel. The director listened to Strogonov's opinions, for he knew their worth.

I asked Strogonov to help me. He immediately offered to employ me as controller in BEZ; no special training was needed. I looked forward to getting a job that would suit me. Strogonov talked to Epstein to arrange my transfer. But Epstein would not budge: he said he had no replacement for me. Then a coincidence came to my aid: Metallurgstroi needed waterproof material to make raincoats for its free employees; this material could only be gotten through BEZ. Strogonov now had leverage to pressure Epstein into releasing me. When Epstein returned to his office after negotiating with Strogonov, he said to Lyam: "I just sold Steiner for twelve raincoats."

Monday was the day for me to start working as a comptroller. I picked up my breakfast. On the way back to my barracks, I was told by the man on duty that the chief overseer had just come to ask for me. What did that mean? I had been told on Saturday that I would have a day of rest on Sunday and begin working at BEZ on Monday. I went directly to Strogonov's office, but he wasn't there, so I went to speak to the chief overseer.

"You want to see me?" I asked him.

"Yes. You're not going to BEZ but to factory number 25."

"How come? I thought an arrangement was made between BEZ and Metallurgstoi whereby I'm supposed to work for BEZ."

"I have orders to send you to factory number 25," the chief overseer said, turning away.

There was nothing to be done. I joined the brigades that marched to work in factory number 25, which was situated at the extreme end of the BMS. The red brick factory buildings stood by the foot of a mountain. Only a few people knew what was being produced there, and those who worked in the factory kept it a secret. My job was to help other prisoners empty a red sludgy substance from lorries into a deep pit. The stuff came from several huge containers on the top floor. I worked for weeks in this factory without having any idea what it was producing. The fact that most of the workers there were criminals showed that the NKVD wanted to keep it a secret, even if it no longer was one.

The work wasn't easy. Three men had to push forty lorries from the great hall to the pit in the course of an eleven-hour day. You could meet the quota if there were no mishaps, but this was rarely the case. Due to the extreme cold in the winter of 1947, the tracks were warped and the lorries frequently derailed and had to be prodded back into place with crowbars and wooden posts. This could take as long as a half hour. Since we had to wade about in the red sludge, we wore regular shoes instead of felt boots. At minus forty-five degrees, your feet could easily get irreparable frostbite, so we had to go into a heated room every hour or so to warm up.

In 1947, American food transports stopped coming in. Our bread rations were severely cut, and so were the portions of warm food. Very little food was brought in from the Russian interior, for there had been a catastrophically poor harvest. To win the peasants' allegiance, the Stalin gang had spread the rumor that the collective farms would be eliminated after the war. It was a deliberate deception of the peasants, and not the first one. The peasants reacted as they had in 1933–34—they virtually went on strike. The organizational structure that had been created to force the workers into the collective farms had been undermined and in some places destroyed by the war and by the German occupation. The harvest of 1947 was the poorest since the establishment of the collective farms. Molotov said in a speech that it was the result of drought; this was one of the many brazen lies the Russian people were fed by Stalin's right-hand man, Ribbentrop's negotiating partner.

Soviet workers manifested the same passivity. The production quotas of 1946 and 1947 were lower than they had been before the war. The Russian workers had expected to be given more freedom and higher wages after the war. Instead, they got promises and more terror. But the workers returning from the front were no longer as timid as before the war. Though they didn't dare speak out openly against the terror and the high quotas, they offered passive resistance. Some stayed away from work for days. The peasants acted likewise.

Once again, an attempt was made to use terror as an industrial incentive. Anyone who stayed away from work for three days without a solid excuse was arrested and put in a camp as a saboteur. A new wave of prisoners came pouring in from the industrial centers. Farmers who had failed to meet the minimum daily quotas set by their kolkhoz were also sent to the camps. Others were resettled somewhere in the Far North.

But terror alone couldn't save the economy. Now Stalin came up with a new device: a currency reform. There were no rich people left in the Soviet Union. Who, then, was affected by the currency reform? The workers, employees, peasants, intellectuals, and, paradoxical as it may sound, the most deprived of all—the prisoners. All free Soviet citizens had to exchange their money for the new currency at a rate of one to one for sums not exceeding three thousand rubles; one to three for sums not exceeding ten thousand rubles; and one to ten for any amount over ten thousand rubles. Only the poor prisoners with their little bank accounts made up of gifts they had received from relatives had to exchange every ruble at the rate of ten to one.

During the war and especially during the last year of the war, the prisoners had been promised a great amnesty after the Germans were defeated. Meetings were held at which NKVD officers and representatives of the camp administration exhorted the prisoners to work hard and endure their hunger: their reward would come after the war was over. I attended one of these meetings. The commander of the Norilsk camp, Colonel Voronov, began his address to the prisoners with: "Comrades!

Yes, yes, comrades—that was not a slip of the tongue. You are temporarily in detention, but after the war you will all be released . . ."

The promised amnesty did come, but only for the criminals. The political prisoners, who had endured greater hunger and had worked harder during the war, were not released.

When I was in the hospital during the war, I met an old acquaintance, David Ivanovich Kiyasashvili, once a member of the Menshevik Central Committee of Georgia. We talked about our prospects for the future. He believed that everything would change for the better in Russia. I couldn't share his optimism and said the Mensheviks had often been mistaken and I feared this was once again the case. Unfortunately, I was proven right. The food shortages in the camp were as severe as they had been before the war. At 5 a.m., you could see long lines of prisoners already standing in front of the kitchen, waiting for their breakfast. The counter opened at six. The prisoners were so hungry that they would begin eating as soon as their food was put in the bowls, instead of taking it back to the barracks first.

When the plight of Soviet prisoners was brought up before the United Nations, Deputy Prime Minister Mikoyan declared that there were no labor camps in Russia and that prisoners were so well provided for that English and American workers had every reason to envy them.

I had now gotten to know almost all the divisions in factory number 25. Its principal product was cobalt. It was taken to the airport in small containers and shipped on from there.

I made efforts to get a better job in the factory, but since the place was run by criminals, I was unsuccessful. So I tried to find a way to return to work on the railroad. On the basis of my work experience in Dudinka, I applied for a job with the railroad administration. I applied directly to the head of the freight division of the Norilsk railroad, Gilels, whose acquaintance I had made when I was working in Dudinka. Gilels promised to hire me, but several weeks passed without any change in my situation. Someone was trying to keep me from working for the railroad. I had to find some other way to get out of the sixth camp section, for in many ways conditions here were similar to those in section 9. I went to my friend Vasily Chuprakov, who had served his sentence and was now chief engineer in the municipal department of Norilsk. Vasily set every possible wheel turning on my behalf, and in the spring of 1948 I was hired as a supposed canalization expert for one of the factories under Vasily's supervision.

On the day of my transfer to the second camp section, the chief overseer came into the factory and called me away from work—I had no idea why. A guard escorted me back to the camp, where I was told to take off the clothes I had been given in the sixth camp section. In replacement, I was given a set of rags to wear. That was the custom in this section. Prisoners being transferred to other sections could pass through the gate only if they had a certificate proving that they had returned all their clothes. Even prisoners who were being released were treated this way: they would be given their documents only after they had shed their prison clothes. As a result, newly released prisoners were faced with nearly insuperable difficulties. Most of them helped themselves by trading bread or other food for clothing. And so, the torn garments they were given on the day of their release were left in the camp.

During the war, prisoners who had finished serving their sentences were not released. Either the authorities would pass over these cases in silence, or else, when the prisoners inquired, they would be told that they would have to stay in the camp for the time being. It happened, then, that prisoners who had finished serving their sentences around the beginning of the war were still in the camp and were still being treated as prisoners as late as 1946 and 1947.

Most prisoners had no money at the time of their release. Some had set aside money they had received from their relatives and expected to be able to take it with them. Then came the currency reform: instead of five hundred rubles, they were given fifty, not enough to buy a shirt. Prisoners were always selling articles of clothing. These sales were illegal and subject to punishment, but it was possible to get around these obstacles.

To escort me to the second section, the guards had to take me across the entire expanse of the BMS grounds. I saw a worker who had broken both his legs while unloading boards. The stretcher was drenched with blood. I was glad I was no longer head of the transport division, as the camp administration liked to blame such accidents on the workers' immediate superiors instead of on the excessively high quotas that forced them to jeopardize their health for the sake of a meal and a little tobacco.

It was getting late. The construction sites had closed down for the day, and from all directions long lines of prisoners came marching back to the various camp sections in rows of five, guarded by heavily armed soldiers. My escorts conversed with other soldiers who were walking in the same direction we were. I recognized some friends among the prisoners; they raised their hands in greeting when they saw me.

After a few minutes of waiting in front of the gate of section 2, I was brought before the chief overseer, who asked me if I had lice. Fortunately, I didn't at the time. The chief overseer gave me a note and sent me to the barracks of the brigade that worked in the mechanics' shop of the communal administration. The brigadier had been informed of my arrival and had reserved a bunk for me just a few meters away from his own— an honor that would raise me in the esteem of the other prisoners. This special favor was due to my friendship with the chief engineer.

I worked together with the locksmiths. We brought iron rods or thick wire into the workshop and worked these materials with chisels and hammers. Two men collaborated—one of them holding the iron and the chisel; the other wielding the hammer. My partner, who pretended to be a professional locksmith, elected himself master and myself the apprentice. Whenever we caused any damage, he would blame me; once, when I protested that he, being the expert, was responsible, he said: "Look, you have to understand why I'm blaming you. You have your friend's protection. I would immediately be sent to do hard labor."

After a few weeks, I advanced to a bureaucratic position in the communal administration. But this involved me in constant quarrels with the drivers, and I had to look for another kind of work. I tried to join the railroad. Once again, an accident came to my aid. The workers of the communal administration were being transferred to the third section because of lack of space. The third section was the railroad workers' division. This made matters a good deal simpler. I made a telephone call to the head of the freight division of the Norilsk railroad administration, and he promised to do everything he could to get me a job in his division. Two days later, I was transferred to the railroad workers' brigade.

My new colleagues welcomed me with the greatest friendliness. The day before, the head of the freight division had told them he would be bringing in a highly qualified worker—he meant me.

THE HOSPITABLE SAMOYEDS

I worked at the Norilsk II railroad station in the center of town. It served as a reconsignment depot for materials destined for the warehouses of the great lumberyard, the central garage, and other enterprises. There were sixty people working at the station, all of them prisoners except for the stationmaster. The prisoners' jobs were subject to daily controls, but there were days when the guards came only once or twice to have a brief look.

We had even more freedom here than in Dudinka. The loading officials were obliged to visit the various destination points to supervise the loading and unloading of goods, and the guards were unable to control them every step of the way. However, the political prisoners only rarely gave the guards a hard time. It was the criminals who took advantage of their relative liberty to enrich themselves at the expense of the free citizens of Norilsk, and occasionally even to murder them.

Near the end of 1947, for example, an entire family was massacred by a criminal convict. He broke into a house near the station. Four children between the ages of four and sixteen were in the house with their grandmother. The old woman was alone in the kitchen when the murderer came in: he killed her with an ax he found in the kitchen. The oldest girl heard the woman scream, ran into the kitchen, and was also struck down with the ax. Then the killer went into the room where the other children were and murdered them in the same manner. After that, he gathered up what few objects he could find in the house. Just as he was leaving, the mother returned. He put down the bundle, attacked the woman, and strangled her. Several days later, the killer gave himself away while talking in a drunken stupor. He was sentenced to death and shot.

Thanks to the unusual amount of freedom I now had, I was able to visit various friends. Some of them were still prisoners in the camp, but others had been released after serving their sentences and were now living in exile in Norilsk and working at various jobs. I met with many of them at the station: they had heard I was working there and came to visit me. But some people avoided my company. Here was a new opportunity for learning about people's real character. It was always those who had been particularly indignant, while they were still prisoners, about the indifference of former comrades once they were released, who now studiously avoided their former fellow sufferers. Others, on the other hand, of whom you would have least expected it, never failed to demonstrate their solidarity with their old comrades. Walter Sorge, a worker from Berlin, had been released and was now employed as a locksmith. After every payday, he would drop in for a visit at the station, make sure no one was looking, and press a twenty-five-ruble note into my hand. Walter Müller, another Berliner, went out of his way to avoid me.

During this period, I was able to visit some friends in their apartments and saw how they were enjoying their freedom. Some of them had married and had children. A few of the wives treated me with particular generosity. The few times I visited Vasily, his wife prepared a good meal for me and stuffed my pockets with food before I left. I was very reluctant to accept the invitations of friends, though, and only rarely visited them, for I knew that if the NKVD found out about it, not only would I lose my job at the railroad, but my hosts would be subjected to extremely unpleasant reprisals.

There was a women's brigade working at the Norilsk II station— thirty to forty women. They repaired tracks, and were guarded by three soldiers. Some of these women offered themselves as prostitutes to the men who worked in the station. With the guards' consent, the couples would meet in the various shacks surrounding the station. Later the women would reward the soldiers with liquor and food. Some of these women had steady customers. A few of them didn't have to work at all; if they weren't busy with their clients, you could see them sitting around relaxing.

After the war, many of the guards who had been sent to the front returned to Norilsk. They were noticeably different from those who hadn't fought in the war. There were definite signs of demoralization, for one. You could see it in their willingness to be bribed by the female prisoners or to become clients of the prettier ones, or to allow criminals to leave the brigade in order to break into some apartment, and share the loot with them later. They weren't afraid of the severe punishments they would be subject to if their superiors found out about these misdeeds. This change in attitude had its advantages for us politicals as well. In the old days, prisoners were constantly beaten and occasionally even killed by guards; now they rarely even cursed at us.

Thanks to the laxness of the guards, small groups of prisoners started fleeing from various camp sections. Most of them were political prisoners. Their hopes for a general amnesty and for radical changes in Russia had proved illusory. Also, the news had spread that the archives of the NKVD had been destroyed during the war and that it was quite possible to disappear somewhere in Russia, especially with the great ebb tide of the returning army and of former prisoners of war making it easier to go unnoticed under an assumed name. Many prisoners who had previously considered any attempt to escape futile were now tempted. Some succeeded. Months later, messages came back to the camp with the good news that the fugitives had survived and were still undetected. Of course, no one knew how long they would enjoy their freedom. Most of the fugitives, however, froze to death in the tundra or in the forest. Some were captured by the NKVD with the help of the nomads who lived in the tundra, and were either beaten to death on the spot or brought back to the camp.

The vast wasteland between Norilsk and Krasnoyarsk is virtually uninhabited. Yeniseisk is the first large town, about four hundred kilometers before you reach Krasnoyarsk. There is only one insignificant little town before that—Igarka, on the western bank of the Yenisei—in an area that is larger than Germany and France put together. There is no sizable settlement on the left bank. The tundra consists largely of marshland and is only passable during the winter months. For this reason, most of the escapes were attempted in the winter. The cold and the snow seemed easier to overcome than the bogs and the mosquitoes, against which there was no protection in the summer. The countless rivers that traversed the tundra and the taiga during the summer months also presented nearly insuperable obstacles. And there were the nomads.

A tribe of nomads called the Samoyeds lived on the Taimyr Peninsula. They raised reindeer and hunted foxes. They would pitch their tents, made of reindeer pelts, near rivers and lakes. Their dogs, which greatly resembled foxes, could smell the approach of a stranger at a great distance. When the dogs started barking, the nomads would stick their heads out of their tents. Any stranger was a welcome guest to them, especially if he had some liquor with him. At night, his host's wife or daughter would lie with him on his bed—a very special honor among these people. No one asks the stranger who he is. He is served green tea, which is drunk with salt and reindeer fat. Later the host, well trained by the NKVD, wants to know whether the guest has a passport. If not, he is treated even more generously.

While the fugitive basks in the pleasure of this friendly reception, someone is already on his way to the nearest NKVD post. (There's a loose network of such posts, each three to five hundred kilometers from the other.) Now the NKVD people come hurrying along on reindeer sleds or dogsleds to arrest the fugitive. The nomad's pay for an escaped convict is the same as for a silver-fox fur.

Escape was not the only way in which prisoners attempted to regain their freedom. The Soviet State Ministries received dozens of letters from prisoners reporting that they had discovered gold or other precious metals. Many of these letters were pure fantasy, but some were genuine. Glazanov, a well-known scientist today, discovered uranium in Norilsk. Another prisoner found oil just outside Norilsk. Others discovered the world's biggest coal deposit near the river Tunguska. Among the more fantastic offers to the government were the invention of a flying bicycle by a prisoner named Glutchkov and the projects of Gorski, a "student of Michurin's," who set out to prove that you could cultivate not only vegetables but corn in Norilsk.

As in Dudinka, when I was working in the harbor, I was frequently approached at the station by women who told me the name of a husband or son and wanted to know if I knew anything about him. Generally, the NKVD did not allow visits to prisoners in the camp, but in a few instances relatives managed to obtain a visit permit. Such a permit was obtainable only from the NKVD in Moscow. It was practically senseless to try to get one through normal official channels. You would get no reply, and an energetic knock on the door could easily lead to a closer acquaintance with the NKVD. A few particularly brave or desperate individuals, who of course had no notion of the way prisoners lived in the camp, ventured the long trip by train or boat in the hope of finding a deported relative. In most cases, they didn't know exactly where to look, for the prisoners' mailing addresses usually consisted only of a post-office box. But even if the name of the town was known, as was the case in Norilsk, the camp was so vast, its territory so extensive, that it was almost impossible to find anyone in it. Still, someone occasionally managed to find a relative after weeks of searching.

The problems began in Dudinka. To enter the Norilsk area, you had to have a special permit. Visitors had to show this permit to be allowed to leave the ship. If you succeeded in slipping through control, you faced new obstacles at the train station, which was strictly supervised by the NKVD. You couldn't get a hotel room in Norilsk without showing proof of official permission to be in the city. But, at a high price, you could find lodging in a private home. Then the search would begin.

We would often see these unfortunate women carrying bundles with food for their loved ones, crying: "Brothers, do you know Petrov?" or whatever his name was. Before anyone could reply, a guard would shout at her or threaten her with his rifle. These women would stand around for days, waiting and seeking in vain. Sometimes they would find a prisoner who knew the man they were looking for but had no idea what section he was in at the moment.

One day, as our group was on the way back to the camp, an old man approached us and asked if we knew someone named so-and-so; we knew him and knew where he was. Our guard happened to be a good man; he even allowed us to take the package the old man wanted to give to his son. We managed to conceal it as we passed inspection at the gate, and we were very happy to be able to give it to our comrade along with his father's greetings. Such cases were rare. Usually, the visiting relatives had to travel the thousands of kilometers back home without having been able to find the person they were looking for.

One day, a terrible thing happened in the camp. The great ore-processing plant BOF collapsed. It had been built by *katorzhniki* who lived in the immediate vicinity of the construction site. They had been forced to work in a great hurry, even when the temperature sank to fifty degrees below zero, because the old ore-processing plant was not sufficiently productive. BOF was a modern factory. All its equipment came from America in crates with the inscription: "From one of the United Nations." The refined ore was supposed to be pneumatically transported to the great metallurgical plant two kilometers away. The accident was almost certainly due to a structural flaw. The building collapsed when the temperatures rose. Naturally, the official explanation was that the *katorzhniki* had committed sabotage.

When news of the catastrophe reached us, I heard the stationmaster asking an officer who was waiting for a train whether he knew anything more precise about what had happened. "Nothing much," the officer replied. The stationmaster asked whether anyone had died. The officer said: "Twenty-three dead and sixty wounded." I was not surprised. For this typical NKVD officer, the number of victims was an incidental detail—"nothing much."

AFTER THE COMINFORM RESOLUTION

NO!

One day in the summer of 1948, I was busy writing out a freight document when the telephone rang. I picked up the receiver and recognized Josef's voice.

"Something tremendous has happened!" he said.

"What?"

"I can't say it on the phone."

"Say it in German."

"I can't do that either. Get hold of today's paper. This is an event comparable to the beginning of the world war or the October Revolution."

I dropped what I was doing. I didn't care what was happening in the station. I had only one thought: to find a newspaper. I hurried to the nearby sales division. I knew some of the employees there, former prisoners who had been released and had access to newspapers. On the way, I tried to guess what sort of world-shaking event Josef could be talking about. Stalin must have died, I thought.

When I arrived in the sales division, I asked myself who I should turn to, and decided to visit Plotkin. But he was not there, and the woman in his office was unable to tell me where I could find him. So I went to Mareyev. He had several visitors who were discussing business matters with him; I was surprised that no one was talking about the great event. When the others left and I was alone with Mareyev, I asked him for a newspaper, and he immediately guessed why, since he knew I was well acquainted with conditions in Yugoslavia. He said: "What courage! They must be amazing people!"

I sat down in a corner and started reading the newspaper. Now I understood. The Yugoslavian comrades had dared to defy Stalin with a decisive "No!" This certainly was an event of global significance.

When I returned to the camp in the evening, everyone was talking about the Cominform, Tito, and Yugoslavia. People had various opinions about the Yugoslav revolt, but everyone was happy about it. Happiest of all were the old communists, many of whom had lost faith in socialism because of their terrible experiences. Now they saw that there were still forces in the world that did not blame socialism for the existence of tyranny in Russia but recognized it as the work of a usurper who, under the guise of Marxism, strove only to maintain his own power. It was obvious to all of us that Stalin would not quietly tolerate this apostasy in his own ranks.

I was firmly convinced that the political prisoners would be the first to pay. It had always been that way. When the Republican Army was losing in the Spanish Civil War, the political prisoners felt the NKVD's grip tightening in the camp. When the Red Army was getting a beating from the German Army, we were the ones who were punished. Why should it be different now? We waited for the first blows.

Soon a rumor started circulating that a mysterious commission from Moscow had arrived in Norilsk. You could see high NKVD officers walking about, people who weren't part of the Norilsk NKVD staff. But that wasn't anything unusual. Every year when the Yenisei became navigable, various commissions and controllers came to Norilsk. This commission stayed for three weeks. Rumors had it that they had visited several camps besides ours. After they left, certain camp sections were evacuated, their prisoners distributed among the other sections. Then we heard that certain camp sections were being converted into prisons.

Some inmates were convinced that the new camps were meant for war criminals. They even claimed to have detailed knowledge about the NKVD's plans: the new convicts would be chained to wheelbarrows, the way *katorzhniki* were in the tsar's days. No one had any idea how true or how fantastic these rumors were. But everyone was on edge. Even the ex-convicts lived in fear now; there was a rumor that anyone who had ever been in a camp would be locked up again. Something was brewing, but no one knew what. Our anxiety grew when we learned that the Norilsk industries had received instructions to make up lists of indispensable workers. This was not a rumor but a fact, and it definitely presaged something unusual in the near future.

I asked a leading bureaucrat in the Norilsk railroad administration whether these lists had really been requested. He told me confidentially that the lists did exist and that my name was on one of them; that was all he could tell me. Near the end of August, I was summoned to the office of the third camp section. The head of the labor section told me not to go to work the next day, to stay in my barracks and wait until I was called. I, too, had been affected by the general anxiety in the camp in the last several weeks, and this order upset me a great deal. I asked some friends whether anyone else had been given a similar order. No one had.

At 7 a.m., the chief overseer came, as he often did, to make sure everyone was ready for work. Turning to me, he told me to stay in the barracks and come to the office after the others had left for work. I reported to the head of the labor section a few minutes before eight. He made a call to the guard building and asked whether the escort for the "operations division" was ready. Now I knew where I was going—to the hated NKVD building.

After a few minutes of waiting, I heard the telephone ringing. Someone announced that the guards were ready. The head of the labor section told me to go to the gate and report at the guardhouse; he expressly said to go there directly and not step into any of the barracks along the way. Then he reflected for a moment and said to an assistant: "Take him to the gate and leave him with the guards."

Two armed soldiers took charge of me at the gate. They discussed which way they should go, the shorter or the longer route. They decided

on the latter. "We're in no hurry," one of them said. We walked slowly
toward the long, two-story NKVD building in the center of Norilsk. Far
away, I could see prisoners rebuilding the collapsed walls of the ore-
processing plant. When we reached the railway crossing, we had to wait
for a train to pass. The soldiers made me kneel while the train rolled by.

AN INTERROGATION

At the entrance to the NKVD building, one of my two escorts told the
NKVD soldier on duty that I was from the third camp section, and gave
him a sheet of paper. The soldier made a telephone call. An officer came
to pick me up and told the two escort guards to wait.

I followed the officer through the dark hallway. He stopped in front
of a door with the inscription "*Nachalnik operativnovo otdela NKVD,*"
stuck his head in, and asked: "May I come in?"

"Come in!" someone inside answered.

I stepped in and said hello. Polikarpov was standing next to a desk.
The moment I saw him, I remembered him taking me by the throat and
screaming: "I'll strangle you!"

A second NKVD man was standing by the window. He was as big
and fat as Polikarpov was. When he turned around, I saw three large
stars on his gold epaulettes. So he was a colonel!

"Sit down," Polikarpov said, pointing to a chair next to his desk. He
and the colonel sat down as well.

"How are you?" Polikarpov asked.

"I am content."

"Content! I didn't expect to hear that from you. Where are you
working now?"

"For the railroad."

"Really? Do you have a pass?"

"No, I'm working in the freight division."

"You can do that without a pass? It must be rather difficult."

"It's all right."

"You should be given a *propusk;* it'll make life much easier for you."

I listened closely. This didn't sound like the Polikarpov I knew. What
was going on?

"How long have you been in detention?" the colonel asked.

"Twelve years," I replied.

"What is your sentence?"

"Twice ten years."

"Why twice?" the colonel asked, as if surprised.

I told him I had been given ten years in 1937 in Moscow and another
ten years in 1943. I began to feel disgusted, for I knew that they were
perfectly well informed about my case.

"Now is your opportunity to get out. It's up to you," the colonel said.

I was astonished. I couldn't imagine what they might be offering me.

"Where did you get to know Tito and the other Yugoslav leaders?"

The colonel, of course, knew very well where I had met the leaders of the Yugoslav Communist Party. But I had to answer his question. So I told him briefly about my activities in Yugoslavia. The colonel interrupted and asked me to be as specific as possible and not leave out any details about my sojourn in Yugoslavia, the communist leaders there, my meetings with communist officials in the West and in the Soviet Union.

"Have you read the Cominform resolution?"

"Yes."

"What do you think of it?"

"I'm a prisoner. My opinion is insignificant."

"When I ask what you think of it, I expect a candid response from you." The colonel's voice was still gentle.

"I can't answer your question. I haven't followed all the events. I've just learned a little bit from the newspapers."

"Do you believe what the newspapers say?"

"You're asking too much of me. You are an NKVD officer, I'm just a prisoner. My situation makes it impossible to speak frankly to you about these things."

"I assure you, you have nothing to fear," the colonel said coolly.

I tried to think, but I couldn't concentrate. What did they want of me? Polikarpov interrupted my train of thought. "Would you like some tea, or something to eat?"

"Yes, I would like some tea. No food, please."

A girl brought three glasses of tea with lemon—the first lemon I had tasted in over ten years.

After I had had my tea, the colonel started talking. He said he had been in Yugoslavia and knew most of the leading politicians there. Every once in a while, he would throw in a Serbian word or two. I had the impression that he really had been in Yugoslavia. Finally, he said: "The gang that sold out to the imperialists won't stay in power for long. The Yugoslavian people are on the side of the Soviet Union. There are uprisings all over Yugoslavia. The days of the Tito clique are numbered."

I listened and kept silent. His phrases sounded very familiar: they reminded me of Soviet newspapers. When he was finished, the colonel asked me: "Are you willing to help us?"

"How could I help you?"

"You can help us by testifying that all those people were in contact with the police twenty years ago, when you knew them."

"I can't do that. As far as I can remember, the opposite was the case. At the time when I left Yugoslavia, both Tito and Mosha Piyade were imprisoned in Lepoglava."

"That's unimportant. If you really want to help us, such details are of no significance."

"I've lost my freedom, sir, but I haven't lost my conscience."

"Don't you trust the Soviet government?" the colonel asked sharply.

"I came to the Soviet Union because I trusted the Soviet government."

"The Soviet government is telling you that the leaders of the Communist Party of Yugoslavia are a band of imperialist agents. Do you believe that, or don't you?"

"I myself was condemned as a Gestapo agent, even though I never had the slightest contact with the Gestapo."

"We are not talking about you now but about the leaders of the Yugoslav party."

"I don't know what has happened in the meantime and I can't judge what is happening today. But at the time when I was in touch with these people, they were all honest communists."

"I repeat: you now have an opportunity to be released. The days of the Yugoslav traitors are numbered. We forced a colossal enemy like the Nazi army to its knees: it won't take us more than a few hours to deal with Yugoslavia. Think about it. We'll talk again. You won't have to go to work for the time being. Take a rest."

I replied that I would much rather go back to work than sit in the barracks.

"No, no. For the time being, you won't be working."

Polikarpov made a phone call. Then the officer came to pick me up and deliver me to the guards. We walked back to the camp.

My comrades besieged me there. Everyone wanted to know where I had been. I confided only in Josef. When I told him about the colonel's offer, he was furious. "Those disgusting bastards! Our freedom isn't enough for them, now they want to take away our honor."

Two days later, I was back in the NKVD building with Polikarpov and the colonel.

"Well, how are you today?" asked the colonel, rubbing his hands.

"As usual," I replied curtly.

"Have you given the matter any thought?"

"There wasn't much to think about."

"How do you mean that?"

"I can only repeat what I have already said: I am not the right man for your purposes."

The colonel stood up, paced the room for a while, sat back down, and said: "Yes, Polikarpov is right. You are an incorrigible element. It's all right, you can leave."

I stood up.

"Have you told anyone about our conversation?" the colonel asked.

"I've told just one person."

The colonel leaped up, his face deep red, his eyes bulging. "Whaaat? Who did you talk to? You ought to be shot just for that!"

I told him Josef's name and added that I kept no secrets from this man.

"Oh, him, I know him! No, that's not your only friend, there's a whole gang of Comintern types still running around thanks to people like"—and he pointed to Polikarpov. Then, addressing Polikarpov, he said: "Have him sign the paper."

Polikarpov went into the next room and came back with a printed sheet of paper. He wrote my name on it and gave it to me to sign. I read: "I declare that I shall not tell anyone of this conversation. I have been advised that if I fail to comply with this order, I will be guilty of betraying a state secret." I signed.

Once I was back on the street, I felt relieved, even though I was convinced that I would be thrown in prison instead of being brought back to the camp. All the way home, I wondered what would happen next. How often had I told myself that my pleasant job at the railroad, where I had so much freedom of movement and enough to eat, couldn't last long, that something would come along to put an end to so much good fortune. Now it had come to pass. What would become of me?

Several days went by. I was sitting in my barracks, eating my normal ration, but I wasn't allowed to go to work. When I tried to return to my office one day, the chief overseer sent me back to the barracks. The same thing happened when I tried again during the night shift. I had already gone through the gate when the commander of the guard noticed me. This can't go on for much longer, I thought to myself; I had never heard of a prisoner who was kept from working without being sick. I wanted to work so that I could resume contact with my friends in the other camp sections. I had reason to fear that the NKVD would take extreme measures against me after my talk with the colonel. I could be shot while "attempting to escape" or die of a "heart attack" in the punishment cell. Despite all my efforts, though, I was unable to make contact with my friends.

Day after day went by. I lay on my cot, reading. No one bothered me, not even the camp commander, who liked to force slightly sick prisoners to work at various odd jobs for three hours every day.

On September 2, something unexpected happened. The head of the labor section came into the barracks, together with a camp guard and a camp policeman. The man on duty leaped up and shouted the obligatory command: "*Vnimanie, zaklyuchonnye*—Attention, prisoners!" The few who were present stood at attention.

"Where is Steiner?" the head of the labor section asked. Then, seeing me, he came toward me. "Pack your stuff! Leave your bedding with the *dnevalny*."

I didn't ask where we were going or why. I knew the answer to that question already: "You'll find out soon enough."

I picked up my bag, containing a set of underwear, a clean pair of pants, a spoon, and a tin bowl, and added my blanket and pillow. I had also set aside four portions of bread, about a kilogram of sugar, and forty rubles. I was led to the office—I assumed, for the formalities preceding a transfer to another camp. Instead, I was locked into a small room next to the office.

I put my bag in the corner and paced back and forth. I didn't want to get comfortable; I assumed I wouldn't be there for long. After about two hours, I felt an urgent need to relieve myself, and knocked on the door. For a long time, no one responded. Only after a great deal of knocking did I hear a voice outside: "What do you want?"

"Why am I locked in here?"

"I don't know. I was told that if you need anything, you should tell me."

"I have to go to the toilet."

The door opened, and before me stood the messenger from the camp office.

"What's going on?" I asked again.

"I don't know."

He led me to the toilet and waited outside. Then he took me back to the little room and locked me in. The window had bars on it, but otherwise I liked the room. I thought to myself: this wouldn't be a bad place to live, perhaps with my wife. I could see myself coming home from work and reading a book or listening to the radio.

In the evening, the messenger brought me soup, fish, and gruel. After eating, I spread my padded coat on the floor, pulled my blanket and pillow out of my bag, and lay down to test my "bed" for comfort. Not bad! Just a little too low for the head. So I put the bag underneath the pillow. Excellent!

I looked out the window. The brigades were coming back from work, walking up the hill toward the barracks. I recognized some friends and called them by name. They came to the window, and I was able to converse with them freely. Everyone was surprised. Many expected something similar to happen to them as well. The news that I was locked in that room spread quickly through the camp. Many people came to my window—people I knew, and also strangers. Most of them asked me to keep them informed if I possibly could. I promised to try. My comrades brought me bread and other food. Some of them gave me money, which everyone was sure would be of real use to me. These demonstrations of support multiplied in the days that followed, until there was no more room in my bag for the many gifts. Even prisoners I had never met took leave of me with such kindness that I was deeply moved.

On September 4, at 11 a.m., the head of the labor section and an NKVD officer came to my room. "Pack your stuff and come along," the section head said. Twenty men were standing in the office. I was told to join them. Among them were a few who had asked me to keep them informed of where I was going—now we would be solving the riddle together.

A large box full of food was brought in from the kitchen. Each prisoner was given two kilos of bread, two salt herring, and five lumps of sugar. We could infer from this that we were being taken on a long voyage, since these provisions amounted to a two-day ration. So we weren't going to the Norilsk prison! I was glad of that. But where were we going? This question was on everyone's mind. We discussed it incessantly.

When we were led out of the office, almost all the prisoners who hadn't gone to work came streaming out of the barracks. The night-shift workers got out of bed. Everyone accompanied us to the gate. The overseers and camp policemen chased the prisoners back, but more and more people crowded around us. As the gate opened, hundreds of voices shouted: "Farewell, comrades!"

FAREWELL TO NORILSK

We were twenty-one, and we were being escorted by twelve soldiers and an officer. We walked toward the train station through the streets of Norilsk. I had been led through these same streets nearly ten years ago. At that time, there had been just a few isolated log houses on either side of the road. They had been replaced by unbroken rows of two-story buildings made of wood and stone. Many people stepped out of these houses to look at us, and as we marched past the central hospital, the patients rushed to the windows and waved as we passed. It was a common occurrence to see prisoners being marched through the streets of Norilsk. I concluded that the extraordinary attention our little group was attracting could only be attributed to the rumors that had been circulating ever since the Cominform resolution.

An unexpected sight awaited us at the station: about three hundred prisoners were sitting on the ground in front of the station building. We joined them. It was a beautiful day. I had never experienced such superb weather in Norilsk. Hundreds of people were standing around the station—free people and prisoners; men, women, and children. Some of them tried to approach us. The guards were infected by the relaxed and animated mood of the crowd. People handed us parcels, and the guards looked the other way. We had been told to stay in line, but we secretly switched places so as to be closer to our friends. I saw Josef waving to me and sneaked over to where he was.

All of us had one question on our minds: Where were we going? For the first time, I heard people surmising that we might be taken back to "the continent." Although Norilsk is not an island, we tended to think of it that way because of the huge distance from the interior of the country and because you could get there only by air or by water. We might as well have been cut off from the world on a desert island.

Most of us, though, including myself, did not believe we would be brought back to the interior. We were all considered "dangerous elements": former leading officials, managers of large industrial enterprises. Almost everyone was a former party member. I thought it equally unlikely that we were being removed to a place with harsher conditions than Norilsk. Some people guessed that we would be taken to an island in the Kara Sea. Others were convinced we would be sent to the coal mine of Kayerkan, fifty kilometers from Norilsk.

When Gilels, the head of the Norilsk railroad's freight division, passed by, I asked him where the cars were headed. "Dudinka," he said. That excluded the coal-mining hypothesis.

For several hours we sat, and we were glad to be in Norilsk a little longer, perhaps because, though we had suffered greatly here, it was also the place where we had spent ten of the best years of our lives. Among the crowd were a few wives and children of prisoners in our group. Since male and female prisoners worked side by side and were sometimes able to move about quite freely, children had been born and close bonds had been established and maintained in anxious expectation of the day of release. Now these families were being torn apart.

As the cars came in and the first names were called, the women and children began to cry. The first car was full: an officer locked the door from outside. Suddenly a woman came rushing toward us: "Comrades, you're going to Irkutsk!" Everyone was stunned.

A prisoner who knew the woman asked her: "How do you know this?"

"The director of medical services told me."

It took a long time to load us on the train. The officer carefully checked the dates in each prisoner's dossier. I cast a last glance at the area around the station. To my left was the *katorzhniki* section; behind it, the giant structure of the new ore-processing plant. On my right was the second camp section, where I had lived for a while. On a hill was the Norilsk railroad administration building, and farther to the right, the Norilsk NKVD building—to this structure and to the people who worked there I addressed a final curse.

It was dark by the time my name was called. I climbed into the freight car and lay down on the floor, where many of my comrades were already. My neighbor was Edi Schreidel, a young Austrian. Someone lit a candle, and I could see the faces of my comrades. Some of them were squatting; others lay prone on the floor. No one talked. Once in a while, someone would say a word or two. We were all lost in thought. We knew our geographical destination, but we were traveling toward the unknown.

Most of us were old hands at camp life. Having served ten years in Norilsk had brought us certain privileges. Gone were the days when we had to perform the hardest work for the least nourishment. By putting to use various professional skills and by acquiring new ones, but especially by acquiring a thorough knowledge of the camp's economic and social structure, we had become indispensable to the authorities, and as a result our lives had become not only bearable but in some cases almost agreeable. Now we were going to a new place where the naked struggle for existence would begin anew. Some of us had just a few months left to finish out our sentences. Others had made arrangements to continue in their positions as free employees after their release, which would have brought them certain advantages. All those hopes were dashed.

The locomotive gave out a shrill whistle, and the train began to move slowly out of the station. Around midnight, someone said we had just passed Kayerkan. Evidently, we weren't being sent to the mines. We arrived in Dudinka at eight in the morning. The soldiers yanked the doors open. "Everybody out!" We had to stand in front of the cars and participate in the usual roll call. Then we were assembled in rows of five. The guard commander announced the customary rules for our march through the town, and we set off toward the transit station. There was lively activity there: transports were coming and going, and the barracks were overflowing. Because of the mild weather at that time of year, it was possible for hundreds of prisoners to sleep outside. Everywhere you looked, people were bartering. The newcomers weren't wise to the criminals' tricks yet, and many lost their possessions without getting anything in return.

We were all put in a separate barracks, under orders from the camp commander of Norilsk, Voronov, who had personally come to Dudinka to supervise the transport of the old Norilsk prisoners. During our stay in Dudinka, we were served our meals at a separate counter. Voronov ordered additional food for us. There was also plenty of makhorka and Papirossi cigarettes. The camp administrators were, altogether, very solicitous toward us. Our removal was highly regretted by the directors of the Norilsk industries.

However, this did not prevent Voronov from continuing to lie to us. When he showed up in the transit station and asked us how we were feeling, some of us dared ask him where we were being taken. He answered with feigned surprise: "You really don't know?"

"No," we replied.

"Why, that's terrible! I told Dvin to tell you." (Dvin was his deputy.)

"Nobody told us."

"You're going to the northern Caucasus."

"The northern Caucasus?" someone said.

"That's right. They're building a nonferrous ore factory there, under Lieutenant General Rapoport's direction. It's he who put in a request for our experts."

Most of us realized this was a lie, but some believed him.

On September 7, 1948, we heard that a passenger ship named *Joseph Stalin* had dropped anchor in Dudinka, with several hundred prisoners on board. As soon as they disembarked, we were to replace them in the lower deck. I was infected by the general excitement. Were we really returning to European Russia?

A few hours later, we saw the newcomers on the other side of the barbed wire, waiting to be admitted to the camp. We recognized them by the variety of clothes they wore. There were German uniforms among them, including caps with the death's-head insignia of the SS. Others had on Soviet Army uniforms. Even though it was warm, some of the prisoners were wearing felt boots—those were people who had been arrested during the winter.

The newly arrived prisoners stood in front of the gate for a long time. Finally, they were called by name, one by one. I could hear the officers mispronouncing the German names. Many prisoners had to be called several times because they didn't realize they were being called. We weren't allowed to go near the newcomers, and a large unit of camp policemen was there to enforce this rule. But the next day we were able to talk with them with impunity, and they were immediately drawn into the usual bartering. They looked starved and were eager to exchange their possessions for food.

On September 8, at eight in the morning, we were told to get ready for transport. I packed my bag; it took just five minutes. I kept my bread bag handy for the usual transport provisions. After we waited for more than two hours, an officer finally shouted: "Line up!" I took my bag and hurried out into the yard. Officers and soldiers were waiting by the gate. As each man was called by name, he had to take off all his clothes and submit to a thorough search. Then we were led out of the camp.

We marched through the streets of Dudinka in rows of five. We could see the *Joseph Stalin* in the harbor. It was a new passenger ship that had been built in the Soviet zone of Germany and now traveled regularly between Krasnoyarsk and Dudinka. When we arrived at the dock, I experienced a sense of relief I hadn't felt in a long time. Ten years ago, when I came to Dudinka and saw the desolate countryside around me, I hadn't believed I would ever leave this place alive. And yet I had survived the most terrible time of my life. I felt both happy and sad— sad because some of my friends weren't here to experience this moment. I was thinking especially of Rudolf Ondratschek and Kerosi-Molnár.

ON BOARD THE *JOSEPH STALIN*

From the gangplank down to the lower deck, we had to walk single-file between two rows of soldiers with submachine guns at the ready. A broad wooden stairway led into an empty room. Everyone tried to grab one of the corner seats. We tried to make ourselves comfortable, but we had to move closer and closer together as more men came in. Eventually, the area was so full that we had to sit shoulder to shoulder. There was no way to lie down. The tiny barred portholes on either side had to be opened to let in enough air. The door was shut, and four armed guards positioned themselves on the stairway in front of the exit.

Gradually, the excitement that had been caused by the lack of space abated; everyone had found a place to sit. Some people took out their bread and started eating. Not until then did I have a chance to see who my neighbors were. On my right was Edi Schreidel, one of a group of Austrians I had gotten to know in Dudinka in 1946. Directly in front of me was Lev Braginsky, the former state prosecutor of Dnepropetrovsk. My neighbor on the left was Viktor Strecker, a mining engineer of German descent who, like many Germans born in Russia, did not speak a word of German. I was only slightly acquainted with my other immediate neighbors.

Late that evening, after the electric lights had been turned on, the ship raised anchor. Looking through the small portholes, we gazed for the last time at the harbor and the houses of Dudinka. After a while, the only sight was the naked tundra. I turned away from the porthole.

After eating a little, we became more talkative. My neighbors and I spoke about the past, about life in Norilsk, about our immediate prospects. Much later, we started to get tired and tried to sleep, leaning against each other or against the walls. Some people succeeded: you could hear the sound of snoring here and there. The next morning, the soldiers opened the wide iron door. We had a glimpse of the free passengers on the upper deck. They were sitting on bundles and wooden suitcases. Some curious folk peered down in our direction but were chased away by the guards.

Several unarmed soldiers came down with baskets full of bread that had been cut into sections. Other soldiers followed with large pails full of tea. My neighbor, Braginsky, was chosen as the elder. Together with some other prisoners, he equitably distributed the bread and the tea. There was no quarreling over the food. After breakfast, we continued our conversations. It was difficult to reach friends who were sitting at some distance from you. You had to climb over the heads of others. We had all taken off our shoes, to be able to move around more easily. We were given a warm meal for lunch, a stew made of millet and beans. The guards promised us a second warm meal for dinner, but it didn't come. In the morning, the soldiers said there was no wood for the stove; we would have to wait till we reached Igarka before a warm meal could be cooked. Late in the afternoon of the second day, we had another warm meal.

On the evening of the first day, I had a conversation with Edi Schreidel. He told me about Austria and about his experiences during and after the war. Edi, the son of a wealthy farmer from Rüdental in Lower Austria, had been drafted at the beginning of the war and had fought in Africa under Rommel's command. When the Afrika Korps was defeated, Edi was imprisoned, first in England and then in America in a camp in the state of Maine. Because he was an anti-fascist, he was put into a school, together with other German prisoners, and was given lessons in the American way of life. After the end of the war, Edi was one of the first to return to his country. Rüdental was in the Russian zone. One day, Edi was summoned to the mayor's office. When he stepped into the room, he found two Russian soldiers there. The mayor said they wanted wine, and he asked Edi to sell them ten liters. Because money was nearly worthless at that time, nobody liked to sell the good Rüdental wines. But Edi didn't want to refuse the soldiers' request. He led them to his wine cellar, which was far from the house where he lived. The Russians took the bottles and paid what they had been asked. Edi went to the village inn with some friends. After a few hours, several villagers rushed in and called out to Edi in great excitement: "You're sitting here while the Russians are plundering your wine cellar!"

He ran to the wine cellar, accompanied by his friends. On the way, they came across a group of people who were beating up three Russian soldiers. Edi, who had had a little too much to drink, pitched in. The soldiers managed to tear themselves loose and took off on a sidecar motorcycle. Only then did Edi learn the details of the Russians' burglary of his wine cellar. They were the same men who had bought ten bottles of wine from him earlier in the day. They had returned to the wine cellar, broken the locks with iron bars, and filled several canisters full of wine. The villagers saw them as they were leaving. After the incident, Edi returned to the inn with his friends to celebrate the "victory."

Three days later, a detachment of NKVD men surrounded the village and arrested eighteen villagers who had taken part in the brawl. They were jailed in Baden and were tried by a Russian war court several weeks later. The court sentenced six men to death and the rest to ten years in prison. Edi was taken to Norilsk, where he remained for two years. Now he was going into the unknown, along with the rest of us.

The ship moved upstream with great difficulty. Occasionally, it would lay anchor near one of the few settlements by the banks of the Yenisei and take on new freight and new passengers. At night, we could hear heavy chains being dragged aboard; they would eventually be used on rafts. This hard work was performed by women. We could tell because we could hear them singing sad songs while they worked. The sound had a depressing effect on us.

IN KRASNOYARSK

On the seventh day we reached the regional capital, Krasnoyarsk. The ship first laid anchor on the left bank; after the passengers had disembarked, it moved over to a makeshift landing site on the right bank. It was a long time before the door was finally opened. The soldiers ordered us to carry out the barrels we had been using as toilets for the past week. We heaved them up the stairs, two men at a time, with a great effort. Some of the contents spilled, leaving a foul-smelling trail on the steps. After this job was done, we were called out by name, one by one. As on the day when we left Dudinka, the soldiers formed a double row on either side of the stairs and along the gangplank as we disembarked.

After an arduous climb up the steep bank, we reached the plain on which the western side of Krasnoyarsk was built. Escorted by armed guards and dogs, we marched through a sparsely populated part of town; we could tell from the factory buildings and apartment houses that a new residential area was under construction. We could look across to the other shore; a railway bridge spanned the broad river. Dozens of factory chimneys stood stark against the sky.

We marched along footpaths toward the tracks of the Trans-Siberian Railroad. Far away, we could see the Siberian Express rushing past on its ten-thousand-kilometer trip from Negoreloye to Vladivostok. We crossed the tracks, and walked past the Yenisei train station. A group of prisoners were unloading logs near the station, with armed guards supervising them. We marched on through a large settlement where there were goats tethered in front of many of the small, untended-looking wooden houses. Women watched us passing by their windows; the expressions on their faces were fearful. Some old women genuflected. Whenever anyone came too close to our column, the soldiers would shout: "V *storonu*—To one side!" and the people would scamper off into the bushes or behind a tree.

Finally, we caught sight of the *ptichniki*—birdhouses, as the characteristic watchtowers surrounding a camp were called. We marched for nearly two kilometers along a tall wooden fence, until we reached the gate of the Krasnoyarsk transit station of the Norilsk camp. A large detachment of camp guards and camp policemen were waiting for us in the yard. Several officials of the camp administration, among them the deputy camp commander, Dvin, were seated at a table. Dvin watched as we were called one by one and stepped up to the table to answer the camp officials' questions. Some of the prisoners greeted Dvin, and he responded in a very friendly way.

After the induction procedures were over, we marched about two hundred steps toward a long barracks with three entrances. We went into the middle entrance in groups of five. The room was square. Two-tiered cots stood along the walls and in the middle of the room. I found an empty spot; none of my old friends was anywhere near me. We made our "beds" by spreading our coats as mattresses and using our unemptied bags as pillows.

Then we discovered that we were locked into the barracks. This gave rise to suspicions that some evil scheme against us was afoot. The barracks was opened at noon. A steaming caldron stood in the yard outside the entrance, and a cook in a white smock was ladling out hot soup. It tasted good. After the meal, we were allowed to walk about in front of the barracks for a while and enjoy the mild and sunny weather. When the overseer came, we asked him why we were being locked in.

"Orders from the commander," he replied curtly.

The next morning, we asked the overseer to call the commander. Later that morning, Dvin came by, accompanied by the camp commander and other officers. All the barracks inmates jumped to their feet and surrounded them. Braginsky—still functioning as the elder—stepped forward and asked Dvin: "Citizen commander, why are we locked in here?"

"I ordered that for your own security," Dvin replied.

"What do you mean?"

"There are many criminals with twenty-five-year sentences waiting here to be transported to Norilsk; they could easily attack and rob you."

"We are not afraid," some men cried out. "We know how to protect ourselves."

"I cannot allow bloody brawls to take place here," Dvin said.

"We ask you, nevertheless, to give us freedom of movement."

"I will think about it. I'll see if there's any way to solve this problem."

The next day, Dvin came back to our barracks, and we asked him again to let us move around freely in the courtyard. He repeated that he was concerned for us and our possessions. He said he would be distressed if anything happened to such accomplished people as we were. We had the impression that Dvin was being forthright. At the end of our conference, he agreed to leave the door open during the day if we would promise only to walk around the barracks and nowhere else. We promised.

As soon as Dvin left, most of us hurried out through the open door to enjoy the fresh air and the sun, and prisoners immediately came out of other barracks to gape at us. All sorts of rumors about us were circulating in the camp: that we were being taken to Moscow, for example, to receive medals and be released for our contribution to the construction of the city of Norilsk. Others claimed they had heard a high-ranking officer say we were being taken to Krasnoyarsk to build a large factory. We were generally referred to as "the engineers' base."

The criminals, who collaborated even more closely than usual with the guards and the camp administration, were in the habit of fleecing all newcomers of all but the shirts on their backs. The stolen goods were then sold outside the camp by the guards, and the proceeds were divided equitably as among brothers. Not only ordinary guards but officers took part in these transactions. As a rule, prisoners stayed in the transit station until the day of their move to another place. Only very sick patients were officially permitted to stay any longer. Nevertheless, there were prisoners in the transit station who were as sturdy as bulls and had been living there for a year or longer—these were people who had established "business relations" with the camp administration. Dvin had made the commander of the transit station personally responsible for our welfare. It was because of him that we remained unscathed, while other prisoners were attacked and robbed almost the moment they arrived in the camp.

A few days after our arrival, a group of young Latvians was attacked by the bandits. The latter had hid under the bunks before the Latvians arrived. The Latvians came into the barracks, made themselves comfortable, but posted sentinels by the gate, probably because they had had bad experiences in other transit stations. But while they were prepared for an attack from outside, the bandits crawled out of their hiding places and began to rob them. The Latvians weren't at all timid, however, and attacked the bandits with boards which they tore off the bunks. The bandits screamed for help, and soon the first casualties ran bleeding out of the barracks. Camp policemen and guards came running to protect their wards against further manhandling. After that, there was peace and quiet in the camp for several days.

There were some newly arrived criminals in the barracks next to ours: they were locked in. The reason was that immediately after their arrival they had committed numerous thefts and robberies. Since they were not part of the clique that was in cahoots with the camp administration, the stolen goods could be retrieved from various hiding places in the barracks.

Most of the criminals had been in a camp before. They had but briefly enjoyed the amnesty Stalin had granted the criminal prison population after the defeat of the Nazis. They had resumed their robbing and murdering right after they were released, and so they were locked up again, this time for twenty-five years. They weren't particularly grateful to Stalin for the amnesty; never before had I heard so much vituperation against Stalin and the Soviet government. Stalin was referred to as the *gutalinshchik*, the shoeshine man (almost all shoeshiners in the large Russian cities come from Georgia or Armenia).

"It'll soon be all over for the *gutalinshchik!*" they would predict, amid volleys of juicy invectives. We stood outside their barred window, listening to their conversation. They were constantly begging us for tobacco and bread.

FRANÇOIS PETIT AND OTHERS

We were joined by several Austrians who were waiting to be transported to Norilsk. It was a special pleasure for me to listen to them talk about recent developments in Austria and Vienna. We informed them about Norilsk, and they told us about the circumstances of their arrest and trial. All the newly arrived Austrians I talked to had been arrested in the Soviet zone of Austria because they had come from the western zones. All of them were accused of "spying for the U.S.A.," and every one of them had been given the same sentence, twenty-five years in a camp. They were, almost all of them, young men from Graz, Linz, or Salzburg. A few of them had in fact been involved with the C.I.A. I tried to console these boys by telling them they would soon be able to go back home. We gave them some of our bread, and they, in return, sang us the newest Viennese songs. This was especially moving for me.

A few days after our arrival, a batch of invalids was brought in from Norilsk. They were being sent to a special camp for invalids. They told us that the infamous judge Gorokhov and a second NKVD henchman had drowned in a boat while crossing the Yenisei. This was gratifying news to our ears.

I was sitting in the sun, consuming the meal I had just picked up, when a thin, bespectacled man of medium height came near me and stood watching me with hungry eyes. I could see by his torn uniform trousers and by his whole appearance that he was either German or Austrian.

"You can come closer," I said.

"You speak German?" he asked with surprise.

"I'm Austrian."

"Impossible!"

"Why impossible? Do you think you're the only foreigner in Siberia?"

"No, of course not. I know there are many here."

"Why don't you sit down next to me—you have plenty of time."

"Time—my God, we certainly have enough time here."

He sat down next to me. I divided the rest of my bread in two and gave him half.

"No, don't bother," he said, embarrassed.

"Go ahead, eat, don't make a fuss."

The man practically tore the bread from my hands. Then he ate it slowly, with reverent attention. I kept silence, not wanting to disturb him. When he finished, he introduced himself. "Dr. Bergmann, from Stuttgart."

I told him my name.

"Have you been here long?" he asked me.

"Unfortunately yes, much too long."

"How long?"

"Twelve years."

"What, twelve years?"

"That's correct, twelve years."

"In camp?"

"Yes, just imagine, twelve years in camp!"

"I can hardly believe it. And where were you?"

"I was where you are going."

Bergmann wanted to know exactly what Norilsk was like, and I told him what I had reported to so many others. Then I went into the barracks and brought out some pieces of zwieback, of which I had a sufficient supply, and gave them to Bergmann. He was very surprised to learn that there were prisoners here whose stomachs were full and who were willing to give bread to others.

I asked him how he had come to be sent to Norilsk, and he told me his story. He had served in the German Army and had been captured by the Russians. He had worked as a doctor in the prison camp. He had a habit of writing down the names of the prisoners of war who had died, so that eventually he could inform their relatives. The NKVD discovered the notebook with the names. Bergmann was tried by a war court and was sentenced to twenty-five years in camp for espionage.

During the weeks I spent in the transit station, Dr. Bergmann frequently visited me, together with other Germans. Our barracks exerted a strong attraction, for we were the only prisoners who could afford to share our food. Bergmann loved the soup that was served in the camp. Every time I met him after a meal, he would ask me: "Did you have lunch yet?" And without waiting for my answer, he would say: "The soup was fabulous today." Or: "The soup is delicious today. I had a piece of meat this big in my bowl!"

One day, after hearing him sing the praises of the "fabulous" soup, I invited him into our barracks and gave him a pot with three liters of soup. After eating about two thirds of it, he put the pot down and said: "I have to stop."

"Why?"

"Because, once you're full, you can taste how miserable this slop really is."

I was happy to see Bergmann finally free of his constant hunger, if only for a moment. Soon after, his transport left for Norilsk, and I never saw him again.

Once a short, black-haired man came to visit me with one of the Austrians. He asked me something in German, but with a strong foreign accent. I didn't have to probe very long to find out where he came from. He was eager to talk, whether anyone was listening or not. His name was François Petit and he had been a captain in the French Army. (I had met very few Frenchmen in the camps, so I was particularly interested in this little *capitain*.) Petit had fought in the Maquis, the French underground, during the war. In the beginning of 1948, he was arrested by the Russians in Potsdam, was tried by a military court, and was sentenced to twenty-five years for "espionage." Now he was waiting to be moved on to Norilsk.

That same day, Petit asked to speak to me privately. We withdrew to a corner. He wanted information about Norilsk. I gave him a brief description of my experiences there.

"Is it possible to escape?" he asked.

The question embarrassed me. I looked at him for a while to make sure he was asking it in earnest. Petit was waiting for my answer. To gain a little time for reflection, I asked him some insignificant question. I wondered: was Petit a provocateur? I decided that the NKVD wouldn't use a completely inexperienced prisoner to entrap a seasoned *lagernik* like me. Petit was a naïve man without any knowledge of the nature of the country he was in, of its vast extent, of the NKVD, and of course had no idea what life in the camps was like. As most foreigners do when they come to Russia, he was applying European standards and concepts to his experience. This error was usually the beginning of a tragedy.

"Do you have any idea where you are going?" I asked.

"To Norilsk."

"That's true, you are going from here to Norilsk. But that doesn't tell you anything. You have to realize that you'll be nearly twenty-five hundred kilometers from the nearest railroad. Once you're in the camp, you'll be cut off from the outside world by several rows of barbed wire. You'll be constantly supervised by overseers, camp policemen, your brigadier, and your own companions. All it takes is for you to be late for dinner and they'll come looking for you."

"And at night?"

"There's no such thing as night and day there."

"What do you mean? Day is day and night is night."

"Not in Norilsk. For four months, the sun doesn't set at all. For another four months, it never rises."

He was amazed.

"Do you see how naïve you are to believe that you can escape from Norilsk? It's altogether impossible."

The Frenchman was stunned. He didn't know what to say. After a small pause, he asked: "Can't you run away while you're working?"

I tried very hard to dissuade him from his futile plans; I didn't succeed. He tried over and over to prove to me that there had to be a way to escape. Petit told me about a mysterious organization called the "cross-makers' league," with members in countries all over the world, including the Soviet Union. He told me how I could recognize the initiates: when meeting a stranger, I should make a sign with my foot, a double cross, somewhat like a swastika. If the stranger was a member of the cross-makers' league, he would respond by making the same sign with his foot.

I listened patiently until he finished, and then asked him: "Let's say you really succeed in finding people who are willing to help you escape from Norilsk; or, to take it a step further, let's say you actually succeed in slipping out of the camp unnoticed—what would you do next?"

"I would try to reach Moscow by train. I'd go to the French embassy in Moscow."

"What you're saying is not only outlandish, it's childish. I have only one piece of advice for you: Don't play with your life. Your situation might change in the course of time, but if you try to follow through on these plans of yours, you'll be dead."

I could see that Petit was disappointed. We met several times after that but never broached this subject again. Years later, in the *spetslager* (special camp) in Tayshet, I spoke to some Germans who had met Petit in Norilsk. They said that, despite his extremely limited knowledge of Russian, Petit had persuaded several prisoners and also the captain of the troops stationed in Norilsk to escape from the camp and from the country with him. Naturally, the NKVD heard about these plans, arrested the entire group, kept them in preventive detention for several months, and then sentenced them all to death. Petit's sentence, however, was not carried out. Supposedly, he was released and allowed to return to France after his government appealed on his behalf.

We had been in the transit camp for a month. The shipping season was drawing to a close. The last transports to Norilsk leave Krasnoyarsk in October. Once the river becomes unnavigable, the town can be reached only by plane. Prisoners were rarely transported by air. The eight planes available in Norilsk were needed for official trips and to transport mail. We were starting to feel at home in the transit station. Some of us had made friendly contacts with the corrupt guards, whose wives brought us tomatoes and other fresh vegetables—something we had never even seen in Norilsk. Those who could pay for it even ordered vodka.

One day, we returned from the bathhouse and discovered our neighbors moments after they had broken through the wall of our barracks and begun to ransack our possessions. We arrived just in time.

In mid-October, the first group of twenty-five was taken away. Their leave-taking was very emotional for all of us, as there was no way of knowing if we would see each other again. We tried to find out where their transport was heading, but couldn't determine anything definite: only that a train was leaving for the Far East at the same time. This seemed to confirm our expectation of being sent to Irkutsk and to invalidate our former camp commander's statement (which some still believed) that we were going to the northern Caucasus.

This happened several times: officials of the camp section would come in the afternoon, read off the names of twenty-five men, and tell them to get ready for transport. Then, at ten in the evening, they would be led out of the camp. My turn came with the fifth group. As usual, we were given provisions for a two-day voyage; this time, however, instead of salt herring, each of us received a quarter of a kilo of cooked mutton. We were escorted by a large detachment of NKVD soldiers and three dogs. We marched at a brisk pace through the darkness. After a while, we were made to run. The soldiers were afraid we would miss the train and goaded us energetically; so did their dogs. Since we were running through the woods, many of us stumbled over roots and fallen branches. Each time this happened, the dogs would lunge at the falling man, furiously pulling at their leashes. The soldiers showered us with the vilest abuse.

When we arrived at the station, the train was just leaving. "Trotskyites, fascists, sons of bitches!" That was the tune to which we marched home. We were glad to get back to the camp.

We left again the next day at the same mad pace. This time, however, the soldiers had made sure to depart an hour earlier, and there was no danger of missing the train. We squeezed through the narrow corridor of the *stolypin* car. The soldiers shoved and pushed us from compartment to compartment. They didn't like the fact that we were carrying luggage.

All the cells of this prison on wheels were filled up. The guards didn't know where to put us. We stood in the corridor for a long time, until the soldiers regrouped the men in the compartments to make room for us.

IN THE *STOLYPIN* CAR

Foreigners traveling through Russia by train don't realize that one of the cars is an NKVD prison. There are few trains that don't have one or two *stolypins*. From the outside, these cars, named after the tsarist minister Stolypin, look like the cars used to transport mail. But look inside, and a shiver runs up your back. The first thing you see is a uniformed man with a dark blue or bright red band on his visored cap—this is one of the tormentors well known to the inmates of NKVD camps and prisons. There are ten compartments, designed to hold either eight or sixteen prisoners, but frequently some twenty men are squeezed into the eight-man compartment, and about forty into the cell intended for sixteen men. The cells have doors with thick iron bars, and there are no windows. The only light comes from the long, narrow corridor, where two armed soldiers stand guard and constantly admonish the prisoners to speak softly.

After a cell had been cleared, all twenty-five of us were stuffed inside with brutal shoves, kicks, and blows. The soldiers didn't seem to care that we would be jammed in that tiny cell for six hundred kilometers. The door was locked. We were literally sitting or standing on top of one another. It took a while for us to accommodate ourselves to some degree. Some of us climbed into the upper bunks, where you could only lie down; others found a place to sit on the benches; the rest sat on the floor. The walls and the floor were reinforced with thick metal plates. It was very cold, despite the overcrowding.

Right after the train left the station, we heard the sound of knocking from the cell next to ours.

"What do you want?" asked a soldier in the hall.

"Let us go to the toilet!"

"I've already told you, you can go only twice a day!"

"What if I have to go now?"

"Do it in your pants."

A woman's voice could be heard pleading from another cell. "*Nachalnik*, please let us go to the toilet!"

"Shut up, you whore, I already told you it's night, no one's going to the toilet now!"

The woman began to cry. "Please let me out. I can't stand it anymore!"

"Shut up!"

Because of the cold, several people in our compartment soon felt the need to relieve themselves. One of them felt such an urgent need that he went to the door and told the soldier, who flew into a rage. "Where the hell do you think you are? You just got in here and now you want to get out! There are people who've been on this train for five days; they come first."

None of us dared repeat the request.

After a while, the sound of knocking came from a more distant cell. "*Nachalnik,* you promised to bring us water, give us some water!"

"Where am I supposed to get water from?"

"I'm thirsty from that salt fish. I can't stand it anymore!"

"If you don't shut up, I'll drag you out here and give you something to drink that you won't forget."

Now everyone started to shout in unison: "Water, give us water!"

An officer came into the car. "What's all this noise? Do you want me to put you in chains?"

"We're thirsty, give us water!"

"You'll get water at the next station."

Now the others started up again. "*Nachalnik,* let us go to the toilet!"

"Shut the hell up, now! You can go to the toilet in the morning, not now!"

Then we heard someone urinating next door. A man in our compartment followed suit: he tried to urinate through a crack in the door into the hallway, but the space was too narrow and most of the urine landed in the cell. Those who were sitting on the floor jumped up, cursing.

Late that night, when the train stopped at a station, the soldiers fetched a pail of water. They walked from cell to cell and gave everyone half a cupful.

At 4 a.m., the soldiers began opening the cell doors and letting the prisoners go to the toilet at the end of the car, one person at a time. You had to run, while the soldiers shouted at you: "*Skorei, skorei, ruki nazad—* Faster, faster, hands behind your back!"

A soldier stood in front of the toilet. He, too, would shout: "Hurry up, hurry up, how long are you going to sit there?"

One of the women asked him to step away from the door. He mocked her: "Why, look at our little virgin! Don't tell me you've never lifted your skirt in front of a man!"

IRKUTSK, A CITY IN THE FAR EAST

We arrived in Irkutsk after a twelve-hour trip. From the platform, we could see the *chorny voron,* the black raven, as the prisoners' transport car is called in Russia. We climbed in. An officer and two soldiers followed us; the soldiers stood by the door. The car drove through the city. We peered curiously through the little window. At first, we passed by many small wooden houses, which began to give way to solid stone buildings as we neared the center of town. We saw buses and a tiny streetcar.

Our destination was a large transit station on the edge of the city. The car stopped in the prison courtyard. Our escorts got out, and we followed them. We sat down on our bundles and waited. We saw men and women wearing armbands with the inscription: *"Prisoner."* To our surprise, none of them asked us where we came from, as camp inmates usually did when new prisoners arrived; they didn't pay any attention to us.

We sat for several hours. During that time, the large gate was opened repeatedly, and trucks, both empty and loaded, drove in and out. The drivers all wore the same yellow armbands. Finally, we were taken to a two-story house next to four large prison buildings—the bathhouse, and also the camp's laundry. After walking up two flights of stairs, we arrived in a large hall with benches in the middle of the room and alongside the walls. A group of women came out of a door and greeted us cheerfully: *"Zdorovo, muzhchiny*—Hello, fellows!" We were surprised to meet women here. They told us to get undressed and hang our clothes over a thick, hoop-shaped wire. One of the women, apparently the brigadier, announced loudly that we were going to receive a *sanobrabotka*, the hygiene treatment, as the disinfecting of clothes was commonly called.

The brigadier was about twenty-five years old, brunette and plump; most of the others were young girls. They were wearing short, sleeveless aprons, slippers on their bare feet, and the yellow band with the word *"Prisoner"* on their left sleeve. Their skirts reached only to their knees.

We were led into an adjacent room in groups of ten. I was standing stark naked in front of ten young women and didn't dare to go near them. "Come along, we don't have forever," one of them said to me, summoning me with a pair of hair clippers she was holding in her hand. I gathered up courage and came closer.

"Sit down!"

I sat down on the bench, and the girl shaved my head. The hair fell on my lap. Then she shaved my armpits. Finally, she went on to shave my pubic hair, and as she did that, she took hold of my penis, moved it back and forth, and made suggestive remarks—how long since I'd been with a woman? Once, she said, her hand had gotten wet while she was doing this . . . I listened to her talk and didn't say a word.

After the haircut, we were taken to the washroom. A woman at the entrance handed each of us a basin and a piece of soap. We washed and returned to the first room, where we had left our clothes. These had been disinfected in the meantime and were lying in a disorderly heap on the floor. I found my clothes after some searching. They were so hot I could hardly touch them.

A guard led us from the bathhouse to a three-story building. We waited in front of the entrance for a while, until another guard came and opened the iron gate with two keys. We had to wait again in the hallway; finally, the chief guard came and ordered us to line up in groups of four. We could assemble in any order we wished. This surprised us considerably, for usually the prison administration determined who would sit with whom in a cell. It's very important for a prisoner to have desirable cellmates. I was put in a one-man cell, together with three other inmates.

The transit station at Irkutsk differed in many ways from other prisons I had seen in Russia. Conditions here could justifiably be called humane. For the first time, I heard the guards and other prison officials reply to the questions and requests of prisoners in a friendly manner, without curses and insults—and this despite the fact that the guards did not have an easy time controlling the prisoners. Of course, I don't mean the politicals, who behaved like normal human beings, but the criminals, who pestered the prison personnel with unreasonable demands and raised havoc constantly, even at night. You could hear the criminals fighting in the neighboring cells, accusing each other of betrayal and deception and cursing so horribly that it could make you sick.

There were adolescent boys on the top floor who carried on salacious conversations with the girls on the ground floor. I found it particularly distressing to hear these young delinquents—mere children, some of them—uttering expressions you would expect to hear only from the most hardened criminals.

We had been in Irkutsk for a week and still didn't know where we would eventually be taken. There was talk of our going to the Alexandrovsky Tsentral, but no one believed it. This ancient prison had such a terrible reputation that none of us could imagine being sent there after we had served the greater part of our sentences. One thing was certain, though: we wouldn't be staying in Irkutsk for very long. We had learned from the prison personnel and from some of the inmates that this was a place for criminals serving sentences of less than five years. These were the people we had seen in the yard and in the bathhouse.

We waited impatiently for our transport. Even though life was bearable here, we were being deprived of some things that were usually granted us. We weren't given any books, weren't allowed to write to our relatives, and weren't given any time to walk around.

One Saturday, when we asked the guard for something, he told us to wait until Monday: "Something's sure to happen by then." Indeed, we were moved to another building on Monday morning. We were brought into a large room, big enough to hold fifty men, and met with some of our old comrades from Norilsk there. After the usual formalities, we were taken back into the yard. There we experienced our first surprise: a detachment of soldiers and an officer stood in front of three trucks. One of the soldiers was holding a bunch of handcuffs. The officer and two soldiers climbed into one of the trucks. Then two of us were told to follow them. Once these men were on the truck, the officer handcuffed the two men to each other and ordered them to sit on the floor. That's a nice beginning, we thought to ourselves.

When the next two men were called up, one of them dared ask the officer: "Why are you shackling us?" The officer acted as if he hadn't heard. "I've been a prisoner for fifteen years and I didn't run away. I don't plan to escape now," the prisoner repeated. "I'm carrying out my orders," the officer replied.

Those shackles were a bad sign. Until then, I hadn't given much serious thought to what was awaiting me after Norilsk. Now I was getting a first taste. I told myself: if I could survive Norilsk, I can endure what's coming as well.

The truck drove through the prison gate. Now we could observe the suburbs of Irkutsk. We were driving slowly, and the soldiers didn't mind our looking around and conversing quietly. There was nothing extraordinary about the sights: low wooden houses like thousands of others in Siberia. Their construction is simple. Naked logs are joined together into "wreaths." Fifteen or twenty such wreaths, placed one above the other, form the walls of a house. The cracks are insulated with moss. The roof, too, is usually made of wood. It's rare to see a tin roof there, and even rarer to see whitewashed or even painted walls.

There was one unusual sight: the large zigzag bridge across the river Angara. It's the only bridge in the area and serves trains, cars, and pedestrians. A little past the bridge, we made a sharp right turn and came to a country road leading in an easterly direction. We drove nearly four hundred kilometers, passing only a few seemingly lifeless villages. Only once in a long while did we see people or animals in front of the neglected-looking houses. Occasionally, a dog would chase the truck for a while.

ALEXANDROVSKY
TSENTRAL

THE HISTORIC CASEMATE

It was getting dark; there were candles burning in the windows. The only places where we saw electric lights were two prison camps we passed. We arrived at our destination late that night. The soldiers jumped off the trucks. While we waited for the order to get off, I looked around. We were in front of a long two-story building with an artfully carved gate. The place resembled the old inns you can find on Russian highways. There was nothing prison-like about it. Both the house and the gate were brightly lit by electric lamps. The surrounding area was steeped in darkness, but I had the impression that the landscape was hilly. Directly facing the big building were several smaller wooden houses surrounded by little gardens. Everything was covered with a thick blanket of snow.

An officer stepped out of the gate. He was the prison commander, as we learned later. He ordered our handcuffs removed. This took quite a while, for some of the locks were defective. Then, one by one, we were led into a large empty room. We were in Alexandrovsky Tsentral, the notorious prison of the tsarist period.

In contrast to the innocuous-looking façade, the interior of this building resembled the description of it by Dostoevsky, who spent several years there: walls several meters thick; long, dark corridors; oppressively low vaulted arches; heavy iron doors equipped with several locks. All these things seemed designed to tell a prisoner: "You'll never get out of here." The yards where the prisoners made their daily rounds were narrow shafts with steep walls above which you could see a small strip of sky. Our steps in the hall made a resounding echo. If you coughed, the sound was so terrifying you'd try hard not to cough again. Otherwise, there was silence everywhere, an uncanny silence.

We were thoroughly searched. Our clothes, our bags, everything we had brought was taken from us. Each of us was given a receipt with a list of his possessions.

Together with thirty-one other prisoners, I was led across long corridors and through several double doors—each of them a heavy wooden door reinforced with metal, followed by a gate with iron bars. Finally, we reached a long hall with two windows looking out on the yard. There were cells on the left and on the right. We stopped in front of a door with the number 1 on it.

A guard opened a large padlock, and then a lock in the door, with a long, thick key. We stepped into a large, brightly lit room with two windows facing the yard. The whitewashed walls smelled of fresh plaster. Alongside the walls and in the middle of the room were wooden beds covered with straw sacks, blankets, and straw-filled pillows. There was also a table with benches, and in the corner a large tile stove which was stoked from the hallway.

The room was warm. Everyone picked a bed, and when the guard was satisfied that we had all settled down, he left, locking the door. Now we compared our first impressions, and found that they were favorable without exception. We had been especially surprised and pleased that here too, as in Irkutsk, there was none of the usual pushing and cursing. We talked for a long time. Finally, the guard lifted the hatch on the door and told us to go to sleep because it was very late.

It was a pleasure to lie on a straw sack. But although I was tired, I couldn't fall asleep. I kept wondering what this all meant: after all these years, I was back in a prison, without a trial, without a sentence, without any explanation. We were driven from one place to another like cattle and weren't allowed to ask where and why. This time, there probably wasn't even a semblance of legality. For the first time, I wished I could fall asleep and never wake up.

At seven o'clock, the guard cried through the door hatch: "Get up!" We got dressed. When the guard opened the door a little later, he didn't have to say anything. Two of us carried out the *parasha* and we followed—to the toilet, which was situated in the middle of the long corridor. That was also the place where we washed. When we were finished, we knocked, and the guard opened the door and led us in a double file back to our cell. Now we waited for our breakfast and looked out onto the yard through the window. We discovered that the kitchen was across from our cell. On our right were the cage-like yards for walking, which reminded us of the Solovetsk Islands. About ten meters farther on, there was a long, one-story building with opaque glass windows—that had to be the hospital.

Two women came from the kitchen carrying a box full of bread. The men at the window announced joyfully: "The bread's coming!"

"Let's see what the food's like here," someone said.

Tall Kharchenko claimed to have seen unusually large portions of bread in the boxes, maybe as much as six hundred grams.

"Good luck, Kharchenko, just wait for your six hundred grams," another man said.

Two other women followed, carrying large, steaming caldrons. Some of us presumed it was soup, while others claimed they had seen a reddish substance, most probably tea. When the food was distributed, each of us got four hundred grams of bread. Now Kharchenko had to put up with a good deal of ribbing: "My, my, six hundred grams he wants. When he was head of construction work in Norilsk, he gave three hundred grams to workers who couldn't meet the quota; but he wants six hundred." Kharchenko tried to defend himself, but the prisoners were disappointed by the small bread ration and vented their anger on him throughout breakfast.

The steaming liquid in the caldrons was tea. Everyone was given a lump of sugar and forty grams of salt fish in addition. The bread had to last for the rest of the day.

"YOU WON'T HAVE ANY DESIRE FOR A WOMAN!"

After breakfast, tempers cooled. We were led out for a walk. We were free to sit on a bench or walk; no one told us how to hold our head and where to direct our eyes. The soldier on the watchtower observed us without making a single remark. After an hour, we were led back to our cells. We were satisfied; in no other prison had we been allowed to walk for so long and at such leisure.

We looked forward to lunch with a good deal of expectation. A siren wailed somewhere—that meant it was twelve o'clock. Lunch was served soon after: half a liter of potato soup and a hundred grams of millet cereal—not enough to fill anyone's belly. A single subject of conversation took up the rest of the afternoon, and once again Kharchenko was made the scapegoat.

"Well, Kharchenko, how did you like the meal?" Babich asked.

"Pretty good—what did you expect, a broiled chicken?" replied Kharchenko.

Someone else said: "Kharchenko, how many portions like that do you think you could eat?"

Kharchenko said nothing, but Babich replied in his stead: "Five, with five hundred grams of bread."

Kharchenko got angry. "You don't have to worry about me; take care of yourselves. I'll get by."

"You'll get by, but you won't feel any desire for a woman," Babich said.

Supper was even more disappointing than breakfast and lunch: it consisted of a portion of potato soup. We waited in vain for a second course. Someone said that perhaps they had forgotten to bring it and asked the guard if there wasn't anything else to eat. He replied curtly: "That was all."

People got more talkative after dinner, and the conversations helped us forget the subject of food. At ten o'clock the guard turned our light on and off three times from outside—the signal for bedtime.

My first days in the Alexandrovsky Tsentral passed quickly. We always looked forward to the morning walk. Between meals, we would sit around in groups or in couples, getting to know one another, sharing experiences, and reminiscing, especially about the war years. Most of the thirty-two of us had been in Norilsk during the war, but some had been at the front or abroad.

One of my most interesting cellmates was Dr. Franz Breuer, a German diplomat who was serving a twenty-five-year sentence for "espionage." He was a former secretary of the German embassy in Moscow. When the war broke out, he was taken to the Persian border together with the rest of the embassy's personnel. From there, they traveled back to Germany via a number of detours. Breuer was a native of Hamburg—a fact I would have detected from his accent if he hadn't told me so himself. He and I became friends. He told me he had joined the Nazi Party, not out of conviction, but to continue his diplomatic career.

Breuer was distinctly different from the other prisoners. Usually, the convicts resembled one another in almost every respect: the same clothes, the same way of life, the same needs. Whenever a prisoner stood out by his appearance or behavior, it was noticed and registered with irritation. Breuer was tall, and his German army boots made him even taller. His long chestnut beard and dark glasses contrasted strangely with his German officer's uniform. The unusualness of his appearance was reinforced by his manner. While the other prisoners immediately devoured the forty grams of salt fish they were given for breakfast, Breuer installed himself at the table to eat his food "at leisure," as he put it. He spread out his towel as a tablecloth, set down his bread and fish and his cup of tea, and tied his handkerchief around his neck. He used the handle of his spoon as a knife, and a sliver of wood as a fork. That was how he ate his breakfast. The tiny morsels he had sliced off with his "knife" were conveyed to his mouth by means of his "fork." Intermittently, he would take a sip of tea and wipe his lips with his "napkin." The other prisoners sat around and watched him eat; they had finished their breakfast long before and had nothing else to do. Some of them made fun of Breuer, but he didn't seem to mind.

Since I often took walks with him and talked with him and was generally considered his compatriot, various prisoners strongly suggested that I try to influence him to change his ways and act "normal." I tried to convince my comrades that it was Breuer's business how he consumed his meager breakfast. But it wasn't only his table manners that fascinated and irritated: every evening before going to sleep, Breuer carefully folded his trousers and placed them under his straw sack so as to preserve the crease. He continued to do this even after his uniform had been exchanged for prison clothes. Some people expressed the hope that Breuer would fail to preserve the crease in his pants for the twenty-five years he would be spending in prisons and camps, but others were convinced that German pedantry would endure much longer than that.

After a few weeks, we were regrouped, and Breuer was moved to another cell. I never saw him again, but I learned later that he was released and resumed his diplomatic career in the Federal Republic of Germany.

Breuer was replaced by a man I already knew, the Austrian Edi Schreidel. Edi was different from Breuer in every respect. He was short, dark-haired, with the round-faced physiognomy of a typical Lower Austrian peasant. We spent nine months together; we were good friends. We talked for hours about Austria and about Hitlerism, which Edi wholeheartedly hated—he called the year of the Anschluss, 1938, the year of Austria's misfortune. Edi's bed was next to mine; we wished each other a good day every morning when we woke up, and a good night every evening before we went to sleep. Our friendship was a pleasing sight to the other prisoners, especially to Dr. Zalkin.

Zalkin had been the head of the sanitary inspection of food supplies at Norilsk. He distinguished himself by his kindness and great willingness to help his fellow prisoners. He was serving a fifteen-year sentence for "sabotage." Zalkin was a small man who walked with a limp due to a crippled leg. He liked to take part in our conversations and regretted not knowing any German. All his relatives except for a sister had been gassed by the Nazis; yet he did not feel a trace of hatred for the Germans. He was one of the few who protected Breuer when he was teased by the other prisoners.

It was from Zalkin that I learned a few things about the fate of the woman I had gotten to know in the kitchen of the second camp section in Norilsk: Taissa Grigorevna Yagoda. He had made her acquaintance when she was put to work peeling potatoes in the warehouse; the unhappy woman had turned to him for protection. Her sentence came to an end in 1947; she was released from the camp and was forced to live in a small town near Krasnoyarsk, where she lived in great poverty. Zalkin asked his sister to help Taissa, and the sister was sending the banished woman a hundred rubles a month.

Zalkin was especially interested in Edi's stories about his experiences as a prisoner of war in the United States. The doctor found it extraordinary that the prisoners were able to buy almost anything in the prison shop, whether it was beer, butter, or gold rings—even while the war was still going on. One day, he asked me whether I thought Schreidel's reports could be believed. When I said I thought they were true, he looked at me incredulously.

Another cellmate I remember was Viktor Strecker, a Volga German who, as I've said, didn't speak a word of German. Edi and I tried to teach him the language, but no matter how much time we devoted to his lessons, all he could say after three months was: "*Ich haben gross Hunger*—I have much hunger." At Norilsk, Strecker had enjoyed a reputation as an excellent mining engineer. Coal shaft number 11B, which had Strecker as a chief engineer, was one of the most productive in the area. Four of the twenty years he had been given for "sabotage" had been remitted for his good work—a rare case. Nevertheless, he was considered a "dangerous element" and was removed from the mine to which he had contributed so much and was sent to prison with the rest of us. He was a stocky, somewhat paunchy man with sharp, perpetually restless eyes. He reacted intensely to any remark he disliked. He didn't get along with most people, but he felt very close to Edi, Zalkin, and me.

His principal enemy in the cell was Babich, who had worked as a technician in the port of Dudinka. Babich got along with only one man, Shusterman, who was semi-illiterate and approved of everything he said.

Both had been sentenced to twenty-five years for "terrorism," even though neither had ever terrorized anyone. Shusterman was said to have stated that conditions in Russia wouldn't get better so long as Stalin was alive; Babich was accused of having remarked, after Kirov's assassination: "Too bad it wasn't Stalin." When Shusterman was arrested, he was not yet nineteen years old.

The quarrels between Strecker and Babich usually originated in disagreements about technical matters and quickly degenerated into personal attacks. Sometimes Babich had to admit that he was wrong and that Strecker knew more than he did; he would then avenge himself on Kharchenko. Kharchenko had only to open his mouth and Babich would cut him with some remark. "His stupidity is proportionate to his length," he liked to say of tall Kharchenko. In Norilsk, Kharchenko had been the head of barracks construction, and Babich liked to remind him of it: "You were born to build prison camps; it suits your character perfectly."

Babich may have been right about that. Every order that came down from the NKVD and the camp or prison administration was holy writ as far as Kharchenko was concerned. He was always worried that someone might break the prison rules, and he was willing to sacrifice everything to avoid offending the prison commander.

An aid committee was formed in our cell. All those who had money were to donate ten percent to those who had none. Of the thirty-two men in the cell, the six foreigners had no money at all, and three or four others had only very little. All except three were in favor of this measure. Two of the three opposed were Kharchenko and Strecker. I was not surprised at Kharchenko and the third man, but I was desperately disappointed by Strecker's decision and couldn't understand it. He was not stingy—on the contrary, he gave more than ten percent of his own accord. When I asked him for the reason, he said he was against any sort of committee. Whoever had money should share it voluntarily with those who had none. He, for his part, was willing to support not just one but two of the needy prisoners. And he did.

During the first months, all you could buy in the prison shop was tobacco and occasionally salt fish and soap. Eventually, you could buy boiled potatoes as well, a kilo for a ruble. We managed to keep our hunger in check for a while, but gradually money became scarce and our hunger increased. The commander of the prison, who was so liberal in other respects, told us he was powerless to respond to our complaints. The funds allotted to him for the provision of the prisoners wouldn't permit his adding even a few more potatoes to our thin soup.

The central prison administration in Moscow had ordered that we be subjected to a "severe regime," and this precluded contact with relatives. For the first time after so many years in prisons and camps, we were forbidden to reveal our address to anyone on the outside. We made written requests for permission to write to our families, but they were never answered.

Our hunger was becoming unbearable. I could no longer read. I slept badly; often, it took me three hours to fall asleep. More and more of us sat on the benches instead of walking during the daily outing. More and more people were getting sick. The hospital was overcrowded. Every month, a medical commission came to check on the prisoners' physical condition. The doctors just shook their heads. When the prisoners complained about headaches, they would prescribe aspirin, even though they knew that a piece of bread would have been better.

Occasionally, a high-ranking officer would come into the room. His reply to all our requests and complaints was: "This is not a sanatorium."

Hunger made us irritable. The most trivial disagreements gave rise to quarrels, not only among us but also with the prison personnel. The punishment cells were used with increasing frequency, and naturally this led to a worsening of our physical condition. Presumably, the prison administrators realized it was senseless to put prisoners of our category together with German and Japanese prisoners of war and subject us to the same regime. But it seemed obvious that Stalin had something special in store for us and was just waiting for the right moment.

One day, when we complained to the officer again, he said: "Who do you think you are to make demands like this? You've already served twelve to fifteen years in a camp, now you're in prison—and not just any prison, but the Alexandrovsky Tsentral—don't you know what that means?"

No, we weren't allowed to ask for anything. All our appeals were either refused or ignored. Since we weren't permitted to tell our relatives where we were, and since we were still wearing civilian clothes, some of us thought we were only passing through. Others believed we would be segregated from the war criminals—until, one day, tailors came into our cell and took our measurements. A week later, we were all wearing the same prison garb: shirt and pants made of the same thin cotton material with zebra stripes, a black padded coat (called a *bushlat*), a matching cap, and pig-leather shoes with rubber soles. Now everyone realized that we were going to be locked up behind these stone walls for a long time.

To prevent prisoners from dying of starvation, the prison administration set up a special unit for the most emaciated. There you were given better and more plentiful food. Once a month, a few lucky men were sent there by the medical commission. You couldn't stay there for more than a month. After that, you'd be back in your cell, starving again. For many people, these brief "vacations" came too late—but we had to give credit to the prison administration and especially to the medical services for doing everything they could to keep us alive.

Our situation was altogether bizarre. If the privations prescribed for us in Moscow had been strictly enforced, we would have died. This was the first time I saw the administration of a prison undermining the plans of the central prison administration in Moscow. In all the other prisons and camps I had seen, the NKVD officials were usually the prisoners' gravediggers. But this was not the case in the Alexandrovsky Tsentral.

Captain Lastochkin, the prison's NKVD chief, did everything he could to ameliorate the suffering of the prisoners.

One day, I decided to apply for an interview with Lastochkin. I conveyed my wish to the guard during roll call. The next day, I was taken to Captain Lastochkin's office. I had discussed with my cellmates the questions I would ask. First, why weren't we allowed to write letters? Second, when would the rations be increased? Third, why were we transferred from a camp to a prison, since most of us had been given camp and not prison sentences?

The guard picked me up at ten o'clock and led me through several corridors to the administration building. I had to wait in front of the captain's office while the guard went inside. After a while, he came back out and summoned me in. This time, he stayed in the hall. There were pictures of Stalin, Beria, and Dzerzhinsky on the walls of the large room. Captain Lastochkin, whom I had met before, was sitting behind his desk. He told me to sit down on a chair three or four meters away from his desk. After examining my features for a while, he said: "So you want to speak to me. What do you want?"

"I want to ask you how long we are going to be hungry."

"I assure you there will be an improvement soon."

"Really? Or are you just giving us a tranquillizer?"

"You will soon be allowed to write to your relatives and receive money from them, and we will see to it that you can use that money for shopping in the prison store."

I questioned him further: "I was sentenced to detention in camp. Why am I in prison?"

"That doesn't depend on me. You could write a complaint to the Minister; maybe that will help."

"Thank you very much. Let's see how long we still have to wait. May I tell my cellmates about our conversation?"

"Yes."

Lastochkin rang a bell. The guard came and led me back to the cell. My cellmates crowded around me, wanting to know what had happened. Someone suggested that we all sit down and that I tell the story from beginning to end without interruption. I told them about my interview with Lastochkin in all its details. Everyone listened intently, and when someone tried to interrupt me, the others very nearly beat him up. The most sensational part of my report was Lastochkin's statement that we would soon be allowed to write to our relatives. As for his suggestion that we write a complaint to the Minister, the general feeling was that this would be useless, and I agreed.

I was the center of everyone's attention for several days. I had to repeat my story several times. My listeners wanted to know whether I had the impression that Lastochkin's promises were sincere. I had the impression that they were.

Strecker, Babich, and Kharchenko wrote petitions to the Ministry: they asked to be taken back to the camp, where they could continue to use their knowledge and abilities "in the service of socialist development."

We had been in that prison for almost half a year. Several of our cellmates had been put into other cells; others had joined us. Some people had been taken to the hospital; others to the special rehabilitation unit. Among the newcomers in our cell was a Dr. Brilyant, the head of the department of health in Odessa before he was arrested in 1937. He had been given a twenty-year sentence for "sabotage." He had been a doctor in the seventh camp section of Norilsk and been very helpful to me and several other prisoners. He had a stomach illness and had to be operated on in the prison hospital. In 1956, I learned from an acquaintance in Moscow that Brilyant had died in the Alexandrovsky Tsentral.

It was the beginning of May when Lastochkin came to our cell. As we assembled in rank and file, my cellmates whispered to me from all sides: "Ask him about writing letters!" I would have done so without their prompting, but Lastochkin knew very well what was on our minds. Without any of the usual formalities, he said: "From this day on, you can write letters home."

An audible sigh went through our ranks. Lastochkin explained that we were allowed to send two letters a year and to receive as many in that time. Some of us thought we hadn't heard him correctly and asked: "Twice a month?"

"No, twice a year," the captain said.

Some other questions were asked, but the most important thing was the permission to write. Now at last our closest relatives would know that we were still alive; they would send us money and we would no longer suffer this terrible hunger. The guard who had come in with Lastochkin distributed paper and envelopes to all except the foreigners. When one of these asked why they couldn't write home, he received no answer.

As soon as Lastochkin and the guard had left, we began to write our letters. They had to be very brief and couldn't say anything about conditions in prison, not even the fact that we were there. The return address was a post-office number. We restricted our messages to saying that we were healthy and to asking for a little money—not packages, as we weren't allowed to receive any.

Now we had a new subject of conversation. There was a lot of conjecture as to whether or when we could expect our letters to be answered. Some people thought the whole thing was a ruse to pacify us; they believed our letters were being incinerated at the very moment that we were talking about them. It turned out that the pessimists were mistaken. Our letters were conveyed with greater speed than was usual in camps and prisons, and after fourteen days, the first money orders started coming in.

POTATOES SAVE OUR LIVES

One day, the hatch in the door was raised and a woman official from the bookkeeping division called out the names of several prisoners to hand them receipts for money orders that had just arrived. An indescribable joy filled the cell; people embraced and kissed one another. My name was the last to be called; I had decided that nothing had come for me, and was steeling myself against the disappointment welling up in me. But a money order had come, after all—a hundred and fifty rubles.

The next day, the guard announced that we could go shopping in half an hour. All those who had received money were let out into the hall. A makeshift store had been set up there, with shelves, a counter, and scales. A young girl sat by the scales—the official who had brought us the receipts. She had a card file with a card for each of the prisoners. A salesman in a blue smock told us what was available and how much each prisoner was allowed to purchase. There was salt fish, marmalade, tobacco, toothpaste, and up to two kilos of bread per person; in addition, you could order potatoes. After the desired merchandise had been received, the woman recorded the cost on the receipt and on the prisoner's card.

I bought two kilos of bread and half a kilo of salt fish and ordered twenty-five kilos of potatoes. After returning to the cell, we gave ten percent of our purchases to those who had no money. We decided to divide equally the potatoes we had ordered among everyone in the cell. Some people didn't like that idea, but they didn't object, for fear of being criticized. Kharchenko was, as usual, one of those who objected most strongly to the idea of supporting the prisoners who had no money.

The next day, the potatoes we had ordered were brought in, boiled but unpeeled, in three barrels. We divided them into thirty-two equal portions, one for each man in the cell. To prevent the potatoes from rotting, we spread them out under the beds. At last, we were able to eat our fill. Some of us gave more than the agreed-upon ten percent to the comrades who couldn't buy any food. I split everything with Edi Schreidel; he praised my brave wife who was sending me money to save me from starvation.

We noticed that since we had received money, the soup had gotten very thin, with rarely more than two or three slices of potato in a bowl. When we asked the guard why, he said: "There are some Japanese prisoners next door; they're not getting any outside support. We're giving them the thick part of the soup, and you're getting the thin part." We never again complained about the thinness of the soup.

After just a few weeks, we were considerably restored. I had received two money orders and now had some cash in reserve, so I could afford to buy some more fish and marmalade, and one day, when some sugar was available, I bought some. The mood in the cell had gotten livelier, with less irritation. Sometimes you could hear someone quietly singing.

This was not the only change. In July, Strecker was removed from the cell. No one knew where he was; all inquiries were unsuccessful. Cellmates coming back from the hospital hadn't heard any news about him from other prisoners there. Not until years later did I find out what had happened to him. In response to his petition, he was reinstated as chief engineer in the coal mines in Norilsk, and eventually died in a mining accident.

Strecker was replaced in our cell by the engineer Ivanov, an old, sick man. His sickness was emotional rather than physical. He had no friends or relatives in the outside world and could not expect, therefore, to ever receive any money. He had brought a hundred rubles with him from Norilsk, where he had worked in the office of the construction division, and now he categorically refused to give the customary ten percent to those who didn't have any money. He was extremely sparing with his funds, and was obviously trying to save as much as possible. But when he noticed that the prisoners who received support from the aid committee were getting more than he was buying for himself, he changed his tactics: he supplied himself abundantly with everything that could be bought in the store. When we asked him why he was suddenly living high off the hog, he replied: "You're better off living at the expense of the aid committee." Several months later, after Ivanov had made his final purchases and spent his last rubles, he looked forward to enjoying the aid committee's support.

In August 1949, a new prisoner was brought in from the hospital. He told us about a group of prisoners that had been transferred to some other place just a few days ago. We presumed this had some connection with Strecker's disappearance. We discussed it for days. Some people didn't believe what the newcomer had told us and subjected him to a regular cross-examination—they wanted to make sure this wasn't just one of the many rumors that constantly spring up in prisons and camps. But the newcomer insisted that he had seen the group coming out of the bath; they had all been wearing civilian clothes. When we asked whether they might not have been new arrivals, he replied that this was out of the question, as he had recognized one of them, a man who had come with our group from Norilsk. Now there could be no doubt that something unusual was brewing. A month later, we found out what it was.

The guard came in September and read off several names, including mine. We had to hand in the receipts we had been given for our clothes on the day we arrived. Nothing else was said. As soon as the guard left, pandemonium broke loose in the cell. We discussed the question of how to pass on the news to those who were being left behind. I told Edi I would leave a note under an empty *parasha* in the toilet. I was worried that Edi might not be able to get by without my financial support. I had once lent Zalkin a small sum of money; I asked him to give that amount to Edi, and Zalkin promised to support Edi from his own funds.

I couldn't sleep all night. My neighbors, Edi and Zalkin, didn't sleep either. We talked all night about what the future might bring. In the morning, the general discussion started again. There were some comrades who feared that we were not going to be transferred but liquidated. I, however, was confident and in a good mood.

After lunch, those of us whose names had been called earlier were taken out of the cell. I took leave of everyone, especially of Zalkin and Edi. I promised again to keep in touch with Edi. I kept this promise twice: once by putting a note under the *parasha;* the second time almost ten years later, after I was free and had gone back to Europe. I wrote to Edi in his home town, Rüdental, hoping that he had survived all his sufferings and found his way home. I received no answer. Two months later, I wrote again. Another two months passed. Then a letter came from Edi in Vienna. He had received my letters after some delay. He was now living in Vienna. He had married and was working for the Chamber of Commerce.

I wish I knew what happened to the other men in our cell, especially Zalkin.

FAREWELL TO THE ALEXANDROVSKY TSENTRAL

We were taken to a dark cell with bare bunks, where we encountered twenty prisoners from other cells. One of them was Josef Berger—we hadn't seen each other for a year. We were happy as children to meet again. He was emaciated but mentally as alert as ever. We sat down in a corner and talked about what the future might hold, and what might be the meaning of our having been incarcerated for a year. We came to the conclusion that it was a preventive measure connected to a planned war against Yugoslavia, which Stalin had eventually renounced for fear of a united response on the part of the free world.

We were obviously being deported—the question was where. The old, experienced prisoners were of the unanimous opinion that we would be put in a camp. We tried to determine the rationale for our selection. It turned out that all of us had originally been sentenced to detention in a camp, whereas those still in their cells had been given prison sentences. Our suspicion was soon confirmed. An NKVD officer came to bring us our mail, and we asked him where we were going. It was the first time in our experience that an NKVD officer answered this question. "You're going to the Tayshet camp."

That frightened us. Tayshet was notorious; that meant hard labor in the Siberian taiga. That evening, when we were led to the latrine, I slipped a note under the *parasha* with the following message for Edi: "We are twenty-five and we're going to Tayshet." Ten years later, I learned from Edi that he had received the message.

We spent the night in the room with the bare bunks. Our old clothes and bags had been returned to us; we used them for bedding. Early next morning, we were given the usual travel provisions: two days' rations of bread, salt fish, and sugar. After the inevitable body search, the officer instructed us to leave the cell very quietly and not make a sound in the hall. Armed guards took charge of us in the administration building. After the usual roll call, we were led outside and loaded onto trucks.

We looked back at the place where we had spent a year of our lives. The trucks were taking us toward the Trans-Siberian Railroad. The little houses in the few villages we passed gave an abandoned appearance. Only rarely did we see smoke rising above a damaged roof. You could still see signs of the fabulous wealth the powerful peasant and merchant families of Siberia had once enjoyed: elaborately carved gates in front of dilapidated farmsteads; large, solid wooden granaries where the world-famous Siberian wheat was once stored. Occasionally, a calf would cross our path, or a dog would bark as we passed. All around us, as far as the eye could see, were fields of tall, beautiful, golden-yellow wheat. Here and there, people were working with combines. The people waved at us, but we weren't allowed to return the gesture.

After driving for several hours, we reached the transit station at Irkutsk. Once again, we were able to soak up the warm September sun for hours in the courtyard before we were taken to a cold, dark cell. This time we weren't taken to the bathhouse, which some greatly regretted, for they would have liked to meet those young "hairdressers" again.

We were in Irkutsk for two days. Then we were crammed into a *stolypin* car which differed from the first one only in that the faces of the guards weren't the same. We consoled ourselves with the knowledge that the trip to Tayshet was only half as long as the distance from Krasnoyarsk to Irkutsk. But the trip turned out to be longer. After three hours, the train stopped in a small station. This wasn't anything so unusual; but soon we heard the soldiers talking about a breakdown. Then our car was uncoupled and moved to a sidetrack. The day passed without any sign of activity. Night came; we were still standing there. We could infer from the conversations of the soldiers that an axle had broken and we were waiting for another car.

By the third day, we had consumed all our provisions. When we asked the soldiers and officers for food, they said they didn't have anything to eat either. We suggested that we trade some of our possessions for food in the nearest village; the guards agreed to that. Some of us donated trousers, jackets, coats; I gave up my good blanket. The soldiers took our stuff to the village and came back with potatoes, flour, and lard. We cooked the food in the car, and the soldiers shared in it.

On the fourth day, a locomotive came with a *stolypin* car; the car was hitched to the next train. Thus, the trip to Tayshet took four days instead of six hours.

AMONG
WAR CRIMINALS

TRANSIT STATION TAYSHET

Halfway between the great Siberian cities of Irkutsk and Krasnoyarsk lies the small town of Tayshet. It is not a town in the European sense of the word, merely an administrative center for several dozen villages and the seat of the regional Executive Committee, the regional party administration, and the regional administration of the NKVD. The old town consists of a single street which is impassable in spring and fall—pedestrians have to hop from stone to stone across the sludge. The usual Siberian wooden houses line this street on both sides. Among these houses are a few general stores where you can buy vodka, among other things. Only in recent years has Tayshet become a forestry center, or rather the center for several large camps whose inmates populate the taiga. Another recent industrial development was the building of the great railroad from Tayshet to Bratsk and from there across the Lena and via Komsomolsk to Yakutia.

Thus, a second Tayshet developed north of the railroad: long rows of identical apartment buildings and, off to the side, some villas—the homes of high-ranking NKVD and army officers. There are wooden sidewalks in the new city, and the streets are better than those in old Tayshet. In the center of town stands the big NKVD clubhouse. There are also several well-stocked stores. NKVD people deserve the very best.

To the south of the railroad lies a huge city of barracks surrounded by a six-meter-high wooden fence. This is the Tayshet transit station, from where prisoners are sent on to various camps far off in the taiga. Tayshet is the first stop for all those who have been selected to cut down trees in the taiga and build the great railroad. Other prisoners are put to work in Tayshet itself: in the lumberyard, in the automobile repair shop, in the locomotive depot, in the construction of houses and barracks, in street building, in making railroad ties. Hundreds of watchtowers line the fence that surrounds the camp. Recently, efforts have been made to conceal these watchtowers behind the fence.

Our *stolypin* car came to a halt a few meters from the wooden train station. We were allowed to get out immediately. Sitting on the ground in rows of five, we waited until some women had gotten out of another compartment and joined us. Even though groups of prisoners arrived every day in Tayshet, many curious onlookers stopped on the station platform. No one was allowed to come near us. A few adolescents who tried to do so were driven back by the guards.

We walked on dusty streets along the camp fence. Some soldiers who were standing or sitting around in front of a gate relieved our guards of their escort duty and marched on with us. As we were passing a factory, we saw prisoners working behind barbed wire: some were piling up railroad tracks; others were loading tracks onto railroad cars. After more than an hour's walk, we reached the gate of the transit station. Some camp officials were sitting behind a long table immediately behind the gate. After the roll call, we were searched, as usual, and were then admitted into the camp.

Some prisoners approached us. Most of them had been arrested recently and had been sent here from various pre-trial detention centers. They told us that all the barracks and tents were filled; hundreds of prisoners were camping outside without a roof over their heads. We were able to confirm these statements very soon. I found some room in the attic of a barracks, together with Josef and some others.

We were especially curious to find out which "elements" were being selected for forced labor these days. Under Stalin, various social strata were attacked in turn. It began in the early thirties with the Industrial Party; then came the Social Democrats, the Social Revolutionaries, the Trotskyites, the followers of Zinoviev, and the alleged as well as the real Bukharinists; after that, the military men who had been arrested in connection with Tukhachevsky and Yakir, the "Gestapo agents" (until the Hitler–Stalin pact), and finally, after the war, those who had collaborated with the Germans. Our initial inquiries established that the transit station was presently full of so-called repeaters, i.e., political prisoners who had finished serving their sentences. In 1948, Stalin had ordered all former political prisoners who were still alive rearrested. In most instances, no new charges were brought against them. They were merely informed that in the opinion of the NKVD they had failed to mend their ways, and for this reason they were being sent back to a camp. It was rare for "repeaters" to be tried and sentenced. The majority were sent directly to the camps; the rest were imprisoned or banished.

There were a large number of Nazi collaborators in the camp. Many of them were women. And there was a third group consisting of prisoners from the Baltic republics, where partisans were still putting up intense resistance. There were many priests among the Baltic prisoners, and also several hundred Germans who had been deported by the Russians.

We were surprised to find only political prisoners here, no criminals. This transit station formed part of a spetzlager called Oserlag, which had been set up in 1948. Before then, there had been only one kind of camp in the Soviet Union, despite some differences in the ways individual camp units were run. Political prisoners and criminal convicts had been locked up together—it made no difference to the NKVD whether a person had been arrested for his beliefs or for murder. Women, for example, who had been arrested because of their husbands' "political crimes" had to work in the same brigade with women who had been prostitutes all their lives. The *spetzlagers* were reserved for political prisoners only. At first, we thought this was something to be welcomed, for we had always felt humiliated by having to live and work together with the criminal underworld. But we soon realized that the *spetzlagers* had not been designed to ameliorate the condition of the political prisoners, but rather to terrorize them more efficiently.

A lively atmosphere prevailed in the transit station. Some prisoners had musical instruments; they had formed a small orchestra. At certain times of the day, in the dining room, the women, who lived in separate barracks, were allowed to meet with the men and dance. A few clever couples managed to slip off into various secluded places. A friend of mine danced with a pretty girl and succeeded in persuading her to climb up to the watertower with him, where they exchanged some hasty caresses for a few minutes. He told me she had refused at first, but when he told her she would be sent to a women's camp in a few days and possibly not see a man for many years, she followed him without a word.

During our very first days, we noticed a new spirit among the prisoners. In the past, no one could utter a word of criticism of the regime without coming into conflict with his fellow prisoners. People were quite different here: everywhere you went, you heard expressions of heartfelt contempt for the government and for Stalin himself. The village elders and policemen who had been installed by the Germans, and especially the Baltic prisoners, almost all of whom had been given twenty-five-year sentences, felt they had nothing to lose; also, most of them expected an imminent war between Russia and the Western powers. We saw a Lithuanian priest making a speech to hundreds of prisoners from the top step of a barracks: he prophesied the imminent end of Stalin's dictatorship and said the United Nations would liberate the prisoners from the clutches of the NKVD. He was able to speak unhindered for ten minutes before the camp police came hurrying along to drag him off to a punishment cell.

Thanks to some helpful contacts, Josef and I soon found shelter inside a barracks. We had to lie on the floor, but we were glad to get away from the loft, which had been indescribably dirty and flea-infested. I got to know the Viennese Dr. Frankl in this barracks. He had been captured by the Russians during the First World War. After his release, he had settled down in Tashkent and worked as a doctor there. In 1926, he visited his mother and sister for several weeks in Vienna and then returned to his wife and child in Tashkent, where he continued to live as a respected doctor and citizen, until he was suddenly arrested by the NKVD in 1940. Like many others, Frankl was convinced he was the victim of an unfortunate error, and was sure that he would be released very soon. Somehow, he even managed to inform his wife that he was accused of having been recruited as a German spy by the Viennese antiquarian Weinberger. Frankl had not seen his school friend Weinberger since 1914.

After Hitler occupied Austria and started persecuting Jews, Weinberger had been deported to Poland and fled from there to Russia. Like many other Jewish refugees, he had been put in a camp near Saratov. He had written to Frankl from the camp, describing his situation; Frankl had sent him packages and money. After the outbreak of the war between Germany and Russia, the Jews were released from their detention camps and were allowed to settle wherever they wanted in the Soviet Union.

Weinberger went to Tashkent in the expectation of finding shelter with his old school friend. When he introduced himself to Mrs. Frankl, she was frightened, for standing in front of her was the man responsible for her husband's misfortune. She told Weinberger why Frankl had been arrested. Together they went immediately to the NKVD to clear up the error. The NKVD officer they spoke to wrote everything down and told them they could go home and relax, he was confident everything would be cleared up very soon. Several days passed. Frankl did not come back, but Weinberger was arrested. Frankl and Weinberger met in a cell decades after their last encounter. Frankl was sentenced to ten years in camp. Weinberger died in prison in Tashkent.

I met Frankl once again in camp 07. After that, I lost track of him.

Once again, we were brought before a medical commission that divided us into work categories; this determined which camps we were sent to. I stood naked in front of three doctors, two women and a man, all of them prisoners; the director of medical services was present but didn't involve himself in the examination. The male doctor put a few questions to me and dictated something to his young, very pretty secretary—all I heard was the word "third." On the one hand I was glad, for the third category meant light labor, but on the other hand I was worried, for it seemed to imply that my physical condition was not good, despite the many potatoes I had eaten in the Alexandrovsky Tsentral.

We stayed five more days in the transit station. Then I was included in a transport of five hundred prisoners. From six in the morning until four in the afternoon, we went through the usual tedious procedure: roll call, search, distribution of provisions, etc. This time we didn't have to walk or be driven to a faraway train station: several freight cars were waiting for us right outside the camp gate. Eighty men went into each car. It was late at night when we finally departed. Our first stop was the station in Tayshet, where our cars were coupled to the locomotive that would take us to our final destination.

The train moved very slowly, for the line was still under construction. We didn't arrive in camp 07 until early in the morning. We could see part of the camp and its immediate surroundings through the little barred window in the car. About two hundred meters away was a high wooden fence, and behind it barracks, most of them painted white. Behind the camp, a dark pine forest. We could clearly see the barrels of the submachine guns in the hands of the soldiers in the two watchtowers that flanked the camp. There was no movement in the camp.

To the right of the camp were two rows of barracks, with a soldier pacing back and forth in front of them, a submachine gun strapped over his shoulder. The train moved on a little farther, making us believe for a moment that we were traveling on; but then the locomotive chugged back to the old spot. Several soldiers and officers stepped out of the guardhouse, and some chairs and tables were brought outside. The first

car was opened. The prisoners slid down the steep incline, assembled in
rows of five, and marched to the gate, where the officer ordered them to
sit down on the ground. Then the second car was emptied, and the third,
the car I was in. We scampered down the incline like goats, glad to be
able to move our limbs after squatting in the car for so long.

The induction formalities lasted several hours. When we were finally
admitted, we still couldn't go into the barracks. We were first divided
into brigades; once again, we had to sit on the ground until our names
were called. Only after this procedure was over were we allowed to go
into the barracks. They looked familiar: double-tiered bunks, just like in
Norilsk, most of them without bedding.

My brigade did repair work on the railroad. It turned out that only
three or four hundred men in this camp were actually sent to work; the
rest hung around the barracks or were occupied in the camp. Since I was
in the third category, the brigadier suggested that I work as a *dnevalny*,
a barracks janitor. I agreed. The work wasn't hard, and I had a partner.
His name was Levchenko. He had been mayor of the Belorussian city of
Rovno during the German occupation. Because one of his legs was shorter
than the other, he had to walk with a stick. That was why he had been
given the post of *dnevalny*, despite his twenty-five-year sentence.

I tried very hard to keep the barracks in order, and I worked a lot.
I had only a few hours of sleep every night. In the morning, when the
barracks door was opened (it was locked overnight), I had to fetch water
from the well a hundred and fifty meters away. Water was scarce, and
the well could not supply enough for the fifteen hundred camp inmates.
I spent the rest of the day cleaning up. My work won me the sympathy
of my brigadier and the other prisoners in the barracks. They were especially thankful for being well provided with water; in the past, there
had always been a lack of it. Frequently, people from the other barracks
came to ours to quench their thirst.

My reputation as a good *dnevalny* led to my being held up as an
example by the brigadiers. My friends, on the other hand, criticized me
for my excessive diligence. People were especially annoyed at the behavior of the "mayor," as my partner was facetiously called; he avoided
work and limited his activities to chasing away prisoners from other barracks who came to drink our water: "I'm not fetching water for the whole
camp!" Yet everyone knew that he never fetched any water at all. The
"mayor" was understandably pleased with my performance; he would
often bring me a larger portion of soup from the kitchen, where he had
a friend among the cooks.

Levchenko, who knew that I was an old camp inmate and a former
communist, told me how he had tried to help persecuted Jews and communists when he was the mayor of Rovno. But the others told me the
opposite was true: he had denounced all the Jews and communists he

knew to the Gestapo, and then ransacked their homes. Nevertheless, a Jew had saved him from execution by testifying at Levchenko's trial that the mayor had given him a pass that enabled him to leave the city and thus escape the Gestapo.

The main purpose of the *spetzlagers* was to isolate the political prisoners from the outside world. In the previous camps, prisoners had considerable freedom of movement and opportunities to make contact with free employees. If you knew any *beskonvoinye*—prisoners with passes entitling them to leave the camp without escort—you could obtain various things that were otherwise unavailable. And the relatively unlimited freedom to correspond with one's relatives made the harsh conditions of camp life a little easier to bear. But in the *spetzlagers* correspondence was limited to two letters a year. Since many letters were lost, it is no exaggeration to say that we had almost no contact with the outside world. At first, only a small portion of the camp population was sent to work: the NKVD had a hard time finding suitable places of work where the prisoners would not come into contact with the free population. It took a while to organize the camps to meet this specification; eventually, all the prisoners had to work.

One of the devices used to ensure our isolation was a uniform that distinguished *spetzlager* prisoners from all others and especially from the free population. Our trousers, shirts, padded jackets, coats, and hats were all of the same dark blue, and every garment had a large number painted on it in oil colors—on the knees of one's pants, on the front of one's cap, on the back of one's shirt, jacket, and coat. No one was allowed to wear garments without numbers, not even inside the camp. The guards were instructed to insist that the numbers be clearly visible. If a number started fading, it was the prisoner's responsibility to restore it; those who failed to do so were put in a punishment cell. My number in the *spetzlager* was CH–462.

Prisoners in the *spetzlagers* were very carefully watched. The old NKVD apparatus was supplemented by the new MGB (Ministry of State Security). Every camp section now had two political officers, one from the NKVD and one from the MGB. Both organizations terrorized the prisoners to the best of their ability; one harassment followed the other. Both the MGB and the NKVD recruited spies among the prisoners and they took note of the other prisoners' minutest impulses and conversations and reported them to their bosses. The prisoners protected themselves against these spies by every imaginable means, including murder. It happened frequently that someone was "accidentally" struck dead by a loose boulder or a falling tree, and sometimes the traitors were dealt with in a no less violent but much more straightforward fashion.

AMERICAN SPIES

Old "camp birds" that we were—and former party members, most of us—we realized from the beginning that we faced an extremely difficult situation. It was unbearable to be forced into the company of former policemen, SS men, and members of the Nazi special detachments. Some of us wrote petitions to the NKVD and the MGB, protesting being locked up with these mass murderers. The reply was that we were in the right place.

Of course, there were people in the *spetzlagers* who wouldn't have anything to do with Nazi war criminals. For example, I met a group of young Germans in camp 07 who had worked for the C.I.A. and had been given twenty-five-year sentences. Among the thousands who worked as spies for the United States, there were naturally many mercenaries and adventurers, but I believe the majority had idealistic motives.

I was very curious to learn how young people in Germany thought shortly after the collapse of the Hitler regime. I noticed in my first conversations with these young Germans that only a few of them condemned the Nazis completely; most of them did not fault everything Hitler had done. They agreed that the slaughter of the Jews and the massacres of other national groups by the SS and the SD were an abomination; they were certain, however, that Hitler hadn't known about these crimes. When I heard this, I thought of the many prisoners who believed that Stalin knew nothing of Yezhov's, Beria's, and Abakumov's crimes. Most of those young Germans regarded their collaboration with the United States as a means to make Germany a powerful nation again. Only very few of them were convinced democrats. My first contact with German postwar youth saddened me. Twelve years of Nazi rule had left the younger generation mentally crippled.

Most of the inmates of the camp were either foreigners or Russians who had voluntarily or involuntarily returned from abroad. Colonel Yarko had been sent to Germany with the Soviet Army; he had been a member of a commission that dismantled German companies and sent the parts to the Soviet Union. Yarko had dismantled the Zeiss optical factory in Jena, a branch company of the Opel concern, several Siemens plants, and others. Not only the machinery was dismantled but also the windows and doors; even bricks and roof tiles were taken away.

Yarko had joined the Komsomol as a young man and became a party member after he enlisted in the army. He had believed all the stories he had heard about the sufferings of workers in the capitalist countries. When he saw the first German villages, he couldn't help comparing them with the collectivized villages in Russia. The sight of typical working-class apartments in Berlin led him to conclude that capitalist proletarian misery could not be as awful as he had been led to suppose. One day, he met with some American soldiers and officers, whose life he could not help comparing with that of their Soviet counterparts. That was the last straw.

Yarko decided to defect to the West. After making thorough preparations, he succeeded in crossing the border unnoticed. He settled down in Düsseldorf, got himself a job, and enjoyed his life in freedom for three months. One evening as he was coming back from the movies, he saw a car standing in front of his apartment. He couldn't remember what happened next. When he recovered consciousness, the car was driving through the streets of East Berlin. He was sitting in the back seat between two men, had a bad headache, and felt blood streaming down his face. He was taken to a jail, where his wound was bandaged. After a hearing that lasted several days, Yarko was brought before a military court and sentenced to twenty-five years in a camp.

Japanese prisoners of war participated in the building of the Tayshet–Lena railroad line. We could still see some Japanese characters on the walls of our barracks. These barracks had begun to rot and disintegrate five years after they were built. Some of them had to be propped up to prevent them from collapsing. The barracks could easily have been renovated or rebuilt, since most of the inmates were idle for months at a time and there was plenty of wood in the surrounding forests. But nothing happened. The camp administration was waiting for orders from above, and no orders were forthcoming. As long as a prisoner worked, he was granted a vital minimum. But here the majority didn't work.

The many NKVD and MGB officers had only one concern: to maintain the strict camp regime. The food was bad and insufficient; we didn't even get the usual *kipyatok*, regularly. The well didn't give enough water. There wasn't even enough firewood. Occasionally, prisoners were harnessed to a cart and had to fetch water in barrels from the nearby Chuna River. But then the MGB chief objected to *spetzlager* prisoners being allowed to go to the river, even under armed escort. So the scarcity of water continued, and our complaints went unheeded.

One day, a lieutenant commander of the NKVD visited the camp and came unannounced into all the barracks. No one dared to lodge a complaint with this grim-looking fellow. I gathered up all my courage and addressed him: "Pardon me, citizen lieutenant commander, is it permitted to lodge a complaint?"

"What do you want?"

"Is it permissible to treat human beings the way they are treated in this camp?"

"This is a *spetzlager* of the MGB, not just some other camp."

"Does that preclude humane treatment?"

"Who is treating you inhumanely?"

"We don't even have enough water to drink."

"You don't have enough water?" He sounded surprised.

"That's right."

"Do you have any other complaints?"

"When can we finally write to our relatives?"

"You can write twice a year." Thereupon, he turned his back to me and pressed through the mass of prisoners toward the exit.

Two days later, my complaint bore its first fruits. We were given stationery and envelopes and were allowed to write our first letter home. I looked forward to giving my wife my new address and asking her to send me a package with some food. That was in the morning. In the afternoon, the overseer came to tell me this was my last day of work as a *dnevalny*. The next day, I would be sent out to work on a bridge.

That job, however, lasted only four days. I was used to help tear down the makeshift wooden bridge across the Chuna River, but didn't have the opportunity to participate in the construction of the new one. The camp commander had taken the first available opportunity to punish me for complaining about his regime. When a commission came to select workers for camp section 033, I was included. As I left, several old friends thought I would have done better not to complain.

Camp section 033 was on the other side of the Chuna, an eight-kilometer march. First, we climbed down a steep slope toward the frozen river; then we walked on the ice. After three or four kilometers, we passed by a village where deported peasants from Bessarabia were piling up driftwood. Then we left the river and marched along a snowed-in trail through the woods, in the direction of the new railroad line. By the time we reached the tracks, we could see the high fence of camp section 033 in the distance. We didn't have to wait long at the gate. Camp policemen and overseers led us to the third barracks and searched us. Then began the usual scramble for a desirable bunk space. I found three spaces on the top bunk and reserved one for Oskar Leptich, a German from Sie-benbürgen, and one for Hans, one of the young Germans I had gotten to know in camp 07.

During the march, I had reflected on what I would probably face in the new camp section. I felt very weak; the medical commission had recognized this when they delegated me to camp section 07, where there was very little hard work. During my few weeks as a *dnevalny*, I had not exerted myself excessively, but neither had it been a vacation. The only purpose in sending me to section 033 was to force me to perform hard labor. I decided to refuse to do any work I was physically unfit for. I knew the consequences this might bring, but that didn't alter my resolution.

It was late when we lay down to sleep in the dark room. I used my clothes as bedding. As we were getting ready for work in the morning, several men—including Oskar and me—were given orders to report for work on the night shift. I was glad to have a day off to look around the camp section. I picked up my breakfast, which was indistinguishable from the fare you got in other camps.

The atmosphere was a little friendlier here than in camp 07, but I found it hard to say what made the difference, since everything looked so similar—the same rotting barracks, the same regime, even the same Japanese graffiti. Maybe it had something to do with the little stream that gurgled along the edge of the camp, or with the hothouse that supplied the NKVD with fresh vegetables.

The men selected for the night shift had to transfer from the third to the first barracks because we would be working with a different brigade. Oskar, Hans, and I found sleeping spaces on lower bunks. I didn't have to search for my brigadier for long. The moment I stepped into the barracks, I heard someone showering the prisoners with expletives. Aha, I thought, that's the brigadier, and went back outside. I wasn't eager to make his acquaintance.

We used our free time to walk about the camp and talk to a few of the old-timers. We didn't learn anything new from them. As we passed the *kipyatilka*, the hot-water kitchen, we noticed a stocky, broad-shouldered man with a long red beard, chopping wood. I took him to be a member of a religious sect—you could usually recognize them by their long beards. Oskar asked him if there was any *kipyatok*. The man answered in Russian, but with a strong German accent.

"Do you speak German?" I asked him in German.

The bearded man dropped his ax and looked at us in astonishment. "Are you Germans?"

We introduced ourselves.

"I come from Styria," he said.

"What town?" I asked.

"Kapfenberg, near Bruck an der Mur."

"I know where Kapfenberg is. I can even tell you where you used to work."

"How could you? Do you know me?"

"You could only have worked for Böhler—that's where most people in Kapfenberg work."

"That's right, I worked for Böhler, in the fire department."

His name was Franz Almeier. He had served in the Volkssturm and had fought against the Slovenian partisans. After the war, he was sentenced to ten years in camp by a Russian military court. He had fallen ill in camp; that was why he was given the *kipyatilshchik*'s job, which was usually reserved for invalids.

Thanks to Almeier, we could have as much hot water as we wanted. There was a stove in the hot-water kitchen which could be used for cooking by prisoners who had received packages from home. The place was generally referred to as the "officers' mess." In the evenings and on work-free days, the *kipyatilka* was full of people cooking their gruel in American tin cans and German and Russian mess bowls, surrounded by kibitzers who had no food to cook and stared enviously at the lucky possessors of oats, millet, and other delicacies. Some people offered to fetch wood in exchange for a bit of gruel. Almeier had difficulty keeping order in his kitchen at such times. I was a frequent guest of his, and often he would murmur into my ear: "Come back later. I've got something for you."

When I became a cook later on, I was able to help him in turn. I spent more than a year in his company, until he was taken from camp 033. Later I heard that he had been seen in section 051.

It was time to get ready for work. My job consisted of loading sixteen tons of gravel in one shift, together with two other men. The work was so hard that, after three months, people were totally depleted and incapable of working. My decision to refuse to do this work was firm. I planned to hide in the third barracks shortly before our brigade marched to work. I confided my plan to Oskar and Hans.

At the first stroke of the gong, we all put on our padded coats. At the last minute, the brigadier and two assistants came in with felt boots they had just picked up from a brigade that had worked the day shift. There weren't enough boots in the camp, so they had to be shared among two brigades. The boots were wet; it took a long time for everyone to pick out a pair. At the second stroke of the gong, I stepped out before anyone else and hurried over to the third barracks. It was pitch-dark there. I groped around till I found an empty space and lay down, fully clothed. I heard the brigade assembling in front of the gate. The brigadier took a count, discovered that someone was missing, and shouted: "Who's missing?" No one answered. As I was told later, the brigadier ran back into the barracks to see if anyone had stayed behind. Since he didn't find anyone, the brigade went to work with one man less.

For one day, I had been spared the grueling work. But what would happen next? After giving the matter more thought, I decided to continue refusing to work. I fell asleep. I got up early next morning, before the brigade came back from work. The brigadier didn't ask any questions, since he had no idea who had been missing. I was new here; he didn't know my face. Oskar and Hans told me about their first night of work: it was so strenuous that they were bathed in sweat despite the frost.

After breakfast, everyone lay down, and so did I. While the others slept, I lay awake, thinking how to proceed. I knew I couldn't repeat last night's maneuver. I finally decided to talk frankly to the brigadier and explain that I couldn't perform any hard labor. I got up quietly and went to visit Almeier in the *kipyatilka*, and confided my plans to him. He was worried for me. "They'll lock you in the punishment cell," he said. I myself knew I couldn't expect anything good to come of this.

I helped Almeier fetch wood. At four, I went back to my barracks; I knew that was when my brigade would be awakened. The brigadier wasn't there, so I turned back. As I stepped out of the barracks, I ran into him. "Brigadier, I have to speak to you." He gave me a questioning look. "It was I who stayed away from work last night, and I'm going to continue to do so."

Nikolai, the brigadier, took me by the throat. *"Yob tvoyu mat*—What did you say!? I'll teach you to stay away from work!" His face was purple with rage.

"Calm down, listen to me!"

He let go of me. "What else?"

"I am an old prisoner and I can predict everything you're going to tell me, and I know the consequences of what I'm doing. I'm telling you this so you won't have to go searching for me again. Report me, and the matter's settled as far as you're concerned."

The brigadier looked at me for a while and said: "You know, I like you. All right, let's go inside, it's cold out here." We stepped back inside, and Nikolai turned away from me without a word.

I picked up my meal along with the rest and waited. Nothing happened that evening. Everyone went to work, and the brigadier passed me without saying a word. I didn't hide. I sat waiting for the camp police to drag me off to the punishment cell. The brigade came back after two hours. Oskar told me the freight cars hadn't come in because of heavy snowdrifts. The brigade would be sent to work during the day. Everyone was happy to be able to go back to sleep.

Early the next morning, the brigade left for work. By now, the brigadier had reported me to the chief overseer. This chief overseer was a "repeater" who had been released in 1946 after serving a ten-year sentence and had been sentenced to another ten years under the same charges. His name was Simin. His repertory of curse words was hardly distinguishable from the criminal brigadier's. Simin was shouting at me before he had even reached the door: "Where is the hero who dares to stay away from work?!"

Everyone pricked up his ears.

I was sitting near the door and could clearly see Simin's red face and nearly toothless mouth. I stepped forward. "It's me."

"We'll soon find out whether you'll work or not. Come here!"

Simin sat down at the table that was in the middle of the barracks. Pointing at me, he said to the brigadier: "Look at him, he doesn't want to work! Now we'll find out what sort of hero he really is!"

"I'm not a hero," I said quietly. "But I'm not going to do this work, because I'm too weak."

"Nobody's asking if you're strong or weak. You're here to work your ass off."

"This time, I'm not working my ass off."

"We'll see about that."

Simin stood up and left. I was sure he was going to get the camp police.

In the meantime, the brigadier and his helpers brought in the felt boots from the drying room. Everyone hurried to get a pair. Two boots remained standing in the middle of the barracks. The brigadier picked up the boots and tossed them on the floor in front of me. "Put them on!"

"I don't need them."

The brigade was already at the gate, waiting for the guards. I sat on my bunk in the barracks. An overseer and a camp policeman arrived. The *dnevalny* hurried up to them.

"Where's the shirker?"

"Here he is," the *dnevalny* said, pointing to me.

"Hurry up, get dressed, the brigade's waiting," the camp policeman said.

"I'm not going to work."

The camp policeman picked up the boots, held them in front of my nose, and showered me with the usual imprecations. I didn't move. Then the overseer very calmly said: "Get dressed and follow me."

I put on my coat, but not the boots, and followed him into the courtyard in my shoes. There we met the chief overseer and other camp officials on their way back to the office after supervising the brigades' departure for work. The chief overseer called out to us: "Take him back to the barracks. He's going to the punishment cell!"

Back in the barracks, I put on the felt boots—I knew I would need them in the punishment cell, an icy hole in the ground where a hundred grams of bread and a pot of warm water would be my only meal in twenty-four hours. The only way to survive imprisonment there was to keep in constant motion. After several hours, the overseer came and told me to follow him. It was very cold outside; the snow was frozen to a hard crust that crunched beneath my boots. I asked myself whether it wouldn't be better to go to work after all, but I rejected this thought: better to freeze to death than collapse under the strain of this terrible labor.

We had to veer off to the right to reach the punishment cell, but, to my great surprise, the soldier accompanying me told me to move on straight ahead. We went to the guardhouse next to the gate. The soldier opened the door and let me walk ahead. Inside were the camp commander, First Lieutenant Sorokin, his deputy, and the soldier on duty.

"Why didn't you go to work?" the deputy asked me.

"I'm very weak and I'm incapable of such hard work."

"You're in the first category and have to do every kind of work!"

"I'm in the third category, not the first."

"How do you know?" asked Sorokin.

"I heard the doctor in the transit station say so."

"That was a long time ago. Now you're in the first category," said the commander.

"Whether it's first or third, I'm too weak for this work."

"There are only two kinds of work here: loading or cutting wood. So tomorrow you're going to cut wood."

"I'm not doing that either."

"I'm sure you would like to sort cake, but we can't offer you that."

"I don't care what kind of work you give me, so long as it isn't too hard for me."

"All right, you can clean the latrines."

"Fine, that doesn't bother me." I just said that, but actually I knew I was no more able to clean the latrines than I was to load gravel.

"Go get the chief overseer!"

I went to the office and got the chief overseer. On the way, he said: "You're going to the punishment cell for five days, then for another five days, and another, until you give up or die."

"Maybe I'll die, but I'm not giving up," I replied with irritation.

The commander said to Simin: "Give him some kind of work in the camp for the time being."

"Yes, sir!"

Outside, Simin said: "By God, you're lucky!" I was happy that my first strike in camp had been so successful.

The next morning, I was taken to the soldiers' barracks together with two other prisoners, a Russian and a Rumanian. We had to chop wood for the soldiers there. We did this for two months. Sometimes the cook would use us for peeling potatoes, even though prisoners were strictly forbidden to enter the soldiers' quarters. Several times, the noncommissioned officer led me into a room where submachine guns and rifles were stored in the eventuality of an alert. There I washed the floor while the guards slept. I was always amazed that the soldiers were foolhardy enough to let us into their quarters: there were quite a few people in the camp with adventurous ideas in their heads.

THE FIRST PACKAGE FROM MY WIFE

February 1950. It was bitter cold, as was normal for this time of year. One day, on the way back to the camp from the soldiers' barracks, we were standing in front of the gate waiting to be let in when a horse-drawn sled pulled up next to us. On the sled, bedded in hay, were several packages.

"Karl, a package for you!" said the Rumanian.

I ignored the remark, for I knew he liked to play practical jokes.

"Your name's Steiner, isn't it?" the Rumanian persisted.

Now I looked. Some of the packages had the labels face up, and there indeed was my name.

I waited anxiously while several officers opened the package and thoroughly examined its contents, slicing the lard into small pieces, pouring the millet onto a newspaper, emptying the carton of sugar. Two little packs of tea were confiscated: we weren't allowed to have tea.

I was very happy when I walked into the barracks with my package. Oskar and Hans had been waiting impatiently. The first thing I did was go to the "officers' mess" and boil some gruel. Then the three of us ate together, chewing the good food reverently. I also gave a plateful to the brigadier. Content and sated, we talked about my wife, who was still faithful to me after fourteen years. It was pleasant to know that for several days we would not be hungry.

Early the next morning, Hans went out to get some *kipyatok*, which we sweetened with sugar and drank with some bread and lard. I put the rest of the food that had come with the package into a knapsack I had made out of a Japanese blanket, put the knapsack under my pillow, and asked the *dnevalny* to keep an eye on it while I was gone. He promised to do so.

When we came back from work, my first glance was at my pillow— the knapsack was gone. The *dnevalny* had no idea where it was. Oskar and Hans were even more upset than I was. I was advised to report the theft, but I knew this was senseless, and did nothing about it. The *dnevalny*, however, ran to the camp police and reported the theft to them. The next morning, I was summoned to the camp police. When I stepped into the office, I saw my knapsack in the corner.

"Is this your knapsack?" one of the camp policemen asked me.

"Yes."

"Take it and sign this paper."

I looked in the bag: it contained a set of underwear and my shoes, but not a trace of the food. So I had had only one day to enjoy the first package my wife had sent me in eleven years.

When we peeled potatoes in the kitchen and the cook had some soup left over, he would sometimes let us have a little. One day, we happened to be sitting in a corner having soup from a pot when a soldier came in, saw us, and said to the cook: "Why are you feeding these fascists?"

That was the last of our supplementary meals. We often saw the cook throwing leftover soup away after that.

One day, we were peeling potatoes again. An iron stove was heating the room. We were hungry. The Rumanian took some potatoes and laid them on the embers. I had gone outside to chop wood, and the cook called me in. When I stood before him, he asked me if it was I who was roasting potatoes in the stove. I thought quickly and decided the others must have blamed me, since they were the only ones in the room. I took the blame. "Yes, I'm the one."

The cook struck me in the face with such force that I staggered against the wall. He continued to belabor me with his fists, and I submitted without putting up any defense. Some other cooks came in, and one of them—a man who had often fed us—said to the hero: "Let him go now, that's enough." Only then did he stop beating me.

I decided to stop working in the soldiers' barracks. That same evening, I went to the office to tell the chief overseer, Simin, about the incident in the kitchen and ask him for another job. He blew up. "Do you think you can pick and choose your work as you please? Where the hell do you think you are?"

The bookkeeper Johann, a Volga German generally known as Ivan Ivanovich, came in from the next room and asked what was the matter. Simin by now had regained his sense of humor. "Look at this guy! First he goes on strike, then he decides he doesn't like working in the barracks!"

Ivan Ivanovich was one of the prisoners who were indispensable to the administration and had some influence on the camp commander. He said: "He was a cook in Norilsk. Why not put him to work in the kitchen?" Simin said he hadn't known I was a master of the culinary arts; he offered to ask the kitchen supervisor to hire me.

That's how I became a cook again. My colleague in the kitchen was a Frenchman; he had come to Russia as a child, together with his father. His name was Berthe, a tall, thin man with a sly, humorous look on his face. He turned out to be a good friend. It was a pleasure to see him laugh: his whole body became convulsed with amusement, while his hands pleaded for respite from whatever story I was telling.

The kitchen supervisor was a Bessarabian Jew, a powerful man of Herculean proportions. He regarded the two of us as his right- and left-hand men. He was proud of having "the whole International" working in his kitchen—a Frenchman, an Austrian, a Russian, a Latvian, and a Jew. He liked to characterize each of us by some dominant trait. To the Russian, for instance, he was always saying: "You are the greatest thief."

The kitchen supervisor was engaged in a bitter struggle against the criminals, who used threats of violence to get better food. Although the *spetzlagers* were reserved for political prisoners, there were a number of ordinary criminals among them—former soldiers of Marshal Rokossovsky's army, which had consisted largely of ex-convicts. There was a gang in camp 033, led by a one-armed man named Vasya. These bandits robbed other prisoners of their packages and strong-armed the cooks into giving them fish, fat, and other food.

Our Bessarabian was determined not to give the criminals a gram more than their allotted portions, and he remained firm despite their repeated threats. His answer was always the same: "I'm not going to deprive other prisoners of their food so that criminals can have more to eat."

Vasya told the kitchen supervisor quite openly that he planned to "do him in" if he didn't hand out some food. One day, he carried out his threat. The kitchen supervisor was sitting in front of his barracks, chatting with a prisoner. Vasya crept up from behind, stabbed him in the back several times, and ran away and hid among his friends. I happened to be on duty in the kitchen when the wounded man came rushing in with blood streaming all over him, and screaming: "An ax, give me an ax!"

We could only guess what had happened. I didn't know what to do—the ax and the kitchen knife were locked up in a closet, and I was in

charge of the key. I gave the kitchen supervisor the ax. He took it and
ran out to find the killer. He collapsed in the middle of the courtyard
and was taken to the infirmary and bandaged. A little later, he was transferred to the central hospital. People said he had died there, but years
later I learned that that wasn't true.

The repercussions for Vasya and his gang were extraordinarily mild.
Vasya was given twenty days in the punishment cell for "violating camp
regulations"—that was all. The camp commander didn't mind prisoners
waging war on one another.

After the Bessarabian had gone, I was put in charge of the kitchen.
At first I resisted, but Berthe and Ivan Ivanovich finally persuaded me
to accept the position. Working in the kitchen attracted both genuine
and false friends. I always helped my friends, and especially my compatriots, as much as I could; this had some unpleasant consequences for
me. But the prisoners liked me; only the camp commander and the people
in the medical services were dissatisfied.

The camp commander, Lieutenant Sorokin, was friendly with the
head doctor, a prisoner named Nikolai Ivanovich Popov; they had known
each other for years. Because of his good relations with the camp commander, Popov had a lot of influence in the selection of the kitchen
supervisor, who in turn was obligated to give Popov and his assistant
plentiful meals. Thus, fat, meat, sugar, and other foods had a way of
moving from the kitchen to the infirmary in fairly large quantities, and
Popov would pass on the lion's share to his friend and benefactor, Colonel
Sorokin.

I, too, gave Popov better food than I gave the others, but he and
especially Sorokin felt it wasn't enough. For this reason, both of them
decided to get rid of me as soon as possible. A few weeks after my
appointment as kitchen supervisor, Sergei Konovalenko, an old friend of
Popov's and Sorokin's, was transferred from another section to ours. I
was summoned to the office. There sat Sorokin, Popov, the victualing
officer, and Konovalenko. "This is the new kitchen supervisor," Sorokin
said, pointing to Konovalenko. "You will yield your position to him."

"Yes, sir, citizen commander," I said.

That same day, Konovalenko came to the kitchen, accompanied by
the victualing officer, and I introduced him to his new domain. He suggested I continue working as a cook, and I accepted. Konovalenko was a
confidence man from Odessa. When the Germans occupied the city, he
stayed and made business deals with them. Then the Soviet Army recaptured the city, and Konovalenko was arrested and given ten years in
camp. He adjusted to camp life quite quickly. With Popov's help, he
established trade relations with the officers of the camp administration:
that is, he sold them clothes he obtained from other prisoners. Later he
was put in charge of the kitchen and used his position to embezzle groceries that were meant to feed the prisoners. Complaints about his per-

formance had been so numerous that he was eventually fired. Now, after a not very long interval, he was being reinstated.

Konovalenko immediately introduced a new regime in the kitchen. According to the camp rules, all the groceries to be used for preparing a particular meal for the prisoners were to be given to the cook on duty. Konovalenko ignored this rule: he gave out the food without weighing it, thus dispensing with the usual controls. He terrorized the cooks by constantly threatening to fire them. They were so intimidated that no one dared say a word of objection to his practices. I couldn't bear to see the prisoners robbed of the little food they were entitled to, and so I was always struggling with Konovalenko, trying to reason with him.

The prisoners' food was getting worse and worse, and the officers came more and more often to the kitchen to pick up their food parcels. Konovalenko was on such good terms with the officers that they invited him to go fishing with them. They even appointed a group of prisoners to come along and help. Boats and large nets were made especially for this purpose. The officers and the guards divided up the catch. Popov and his medical assistants were also eating their fill: they appropriated a good part of the prisoners' meat and butter. Sorokin, of course, got his share.

I wanted to quit working in the kitchen because I could no longer stand being near Konovalenko. But my friends begged me to stay; they were afraid of what might happen if they lost me as an ally in the kitchen. I tried as hard as I could to help these people, who as foreigners were even worse off than the Russians. But there were also "friends" who weren't worthy of assistance. It happened that prisoners received packages from home and still came to the kitchen window to beg. One day, I was returning to the barracks from the kitchen when a prisoner accosted me in the courtyard. He had evidently been waiting for me. I knew him; he was a priest from Carpathian Russia.

"Forgive me," he said in good German. "My need is pressing."

"What can I do for you?"

"I would like to ask you to give me some food now and then."

I promised to do what I could and suggested he come to the kitchen window. For several weeks, the priest came to my window, and I gave him soup and occasionally gruel. One day, I mentioned him in a conversation with Oskar. Oskar told me the priest behaved in a thoroughly unchristian manner; he received many packages in the mail and never shared with his fellow prisoners. While he was begging me for soup, lard was rotting in his knapsack. I never gave the priest food again.

One of my steady customers was the Ukrainian writer Maystrenko. In contrast to the priest, Maystrenko had not wanted to ask me for help. I had gotten to know him earlier, and when I became a cook, I tried to help him. It took some effort to prove to him that it isn't immoral to accept help when you need it.

Maystrenko had stayed in Kiev during the occupation and hadn't written a line during that time. To make a living, he had worked in a secondary school. When the Soviet Army returned, Maystrenko was arrested and sentenced to five years for "collaboration with the enemy." Maystrenko hated the fascists wholeheartedly; whenever we talked about the occupation, he quivered with rage at the crimes commited in Kiev by the SS. Until 1941, he said, Kiev had been an anti-communist city; one year of occupation had been enough to turn everyone into a communist. Even those who had enthusiastically welcomed the German Army when it first marched into the city turned away from the Nazis after they murdered more than fifty thousand Jews in the gorge of Babi Yar on the outskirts of Kiev. Maystrenko fell ill in 1951 and was taken to the central hospital. I don't know what happened to him after that.

One of Konovalenko's intimate friends was First Lieutenant Komarov, head of the KTTch, the department of education. He was a regular guest in the kitchen. When he came, he would usually berate the cooks in a particularly foul-mouthed manner, lecturing them on the need to give the prisoners the precise amount of their official rations and not a gram more. Before leaving, he would go into the pantry with Konovalenko and stuff his pockets with the prisoners' food.

The officers often caroused and drank with a young woman who lived near the camp. Komarov, who was married and had a seventeen-year-old daughter and a twelve-year-old son, was one of the more frequent visitors at her house. One of the prisoners, an artist, was permitted to paint pictures, which were then sold on the market in Tayshet. The officers would buy their vodka with the proceeds. Komarov brought along chickens he had stolen from his wife. Her suspicion fell on some prisoners who had been chopping wood near her house. The camp police came into the "officers' mess" to see if the prisoners were broiling chickens there.

One day, two prisoners disappeared. They were Latvians who had deserted the Red Army to join the Germans. In 1944, they had been captured, tried by a military court, and sentenced to twenty-five years for "high treason." It seemed extremely unlikely that they had escaped, since the two had worked as *dnevalny* and never had an opportunity to leave the camp. After several days of investigation, the NKVD found out that the two had used a fire ladder to climb over the tall camp fence on a foggy night. Their footsteps led to the Chuna River. The fugitives hadn't been able to cross it; most likely, they were hiding in the forest, but a manhunt involving a large number of men and dogs failed to find them. One day, two NKVD officers who were hunting in the taiga stumbled on the two Latvians as they were making a fire. The Latvians tried to run away, but it was too late—one of them was shot; the other was captured alive. Both were brought back to the camp; one of them was put in the morgue and the other one into the punishment cell, where he died of a "heart attack." The hospital attendants said his entire body was black and blue; apparently, he was beaten until his heart failed.

My relationship with Konovalenko got so bad that I finally decided to leave the kitchen. An opportunity soon presented itself. When Konovalenko gave me the food for supper one day, there wasn't a gram of fat included, even though, according to regulations, I was supposed to get four kilos of oil. I told him I wouldn't cook dinner. "Then go to hell," was his answer. I threw my white apron on the floor and ran to my barracks. In the evening, I went to the chief overseer and told him I would no longer work in the kitchen. Simin turned to the camp commander to ask *him* for instructions. The camp commander had no objection to my leaving the kitchen and working in Chernyavsky's brigade, as I had requested.

Chernyavsky's team made repairs on the railroad line. I had a good understanding with Chernyavsky, as I had done him many a good turn when I was a cook. He treated me in a very friendly fashion and even reserved a good bunk space for me. My work was considered one of the easier jobs in the brigade. Many people wanted Chernyavsky as their brigadier, but he was selective, and if the camp administration forced him to accept a prisoner he didn't want, the latter could count on being given the hardest work. Chernyavsky was a peasant from Belorussia. Small, thin, with prominent cheekbones and deep-set eyes; he looked like a killer. He had joined the police during the German occupation and was appointed police chief of a small regional city, a distinction he had earned by devoting himself with particular zeal to the destruction of Jews and guerrillas.

His first assistant in the brigade was a compatriot, Kopak; he, too, had been a policeman under the Germans and bore a great resemblance to his chief, except that he was stronger and even more bloodthirsty. The third man on the "staff" was Leshchenko, a Ukrainian from Volhynia; he liked to eat dog meat and would probably have enjoyed eating human flesh as well. The fourth member of the club was a priest who tended to the souls of the faithful and regularly supplied his chief and his two assistants with food he had obtained from members of his congregation.

The entire brigade constituted a criminal gang that was just waiting for a word from their leader to murder and pillage. They especially wanted to gas the Jews Hitler had overlooked—this was a wish Chernyavsky frequently expressed—and would not forget the communists either.

I made the acquaintance of an Austrian in this brigade: Franz Stift, a former leading official in the Austrian Hitler Youth. He had started his career in the small Lower Austria city of Scheibbs, where he had lived together with his father, a peasant. I soon discovered that Stift and his brigadier saw eye to eye on the question of Jews and communists, for Stift liked to voice his opinions in broken Russian. After the collapse of the Hitler regime, Stift had tried to flee to the West with his bride and would probably have succeeded if a woman hadn't recognized him and denounced him to the Russians, who sentenced him to fifteen years in a camp.

Stift and I became friendly. Many were unpleasantly surprised to see me chatting with this Nazi during the noonday breaks, or drinking tea with him, or walking about in the courtyard in his company. They found it altogether strange that I was working in Chernyavsky's brigade, which consisted entirely of bandits with Nazi sympathies. The reason was simple. Most prisoners in camp 033 were used for loading or for chopping wood. The only work I was physically capable of performing was with Chernyavsky's brigade in the railroad division. I had no choice but to avail myself of his "protection." If I wanted to survive, I had to gain the allegiance of even the most repulsive characters.

THE ADVENTURER KARL KAPP

Listening to Stift, I could see that he hadn't learned anything from the past and still adored Hitler, whom he considered infallible. The German defeat was the fault of traitors in the General Staff of the Wehrmacht. There was only one thing he did not defend: the mass extermination programs—he simply denied them. He said they were lies invented by Hitler's enemies: the Nazis had never done any harm to anyone, including the Jews.

Stift was a good worker, even though he had a crippled hand. We often talked as we worked, and when I said something funny, he would laugh aloud, opening his toothless mouth wide.

My friendship with Stift ended in the summer of 1951, when a new group of German prisoners arrived. Among them was a man named Karl Kapp; he was put into the brigade led by the former kulak Schmidt, and he lived in our barracks, together with the rest of his brigade. I got to know Kapp a few days after his arrival. I soon realized he was a dangerous adventurer—not just because he proposed an armed revolt to his fellow prisoners, but mainly because the NKVD and the MGB used such people as bait to attract other adventurers and gullible souls. Their victims were often sentenced to death. I knew this from experience, but Franz Stift did not recognize the danger and was taken in by Kapp's plans.

As a former cook, I was able occasionally to get extra food. I would bring soup and gruel to Kapp, who was suffering from hunger. After he ate, he told me how the Russians had put him in pre-trial detention in Leipzig and finally sentenced him to twenty-five years in camp. I observed him as he spoke: he was short and stocky, with a stout neck and a large head with a narrow forehead. His nut-brown hair was turning gray; he may have been fifty. Our conversation was interrupted when Schmidt, the brigadier, joined us.

That same day, Kapp came to talk to me and said: "Karl, I'm fortunate to have met you. I have an assignment for you." I found it strange that Kapp was addressing me with the familiar *du* as if we were old acquaintances; we had just met three hours before. He asked me to tell him where and when we could talk without being overheard. We agreed to meet in the *kipyatilka* the next day after work. But when we got there, the place was full of people, so we decided to go elsewhere. A new barracks was being constructed nearby, and the workers had already left. We went in and sat down. After making sure we hadn't been noticed, Kapp began to speak: "As I said before, I have a special assignment for you. But first I want you to know who you're dealing with. You already know my name. Everything I told you yesterday about my arrest and investigation was deliberately staged in order to get me into a Russian camp."

"What do you mean?"

"I was a factory owner and could still be one if I wanted to. It's my mission to organize Siberian camp prisoners and prepare them for an uprising in case of a war."

"Who are you working for?"

"Can't you guess?"

"What you're saying sounds so fantastic that I don't understand anything."

"All right, I'll express myself more clearly. I'm working for the Americans. It's they who sent me here."

"But surely it's an accident that you're in this camp and not in some other camp or in prison."

"Not at all. Thanks to our contacts in the NKVD and the MGB, we managed to have me placed where I was most needed."

"So when you were arrested you already knew you would be sent to the Oserlag?"

"Not only that. I even knew I would find you here."

"I have to tell you honestly—what you're saying strikes me as so outlandish I'm having a hard time believing it."

"That's because you have no conception of the American genius for organization."

"So what do you intend to do, specifically?"

"First of all, I want to come to an understanding with you; I need to know if I can count on you."

"I can't imagine how I could help you."

"I am the commander in chief of the underground army of prisoners I am here to organize. You are expected to be its political officer."

"What, without being asked?"

"Circumstances did not permit us to discuss it with you first. But I was assigned to tell you. Your monthly salary will be $3,000; it's been in effect for a year. As soon as you get to Europe or America, you'll get your money."

I was bewildered. "This is all so unbelievable; I don't know what to say," I said, embarrassed.

"Do you want some confirmation?"

"Who's going to confirm it? Are there other people here who know about your plans?"

"Not yet, but I can contact my superiors any time."

"How are you going to do that?"

"A plane will fly over the camp, and I'll signal."

Our conversation lasted for several hours. Kapp told me that as soon as he finished organizing camp section 033, he would have himself transferred to another section and get to work there; and so on. He intended to organize several camps. When the time came, planes would drop weapons, food, and instructions. At the end of our talk, Kapp gave me twenty-four hours to consider my "nomination" as political officer of the underground army.

We left the barracks separately. When I returned to my barracks, most people were getting ready for the night. I lay down, too. What I had just heard was too much for my already strung-out nerves. I couldn't sleep all night. I had met adventurers and provocateurs before, but I wasn't sure which of these two categories Kapp belonged to. It seemed unlikely that the MGB or any of the other official agencies had sent him to talk to me. I came to the conclusion that Kapp was one of the many petty agents who were recruited in West Germany after the war and were then sent across the border on all sorts of insignificant missions in exchange for a few hundred dollars and a promise that the Americans would liberate them in case they were captured by the Russians. They were expected to continue recruiting spies in the camps and to promise them ample rewards after they returned from Russia. These people usually disappeared after their first assignment; others were caught after two or three missions. It was rare for this kind of agent to last longer than a few months. The Americans counted on these small fry luring the NKVD and the MGB off the trail of the really important agents. Also, they wanted to have as many such people in the Russian camps as possible, so that, in case of a war, they would constitute a "fifth column." Karl Kapp was evidently eager to accomplish more than his employers had asked for. There was only one small thing he hadn't considered: the NKVD and the MGB had their own spies among the camp inmates.

But how to react to Kapp? There was only one sensible response: resolutely refuse to take part in his plans. I was even determined to break off all contact with Kapp before anyone noticed that we had had anything to do with one another.

When I awoke in the morning, I wasn't able to stand. My knees wobbled; I lurched about in the room. I didn't pick up my breakfast but went directly to Popov in the infirmary. Popov asked no questions but simply told his secretary to include my name among those who were excused from work that day. After the others left, I got my breakfast. Later I sat on my bunk and tried to read, but I was unable to concentrate and had to put the book away. The question that obsessed me was how

Kapp had known of my existence. Either his agency knew the names of certain prisoners in the camps, or else someone had told him about me in the transit station. Eventually, I managed to sleep a few hours. After that, I felt better.

When Kapp returned from work, he greeted me loudly from the other end of the barracks. I answered with a nod. In the course of the evening, he passed me several times. He was probably waiting for me to give him a sign that we should meet; I ignored him. On the following morning, I avoided him as well; in the evening, we barely greeted one another. To my relief, he didn't try to talk to me again. Apparently, he understood and accepted that I didn't want to have anything to do with his plans.

I soon noticed that Kapp and Stift were becoming friends. Every day, you could see them sitting together or walking about in the courtyard, engrossed in a lively discussion. One day, during the noon break, I sat down next to Stift, as I usually did. Suddenly he asked me: "Herr Steiner, what do you think of Kapp?"

"I can't form a judgment of someone I hardly know."

"Do you know that he's a very important man?"

"I don't know that, and Kapp doesn't interest me more than any number of prisoners I've briefly met."

Stift seemed to be insulted on Kapp's behalf; we stopped talking about him. From that day on, Stift's interest in me diminished, and we were no longer friends. I was glad about that, and I was especially glad that I had succeeded in breaking with Kapp.

It didn't take long for Kapp to become a glamorous personality in the camp: everyone was talking about the "commander in chief of the underground army." Many prisoners approached me to ask my opinion about Kapp. I spoke only to my best friends about him; I told them I considered Kapp a dangerous adventurer who was trying to exploit the prisoners' desperation. My response to the others was simply that I didn't know him and didn't want to know him.

The two brigadiers in our barracks, Chernyavsky and Schmidt, were enthusiastic followers of Kapp. When I once made a deprecating remark about him in their presence, they nearly beat me.

It wasn't only the prisoners who were interested in Kapp, but the MGB. He was a frequent guest in the infirmary, where he described his plans to Drs. Popov and Sokolovsky. They listened with eager curiosity, pumped him for details, and rewarded him with vitamins. As soon as Kapp left—I learned this from Popov's secretary—everything he had said was written down and passed on to the MGB. Pretty soon, Kapp could not only take sick leave whenever he wanted but arranged for other prisoners to take a few days off from work; he regarded the doctors as members of his organization.

He used all sorts of tricks to strengthen his authority. Frequently,

NKVD planes would circle the extensive camp territory and the work sites. As soon as their motors became audible, Kapp would go into the courtyard and make signals with his arms. The prisoners who saw this believed the planes were American. Sometimes Kapp did not go into the courtyard at the first sound of approaching airplanes. His followers would alert him: "The planes are here!" He would step outside, peer into the sky with a hand shielding his eyes, and then shake his head and say: "Those aren't my planes."

Kapp lived an absolutely parasitical life in the brigade. He didn't have to work; neither the brigadier nor his teammates objected to his laziness. He never went hungry either. He always got the biggest portions, and everyone who received a package from home considered it an honor and a duty to give some of the food to Kapp as well as to the brigadier.

The Kapp comedy went on for a few months. Then the great man was transferred to another camp. His followers were upset, but Kapp reassured them: he was being transferred on his own instigation; he had to "inspect" other camps. He appointed Franz Stift as his deputy. Life went on in camp 033, and the Chernyavsky brigade turned its attention back to practical matters. A lively trade in clothes began to flourish. Every morning, the brigade would go to the stationmaster's house to pick up their tools from a shed. While some of the prisoners were in the toolshed, surrounded by the guards, the others were busy bartering with the stationmaster's assistant, a free employee. He would buy all the clothes the prisoners brought—mostly prison clothes that hadn't had numbers put on them yet—and resell them to some banished Bessarabians who lived in a nearby village. Felt boots were in especially high demand; though they were indispensable in Siberia, they were rarely available in regular trade.

The prisoners of the Chernyavsky brigade sold not only their own clothes but also the clothes of other prisoners, for which they received a "commission." It was fairly easy to smuggle the garments out of the camp: all you had to do was wear them under your numbered clothes. When the camp administration got wind of these dealings, the guards at the camp gate were instructed to exercise tighter controls. Anyone discovered wearing or carrying unnumbered clothes was sent to the punishment cell. But the trade in clothes continued. Sometimes the military guards took part. They would use the money to buy bread, sugar, tobacco, and sometimes vodka.

Since we worked on the railroad, we were able to observe the trains passing by. Most of them were prison transports bringing their freight to the camps near the Tayshet–Lena line. We also saw trains full of peasants who had been deported from the Baltic countries and Bessarabia and were being resettled in the taiga near the railroad. Some of those trains were virtual cities on wheels: fifty or more closed sixty-ton cars bearing six or seven thousand prisoners. The trains had their own kitchens and their own electricity. Three of the cars housed guards. On top of each car was a raised compartment where a soldier with a submachine gun was always on guard, with a telephone next to him in case he needed to call for reinforcements. Searchlights mounted on the front and back car lit up the entire transport at night.

Often, NKVD recruits were driven past on their way to the training camp in Bratsk. We were replacing the tracks at station kilometer 129 when one of those recruit transports stopped right by us. The recruits looked at us full of curiosity, and we, too, looked at the future soldiers. Suddenly a rain of bread, makhorka packets, and other gifts came down upon us—so many that we couldn't pick everything up fast enough. The guards were speechless with astonishment. Then they shouted at the recruits to stop and forbade us to pick up the presents. But the recruits kept throwing things down to us. Finally, the commander of the guard had us removed. We didn't get back to work until after the train left. Three months later, after graduating from the NKVD training school in Bratsk, those fresh-baked soldiers were stationed in our camp as military guards. They were now as inhumane as they had been compassionate when they first met us. It was hard to believe these were the same people.

The chief overseer, Simin, was demoted and made a brigadier. His brigade worked in the gravel pit. One day, the brigade had to load some cars that stood outside the usual work area. Before they could do this, they had to obtain permission from the military guards. Simin talked to the commander and obtained permission to move the "forbidden zone" sign. He dug out the sign, walked a few steps, and was shot down by one of the soldiers. The commission that came a little later found him dead. The soldier claimed that his commander hadn't told him that Simin was authorized to move the sign. This was such a transparent excuse that the camp commander, Sorokin, spoke in front of the prisoners of a "senseless murder."

The prisoners knew the real reason. A few weeks before, Simin had testified against a soldier who had shot down a girl who was walking past the gravel pit. This girl happened to be the daughter of a party secretary. The soldier hadn't known that; he said he had thought she wanted to communicate with the prisoners. The soldier was sentenced to two years in prison. Simin, who had witnessed the incident, described it accurately at the trial. The condemned man's friends, who also appeared as witnesses, told Simin that his days were numbered. They kept their word.

Two months had passed since Kapp had been removed from camp 033. No one knew where he was. His followers indulged in the most extraordinary fantasies: some thought he was free by now and would soon arrive at the head of a victorious army to liberate all prisoners. This prophecy was mainly the creation of former Vlasov soldiers. Chernyavsky and Schmidt were also girding their loins for battle.

All these people gave the appearance of having been struck blind by hope and desperation. They couldn't see that there were NKVD and MGB informers in their own ranks. They were oblivious to danger. Many didn't care how things ended. All they could see was the awful number 25: no one could imagine living that many years under these conditions— better to die! Just as many had once pinned their hopes on Hitler, now there were many who waited for their deliverance by the Americans.

Newly arrived prisoners added to these illusions. Germans and Austrians came in with every transport; most of them had been sentenced to twenty-five years for working as American agents, and all of them brought the same message of imminent liberation. Some of them even knew the date: "We'll be back home by Christmas at the latest," or "by New Year."

I wondered why the authorities did not intervene. Apparently, the NKVD and the MGB were afraid of having recourse to mass executions. So long as individual prisoners dared to dream of insurrection or liberation, the authorities slammed down their fist very quickly. But now they would have had to slaughter the majority of the inmates, and apparently they couldn't bring themselves to do it.

One day, I saw Kapp among a small group of prisoners who were being brought into the camp. I didn't recognize him immediately; he was emaciated and his clothes were rags. The news of Kapp's return spread like wildfire in the camp. His friends brought him bread, and the priest in Chernyavsky's brigade gave him a large piece of lard. Kapp was very taciturn, which surprised everyone, for he used to be very talkative. While Kapp and the other newcomers were in the bathhouse, dozens of prisoners assembled outside to get a glimpse of their "commander in chief." Then Stift came and ordered the spectators to return to their barracks. He would speak to Kapp and find out the news.

For two days, no one heard anything about Kapp. Then the first rumors began to circulate: Kapp had "inspected" four camp sections and was more than satisfied with the prisoners' readiness for combat; he had instructed his followers to be more careful; he was supposed to have told his closest confidants, Stift, Chernyavsky, and Schmidt, that a large underground army led by a Russian general was already in operation on the other side of the Chuna River. As I learned from other prisoners, however, Kapp had not been in four camps but just in one—camp section 05— where he had worked as a woodcutter and where most of the prisoners had not been so gullible. After a while, some of camp 05's operations were suspended, and various prisoners, especially people who had become too weak to be useful, were transferred. But, for Kapp's followers, his return was no accident but rather a new proof of his power. I avoided all contact with Kapp and walked past him as if he were a complete stranger.

Around this time, a commission from Tayshet came to inspect our kitchen. Probably there had been too many complaints about the bad food and about Konovalenko's embezzlements. The commission arrived in the evening and spent all night in the kitchen. The next morning, they recommended to the camp commander that he remove Konovalenko from his post. There was a lot of guessing as to who would replace him, but no one had any clues. A few days later, I came back from work and was told by a messenger from medical services that the head doctor, Popov, wanted to speak to me. I was very hungry and wanted to eat first, but as I passed the medical-services barracks on the way to the kitchen, the messenger called out to me that Popov wanted to see me immediately. I stepped into the infirmary barracks with my tin bowl and wooden spoon. Popov said: "Throw away your bowl and go to the kitchen. You're the new kitchen supervisor."

I wasn't at all pleased. I knew I wasn't the right man either for Popov or for the camp commander. But when I tried to object, Popov interrupted me: "Stop jabbering. Go to the kitchen, I'll be right there. I want to be present when you assume your post." On my way to the kitchen, I passed several prisoners who obviously already knew I was in charge of the kitchen now: they greeted me politely.

In my capacity as kitchen supervisor, I made an effort to prepare palatable meals from the available stock of food. I broke with the camp tradition of serving only soup and gruel and devised a varied menu. Although there was very little meat or fat, we sometimes made meatballs or goulash. The prisoners were very pleased with these changes. I also made sure the cooks had no way of stealing food. Even the most severe critics had to admit that the kitchen was being run efficiently. I helped my friends and especially the foreigners as much as I could. My main concern was that no one should be hungry.

Franz Stift now regarded me as an "enemy" and thought it beneath his dignity to accept my help. This was no great sacrifice, however, for as a friend of Kapp's, who was always well provided, he had enough to eat. One day, the man in charge of heating the kitchen called me into the boiler room. A "delegation" was waiting for me there—two members of one-armed Vasya's gang. They wanted to know if I was prepared to give them some "decent" food. I was ready for that question and didn't have to search for an answer; I replied that I wished to live in peace with them. They threatened to "send me to glory" if I didn't keep my promise, and left. That same day, they sent a messenger to the kitchen to pick up the "decent" meal they had requested. I gave it to them.

Several days later, I was summoned by the NKVD officer. The boiler man had reported to him that the criminals were getting additional food from me. He asked me if this was true, and I replied frankly that I was not going to risk my life for the camp kitchen. I reminded him that the man who had murdered the Bessarabian was given a joke of a sentence. The NKVD officer showered me with curses that were in no way different from those of Vasya, the bandit chief, and dismissed me with all sorts of threats—none of which he carried out, despite the fact that I didn't change my attitude toward the criminals. Here was an instance where I had to compromise my conscience—my life was at stake.

My predecessor, Konovalenko, couldn't face the fact that the kitchen was functioning without him. He had reason to hope that I would be demoted and that his benefactors would reinstate him before very long. His impatience was obvious. The officers who regretted his removal from the kitchen visited me daily; however, they didn't leave with food packages as they had during Konovalenko's time. They made sure the prisoners received the precise number of grams they were supposed to, and they never forgot to check whether the prescribed amount of fat had been used and whether the caldrons and the floors were meticulously clean. Even if everything was perfect, they would complain about the "mess" and mismanagement in the kitchen. Komov, the head of the education division, openly said it was time to get Konovalenko back into the kitchen.

One day, the secretary of the medical services told me about a conversation between the head doctor, Popov, and Konovalenko. Popov had assured Konovalenko that it was just a matter of three days before he would be back in his old position. Sure enough, a few days later a commission of officers headed by Komov came into the kitchen very early in the morning to supervise the distribution of breakfast. After all the prisoners had received their food, the commission discovered that fifteen portions were left over. Komov exploded. "Why is there so much gruel left over?" he shouted.

"When you're cooking for fifteen hundred people, it's impossible to calculate everything precisely," I replied.

"What do you mean, impossible? Don't think you can fool me!"

"I'm not fooling you. Ask your own wife. Even if you're cooking for four people, you can't calculate the precise number of grams of gruel you need. And here we've got fifteen hundred people."

"And you're insolent, too! Don't try to tell me you weren't keeping the rest for yourself and your friends!"

I said nothing more. It was obviously useless to argue. Konovalenko's return to the kitchen was a settled matter. An hour later, I was informed of the camp commander's decision: I was being removed from my post in the kitchen for squandering food. This time, Konovalenko did not offer me a job as cook. I was put in Yakovliev's brigade. This was the worst one of all. We had to build a railroad that penetrated far into the taiga, where a group of deported collective farmers from the western Ukraine were building a village (they would be working as woodcutters from now on). The railroad was five kilometers long when I joined the brigade; we had to extend it by another six kilometers. Probably it would be extended even farther than that. Our work site was eight kilometers from the camp.

We had to cart gravel on wheelbarrows from a nearby hill to the railway embankment. It was hard work; nevertheless, I was glad to be out of the kitchen. I now preferred working in the forest to the constant conflict with soldiers and criminals who wanted to rob the prisoners of their tiny rations. Also, I had regained my strength, and my fellow workers in the brigade were helpful; they told me again and again how thankful they were for what I had done as kitchen supervisor.

I worked in this brigade for three weeks. Then a group of prisoners was transferred to a nearby camp, and my name was included on the list. By a peculiar coincidence, I left the camp on February 20, 1952, precisely two years after my arrival. It was hard for me to part from my friends. Also, I was apprehensive. For a prisoner, any change can mean a turn for the worse.

IN THE TAIGA

Camp section 030 was six kilometers away from camp section 033. We marched through the forest on a path along the railroad tracks. We didn't feel the cold because we were marching very fast. We made one stop to relieve ourselves. It was 10 a.m. when we reached the gate of camp 030. We were exactly a hundred men. We had been sent here to speed up the clearing of trees in the area.

The camp commander took the roll call. He asked each one of us for his profession—but no matter what you had once been, a doctor, a lawyer, or a carpenter, you were sent to chop down trees. So why did he spend hours asking all those questions?

I was put in Nikolenko's brigade. When I reported to the brigadier in the dark barracks room, he asked me what my profession was. This struck me as so comical that I had to laugh, and he laughed too, because he realized how pointless the question was. We soon became good friends. Nikolenko had been a schoolteacher in a Ukrainian village and had continued teaching during the German occupation. When the Russians recaptured his village, he was sentenced to ten years in camp.

Camp 030 was situated in a ravine; it looked as if the barracks had been dug deep into the earth. The nearby cemetery contributed to the depressing look of the place. Roughly two thousand prisoners lived in twenty-two barracks. Almost all of them were used for woodcutting; only the weakest were used for repair jobs in the camp. When we arrived, the barracks appeared uninhabited. I was surprised to learn that they were overcrowded. The camp seemed almost dead until people started coming home from work.

I heard a good deal of distressing news on the first day. The camp commander, First Lieutenant Kovalyo, was feared. Wherever he turned up, in the camp or at the work site in the woods, people were overcome by terror. The prisoners were worked to exhaustion. There was no way to get easier work, except by getting sick. Every Tuesday, the sick were taken to the hospital, where they were given a brief respite from the

murderous pace and the constant exertion. Every month, a new group
of prisoners arrived to replace the ones that had dropped out.

We went to work on the day after our arrival. I had slept soundly
despite the hardness of the bunk. Together with the other members of
my brigade, I went to the long, narrow mess hall with its long wooden
tables. Ten brigades could eat here at one time. Prisoners who had been
assigned to fetch food by the brigadier carried tin bowls full of soup on
wooden platters. We had all been given six hundred grams of bread in
the barracks; this was a newcomer's ration for three days. After that, the
size of your portion depended on your ability to meet the quota.

The prisoners ate their herb soup and chewed their bread with a
meditative air. But we had to hurry, for other brigades were waiting their
turn. The two hundred grams of gruel were consumed quickly. Then we
went back to the barracks to conclude breakfast with a bowl of *kipyatok*.
The second gong sounded before we finished drinking—off to work!

People left the barracks reluctantly and assembled outside. It was
still dark when we marched out the gate. A strong guard contingent
received us there. We marched along a broad street until we crossed the
railroad embankment and entered the woods, treading a narrow path.
After about four kilometers, we reached a large clearing, the center of
the camp's forestry operations. Our tools were stored in wooden sheds.
The necessary electricity was supplied by a mobile generator. There was
a barracks office for the managers and another barracks for the guards
and for a first-aid station. An open shed contained several field kitchens
in which lunch was prepared for the prisoners.

Hundreds of prisoners worked in an area comprising several dozen
square kilometers. Guards were posted on the perimeters of the work
area. Glades had been cut into the forest to facilitate a more thorough
control; you couldn't leave the work site without crossing one of these
glades, and you would be seen by the guards. I never heard of a single
successful escape from that place.

After receiving their tools, the various brigades went to their respective places of work. We were divided into groups of three. Two men
felled the trees by first chopping a groove into the trunk and then applying
an electric saw or a handsaw; the third man cut off the branches. We
worked for twelve hours a day, often standing up to our chests in snow.
Only rarely were the necessary safety measures observed; the high quotas
didn't allow it. One's food ration was more important than life and limb.
To meet the quota, three men had to cut down forty meters of solid
timber, remove the branches, and cut the trunks into six-meter sections.

Unbelievable as it may sound, cutting down a tree was easy compared
to chopping off the branches. Within a short time, one's body was drenched
in sweat, even if the temperature was forty or fifty below zero. And if
you could afford to take a little break, you had to hurry over to the bonfire
where the brushwood was being burned, so as not to catch pneumonia.

Not everyone was concerned about his health: many did their best to get sick. The number of accidents that occurred every day could not be attributed to errors of judgment; some prisoners deliberately injured themselves so that they could go to the hospital. Many yearned for death. You could often hear the bitter song of the captive woodcutters:

> *Sawing, chopping, felling trees!*
> *This curse I send to the whole world!*
> *Mother, I am lost here!*
> *Why did you give birth to me?*

The brigades that transported the wood had as hard a time as the branch cutters. Each group of three men had a horse that dragged the logs to a central pile. The poor horses lasted no more than three months; exhausted and emaciated, they all ended up in the camp kitchen. Of the three hundred and forty horses in camp section 030, about two hundred and twenty were usually receiving veterinary care. Most commonly, they had trouble with their legs. One's own suffering was more than enough to deal with, but it hurt to see those poor lame animals dragging their heavy loads and being beaten because their master had to worry about meeting the quota.

The wood was loaded from the central pile onto the small cars of the narrow-gauge railroad, which was being extended a few feet every day. Then a tiny locomotive pulled the load to the lumberyard or delivered it to the consignment station of the normal-gauge railroad.

While we were working and during the breaks, we were able to talk about our situation. During the war, prisoners who dared to express their political antipathies would usually direct their anger against Stalin and his clique for plunging Russia and her people into barbarity; and the communists had been especially incensed that all this was being done in the name of Marx and Lenin. Now, after the war, it was Roosevelt, Churchill, and other Western statesmen who were blamed. Many prisoners found it incomprehensible that the West, after conquering Nazi Germany, was willing to make common cause with Stalinism, and wondered how the interests of the civilized world were being served when hangmen like the former Chief Prosecutor and the current deputy commissar for foreign affairs, Vyshinsky, were treated with respect at the conference table. Many predicted that the day was not far off when those "great statesmen" would stand beside us in padded trousers and coats, chopping wood in the forest and wishing that by some miracle they might find a large piece of black bread.

There were many Germans in camp 030; one of them was Hans Baltes, a young doctor from Siebenbürgen. He had likable features and was a good-looking man even in his ill-fitting prison garb. He had served in the SS during the war; this puzzled me. How could this kind and generous person have joined a band of murderers like the SS? One day,

I put this question to him, and he replied: "I didn't join the SS because I wanted to take part in mass murders. I joined them because I was young and foolish and believed I was serving a good cause, as did many others." Then he added: "Karl, I would like to ask you a question, too. Did you communists join your party with the idea of creating all of this?"

The camp administrators used Hans as a doctor only when no one else was available. When I got to know him, he was part of the wood-piling brigade. I admired the way this intellectual moved the heavy logs with apparent ease, while others who had done physical work all their lives groaned under the strain. Hans and I always walked side by side on the way home. The march home was always the worst part of the day. The sun was setting by that time, and the guards, fearing that it would be dark before we reached the camp, forced us to run through the woods, with the sound of barking dogs at our heels and the voices of soldiers shouting: "Faster, faster!" You couldn't help stumbling over roots and logs; if you fell, you ran the risk of being trampled by those behind you. Hans would take my arm with his strong hand and pull me along so that I didn't fall back.

After supper, he would come to my barracks, and we would chat or take a walk in the courtyard, if it wasn't too cold, until the gong called us back to our barracks. Hans told me many stories about his experiences as a student at the University of Vienna and especially about his bride, an actress from a Viennese theater. I promised him to inform her of his fate if I ever returned to Austria.

One evening, when I came back from the forest, I was very surprised to hear that a package had come for me. I assumed this must be a mistake. I had recently asked my wife not to send me any more packages. I had everything I needed, and I knew she didn't have enough for herself. But who else would send me a package? I went to the camp office. It wasn't a mistake: there was a small package, addressed to me, containing half a kilo of honey, half a kilo of butter, and five packets of makhorka.

The officer who handed me the package gave me a pitying look. But I was happy, for the package came from my friend Josef Berger. Now I knew that he was alive. His sentence had been completed in 1951; we had agreed that he would send me a small packet from his place of banishment, so that I would have his address (since it was unlikely that I would be allowed to receive a letter from him). So Josef was letting me know that he was living in the village of Kazachinskoye.

I hurried to share the good news with my friend Hans. We sat down together and celebrated the New Year, even though it was already March— for Josef had sent the package before New Year's Day. It had been delayed because of my transfer to another camp. After eating our fill, we took a walk in the courtyard. It was on that evening that Hans, who was ordinarily so sober-minded, confided to me that he planned to escape. His plans struck me as utterly fantastical, and I had a very hard time convincing him of their futility. A few days after that conversation, there was a major alarm in the camp. All the brigades were returned immediately to the camp. We found out why several days later: sixteen prisoners had tried to escape from a neighboring camp section.

Several hundred men were used for piling up logs by the bank of the Chuna. Almost every evening, at the end of the day's work, the leftovers were loaded on a truck and transported back to the camp to be used as firewood in the kitchen; the prisoners who helped load and unload the truck got an extra meal from the kitchen supervisor. Some twenty-five prisoners decided to use the truck to escape. One evening, as the firewood was being unloaded, the driver of the truck was sitting in the kitchen, warming up while he waited for the prisoners to come in and tell him they were finished. But they didn't come. One of them sat at the steering wheel, and the others on the loading platform in the back (only sixteen of the original twenty-five went along; the others had changed their minds). The truck rammed through the locked camp gate. The guards opened fire from the towers, but the car drove on and reached the edge of the frozen river. When the guards got to the truck, they found four men dead and three severely wounded; the others had fled into the woods. That same night, four were captured, two of them slightly wounded. Later we learned that the other five had gotten away. In 1953, I was told that one of them was eventually arrested in Khabarovsk by the river Amur and was sentenced to another twenty-five years in a camp.

After this, our brigades were regrouped. I was put into the Pavlov brigade. It consisted of prisoners whose sentences would expire in two years. The work consisted of loading wood on freight cars or trucks, always at night, in the taiga. On my first night, I realized that I would not see the day of my release if I didn't succeed in getting into another brigade.

Pavlov was one of those men who are called "wolves" in the camps. His motto was: "Survive at all costs; let everyone else go to hell." He boasted that he had done only two days of hard work in the fifteen years he had spent in camp; during that time, he had worked almost exclusively as a camp guard, a brigadier, and a foreman. Once he fell ill and was put in a hospital. After his recovery, he continued working there as an orderly for the next two years, until the authorities discovered that he had col-laborated with the hospital's managing supervisor in removing gold teeth and fillings from the mouths of dead prisoners and trading the gold for money and vodka. He regularly collaborated with the NKVD and the MGB, and it was they who protected him from prosecution in the affair of the gold teeth and spared him the ordeal of hard labor.

In 1937, Pavlov was sentenced to fifteen years in camp under Article 58, paragraphs 7 and 8. He claimed that he had never committed a political crime, and that it was his attractive wife and his beautiful apartment that were the cause of his misfortune. His wife had wanted to divorce him but didn't want to lose the apartment. Her lover advised her to tell the

NKVD that Pavlov had been defaming the Soviet government. The wife followed the lover's advice, and soon her problems were solved: Pavlov was arrested. The two crown witnesses against him were his wife and an apprentice in the factory where Pavlov had worked. One of the apprentice's accusations was that Pavlov had once called him a "lousy kolkhoz peasant."

After Pavlov's arrest, his wife's lover moved into her apartment. Later she wrote letters to Pavlov in which she asked his forgiveness; she had kicked out the "bastard" and couldn't wait for the day when Pavlov finished serving his sentence and could join her.

When we assembled in front of the gate, brigadier Pavlov roared in his resounding bass voice: "Get a move on, you sons of bitches!" Or: "Motherfuckers, swine, when are you going to stand still?" That was how he treated people. His assistant, who was also his best friend, imitated him in every way.

When more than thirty prisoners went to work in one group, the number of guards was increased as well—one guard per prisoner. They goaded, pushed, cursed, and abused us constantly. By the time we reached our place of work after an eight-kilometer march, we were as tired as if we had been working for hours; and the worst was yet to come.

Usually, the cars stood ready for loading when we arrived. We were divided into groups of two or three to each railroad car, depending on the girth of the stems. Two soldiers stood in front of each car with their fingers on the triggers of their guns. The badly lit loading site resembled a mousetrap—you had to be very careful to avoid falling into a pit and being killed or permanently crippled by falling logs. We rolled the logs along several beams that connected the car to the woodpile. As long as we were rolling them downhill or even on a horizontal plane, it wasn't so bad, but it took a tremendous effort to roll the logs uphill, and the last rows were sheer hell. Throughout the day, the brigadier, the soldiers, and the supervisor insulted us in the foulest terms they could think of: "Whoresons, motherfuckers, fascists, Trotskyites . . . *vashu mat!*" The abuse became much worse if we didn't have the strength to roll the last logs into the car and had to ask others for help.

Once the cars were loaded, we were allowed to light a fire and rest until the locomotive came to bring empty cars and take away the loaded ones. Those breaks usually lasted a half hour. Once in a while, the locomotive took as long as two hours to show up, but that was rare.

Most of the accidents happened during the second phase of loading. Partly from exhaustion, partly because of the lateness of the hour, the workers' attention began to flag. We all knew how important it was to stay alert, but the general apathy was so great that after a while you stopped thinking of the danger. Body and soul yearned for rest, even at the price of injury or death. I, too, thought of dying a lot of the time. My sentence would end in less than two years—but would they let me go? Hadn't I seen hundreds of prisoners reach the end of their sentences only to have them renewed? And once I was out of the camp, would I be living in freedom? If I was lucky, I would be banished to some remote Siberian village. Was it worth living there as a slave of Stalin's "socialism"? These questions tormented me, and again and again I came to the conclusion that death was the only solution. But then an inner voice reproved me: Karl, don't lose heart! You've gone through such terrible trials, you'll get through this one, too.

We trotted back to the camp at dawn. Often, we had to work as much as two hours overtime. Usually, the camp commander would be waiting by the gate to ask the brigadier how many cars had been loaded. If the results were satisfactory, the camp commander wouldn't say anything; but woe to us if we had failed to meet the quotas—even if it was the railroad division's fault because they had failed to send enough cars. "You good-for-nothings, you fascists!" he would shout. "Who do you think you are, you eat while others work for you! Just you wait, tomorrow you're getting only three hundred grams of bread!" And he always kept his promise.

We would hurry back to the barracks, toss off our heavy padded coats, and run to the kitchen without washing, quickly eat our paltry meal, return to the barracks, and crawl into our bunks to enjoy the rest we'd been yearning for all day. I usually covered my head with my coat so as not to be awakened by the noise in the barracks. But even if you managed to sleep for six hours—more often, it was five—it wasn't enough to restore you for another night of hard work.

There came a day when I couldn't go on. We didn't get back to the camp until 11 a.m. after our thirty-man brigade had loaded forty-five cars. What a night that was! Even the brigadier's protégés, who were usually assigned the most desirable loading sites, had enough. While one of the last cars was being loaded, two props broke down and the logs rolled off and fell on two workers; the third man jumped to one side just in time. One of the two was dead—his head squashed by the weight; the other had both legs broken. Since the workday wasn't over yet, the guards did not permit the two victims to be carried back to the camp. Everyone had to go on working. And very soon after, there was a second accident. The brigadier had ordered two prisoners to take the place of the two casualties and finish loading the car. One of them slipped and fell; nothing happened to him. But the second man, who had been carrying the other end of the log, broke his collarbone.

Thus, we came home with one dead comrade and two others severely injured. The commander didn't say a word. Forty-five cars had been loaded; nothing else interested him.

Even before the end of that night, I had told myself that this was the last time I would come here, no matter what the consequences. But I had no clear idea how to extricate myself. Simply refusing to go to work was senseless; I would be put in the underground dungeon that served as a punishment cell here. I had to find another way. But I was so exhausted that I was incapable of reflection. I got my breakfast, as usual, and lay down on my bunk after eating, but I wasn't able to fall asleep right away. The question of how to avoid this murderous work kept recurring, but there seemed to be no answer. It was completely quiet in the barracks. Not until two o'clock did the *dnevalny* start scrubbing the floor with a rubber brush. It occurred to me that I could try to get a job in the kitchen. But this wasn't a simple matter at all. You had to have friends in high places, and I had none in this camp. So I decided to take the official route. I got up and washed myself, with the intention of visiting the camp commander. On my way to the office, I was stopped by the chief overseer, who returned my greeting with the following question: "Why aren't you working?"

"I'm in Pavlov's brigade. I worked all last night."

"Oh, you work at night. All right."

I walked on. When I opened the office door, I heard the camp commander, First Lieutenant Kovalyo, talking to the camp's bookkeeper in a scolding tone. It seemed a bad moment to make my plea. But as I started to leave, the camp commander called after me: "What do you want?"

I turned back and looked at him. Probably he could read the despair on my face, for he said in a friendly voice: "Go ahead, speak up—what do you want?"

I noticed that at first he had used the familiar address, and in his final question had used the polite form. This seemed a good sign—at least of his readiness to hear me out.

"Citizen commander, I'm from the Pavlov brigade, and—"

He interrupted me: "Another guy from the Pavlov brigade!"

I continued: "The work is too hard for me. I'm completely depleted."

"Where am I going to find strong people? They're all saying they're too weak."

"I really can't go on," I said, in despair.

"That's the only work there is."

"I'm a cook. Perhaps I could get some work in the kitchen?" I asked halfheartedly.

"You're a cook? In that case, we might be able to do something. But I need people for loading. I can't send a man on night duty who has twenty-five more years to go."

"Just for a while, until I pick up a little, then I can go back to the woods," I said.

"I'll tell you what. Stick it out till the first, then I'll hire you as a cook."

That was the end of my interview. I thanked him and left. The prospect of working in the kitchen after the first gave me some courage, but I couldn't see myself lasting through another two weeks of this unbearable labor. What to do? There were only two hours left until the gong called me back to work. What if I didn't think of a way before then? Hide in another barracks? They would find me by the next morning at the latest and throw me in the punishment cell.

Then I had a brainstorm. I knew that the brigadier, Pavlov, was fond of money. What if I offered him fifty rubles if he let me stay away from work for a week? This wasn't impossible during the night shift, because the controls were less stringent—one man more or less wouldn't be noticed by the guards. I decided to accost Pavlov on his way to the camp office. First, I went back to the barracks to warm up a little and to see if the brigadier was still asleep. He was gone. The *dnevalny* said Pavlov had left for the office. I met him in the courtyard. He ignored me.

"Brigadier, could I speak to you for a moment?"

"What do you want?"

He didn't stop, so I stepped in front of him.

"Let's go back to the barracks," he said. "It's too goddamn cold here." And he started to push me aside.

"I have to talk to you in private."

He looked surprised. "What do you want? Say it quickly."

"You're going to be free soon. I have fifty rubles, and I think you could use them." I could see that I had caught his interest. "I want to give you those fifty rubles. Please let me stay home for a week!"

"What are you talking about? I can't do that."

"I understand. You don't trust me, you don't know me well enough. I've been in camp for sixteen years, I know what can and can't be done. I won't disappoint you."

"I'll think about it. Come and see me before dinner," Pavlov said.

I had won. I knew that Pavlov was postponing his reply to avoid showing how much he liked deals like this one. Only one problem remained: I had sewn my fifty rubles into my padded pants—how to get them out without anyone's noticing? I crawled into the bunk, took off my pants, found the place where the money was hidden, and started to cut and loosen the thread, stopping each time I was interrupted by my neighbors. Finally, I was holding the two twenty-five-ruble notes in my hand. It was time for dinner. The brigades were going to the kitchen, with the brigadiers at the end of each line. I placed myself behind Pavlov. He must have expected me to do that, for he didn't seem surprised.

Before I had said a word, he said: "You can stay home."

"Thank you," I replied, and gave him my hand with the money.

The brigadier took it, saying: "Let's see what kind of person you are."

"Don't worry," I said. Then, to reassure him, I added: "I'll be working in the kitchen soon, and I'll be sure to remember you then."

"Yes, try to get a job in the kitchen, that's a good job!"

At long last, I could get a real rest. I was happy. But I had to make sure no one noticed. I had to steer clear not only of the overseers but of my fellow prisoners. It helped that only a few brigades worked during the night. I wouldn't be particularly conspicuous if I was seen in the camp at night; and if I was seen during the day, I could always say I had worked at night. To be really cautious, I had to sleep in another barracks. That wasn't easy: when the gong struck, all visitors had to leave and the barracks was locked until the next morning.

I turned to Hans Baltes for help. I told him about my arrangement with the brigadier and asked if he could help me find a place to spend the night. He offered to let me sleep between him and his bunk neighbor, another German. Thus, a week passed without anyone's noticing my absence from work. Then the problem became acute again. Pavlov and I had agreed on a week, and I had no money to pay for a second week. So I made an inventory of my possessions: two sets of underwear and a pair of shoes were all I could offer Pavlov. Again, I asked the brigadier for a private talk, and he granted it. At first, he rejected my proposal outright; he had been forced to split his fifty rubles with the chief overseer, who had noticed my absence on the second day. But in the end I succeeded in buying a second week of "vacation" from Pavlov.

The end of the month finally came. I went to the camp office to remind the commander of his promise. I showed up just as he was giving a group of brigadiers a lecture for their insufficient productivity. I waited until they left; then I repeated my request for a job in the kitchen. He pondered for a long time. I stood before him rigid with apprehension. It must have taken him five or six minutes to answer. Finally, he mumbled something inaudible; all I could make out was that I should call my brigadier. At that moment, as if by arrangement, Pavlov stepped in.

"Pavlov, is this one of your people?" asked the commander.

"Yes, citizen commander, he's in my brigade."

"How's his work?"

"Very good, citizen commander."

"He wants to work in the kitchen. What do you think, will he comport himself decently there, or is he just going to spend his time stealing food?"

"He's a very conscientious worker, and he doesn't look like a thief," Pavlov replied.

"Sure, sure, I know these goody-goodies. In the long run, they're just as bad as the rest."

"The people who came with him from the other section say he was a good cook and was really conscientious."

"All right, let's give him a try. He'll stay with you till the third. Then we'll switch him to the kitchen," the commander concluded.

It wasn't hard to buy another three days of "vacation." On the third day, the chief overseer came to tell me that I was expected at medical services. There I was thoroughly examined by Dr. Shevchuk in the presence of the director of medical services. One of his questions was whether my parents had ever had venereal disease. Then the director of medical services exhorted me to work hard and stick to the rules and especially to forget that I had friends; the slightest irregularity would be severely punished.

I reported to the kitchen supervisor, a native Caucasian, and gave him a note from the director of medical services. The kitchen supervisor asked with a slight Caucasian accent what my previous experience as a cook had been. When I told him that my experience was restricted to the usual "camp menu," he smiled with pleasure and said: "Finally, someone who tells the truth! Everyone else claims they worked in the best restaurants of Moscow and Leningrad."

I gained his complete sympathy when I told him I wasn't Russian. (He spoke Russian so badly that he hadn't noticed that my Russian wasn't fluent or accent-free either.) We agreed that I should start work the next day. I went to tell Hans Baltes the news, but he received me with the following words: "I already know!"

"So I don't have to tell you?"

"No, no, please tell, how was it?"

I told him everything in the minutest detail. Hans warned me against trying to help the many foreigners by giving them additional portions, as I had in the other camp section. He expressly forbade me to do him any such favors, for the whole camp knew that we were friends, and everyone would watch with eagle eyes to see if I was giving him preferential treatment. I could not accept this counsel; I said I would rather work in the forest again than refuse to help my fellow sufferers.

The kitchen where we cooked two meals a day for two thousand people was situated in a long barracks. There were no side rooms, just a cellar where ten invalids cleaned the vegetables. The water was fetched in pails from a well fifty meters from the kitchen. All the work had to be performed by two cooks during the day shift and one during the night shift, with the help of two assistants. The kitchen was miserably equipped: three large caldrons and a stove, that was all—and there were fifty sick men for whom we had to cook separate meals. There was no ventilation; the kitchen was always full of steam, especially when several caldrons were being used at one time. As in all the camps, the prisoners' food consisted only of soup and gruel. The bonus for exceeding the quota was a piece of salt fish or, very rarely, fifty grams of salt meat.

After my first day in the kitchen, I asked myself whether this was any better than working in the woods. My answer was unequivocal: if I could be sure of being sent out to cut trees instead of loading logs at night, I would go back to the forest tomorrow. After a few days, though, I started getting used to conditions in the kitchen and found the work a little easier.

During the first days, I was spared the entreaties of my "country-men," thanks to Hans Baltes, who had urged all the foreigners to avoid getting me into trouble, at least in the beginning. But then there was a veritable onslaught: there was hardly a foreigner who didn't come to the kitchen window and beg for additional food. I gave what I could: a little soup for one man, some gruel for another, and if I could, a piece of fish.

It wasn't long before the camp administration was informed by its spies that I was giving extra food to the foreigners. The kitchen supervisor admonished me to be careful. I tried to refuse this or that request, but it wasn't easy: the hungry prisoners hung around the kitchen, waiting for a propitious moment to accost me. All I had to do was go to the toilet and I would be surrounded by several pleading men: "Can't you give me something to eat, I'm so hungry!" I heard this plea in many languages: German, Hungarian, Polish, and Russian. I wasn't always able to help. Those who got something thanked me; those who didn't cursed.

IN THE PUNISHMENT CELL

Three weeks passed. One evening, when I was already in my bunk, an overseer came and ordered me to put my clothes back on and follow him. I obeyed unwillingly, for I was tired and wanted to rest. On the way, I wondered where he was leading me; perhaps the commander had some urgent question, or else someone had denounced me—whatever it was, it didn't bode well. We reached the fence surrounding the pit that served as a punishment cell. The overseer stopped and opened the gate. I stood there watching him; I hadn't considered the possibility of being put in the punishment cell.

"Come along," the overseer said. I followed him to the pit. A steep stairway led down into a badly lit room. The overseer pulled a piece of paper out of the pocket of his long coat and handed it to me. I read:

> It has come to the attention of the camp administration that the prisoner Steiner, employed as a cook, has been giving supplementary food to a gang of foreigners. For this violation of camp regulations, Steiner is being sent to the punishment cell for five days.
>
> Commander of camp section 030
> First Lieutenant Kovalyo

The overseer opened one of the four punishment cells and let me in. It was pitch-dark; after a while, I was able to make out the forms of two men sitting on a bunk. One of them was a Russian; the other, who spoke very little Russian, was a Korean. I lay down on the bunk, and since I was very tired, I fell asleep. Around midnight I woke up, rigid with cold. To warm up, I walked back and forth in the narrow room, but that didn't help much. I noticed that the others couldn't sleep either. In the morning, a little bit of light came into our pit. Three hundred grams of bread and a potful of hot water—that was the usual punishment ration for a twenty-four-hour period. We weren't taken to work in the morning, but at two o'clock a supervisor took us to the guards' barracks, where we had to dig deep holes for lampposts. By 8 p.m., we were back in the pit.

Suddenly there was a timid knock on the window. The Korean climbed up on his bunk, clinging to the bars with both hands. "Is Karl Steiner here?" a voice asked from outside. I pulled the Korean's leg, explaining with gestures that I was being called. He gave me his place after some hesitation.

"Karl, are you there?" Now I recognized the voice—it was Hans Baltes. "I have some bread for you. How can I give it to you?" he asked.

Although he was speaking very softly, the Korean heard him and called out: "Break window!" We heard the sound of shattering glass, and a cold stream of air penetrated the cell. With some difficulty, Hans managed to squeeze a piece of bread through the little aperture he had made; then he added a few more pieces. We exchanged a few more words; then he left.

While I was talking to Hans, the Korean ate one of the pieces of bread. For this reason, I gave the Russian a bigger piece than I gave him, and this angered the Korean. I was extremely impressed by Hans and grateful to him for having the courage to crawl through several barbed-wire fences, risking severe punishment, to bring me a little bread. The Korean was very eager to know the donor's name. When I said I hadn't been able to recognize him in the dark, the Korean said: "I know who it was: your friend, the German doctor." The Russian retorted in my stead: "You already ate the goddamn bread, what more do you want?"

The next day, Hans came back. I stood on the cot and pulled out the rag we had stuffed into the hole. Again, Hans brought us some pieces of bread, and also a piece of sugar. I divided everything into three equal parts. I wondered how Hans could afford to give us so much bread—he didn't have enough for himself.

The next day, when we went to work, I saw the Korean lagging behind and then saying a few words to the camp guard. I had a hunch that he was denouncing me and Hans. The Russian had the same impression: "I bet the Korean ratted on you because of the bread."

"But he got his share."

"That's the way he is. You can't do anything right for people like him."

"I could understand it if I had eaten it all by myself and he was denouncing me out of envy."

"Some people do it because it's their nature to denounce you. There's no other reason."

When the camp guard let us back into the cell after work, he looked up at the window and asked who had broken the glass. "It was broken when we got here," the Russian replied. "We just stuck a rag in." To my great relief, the guard left the cell without a word.

On the fourth day, a Saturday, I was called out of the punishment cell. The overseer said I was being taken to an MGB officer. That surprised me; I couldn't imagine an MGB officer interrogating me about my work in the kitchen. But at least I would have a chance to warm up a little— that seemed more important than anything else at the moment. The overseer led me to a room right next to the camp commander's office. Behind a desk sat an officer with the bright red epaulettes of the MGB on his uniform (in contrast to the blue epaulettes of the NKVD). He smiled at me as if we were old acquaintances. I didn't know how to react to this, so I looked back at him with an indifferent expression.

"How do you feel?"

I had met with this question before. Coming from an MGB or NKVD officer, it was meant to signify a high degree of sympathy.

"Not very well," I said.

"Why not? You're working in the kitchen, aren't you?"

"First of all, I'm not working in the kitchen at the moment—I'm sitting in the punishment cell—and second, working in the kitchen is just the lesser of two evils."

"Why are you in the punishment cell?"

"For giving some countrymen of mine a little soup and some spoonfuls of gruel."

"I will order you removed from the punishment cell," he said.

"That's not necessary. Tomorrow's the fifth day; I'll be let out anyway."

The officer lit a cigarette, stood, and began to pace the room. After smoking half his cigarette, he asked me if I wanted to smoke. I thanked him, explaining that I was a nonsmoker. He continued walking back and forth, and I sat still, following him with my eyes and trying to think. But I wasn't able to concentrate. I was completely confused and couldn't imagine what this was all about. So far, I had had dealings only with the NKVD (later called the MVD); now I was getting to know the other variant of Stalin's police apparatus, the MGB. The officer was broad-shouldered, had a round face and blond hair; he was wearing the insignia of a major.

After a while, he sat down in a comfortable position and leaned his head in his hand. "Have you been in this camp for long?" he asked.

"About two months."

"You came here from camp 033?"

"Yes."

"I know you, I know you were in camp 033."

"You know me? I've never seen you before," I said, surprised.

"That is to say, I know about you," the major corrected himself. Then he continued: "Who else came here with you from camp 033?"

"About a hundred people, but I only know a few of them."

"Tell me their names."

I told him two or three names that occurred to me.

"Who were you friendly with in camp 033?"

"I didn't have any close friends there. My only friend was Josef Berger, but he left there long ago."

"And Kapp and Stift, weren't they your friends?"

"On the contrary, they were my enemies."

"How come?" The major seemed surprised.

"Because I didn't want to have anything to do with those adventurers."

"According to our information, the three of you were very close friends."

"In that case, you have been falsely informed, as usual. I repeat, I have never had anything in common with those adventurers."

"Very well. We'll talk about this again. I don't have the time right now."

With those words, I was dismissed. I went back to my barracks with the intention of waiting until the evening before I reported back to the punishment cell, since I assumed that the overseer wouldn't know how long my hearing had lasted. The barracks was empty; everyone had gone to work. Only the *dnevalny* was lying on his bunk near the door. When he saw me come in, he raised his head: "Ah, it's you. Is your time up?"

"Not yet. I have to go back."

"Vacation?"

I didn't reply and crept into my bunk to reflect quietly on my situation. It was happening all over again: another inquest. When Gorokhov had served me with an extra ten years in 1943, I had three years left on my first sentence; this time, I had only sixteen months left. It seemed as if I would never escape the clutches of the NKVD, the MVD, the MGB, and whatever other acronyms they chose to give themselves. Were they accusing me of being a member of the group around Kapp, Stift, and Chernyavsky in order to finally finish me off?

I lay immobile for several hours. I had no appetite, despite the fact that I had eaten hardly anything in three days; nor did I feel sleepy, though I had hardly slept for four nights. First, I was seized by despair; then I sank into apathy. Let come what may, I said to myself; I can't do anything about it.

After a while, I thought of telling Hans Baltes the news, but then I realized it was too early; he wouldn't be back from work yet. Suddenly, I felt hungry. I went to the kitchen. There I ran into the overseer, who wanted to know if my hearing was over. My colleagues in the kitchen served me a plentiful meal, and the overseer let me eat it in peace. Then he led me back to the punishment cell.

The Russian and the Korean asked me where I had been for so long, but when they saw that I didn't feel like talking, they left me alone. Suddenly, I remembered that two acquaintances from camp 033 had visited me a few days before and had told me, in strict confidence, that they had been interrogated by the MGB, and that they had been asked to testify that I had tried to organize an armed uprising in the camp. At the time, I had been sure they were merely trying to extort food from me—a fairly frequent occurrence in the camp. Apparently, they had been telling the truth: the MGB was looking for witnesses against me. When the MGB needed witnesses, they found them. There is an old Russian proverb: "Where there's a head, there's a yoke."

At ten o'clock on Sunday morning, the guard let me out of the punishment cell, even though according to regulations I was supposed to be there until 9 p.m. He asked me to keep away from the courtyard; if anyone saw me there before nine, he could get into trouble.

The first thing I did was visit Hans, who was glad this unpleasant episode was over. He wanted to get some bread for me right away; I almost had to use force to restrain him. He couldn't believe that I had eaten a big meal in the kitchen the day before—such a big meal that I had given my bread ration to my two fellow prisoners in the punishment cell. Hans and I tried to guess what sort of work I'd be put to next; we were both fairly sure I'd be given the hardest labor available: piling up wood in the night shift. I didn't tell Hans anything about the hearing.

My first concern now was to get some warm clothes. When I was transferred to the kitchen, I had had to give up my padded pants and my felt boots for a pair of summer pants and light shoes. To get my warm clothes back, I had to ask the chief overseer for a special paper. The chief overseer told me he hadn't received any instructions from the commander to send me back to the forest brigade; he suggested I wait until the morning.

The morning came, the gong sounded, and I still didn't know which brigade I belonged to. Again I went to the chief overseer, and again he told me to wait. The barracks was empty when I came back. Everyone had gone to work. When the head of the labor section came by on his inspection tour of the barracks, the *dnevalny* reported: "Citizen commander, twenty-four-man brigade departed for work!"

The officer cast a perfunctory glance into the barracks, overlooking me on my bunk. The *dnevalny*, too, had forgotten that I was there. About an hour passed, and the chief overseer came and asked for me. Only then did the *dnevalny* remember me. I was dozing on my bunk. The chief overseer shook me awake. "To the commander!" he said.

I followed him to the camp office. When I knocked on the camp commander's door, Kovalyo called "Come in!" in his bass voice. The chief overseer stayed outside. Kovalyo examined me from head to foot. I stood two meters away from him.

"Well, what's up?" he began.

I said nothing.

"Did you deserve being put in the punishment cell?"

I didn't answer.

"Have you lost your voice?" he asked impatiently.

"From your point of view, I deserved it," I finally replied.

"I see. From my point of view, you deserved it, and from your point of view, you didn't. So you think it's right to give your friends food that's supposed to be for everyone?"

"Citizen commander, I only gave away leftovers."

"No one is to receive a gram more than he deserves! Otherwise, no one's going to bother meeting the quota. Why should they? There's that nice guy in the kitchen who gives them what the commander doesn't let them have!"

I decided to hold my tongue, for I knew that no commander would want his prisoners to contradict him.

"All right, off with you, back to the kitchen! But God help you if I hear about your giving away even a spoonful of soup!"

I went without really feeling glad that I was being allowed to go on working in the kitchen. The kitchen supervisor was happily surprised to see me again. When I handed out supper through the kitchen window that evening, most people stared at me as if I had risen from the dead. Hans told me later that my being reinstated in the kitchen after being sent to the punishment cell was unprecedented. It appeared that my work as a cook was appreciated, after all.

IN PRE-TRIAL DETENTION . . . FOR THE THIRD TIME

Four days later, the chief overseer came to the kitchen at lunchtime. "How about giving me one more meal. Then go back to the barracks and get your stuff together. You're going to section 025." At first, I thought he was joking. "I mean it, you're going to the transit station!"

That's how I learned that section 025 was the transit station of the Oserlag. I wanted to say goodbye to Hans Baltes, my only friend in this camp, but he was at work and wouldn't be back before 8 p.m. at the earliest. But by chance the escort that was supposed to take me to the train arrived late, and I was able to speak to Hans after all. For the first time, I told him about my hearing. He suspected I was being taken to prison. He was as moved when we parted as if we had been friends for years. I never saw Hans again. In 1955, a man who came from Tayshet told me that the MGB had delivered Hans to the Rumanian authorities together with a group of Rumanian citizens.

It was 9 p.m. when two soldiers picked me up to take me to the station at kilometer 129, from where I was supposed to go on to Tayshet with the regular passenger train. It was a cold, clear night. Millions of stars were scattered across the sky, and the full moon was shining as if to illuminate the path we were taking through the dark forest. We walked slowly. Probably there was plenty of time until the scheduled arrival of the train, for the soldiers allowed me several times to set down my Japanese knapsack and rest.

We reached the station at ten-thirty. The train was expected at eleven. I sat down on my knapsack in front of the station building. The soldiers took turns going inside to warm up. A few minutes before eleven, two soldiers arrived with a prisoner from camp 033, where I used to be. The prisoner was given permission to sit down next to me. It was Dr. Dulkin, the man who had examined me in Tayshet and put me in the third category. He, too, was on his way to camp 025.

Our train arrived forty-five minutes late. A soldier appeared in the door of a *stolypin* car, and one of our escort handed him some papers. Then he ordered us into the car. The train left as soon as we were inside. We arrived in Tayshet early in the morning. Some soldiers received us at the station and herded us into the camp with a great deal of cursing.

Even before passing through the gate, I could see that the place had changed over the past two years. The gate had been reinforced, and several roadblocks had been set up to make vehicles approach the gate from the side. Two rows of barbed wire had been attached to the top of the six-meter-high fence. Four soldiers with submachine guns patrolled the gate, two on each side.

A hundred twenty men had arrived with us in the train. A few officers and several camp guards received us with unusual dispatch. The camp police were already waiting for us inside and immediately began to search our baggage. Dr. Dulkin and I were segregated from the other prisoners and taken to a barracks which, we were told, was reserved for prisoners who were being indicted or who were witnesses for the inquest department.

The transit station of the Oserlag was almost unrecognizable. There used to be a lot of activity there. Prisoners had wandered from one barracks to the next. Now the women's unit, which used to be separated from the men's barracks by a single barbed-wire fence and guarded by an invalid, had been moved to another barracks which was separated from the men's camp by a six-meter-high wooden fence. Gone were the days when you could make music and dance with the women. A male prisoner had only to walk past the women's unit and off he'd go for five days in the punishment cell.

Where in the past you were near to suffocating in dirt and cramped quarters, now everything was meticulously clean, and there were enough barracks to provide plenty of room. The only crowded barracks was ours.

I met many people from other camps who were now waiting to be remanded, either as witnesses or as defendants. I made the acquaintance of Heinz Gewürz, an Austrian who had fled to France with his parents when Hitler marched into Austria. When the war broke out, Heinz volunteered for service in the French Army; he was decorated several times for bravery. After the war, he returned to Austria with the occupation troops. In 1947, he was deported by the Russians; he was sentenced to twenty-five years in camp by a military court in Moscow. Now he was being interrogated again: he was supposed to testify against alleged "French agents." The second Austrian I met in the transit station was a young fellow from Styria. He had been sentenced to ten years in camp for being a member of the Hitler Youth; now he was being tried in connection with an alleged "conspiracy" in the DOK camp.

Several groups of Germans were brought in who had been arrested in East Germany and had been sentenced to twenty-five years for espionage. They were convinced that they would be liberated by the Americans very soon. They kept talking about John Foster Dulles—all their hopes were pinned to that name. When I told them I had been waiting to be released for sixteen years, they shook their heads incredulously; they thought I was exaggerating, trying to make myself important.

A week after my arrival in Tayshet, I was taken to a hearing. The MGB department was situated in the administration building. The hearing lasted more than two hours, but the questions were basically the same ones I had been asked in camp 030. My interrogator was Major Yakovliev. At the end, he admonished me to be "reasonable" and admit everything at the next hearing, since, he said, the MGB knew everything already.

A few days later, I was summoned again—but this time I was told to bring all my "things." I quickly took leave of my old and new acquaintances and brought my Japanese knapsack to the gate, where Major Yakovliev was waiting for me in a jeep. A second officer was sitting next to the driver. The jeep rumbled straight across Tayshet to the section of town where the MGB and MVD officers lived. The snow was so deep in places that we had a difficult time plowing through. We had to wait at the railroad crossing—the Moscow–Peking Express happened to be passing by. Then we drove on.

We stopped in a large back yard. Major Yakovliev got out, and I stayed in the car with the driver and the other officer. After ten minutes, I was told to get out. We entered the house, passing a sentry posted at the side of the door, and reached a long, thickly carpeted corridor with white doors on either side; some of the doors were padded. I sat down on my knapsack and waited. Officers walked in and out of the rooms. I saw some women, too; one of them was crying as she was led out of one of the padded doors. I was told to turn my head to the wall so I wouldn't see her; but I heard her sobbing voice: *"Bozhe moi, bozhe moi!*—My God, my God!" A little later, a man in the usual prison garb was led past me, and I was again told to turn my face to the wall.

Then the officers seemed to be taking a break. Two young girls in black skirts and little white aprons walked past me with tea and sandwiches on wooden trays. The smell of the food made me hungry.

After a long wait, Major Yakovliev called me. I wanted to take my knapsack with me, but he waved his hand, saying: "*Ne nado*—Not necessary."

A man in MGB uniform without any insignia was sitting behind one of two desks. I could tell by the subservient tone with which Yakovliev addressed him that he was the major's superior. He told me to sit down. Now I expected the usual "How are you?" but instead he said: "You don't seem to want to get out of here?"

"Do you think there's a creature alive who doesn't want to be free?"

"Why do you force us to prosecute you for the third time?"

"I wondered about it the first time. By now, I'm used to it."

"I'm glad you're getting used to it; but you should consider the possibility that it might end tragically for you."

"So much the better, I'll finally have some peace," I said quietly.

"I can see that you don't appreciate life very much."

"What sort of life are you talking about? Do you call this a life, being dragged from one camp to another?"

"This isn't going to get us anywhere. You must help us bring this inquest to a conclusion without any undue delays."

"I don't even know what I'm accused of. I'm not conscious of having committed any crimes."

"You were surrounded by a band of American agents who were planning an uprising. We have to liquidate this nest of spies, and if you really have nothing in common with these agents, I'm sure you'll be willing to help us."

"You are mistaken if you think I'm in a position to help you. I have always avoided even saying hello to people who spread those kinds of ideas."

"Think about it. I'll give you some more time."

"Where am I going now?" I asked.

"I'm forced to keep you in custody for the time being."

He picked up the telephone. A young officer came in and led me out of the room. I took my knapsack and followed the officer to a jeep. He sat down next to me. The officer who had accompanied Yakovliev and me on the drive from the camp sat down next to the driver. I later found out that he was the prison warden.

I could see the large wood prison house and the obligatory watchtowers, those Siberian landmarks, long before we stopped in the courtyard. Some prisoners were sawing wood near us. As we passed, they turned their backs to us. The prison looked virtually identical to the one in Norilsk, probably because it was built to the same architectural design. As usual, I had to take off my clothes and submit to a search. I wasn't allowed to take any of my possessions with me into the cell, not even my blanket.

The guard let me into the cell. Here, too, everything looked familiar, not only the naked bunks, but the prisoners' faces, even though I had never met them before. After a half hour, I knew their names, their background, and the reason they were in pre-trial detention. One of them said he had heard about me in another camp; under the circumstances, I wasn't happy to hear this at all.

Three of the five men in our cell were foreigners; this wasn't an unusual ratio in the Oserlag. Abdulla, an Uzbek, immediately forced me to focus on him by his provocative behavior. Szilasi, a Hungarian baron, spoke German with a Hungarian accent. He was eager to speak German with me, even though I advised him not to, since Abdulla was the only one besides us who could understand the language. The other two prisoners were Russian criminals.

Abdulla had been a shepherd in the mountains of Uzbekistan before the war. Before he was drafted, all he had seen of the world was his collective farm and his sheep. He was captured by the Germans, nearly starved to death in a POW camp, and allowed himself to be recruited into the Moslem legion organized by the SS. He was assigned to guard duty in the extermination camp of Auschwitz, where he helped the SS murder tens of thousands of people. Abdulla wasn't able to flee in time. When the Russians liberated Auschwitz, he was arrested and sentenced to twenty-five years of *katorga* for his crimes. He was sent to the *katorga* section of the Oserlag on the other side of the Lena. After a few years of forced labor, he decided he needed some rest. Toward this end, he wrote a petition to the MVD in which he claimed to have collaborated with an SS man in burying a case full of dead prisoners' jewelry in the main courtyard of Auschwitz, and offered to show the authorities where the treasure was. A few months later, Abdulla was taken to Auschwitz. After a good deal of digging, the MVD realized that Abdulla had been leading them around by the nose. They sent him back to Tayshet, instituted new proceedings against him, and suddenly discovered that he had been too mildly punished for his war crimes.

Szilasi was fifteen years old when his father died. He inherited his baron's title and a fortune, which he lost in 1945. When he was twenty, he moved from his native province to Budapest and enrolled in the university. He probably would have been able to conclude his studies if an aunt who lived in the West hadn't repeatedly sent him money. He had successfully concealed his aristocratic title, but the money transfers did not pass unnoticed. The authorities began to take an interest in Szilasi. One day, he was arrested; he had to reveal his family history. He insisted in vain that the money had been sent by his aunt. He was sentenced to twenty-five years in a camp as a "foreign agent" and was sent to Siberia.

He was put in camp section DOK, which was part of the Oserlag. There prisoners built prefabricated houses, window and door frames, and other objects from the wood that was cut down by other prisoners. Szilasi couldn't face the prospect of twenty-five years of hard labor and hunger. He founded a "secret society" which he called the Avengers. Before long, he had convinced twenty-four gullible souls that they could topple Soviet power if only they set their minds on it. Once a week, the conspirators met in the drying room of their factory (the boiler men were part of the organization). Their behavior was so blatantly conspiratorial that the MGB soon had knowledge of every step they took. One day, the MGB pounced on the Avengers and arrested all twenty-five of them. Twenty-two went straight to prison; the other three were transferred to another camp—these were the MGB's spies, former SS men. They appeared as witnesses for the prosecution, and on the basis of their testimony, eight of the accused, among them Szilasi, were sentenced to death. The other seventeen were given twenty-five years of *katorga*. One of those seventeen was the young Styrian I had met in the transit station.

A week passed and I was brought back for another hearing. This time, I was questioned by an officer in civilian clothes.

"You are Viennese?" was his first question.

"Yes, I was born in Vienna."

"When were you last in Austria?"

"1932."

"I was there much later," he said. When he saw my surprised expression, he explained: "I was there with the occupation forces."

From then on, he spoke to me in a manner that was most unusual for an MGB officer. He was highly enthusiastic about Austria, especially about the city of Baden near Vienna—that was where Marshal Konev's staff had been quartered. As I listened to the officer singing the praises of my native country, I wondered if it was his love of Austria that had brought him from Baden to Tayshet. After approximately two hours of conversation, he ordered two glasses of tea and sandwiches.

After we finished eating, he said: "What should I do with you?"

"Send me back to the camp so that I can finish my sentence and finally get out of here."

"You make that sound so simple. Look at this." And he showed me a fat bundle of dossiers. "Your name crops up in these reports at least a dozen times."

"Why can't you just believe that I didn't have anything at all to do with those adventurers! I'm experienced enough to keep my nose clean of that kind of nonsense—especially now that I'm just a few months away from being let out."

"Yes, if all that was needed was my believing you, there would be no problem: you could quietly wait for your sentence to run out."

"I am sure you could do something to get me off the hook—especially since I really didn't have anything to do with this business."

"I will try to talk to the boss. Go now."

When I returned to my cell, my place on the bunk was occupied. The newcomer was a "jackal"—one of those people who didn't recognize the rights of their fellow prisoners. I didn't feel like fighting him, but neither did I want to lie on the cold stone floor. So I knocked on the door until the guard came, and demanded to be given a place to sleep on a bunk. It didn't help—I had to sleep on the floor that night. When our cells were inspected the next morning, I asked the prison warden to find me a place to sleep. A little later, I was transferred to another cell.

THE ADVENTURES OF RAUECKER AND HIS WIFE

The first thing I saw when the guard opened the door of the cell was a pair of crutches leaning against the wall. I stepped in and greeted the man lying on the top bunk. There was no one else there. He returned my greeting with a hard accent: "*Tobri dan [Dobry den]*." He's not Russian either, I thought. It turned out he was an Austrian named Rauecker. In the course of the two weeks I spent with him in that cell, I learned his story.

He had been a member of the Austrian Communist Party. In 1946, the party helped him obtain a post in an agricultural enterprise run by the Russians near Ybbs, in Lower Austria. There he met his future wife, Trude Rauscher. They worked together for a while, until they were fired because of certain irregularities. They were unemployed for several months, supported by Trude's parents, until their friends in the party found them jobs in another Soviet-run company, this time in Vienna. They didn't last long there either: again, they were found to have "misplaced" several thousand schillings belonging to the company. After that, the party was no longer willing to help them, and they were expelled. Rauecker tried threats to regain his party membership and obtain a new post, but he didn't succeed.

Now Trude conceived of a way to make some easy money: work for the competition. Since the Soviet and Austrian communists would no longer help them, they would try their luck with the C.I.A. They went to the Viennese office of the C.I.A. and offered their services. After a one-hour interview, they left the building with a hundred-dollar bill and an assignment to penetrate the Soviet-run oil refinery in Zistersdorf, make sketches of certain apparatus, and steal various documents from the management. Trude's brother was the head of the company police in Zistersdorf; they asked him for permission to visit the plant. He consented reluctantly, and everything proceeded according to plan: Trude's brother let them into the plant on a Saturday afternoon, and while Rauecker made his drawings in the machine room, Trude rummaged through the office files and found the desired documents.

All the while, however, the two were being watched by MVD agents. At an appropriate moment, the couple were arrested, interrogated on the spot, and sent to the MVD prison in Baden. Rauecker immediately gave a full confession. Trude was more stubborn; it took a week of beatings to get her just to talk. Eventually, she retracted her confession in a letter to the Soviet Secret Service. Their response was to drag her into the punishment cell at night, undress her, and beat her with a whip. Although she begged for mercy and promised on her knees to admit everything, they beat her until she lost consciousness. After she recovered, she was questioned again, and this time she made a detailed confession.

Then they were tried by a Russian military court and were sentenced to twenty-five years in camp. They saw each other again in the transit camp in Lemberg. Trude made one more attempt to avoid being transported to Siberia: she sent the MVD a petition containing some tall tale or other. The officer to whom she gave the petition read it in her presence and said with a sarcastic smile: "You don't seem to realize who you're dealing with."

As I listened to this story, it came to me that I had heard the name Trude Rauscher before. In camp 033, I had once helped put a derailed car back on the tracks. Some female prisoners were unloading building material near the site of the accident. The guards were lenient: we were able to talk to the women without being chased away. I had a conversation with a red-haired Hungarian woman who told me there was an Austrian prisoner in the camp, Trude Rauscher, who was in such bad health that she was never sent to work outside the camp. When I told Rauecker about this, he was very surprised. He was convinced there weren't enough locks and barbed wire in the world to prevent her from regaining her freedom.

In the transit station at Lemberg, Rauecker continued, he had been relatively comfortable. He was glad to have emerged from solitary confinement in the cellars of the MVD. Life was never boring in Lemberg: prisoners' transports, large and small, came in continually from all the countries where Soviet troops were stationed. You could walk around freely in the camp compound, and the only work you had to do was pick up your food three times a day. As for his twenty-five-year sentence, Rauecker didn't take it seriously. I'll have a look at Siberia, he thought, stay there for a few weeks or a few months at the most, and then go back home in a sleeping car and be welcomed with flags and music. I'll recuperate from the stress and strain of captivity for a few days and then go back to the Americans and tell them over a glass of whiskey what it was like in Siberia, till we get to the most important thing—the check, with a nice round sum written on it. After that, I'll go shopping with Trude, and then we'll go to the Riviera.

That had been Rauecker's fantasy, not unlike those of Kapp, Stift, and many others. The first doubts assailed him when he was crammed into a cattle car with sixty other men and sent off into the unknown. The trip seemed endless. Once a day, the door of the car was yanked open for feeding: sixty portions of bread, sixty pieces of salt fish, a hundred and twenty lumps of sugar, two pails of water. After that, the door was shut for another twenty-four hours. At night, when the broiling heat of the day gave way to some pleasant coolness, you managed to fall asleep, but pretty soon the guards would wake you up by pounding on the walls of the car with sledgehammers. As long as the train was going through European Russia, the prisoners were fed regularly, but after they crossed the Urals, the daily provisions began to diminish. There was no more sugar, and the only way for the prisoners to get water was to shout in chorus every time they pulled into a station: "Water! Give us water!"

And all the while you were being eaten alive by lice. Not until the transport reached Chelyabinsk were the prisoners brought to a transit station where they were bathed and their clothes deloused. They also got hot meals during their three days in Chelyabinsk. Then they went on. They traveled for thirty-four days, in the course of which Rauecker's dreams went up in smoke—all he could think of was water and bread and a chance to get a real rest; he didn't even think very often of Trude, who was in another car on the same train.

When they finally reached Tayshet, Rauecker was glad to stretch his legs, walk about in the courtyard, and occasionally talk to Trude across a barbed-wire fence. The stories he heard from prisoners about the various sections of the Oserlag were so frightening that thoughts about escaping and finding his way back to Europe began to obsess him. He discussed these ideas with other prisoners. One of them was naïve enough to take him seriously; others listened attentively so as to be able to furnish the MGB with a detailed report. That was how Rauecker's name was entered in the MGB's blacklist just days after his arrival in the camp.

He was put in section 05, where he worked as a woodcutter. He never tired of searching for people to help him escape. He planned to disarm the guards. One day, something happened that made a shambles of all his plans. He failed to heed the warning cry when a tree was cut, and the tree fell on him. His fellow prisoners took him for dead; but when they came closer, they heard him groaning. After pushing the tree aside with great effort, they were astonished to see Rauecker lying on his back with his eyes open, seemingly uninjured. Only after they helped him to his feet did they realize that his left leg was broken.

Rauecker was hospitalized for two months. When he was released from the hospital, the fracture had healed, but the leg had gotten shorter; he could walk only with the help of crutches. He was put in a camp for invalids and resumed planning his escape there. He found followers among the invalids as well. Maybe the many MGB officers were experiencing a lull in their daily work: Rauecker was arrested and put in prison, and the MGB began an inquiry into his "preparations for an armed revolt." At first, Rauecker denied everything. Then the MGB produced witnesses who repeated word for word what he had said in the transit station. Others told him to his face that he had recruited them in camp 05. To all these accusations, Rauecker had a single answer: "Those are all lies and calumnies. How could I, a cripple, lead an insurrection!"

In the meantime, Rauecker had learned how to move around without crutches, and he often walked back and forth in the cell. The guards seemed to know that. Every time we were taken out for our walk in the yard and Rauecker took along his crutches, the guard would say: "Why don't you leave your crutches, we know you don't need them! Just wait, we'll take them away from you one of these days."

On the twentieth day after my incarceration, I was called back for a hearing. I had to sit in a waiting room in the MGB building. Finally my interrogator, the officer in civilian clothes who had been in Austria, came up to me and said: "The chief will see you now. Follow me." I followed him into a room where a young woman in an MGB uniform stood up as we entered. She knocked on a door and stepped into an adjoining room. She came back out shortly and let us in.

It was a large room, thickly carpeted, with pictures of Stalin, Molotov, and Beria on the walls. A portly, round-faced man with blond hair was leaning back behind his desk. He was wearing a colonel's uniform. This was Salamatov, the MGB director of Tayshet. He pointed to a chair and told me to sit down. My interrogator sat to the right of the colonel.

"How do you feel?" the colonel asked.

"Not well."

"Why not? Did someone hurt you?"

"The fact that I'm back in pre-trial detention is reason enough for me to feel upset."

"You won't have to be there for long. All we need is a little information about our patient, the fellow who's in your cell."

"You mean Rauecker?"

"Yes."

"But I hardly know the man," I said.

"But he's Austrian, as you are!"

"Of course, but that doesn't mean that I know him."

"Why not? You've been in the same cell for two weeks."

"If you want to hear my opinion about Rauecker: you shouldn't take him seriously. He's a fantasizer and an adventurer, like many others I've met in the camps."

"You are very naïve not to take seriously people like Kapp, Rauecker, and others."

"The inquest authorities have the right to judge these people as they see fit, but if you ask me, I can only repeat: what they're doing is childish and insignificant."

The colonel asked the interrogator whether he had any questions, and the interrogator shook his head. "All right, we're finished," the colonel said.

The interrogator led me into his room and asked me a few more unimportant questions; then he led me to the waiting room. Half an hour later, I was taken back to the prison.

Rauecker asked me if I had brought him anything to smoke, and when I asked him where he thought I could have gotten any tobacco, he said: "You could have asked the interrogator to give you some." I replied that this was beneath my dignity. Rauecker grumbled: "Beneath my dignity . . . beneath my dignity." Then, deeply insulted, he turned away from me and faced the wall. During the walk in the yard, he found a cigarette butt and picked it up. When we got back to the cell, he lit and smoked it without saying a word to me.

The next morning, the guard handed me my bread, saying: "Eat your breakfast and get your stuff ready." This could only mean that I was being taken back to the camp. I didn't eat my bread and gave it to Rauecker as a goodbye gift. He was very moved. He stayed behind in the cell. As I left, I saw his crutches leaning against the wall in the corridor outside the cell. I never saw Rauecker again, nor did I hear anything more about him.

After I was given back my Japanese knapsack with its contents, I walked through the filthy streets of Tayshet, wondering where I was being taken now; probably back to that terrible place, section 030. When we crossed the tracks instead of walking on to the station, I suspected we were going to the transit camp—but that wasn't the case, either.

SECRET ORGANIZATION IN CAMP 048

After a two-hour march, we reached the gate of a camp that was not known to me. I could see a large chimney to my right. A terrible thought flashed through my mind: Had the MGB built extermination camps along the Nazi model? Was I going to end up in a gas chamber?

After I sat for a long time in the waiting room of the little guardhouse, an overseer came to fetch me. I looked around as we crossed the compound. This was the largest camp I had seen in the Oserlag complex. There were rows and rows of barracks in straight lines, with street-like areas between them. We walked along the broadest of these lanes, a sort of main road; it was actually lit by electric lamps. Turning off to the left, we reached the camp office. After the usual formalities, I was given a piece of paper with the number of my brigade and the name of its brigadier.

But first I had to leave my knapsack in safekeeping with the camp office. I was still wearing felt boots and padded pants; I had to exchange my winter clothes for shoes and summer trousers. Then I went looking for my barracks. It was empty. Only the *dnevalny* was there; everyone else had gone to work. The *dnevalny* read the paper I had been given and assigned me a place on the upper bunk.

I was surprised by the cleanliness and order that prevailed here. The bunks were arranged like sleeping-car bunks, with four men in each compartment. Each prisoner had a straw sack, a blanket, and a pillow stuffed with straw; some even had sheets. To the left of the entrance, there was a washroom containing two metal buckets, one of them filled with *kipyatok;* the other with fresh water. There were also two clothes racks there. The floor was scrubbed clean. I asked myself why the outside camps were so dirty whereas the camp in Tayshet was so clean and orderly. The answer was easy to determine: Tayshet was near the main railroad line, and VIPs from Moscow occasionally came to inspect the camp. None of them would ever stray into the taiga.

There was enough time for me to take a walk around the camp. Here in section 048, the largest of the Oserlag complex, there were more than four thousand prisoners. Most of them were employed in large workshops repairing locomotives and automobiles and building gas tanks. Other prisoners were sent out to the city to do construction work. The workshops were next to the camp. The prisoners worked there without armed supervision, but there were watchtowers all around, and MGB people guarded the camp's gate. Civilians had to have special MVD passes to walk in and out. As I was strolling through the camp, I was twice accosted by guards and asked why I wasn't working.

In the evening, the brigades returned from work. I stood near the gate and watched the masses of prisoners streaming in. The first to enter were the people who worked in the plant. Before the gate was opened for them, a dozen camp guards lined up in front of the gate. Then the prisoners were let in. Each man was searched by the camp guards. Some of them did this in a perfunctory manner; others were very thorough. Some even forced the prisoners to take off their shoes. Many of the prisoners had so much dirt smeared on their faces that you couldn't distinguish their features—these were the people who worked in the locomotive shop.

I kept a lookout for familiar faces. For a long time I didn't recognize anyone, but then I saw Heinz Gewürz, whom I had only recently met in the transit station. We were both glad to meet again, even though we scarcely knew one another. Heinz told me that Oskar Leptich was here, too.

My brigade came back late in the evening. I reported to my brigadier, a young Ukrainian. The next morning, our brigade—number 31—assembled at the gate. A long column of trucks was waiting to transport prisoners whose work sites were at some distance from the camp. I wasn't used to this, either. I was accustomed to marching and sometimes running five to eight kilometers to work and back to the camp. Twenty-five men went into each truck. A soldier holding a submachine gun with the safety off stood next to the prisoners on the loading platform, and another one sat next to the driver.

My brigade was used for construction work in the city of Tayshet: we were building apartment houses for MVD and MGB officers. That entire section of town was surrounded by guards, but we were able to move around freely in the work area. At first, I helped dig foundations; later I worked with a team laying concrete. The conditions of work were fundamentally identical to those in other labor camps; the quality of the food, too, was the same. Yet there was a difference: the brigadiers treated us in a very decent manner, and this made the work much easier to bear. The brigadiers gave all prisoners their full ration—even those who hadn't met the quota, and there were quite a number who didn't or couldn't.

The brigade consisted mostly of former Vlasov soldiers. It was called the juvenile brigade, because most of its members were serving ten-year sentences, whereas the majority of the prisoners in the rest of the camp were serving twenty-five-year sentences. The men in our brigade got along well with one another; but you couldn't tell anyone that you were a former party member—communists were as hated as Nazis.

I learned on my first day that the popular Moscow actress and singer Ruslanova had been in this camp a year before. She had been arrested together with her husband, a general; he had been sentenced to twenty-five years for high treason, and she was given ten years in camp. She appealed to the Supreme Court. The result: an extension of her sentence to twenty-five years. General Ruslanov had been in Germany with the occupation troops and had cleared out the apartments of Germans who had fled, taking furniture, paintings, and jewelry for his own use in Moscow. Some envious colleague had denounced him, and the MVD decided to lock up his wife as well.

Ruslanova worked as a seamstress in the camp. As a way of ameliorating the constant hunger, she developed a relationship with the cook, Misha Novikov, visiting him regularly and always returning to her barracks with a little food package. The guard who served as their intermediary was also rewarded with food. When the affair was eventually discovered, Misha lost his post in the kitchen, the guard was transferred to another camp, and Ruslanova was sent to a women's camp where she had to work as a woodcutter. After Stalin's death, the actress was released; today she is again enthusiastically applauded by audiences in Moscow.

On the day after I arrived, Heinz Gewürz brought me and Oskar Leptich together. Leptich was surprised to see me here and expressed concern about my unhealthy appearance. He soon introduced me to his companion in arms, Helmut Roth, a German from Hungary. Both had served in the SS. In 1944, Oskar, Helmut, and a third SS man had parachuted into Transylvania, in the rear of the advancing Soviet troops. They reached the city of Klausenburg unnoticed, and hid in the home of a Dr. Bauer, a longtime secret Nazi sympathizer. There they set up their radio equipment and kept the German Army commanders informed about Soviet troop movements. But one day Dr. Bauer went to the NKVD and denounced the three parachutists; they were arrested, and so was Dr. Bauer. All four were tried by a military court. Bauer was given ten years; the other three received heavier sentences. Helmut Roth was sent to Norilsk; Oskar to Tayshet; the other two to other camps.

Helmut Roth had taken part in the prisoners' uprising in Norilsk in 1950. This desperate revolt was initiated by old inmates who had worked hard during the war and had counted on an amnesty after the victory over Nazi Germany. There *was* an amnesty, but it applied only to criminals—the politicals had to stay in the camp. The revolt began in camp number 5, a copper mine. Five thousand prisoners succeeded in disarming some of the guards and routing the rest. By the time they marched to camp number 9 and attempted to storm it, the NKVD and the MGB, as well as the tank regiment that was stationed in Norilsk, had mobilized all their troops against the rebels. After two days of heroic resistance, the prisoners were forced to capitulate. Hundreds of them had died, and thousands were wounded.

The authorities' revenge was harsh: hundreds of prisoners—including people who had had nothing to do with the revolt—were thrown into cells. Some were killed right off; the rest were summarily given twenty-five-year sentences. Among the latter was Helmut Roth, who had originally been sentenced to fifteen years. Most of the surviving rebels were transferred to the Steplag in Kazakhstan or the Dallag by the river Kolyma; a few were sent to Tayshet.

Here in camp 048, there were hundreds of foreigners, mainly Germans. I noticed after just a few days that here, too, there were groups of prisoners with plans similar to those of Kapp and Rauecker; and Oskar told me about a secret organization, of which he was a member. Several groups were wooing him, for everyone knew he had been a wireless operator in the Wehrmacht. The majority of the prisoners didn't know anything about these secret groups until one of them was exposed and its members were arrested. Just a few weeks before I arrived, a group of MGB officers headed by Colonel Salamatov had stormed the camp's fire station. No one was there, except for the man on duty. After searching the place thoroughly, they left, taking the fireman and parts of a radio transmitter with them. There was a rumor that the fireman had belonged to a secret organization of locomotive workers, and that it was they who had built the components of the radio transmitter. Supposedly, the transmitter was going to be set up in the fire station.

This event was the subject of animated discussions, but it would probably have been forgotten very quickly if it hadn't been for a bloody incident shortly after. One evening, just before everyone prepared to go to sleep, an electrician, a prisoner from another barracks, came into our barracks, walked up to a young man who was unsuspectingly lying on his bunk, and stabbed him repeatedly in the chest with a knife. The boy died instantly. The murderer left and went to the guardroom, where he told the chief guard that he had just executed a traitor. The murdered man had been a member of a secret organization and was suspected of having betrayed his group to the camp administration. The murderer and two close associates were sentenced to death and shot; several others who were involved in the affair were sentenced to twenty-five years of *katorga*.

In view of incidents like these, I decided to restrict my circle of acquaintances to just a few people. All I wanted now was to get through the last year of my term. I confided only in Oskar, and maintained a more reserved contact with Heinz and Helmut. I avoided talking to the members of my brigade, and this attitude earned me the reputation of being untrustworthy. They couldn't understand how someone could live through seventeen years of bitter injustice and not feel the urge to vent his hatred of the regime with at least an occasional curse on Stalin.

BAPTISTS IN THE TAIGA

There was one other man I enjoyed talking to, especially since I knew it was safe to do so. This was the old *kipyatilschchik*, Nikifor. He was seventy-six years old and had been sentenced to twenty-five years in camp for being the "leader of an American spy and sabotage ring." This broad-shouldered, patriarchal figure with his white beard had immediately caught my eye. Because of his advanced age, he had been given the relatively easy job of keeping a caldron of water hot. On warm days, he would sit in front of his hut and chat with other prisoners. One day, I greeted him in passing, and he said: "I bet you're not Russian!"

"Correct," I replied. "I'm Austrian."

"So many nationalities here," the old man said, shaking his head.

"Yes indeed, we have quite a colorful group."

"How did you get here?"

"That's a long story; maybe I'll tell it to you someday."

"Why don't you come in?"

I accepted his invitation, and we talked for a while. After that, I visited him whenever I had the time. It was a pleasure to talk with this intelligent old man. He had been interned for belonging to a religious sect, like many others; but his case was unusual and deserves to be recorded. Nikifor and forty other peasants had been banished to Siberia by the tsarist authorities in 1907 for belonging to the Baptist Church. They were settled near the city of Achinsk, where they farmed and raised livestock, as they had on their old homesteads. Each family was given as much land as they could cultivate by themselves. The peasants' material existence was secure, for the earth was fruitful and brought forth rich harvests; and they were allowed to continue practicing their religion and even build a house of prayer. When the war broke out in 1914, all the men of conscriptable age were called up for military service. They refused to be inducted; none of them was punished. The revolution of 1917 scarcely touched their lives either. Between 1918 and 1923, Achinsk was governed successively by the Soviets, by Kolchak, then by the Mensheviks and the Czechs, and finally by the Bolsheviks again. So long as the peasants were left in peace, they hardly cared who was in power at the moment.

In 1929, the drive for collectivization began. This, too, would have been acceptable to them, for they were used to collaborative farming; but when one day an agitator came into the village to talk about the poisonous nature of religion, people started to get upset; and when their prayerhouse was turned into a clubhouse (which no one went to), the peasants decided to move elsewhere. After careful preparation, the entire community—nearly two hundred men, women, and children—set off with their livestock, tools, household goods, and some provisions. They went deep into the forest, marching for ten days, with only three or four hours of rest every day. Not everyone survived this ordeal. When they finally decided to establish their new village on a meadow by the side of a river, there were only a hundred and eighty people left.

They lived for a year off the grain they had brought along. The new homes were built in the course of the summer, and the winter was spent clearing the forest to obtain more arable soil. The very first harvest yielded enough corn and vegetables to last three years. After several years, the peasants were so well off that no one regretted having abandoned the old village. As for the rest of the world—they couldn't have been less interested. "We made clothing out of the pelts of animals we hunted with bows and arrows," Nikifor said.

When they started running out of salt, the peasants found an herb that served as a salt substitute. They fueled their lamps with resin. For more than twenty years, the Baptists lived in complete seclusion. They didn't hear about the war until six years after it was over.

"One day in the winter of 1951, our dogs started to bark louder than usual. We were frightened, because we realized it couldn't be the wild animals which sometimes came close to the village. Eventually, the barking stopped and we calmed down. A week later—we happened to be in the prayerhouse—the dogs started barking like crazy again. Some people came rushing into the prayerhouse, so scared they couldn't say anything; all they could do was point out the door. Outside was a detachment of soldiers on skis. We stood facing each other without talking for a few moments: there the soldiers were, and here was I with four other men and my only daughter. One of the soldiers came up to us and asked who was our leader. I told him we didn't have a leader, that we were all equal, that our only leader was God. When I said this, one of the soldiers laughed aloud. Then they drove us back into the prayerhouse. A few of them came inside with us; most of the others stayed outside.

" 'What are you doing here?' one of them asked. I guess he was their commander.

" 'This is our prayerhouse, we are praying to God.'

" 'I see, your prayerhouse. And where are your radios?'

" 'We don't have radios.'

" 'We'll see about that!'

"We were all pushed into a corner and weren't allowed to move. The soldiers searched the prayerhouse, and then each of us had to step

352

forward and let himself be searched. After that, the soldiers went out, except for two, who kept watch at the door. A few hours later—it was night by now—we were all interrogated. My turn came in the early morning. It happened in one of the houses. The room was full of soldiers. An officer was sitting behind the table.

" 'Come on, grandpa, tell us the truth nice and easy. Your buddies have confessed everything.'

" 'What do you want to know?'

" 'Everything, but especially where you hid the radio and the weapons.'

" 'I didn't hide anything. What we have is what you see.'

"Then the officer grabbed me by the beard and pulled me down till my head was on the table. He drew out a long knife and said: 'If you don't admit everything right now, I'll cut off your head!'

"I didn't say anything. Then he yanked my beard so hard that a clump of hair was left in his fist.

" 'I'll give you an hour. If all of you don't admit everything by then, we'll lock you up in your houses and set them on fire.'

"After several hours, I was called again. 'What a shame for such an old man to be a saboteur.'

"I didn't know what to say, so I didn't say anything.

" 'When the hell are you going to talk?!'

"I told him how we had fled to the woods so that we could start a new life far from other people. The officer wrote everything down in a little notebook. The hearing went on for several hours. Then they let me go home. There I found my son and my daughter-in-law. Both of them had been interrogated for hours.

"There was a soldier posted in front of every house. We had to ask permission to step out. We couldn't feed the animals without soldiers watching us.

"This went on for three weeks. The soldiers got used to us and let us serve them food, whereas in the beginning they had cooked it themselves or eaten from provisions they had brought along. They told us the commander had gone to the regional center and that when he came back we would be allowed to go on living as before.

"The officers came back with more soldiers. After resting for two days, the officers called the peasants together and told them the decision of the regional authorities: we would have to move closer to the regional center, closer to civilization; otherwise, we would end up living like wild animals. Why, the children didn't even have the opportunity to go to school! We were given three days to get ready for the move. After he finished talking, we knelt down in the snow and prayed. Some of the women were sobbing.

"On the third day, at the break of dawn, we were all ready; so were the soldiers. We fed the animals for the last time and started off into the

forest, two hundred adults and eighteen children. The children and some
of the women sat on sleds, covered with bear pelts. The men followed
behind on foot. The soldiers escorted us on skis.

"We marched by day. At night, the soldiers pitched tents for themselves and for us.

"After ten days, we reached Achinsk, where we were all locked up
in two big prison cells—one for the women and children; the other for
the men.

"We were investigated for two months. We were accused of having
had contact with American spy rings and of working for the overthrow of
the Soviet government. Only two of us could read and write; the rest
were illiterate. We signed the papers they asked us to sign—that is, we
marked them with three crosses, without having any idea what the paper
said. When we were put on trial and told the judge that we hadn't seen
anyone outside our village for the past twenty years, he said that almost
everyone had admitted that an American courier had visited us several
times and given us dollars. And he showed us the crosses we had made.

"We were all given twenty-five years in camp, and this is the place
where they brought us. They took our children away from us."

After Nikifor had ended his tale, I asked him: "How was your village
discovered? Did one of you go too far out into the woods?"

"That's not possible," he said. "There was no reason to go more than
ten kilometers away from the village. We had everything we needed right
around us."

"And no one ever came to your village in all those years?"

"Never. We heard a few shots, but that was far away. We assumed
someone was hunting."

"You said the dogs started barking very loud one night. Do you think
there might have been hunters nearby?"

"Probably. And that's what we assumed. Probably some hunters
discovered us and reported us to the authorities."

"How is your health?" I asked.

"Excellent. I have to keep myself in good health. I'm seventy-six
years old, and if I want to pay off my debt to the Soviet Union, I have
to live another twenty-five years."

MAJOR SCHÜLLER'S GROUP

There were two groups of Germans in the camp. One of them consisted
of Nazis who had been condemned as war criminals; their leader was the
former police commissioner of Berlin, Steinemann. They didn't carry out
any political activities in the camp. Steinemann had been the regional
commissioner in the Ukraine and was guilty of horrendous crimes. The
Austrian Stecher was another prominent member of this group. He had
been an SS officer in a Nazi concentration camp and regretted not being

there any longer. These incorrigible Nazis who had learned nothing from the past and still secretly adored Hitler were too cowardly to openly oppose the Stalin regime. They whispered among themselves but kept silent otherwise. Nor was there any sign of camaraderie among them: whoever managed to get an easy job took advantage of his privileges without giving another thought to his former party comrades.

The second group consisted of the "Americans"; that is to say, people who had collaborated with the American occupation troops after the war. Among them were many people of genuine democratic persuasion. The Russians had deported them from Germany and sentenced them all, without exception, to twenty-five years. Some had really been C.I.A. agents, but most had been arrested because of their democratic activities and were accused of being "American spies." The most striking personalities among these spies were Majors Schüller and Schröder.

This group engaged in feverish clandestine activity; their goals were the same as Kapp's and Rauecker's. But while the latter were simple adventurers, these people seriously believed in the possibility of overthrowing the Soviet government. Their naïve confidence was largely due to the fact that they were foreigners completely unacquainted with Russian conditions. That is why their plans were doomed to failure from the start. They were convinced there would be a war between Russia and the United States within the next few months, and they wanted to do their utmost to contribute to an American victory.

Rumors of an imminent war circulated throughout the camp. Some people said they'd been informed by a reliable source: Major Schüller. I warned Schüller of the danger he faced. He told me that before his arrest he had been told by Field Marshal Halder that a war would break out no later than 1953; he said the Americans had reliable information that the Soviets planned to invade Yugoslavia in 1953. If they did, it would definitely lead to a new world war. But 1952 was coming to an end, and there was no sign of an imminent liberation. Major Schüller's group decided to risk all by trying to make contact with the West. If one man could escape and cross the border, he could give the Americans a firsthand situation report and let them know that millions of prisoners in the Siberian camps were only waiting for a go-ahead to rise up against the Stalin regime. Here was further proof of their naïveté: they believed that if someone succeeded in escaping from the camp, he wouldn't find it too difficult to get to the West. Granting even the possibility of crossing the Russian border (a virtually inconceivable feat, in reality)—how would a fugitive without any knowledge of the Russian language reach the border from eastern Siberia, thousands upon thousands of kilometers away? Even a Russian with false papers would have a very hard time avoiding detection in Stalinist Russia; the country was swarming with undercover agents.

None of these problems was even considered. A young German who worked as a locksmith in the locomotive factory had been elected for the mission. He was supposed to hide in the water tank of a locomotive when it was leaving the camp. The boy was equipped with a little money and bread. He covered his whole body with grease to protect it against the effects of prolonged immersion in water, and as the locomotive was being heated, he crept into the water tank. The locomotive was searched at the gate of the camp, much more thoroughly than usual; the military guards even poked long iron rods into the tender, but found nothing. Their commander was about to allow the engineer to drive on when an MGB officer ordered a second search. This time, the soldier poking the iron rod into the water tank struck the prisoner, who cried out and rose up out of the water, his features disfigured by soot and grease. No doubt, the MGB had infiltrated Schüller's group and knew about the escape plans.

The follow-up was the usual: more than twenty German prisoners, among them Majors Schüller and Schröder, were locked up and put on trial. I wasn't able to learn any more about their subsequent fate than I did about Kapp's and Stift's.

THE ANNIHILATION OF THE JEWS

Several months before the public in Russia and in the world at large learned about the anti-Jewish campaign instituted by Stalin, the prisoners in the camps had witnessed it firsthand. The official news of 1952 was not the beginning of the tragedy but its continuation. The affair of the Jewish doctors was but a minor episode in a large-scale operation, the purpose of which was to complete what Hitler had begun.

Starting in the spring of 1952, there was a noticeable preponderance of Jews among newly arriving prisoners; in the past, the various nationalities that make up the Soviet Union had been more or less proportionally represented. At first, we thought this must be a coincidence, but when entire "Jewish transports" began to come in, the anomaly couldn't be overlooked.

Brigade 31 was increased by several workers, among them two Jews. I worked with one of them, and we got into a conversation. At first, he was taciturn and didn't want to talk about himself. Since I was acquainted with thousands of cases that scarcely differed from one another, I wasn't particularly interested in my partner's story. Weeks passed. My new acquaintance had had to ask for my help several times, and after I protected him from anti-Semitic attacks on the part of some fellow convicts, he came to trust me. From then on, he constantly came to me for advice. My new acquaintance was Colonel Rovinsky, a former commander of the railroad guard in Moscow. He had joined the Komsomol as a young man and had later been accepted in the Communist Party. He had fought in the Civil War. Later he joined the railroad guard; his special task was to ensure the security of traveling party officials. The railroad guards were subordinate to the MGB.

Colonel Rovinsky had been born into a Jewish family but had completely removed himself from Judaism, mainly as a result of his marriage to a Russian woman. Both his children were raised in the communist spirit and were considered Russians in school. They hadn't known their father was a Jew until a year before—when all of a sudden Jews could be called *zhid* with impunity: Rovinsky's young daughter came home from school crying because her classmates had called her *zhidovka*. Her indignant mother went to school to complain to the principal and to give him documentary proof that neither she nor the children were Jews. The principal replied that the children had a pretty good idea whom they could consider a Jew, and that he didn't want to get involved.

Rovinsky himself wasn't called a *zhid*, but one day he was summoned by his superior, a general, who introduced him to his successor and ordered him to relinquish his post immediately. No one gave him any explanation as to why he was being dismissed after three years of service. Since he also had to give up the apartment that came with the job, he found himself literally on the street with his family. He went from one municipal office to another but was given the cold shoulder everywhere. Finally, he contacted an old friend, a Vice Minister. After the friend had heard Rovinsky's story, he stood up, locked the door, and said in a low voice: "There's a secret order from Stalin to remove all Jews from official positions. I hope you understand that my hands are tied. You'll eventually have to leave Moscow as well. The Politburo decided as far back as 1940 to evacuate Jews from all the large cities, especially Moscow. The only thing that prevented that decision from being put into effect was the outbreak of the war."

As they took leave of each other, the Vice Minister said to Rovinsky: "Please don't be angry. But from now on I cannot accept any visits from you."

Soon Rovinsky noticed that he wasn't the only one: Jews were being dismissed from all official positions. The various cadres of the Ministries, the major governmental departments, and the centers of higher education drew up lists of Jewish employees, who had to leave immediately or as soon as replacements were found. Many Jews in Moscow and Leningrad were now unemployed. There was only one Ministry that didn't have to dismiss its Jewish members: that was the Foreign Ministry, headed by Molotov. He had gotten rid of the Jews in his ministry long ago. The last Jew in the Foreign Office had been Losovsky, who had promised the first ambassador of the State of Israel to Moscow, Golda Meir, to grant emigration visas to all Jews who wanted to leave the country. For this promise, Losovsky was arrested, and Molotov could boast to Stalin that his ministry had been completely "purified" of Jews. He "purified" his own family as well, by divorcing his Jewish wife, with whom he had had two children, and simultaneously divesting her of her position as Minister of the Chemical Industry and having her arrested.

At the end of 1952, the Soviet press and radio announced the discovery of a conspiracy of Jewish doctors to murder leading personalities in the party and the government. The doctors were said to have confessed to having murdered several prominent politicians. Only thanks to the vigilance of a Russian woman doctor had the conspirators' plans to kill the other leaders been foiled. The effect of this announcement can be imagined only by someone with an intimate knowledge of Russian history. It was the signal for a pogrom. Henceforth, Jews were fair game in Russia; they were thrown out of offices and factories in large numbers, without any notice and without compensation. All Jewish students were dismissed from the universities and trade schools. The NKVD and the MGB worked at a feverish pace. Soon the prisons were filled with Jews who had been condemned as "American spies," "Zionists," and "terrorists."

The mob was given free rein to vent its rage. Jewish or Jewish-looking passengers on trains were abused, manhandled, thrown out. The fate of Russians who tried to protect Jews was not much better. Russians no longer dared to have friendly relations with Jews. Prominent Jews who were famous outside Russia couldn't be arrested willy-nilly; but there were an increasing number of "accidents." A small notice appeared in the newspapers one day telling that the celebrated actor Michoels and a friend had been run over by a truck and killed. In reality, they had been murdered in prison because they refused to admit that they were American agents. Jewish literature, too, was decimated. The writers Markish, Gorstein, Bergelson, and Kvitka were arrested, murdered, worked to death in camps. Yiddish newspapers, of which there had been a great number until then, were shut down.

The fate of Jews in the camps was similar to that of Jews on the outside. Jews who had more desirable jobs were transferred to hard labor. All Jewish doctors were sent to work in quarries and sand pits, in mines, or cutting wood in the forest. The fascist mob that had apprenticed under Hitler now had ample opportunity to vent its hatred of the Jews. But there were enough brave prisoners to protect their Jewish comrades against those who wanted to instigate pogroms in the camps. In the barracks where the factory workers of the camp lived, a group of Ukrainian fascists tried to attack a Jewish tailor. The head of the shop, Chinchuk, and other workers rushed to the victim's aid. The fascists were so badly beat up that four had to be hospitalized. A similar scene occurred in the mess room when a Jew was shoved out of line by other prisoners. He defended himself and injured one of his assailants with his bowl. Then they all attacked him at once—whereupon the kitchen supervisor and the cooks simply threw the bullies out.

There is only one reason why the Jews were not exterminated in Russia: the "beloved leader" suffered a stroke on March 1, 1953, and died on March 5. The oppressed people had been waiting for this moment for more than two decades; a sigh of relief spread through the land. Not only the people but Stalin's closest collaborators were relieved of the ever-present threat of sharing the fate of Bukharin, Rykov, Tomsky, Pyakatov, Yagoda, and other former confidants of the tyrant. Every time Stalin sent one of their colleagues to his death, they must have asked themselves: Who will be next?

AFTER STALIN'S DEATH

On March 7, 1953, Soviet newspapers appeared with a heavy black border. The "great leader" had died on March 5 at 9:50 p.m. While the newspapers and the radio lamented the party's and the people's irreplaceable loss, a struggle began in the Kremlin among Stalin's political heirs. Before the tyrant's body had turned cold, people were already concerned about safeguarding themselves against his successor. None of the members of the Politburo wanted another "beloved leader" who would make them quake for their lives. Khrushchev made a statement at a meeting of the Central Committee after Stalin's death that gives us a glimpse of the state of mind those people lived in. In response to the question: To what extent are members of the Central Committee responsible for Stalin's crimes? he replied that he had taken leave of his family before every meeting of the Central Committee because he could never be sure that he would see them again. This statement was strongly applauded.

On the day Stalin was buried, hypocrisy reached its pinnacle in the camps. A day of rest was announced, which of course pleased the prisoners. Some of them said: "I wish a beloved leader would die every month; we'd have an extra day off." The alarm gong was sounded; the prisoners assembled in the camp yard, arranging themselves by brigades. An MVD officer who was more feared and hated than anyone in the camp climbed up on a table in the middle of the yard and commanded: "*Shapki doloi*—Off with your caps!"

Bareheaded, their caps in their hands, the prisoners stood still. The officer's voice resounded through the yard: "At this hour, the great leader of the Soviet people and of free human beings everywhere . . ."—at this point, some prisoners coughed loudly; the MVD officer looked about and continued—". . . Joseph Vissarionovich Stalin, is being in the Mausoleum in Red Square. We join the people throughout this land in mourning for our beloved leader and vow at this difficult moment to work even harder and even more productively than before."

A long pause followed. Then a prisoner raised his hand. "Citizen commander, my wife sent me some money, it's in my account. I have no use for it here, so I would like to spend it on a bouquet for our beloved leader. Can I do that?"

"Send a written petition to this effect to the camp commander," the officer said.

We returned to our barracks and secretly laughed at the seemingly boundless cynicism of the MVD.

Everyone discussed Stalin's death, and there was general agreement that the stroke he had suffered was not the real cause of his death; the actual, internal cause was the blow he had been dealt by Tito and the Yugoslavian communists. Stalin had never regained his balance since 1948, and people who were close to him reported that he contemplated vengeance against the Yugoslavians day and night. At first, he planned a military attack; this was confirmed by his right-hand man, Molotov, when he said: "In a few weeks the Tito clique will be swept to oblivion by the Yugoslavian people." The "people" he was talking about were the NKVD's hirelings and the NKVD itself. Stalin had hoped that a few hundred of his agents would succeed in setting off disturbances that would provide him with a pretext for military intervention in Yugoslavia, to be followed by the establishment of a puppet regime. He did not count on the massive support Tito received from virtually the entire population in Yugoslavia.

The Korean War was a second blow to Stalin's ambitions. He had hoped to solve the Korean problem with a blitzkrieg à la Hitler. In defiance of all warnings—and despite the fact that the American Secretary of State, Dulles, had gone to South Korea to demonstrate that the United States would not allow an annexation of that country to the Soviet bloc—Stalin started the war in the hope of "driving the Americans into the sea," as he put it in a speech. This, too, he failed to achieve.

There remained the possibility of a new world war. In preparation for it, Stalin set about persuading the world of his desire for peace. Ilya Ehrenburg, Frédéric Joliot-Curie, Hewlett-Johnson, the Dean of Canterbury, and others were assigned to organize Congresses for World Peace dedicated to attacking the Western imperialists. Many honest people allowed themselves to be misled, for who does not desire genuine peace, and who would believe that the sacred word "peace" would be used to conceal preparations for war? Nevertheless, in the end Stalin and his supporters failed to hoodwink the world. This final failure was the ultimate cause of his death, the one that remained unmentioned in the medical reports.

Stalin's death gave rise to great hope in the camps. They knew what had happened even before the news was officially announced—for the guards, the overseers, and the other camp officials sensed that a new era was dawning, and the prisoners could feel the difference. There was, above all, a relaxation of discipline. Until then, no prisoner had dared to protest against the daily bullying and harassment, since even the slightest objection would be brutally punished. Now you could see people quite openly refusing to perform the most strenuous work, and no one thought of punishing them for it. Prisoners who had been given punishment rations for failing to meet the quota declared that they would refuse to work on an empty stomach—and they received their full bread rations. There was a big increase in our days of rest—four a month now—and instead of four letters a year, prisoners could now write two a month.

You could sense that the camp administrators were floundering. After two months, they tried to tighten the reins: prisoners were thrown into the punishment cells again, and there were instances of brutality on the part of the military guards—but the old conditions could not be restored. The stream of newly arriving prisoner transports, once a steady flow, diminished radically. The few prisoners who came into the camp from pre-trial detention told us there were hardly any new arrests.

Rumors and reports about the power struggle in the party leadership filtered through to the prisoners in the camp. The appointment of Marshal Zhukov as Minister of War provoked great excitement. The prisoners knew that Stalin had sent the marshal into exile, usually the first stage before liquidation—as had been the fate of Tukhachevsky, Gamarnik, Yakir, Blücher, and other Soviet military leaders.

I was counting the months that were left until my sentence expired. I pictured myself living in freedom again and tried to prepare myself for "perpetual exile" in some Siberian village. I realized, of course, that I would still not be truly free; I knew only too well that political prisoners were unable to return to their families after their release, and that their place of residence was determined by the MGB. But life would be different, and I longed for the day when I would no longer have to contend with overseers, camp policemen, and commanders.

I had heard from people living in exile that they were so badly off that some of them wished they could be back in the camps. There were many exiles living in Tayshet, and once in a while we had a chance to talk with some of them when we went to work; frequently, they would ask us to sell them some clothes. When we marched through the streets of Tayshet, we could see the long lines in front of the stores—and the happy faces of those who had finally obtained a piece of bread or some other staple after hours of waiting. Through the windows of the houses we passed, we could see people sitting in their candle-lit rooms. That was our first impression of the life of Siberian exiles.

All this filled me with worry about the future—but still I longed to get out, yearned for the bit of freedom, illusory freedom perhaps, that would soon be mine. I often looked down at my dirty, torn clothes and ruined shoes and asked myself: Is this how I'll walk out into the world? I knew that prisoners were released in their prison clothes; only the number was removed.

I wrote to my wife, telling her how happy I was at the prospect of soon being free to embrace her again. It wasn't the first time I had expressed this hope to Sonya in the course of our seventeen-year separation. Probably she would not really believe that I was getting out; nevertheless, she sent me a package which arrived a month before I was to be released. It contained a suit that had belonged to her brother, who had been killed in the war, as well as two sets of underwear and a pair of boots she had bought with her meager salary.

I was very glad: now I was prepared for at least the beginning of my life in exile. My friends in the camp also helped as much as they could. Oskar Leptich, who worked as a turner in the gas-tank factory, made me two pots and two cans out of aluminum. Helmut Roth made me a spoon and two fountain pens that were in no way inferior to factory-made products. Heinz Gewürz secretly raised money among the other prisoners, collecting three hundred rubles for me.

All this gave me courage and hope. My fellow workers, including the brigadier, encouraged me to relax and not work so hard on the job. They said: "You'll have plenty of work once you get out."

I started counting days, no longer months or weeks. Ten days, eight, five, two . . . Finally, there was just one day left. That evening, the chief overseer came to the barracks and said to me: "Tomorrow you don't have to go to work."

My friends surrounded me, congratulating me. They knew I still doubted that I would really be let out; now they were happy for me. Oskar Leptich, Heinz Gewürz, and Helmut Roth asked to be put on the night shift so they could keep me company during my last hours in the camp.

THE LAST DAY IN THE CAMP

September 22, 1953. Immediately after the first stroke of the gong, the signal for reveille—the last one for me in the camp—my friends came into the barracks. "Today we're having breakfast with you here."

Oskar pulled a can of compote out of his padded coat; Heinz produced a bag full of sugar, and Helmut a large piece of lard. I have no idea how or where they managed to get these treasures. Shortly after we finished our festive breakfast, the chief overseer came in: "Where's Steiner?"

I followed him to the storage room, where I was given my knapsack and my clothes. From there, I went to the guards' room, where I had to strip in the presence of an MVD officer and submit to a search. The officer told the guards to search my clothes closely for "notes"; by this, he meant messages or addresses given to me by other prisoners. After the search was over, the MVD officer gave me a printed form stating that all my possessions and money had been returned to me and that I had no further claims on the camp administration. I signed the statement, even though some of the money and clothes that had been taken away from me seventeen years before were missing.

My three friends were waiting in the yard. They accompanied me to the gate. While the chief overseer conversed with the soldiers, we took leave of one another; we were very moved. As I learned later, Roth and Leptich were delivered to the Rumanian authorities. Heinz Gewürz stayed in the Oserlag.

The large gate opened. Two soldiers escorted me along a field path to the transit station. This would be my fourth stay there, but this time I wasn't on my way to another camp, but on the way to freedom. I was housed in a barracks reserved for prisoners whose sentences had expired and who were about to be released. Some of them were there for several months. Life was especially hard here for those who had become incapable of working in the camp. They had to furnish written proof that their relatives were willing to support them. But how many families were prepared to take care of a man who had spent the last ten or twenty years in a camp? And some prisoners had no families to return to. Those who could not come up with the required guarantee were eventually housed in a home for invalids run by the MVD.

Foreigners had possibly an even more difficult time. I met a Viennese in the transit station, Major Schüssler, who had been arrested by the Russians when they marched into Vienna in 1945. He had directed the War Ministry's division of industrial control; this division had been subordinated to the Gestapo two years before the end of the war, and Major Schüssler moved into the Hotel Metropol, the Viennese Gestapo headquarters. A Soviet court sentenced him to eight years in camp. His sentence expired in March 1953, but he wasn't released, for two reasons: he was Austrian and he was sick. He asked to be allowed to return to his country. After a waiting period, he was summoned to the office of the camp administration and given a form to sign. Since Schüssler could read only a few words of Russian, he asked what it was he was signing. The official said it was a statement authorizing his return to Austria. Schüssler signed it gladly. Weeks passed, and he was still waiting in the transit station.

When I entered the barracks and looked around for a familiar face, I discovered Major Schüssler in a corner; we had met in 1949. When I greeted him, he stared at me as if I were an apparition. "Steiner!" he stammered, embracing me and crying. The broken old man told me about his misfortune. We decided to go to the office together; I would serve as his interpreter. When I explained to the head of the labor and records section why we had come to see him, he replied harshly: "What's Schüssler to you? Get the hell out of here!"

"We're both Austrian. Schüssler doesn't know any Russian, so he asked me to translate for him."

"Out!"

We conferred in the hallway and decided to try our luck with the camp commander. When we entered his room, I saw the MGB officer in civilian clothes who had been my last interrogator.

"What are *you* doing here?" he asked.

I explained why we had come. At that point, the camp commander pricked up his ears. He called his secretary: "Bring me the Schüssler dossier." She brought it. The commander opened the folder and read the statement Schüssler had signed: it said that Major Schüssler did not wish to return to his native country. I translated, and Schüssler cried out: "For God's sake, I never signed anything like that!"

The commander pointed to his signature. "Is that your signature?"

"Certainly, but I had no idea what it said there!"

"This matter is settled. Go back to your barracks," the commander said.

Schüssler had a crying fit. I had to support him all the way back to the barracks. He dropped on his bunk, groaning. "Such a lie, such a lie," he kept repeating.

During the four days I spent with Schüssler, I had to promise him dozens of times that I wouldn't forget him and especially that I would tell his wife about him—she lived in the Seidengasse, in the seventh district of Vienna. When I took leave of him, he was crying so loud that everyone in the barracks crowded around us. When people learned what had happened, they exclaimed: "Poor bastard! How mean can you get!" As I learned at the federal chancellery in Vienna in 1958, Major Schüssler died in Tayshet.

For the last time, I saw recently arrived Germans, Austrians, and Hungarians, all of them sentenced to twenty-five years and all convinced they would be home by Christmas; and I thought to myself that many of them would never see their homes again.

That day, forty-two prisoners who had served their sentences were released from the Oserlag. I was summoned to the office, where the following resolution of the MGB in Moscow was read to me: "The Special Tribunal of the MGB has resolved to banish Karl Steiner, who has served sentences totaling seventeen years in prison and in camp for offenses punishable according to Article 58, paragraphs 6, 8, 9, 10, and 11, to the Krasnoyarsk area forever. The regional administration of the MGB in Krasnoyarsk is instructed to designate the location where Karl Steiner is to take up permanent residence. Karl Steiner is instructed to remain in the location assigned to him, failing which he shall be punished with twenty years of *katorga*." I had to indicate with my signature that I had taken cognizance of the MGB's resolution.

So this is "freedom," I thought to myself. Well, I hadn't expected it to be different.

I had assumed I would travel to my place of exile by myself, but I was mistaken. Once again, I was thoroughly searched. Once again, I was stuck into the "black raven," which drove me and other "free" men to the train station in Tayshet, where we waited for the regular train on the Khabarovsk–Moscow line. We were crammed into a *stolypin* car which was already jammed full of prisoners from the giant camp of Kolyma who had contracted scurvy.

The sick men greeted us: "Hello, brother! Where are you heading?"

"To Krasnoyarsk."

The sick men were on their way to a camp in Karaganda, where they hoped their terrible disease would be cured. Most of them had lost all their teeth; there were youths who sounded like mumbling old men. There was a terrible stench in the car, for many of the men had open sores, some of them as large as the palm of a hand.

HOW DO YOU LIKE FREEDOM?

I was glad when we arrived in Krasnoyarsk the next morning. A large truck was waiting in front of the station, with room for eighteen men. We drove to the other side of the city, where the big prison was. The car stopped in the yard, and the heavy gate closed behind us; only then were we allowed to get off. I sat down on my knapsack and looked about: I was surrounded by four-story houses with hundreds of barred windows. So this is the first stage of freedom, I thought to myself. And my neighbor said it aloud: "Well, how do you like freedom?"

"Have patience, my friend," I said. "This takes a while."

Some guards came out of one of the buildings. We were called up by name. When it was my turn, the guard asked me: "Paragraph? Length of sentence?"

"I've served my sentence."

"Makes no difference. To me, you're a prisoner."

My knapsack was searched, and a body search followed. This went on for more than an hour. If it hadn't started to rain, it would have taken longer, for the guards were doing their work with extreme thoroughness. We were taken into one of the buildings and locked into cell number 9 on the ground floor. We had our possessions with us. This wasn't the usual kind of cell; it was a huge hall divided into four sections. There were two rows of bunks with room for hundreds of people. The place resembled an Oriental bazaar.

Hardly anyone took notice of our arrival. Each of us had to find an empty place on the bunks. I found one near the door, next to a Lithuanian and a Belorussian. Our neighbors, most of whom had come here from Tayshet, as we had, told us they had been waiting for a week to be sent to their places of exile. Some had been there for several weeks. Most of us, we heard, would be sent to *lespromkhozi*, collective forestries—to work in the woods!

I noticed that the bread was lying around unguarded. I asked one of those who had been here the longest whether there was any stealing in the cell, and he replied: "No one touches the bread, but you've got to watch out for your things."

The door was opened for lunch; we had to step out and fetch it in our bowls. Young girls wearing yellow armbands with the inscription "Prisoner" served the traditional Russian vegetable soup from a metal container. They knew we were "free" men; they teased and flirted with us as they ladled out the soup, and we responded in kind.

After two days, I was summoned to the prison office, where an official filled out a questionnaire which contained no new questions. Once again, I had to indicate my name, the article under which I had been judged, the length of my sentence, and my profession. The official once again recited to me the MGB's resolution to banish me to the Krasnoyarsk region "forever," and once again I confirmed that I had read and understood this document. When I asked where I was being taken, I received the stereotypical answer: "You'll find out in due time."

Finally, the day came when about fifty names were called up, mine among them. We were led into one of the many courtyards in the prison. Some fifty women were already there. Two of them had babies with them. Next to the guards stood a "buyer" who inspected us as we were led past him. Once in a while, he asked a few questions. He accepted most of us. Eight were rejected; they had to return to the cell. Among the rejected ones was one of the two women with children. Her baby had been crying, and this had irritated the "buyer." He was a representative of the construction company that was building a large hospital for disabled soldiers near Yeniseisk. He was picking out able-bodied workers—no different from any slave master. Having selected his merchandise, he went to the prison office to pay the price of his purchase.

MY FRIEND GETS MARRIED

While we were waiting for the "buyer" to come back from the office and take us away, we talked with the women who would be working with us. The young Lithuanian who had attached himself to me said: "I've already found a wife."

"Which one?" I asked.

"The second one in the third row."

"You have good taste."

The "buyer" came back with two soldiers. The gate was opened, and two trucks came rolling in; but it was another hour before we could climb aboard. The young Lithuanian used this time to introduce himself to the woman of his choice. He stepped up to her and said: "Do you realize you're going to be my wife?"

The girl looked at him in astonishment.

"I'm serious. I like you. What's your name?"

"Fanya."

I could tell by the manner of her response that she wasn't averse to his proposal. After some conversation, she called over to an older friend: "Katya, I've already found a husband!"

Katya shook the Lithuanian's hand. Then Fanya pointed at me: "That's my husband's friend."

Katya behaved as if she and I were engaged to be married as well, calling me by my first name and addressing me with the familiar "thou."

We split up into two groups and climbed into the trucks; only with difficulty did we all find a place to sit. Then we drove off, through the city and farther on in a northerly direction along the old postal route, which of course had not been built for cars, so that the trip became a torment for us. An icy wind was blowing. Now the lack of space on the truck didn't bother us any longer: we tried to warm up by moving closer together, but it didn't help much. The only ones who apparently didn't feel cold were my Lithuanian and Fanya, who were all but celebrating their wedding night on the truck.

When we reached a village, we knocked on the front of the truck and begged the escort soldiers to let us step into a *chainaya*, a teahouse, to warm up a little. We were frozen stiff when we climbed out of the truck. The spacious *chainaya* was half empty; we all found a place to sit. Those who had money ordered tea, and some ordered vodka as well, despite our escort's prohibition; but then he himself poured a tea glass full of vodka down his throat. Some of the guests inquired where we came from and where we were going. They, too, were exiles; some of them had been living here for years. They treated us to more vodka.

For two hours we sat in this warm, convivial atmosphere. Then we drove on. It was late in the evening when we stopped in front of a teahouse in another village. Our escort delivered four women to the local MVD commander; this village was the permanent place of residence they had been assigned to. Again, we drank tea. Then we drove on through the dark night. There was a little more room in the truck now. We were driving through the taiga. Only rarely did we pass through a village. Often we would see lights in the distance and assume we were nearing a settlement, but it turned out to be an illusion. The light would disappear and it would be hours before we came to the next village. It wasn't until the following day that we reached our destination, which was simply called Novostroika—New Construction; the settlement hadn't been named yet. We had driven the thirteen-hundred-kilometer stretch from Krasnoyarsk in twenty-four hours.

Thirteen hundred kilometers from Krasnoyarsk and thirty kilometers from Yeniseisk, about fifty square kilometers of primeval forest land were being cleared to make room for the new settlement. When we arrived in Novostroika, there were only a few half-completed two-story wooden buildings and half a dozen one-story office buildings, also of wood. The only brick building (which was still unfinished) was the bathhouse. Compared to the dilapidated peasant houses we had passed on the way, the new settlement for disabled soldiers made a favorable impression.

The director, who was an invalid himself—he had lost his left leg—
was waiting for us in the yard. An MVD officer delivered the new work
force to him. We were quartered in one of the houses; there were two
to four people in each room. The Lithuanian moved into a separate room
with his Fanya, and Katya suggested that she and I live in the room next
door. Instead of answering her, I asked an official who was standing near
us, in a loud enough voice so that Katya could hear me, where I could
send a telegram to my wife. Katya understood, took her suitcase, and
joined the women.

Each of us had a bed with a down mattress, a blanket, a pillow, and
a sheet. I lay down in my bed for a moment: how wonderful to be able
to sleep like a human being! Then the director led us into the dining
room, where we were served a plentiful meal. Later the MVD officer
came to inform us that we were free now and would be living and working
here. Those who wished to start a family could do so; those who already
had one could arrange for their relatives to move to Novostroika. Finally,
he reminded us that we were not allowed to leave the settlement without
permission from the MVD; trips to the regional capital could be arranged,
but no one could go there without permission.

LIVING

IN EXILE

AMONG CRIPPLES

We rested for a day and took the opportunity to get to know the settlement and its inhabitants. The place was surrounded by a wooden fence, on the other side of which were the construction workers' barracks. Almost all these workers were former prisoners who had been forced to settle here. Most of them had families. Some of the women were former prisoners; others were natives of the region. The married couples raised cows and pigs.

We observed the way people lived here. After work they ate, fed their animals, and then sat down in groups of three or four to play cards. The stake was vodka, and there was a good deal of drinking and eating of pickles during the game. The women looked over their husbands' shoulders and proffered advice. If a man refused to heed the advice and then lost the game, there would usually be a fight, and quite frequently these quarrels degenerated into physical violence. On Sundays, people played cards from morning to night or danced to the sounds of an accordion.

The morning after our arrival, the cashier of the disabled veterans' home gave each of the newly arrived workers an advance of fifty rubles, which was supposed to tide us over until we received our first wages. There was a small shop in Novostroika where, in addition to a never-ending supply of vodka, you could buy flour, margarine, and sometimes sugar. There was an outdoor stove where you could cook.

We newcomers were not employed in construction work but in cutting firewood in the nearby forest. Just as we had in the camp, we formed three-man "teams"; two of us felled trees and the third man removed the branches. The trees were sawed into sections one and a half meters long, which were then split into smaller pieces. The firewood was stacked in a large pile. For one cubic meter of wood, we received eight rubles. The most we could cut was six to eight cubic meters a day, so that our maximum daily wage amounted to sixteen to eighteen rubles.

Two kilometers from Novostroika was the little village of Kuzminka, consisting of a few dozen peasant houses. Part of its once prosperous population had been deported during the collectivization drive of the early thirties; the rest had abandoned their farms and gone to work in the nearby sawmills. The houses stood empty for years, until the MVD converted them into a home for people whose health had been ruined in the camps. Here lived human wrecks who had survived the gold mines of Kolyma, the uranium and copper mines of Norilsk, the coal mines of Vorkuta and Chelyabinsk, and the Siberian taiga. The main contingent consisted of men and women who had lost eyes, arms, or legs; the rest were victims of scurvy or epilepsy. I talked to many of them. Among them were university professors, priests of all denominations, workers, and peasants. Quite a few of them yearned for death.

A large dining hall supplied the invalids with plentiful meals. Those who could work cleaned the rooms; the others took walks, with or without help, or read books and newspapers. These people were enjoying a degree of freedom that was otherwise unknown in Russia. They had nothing to lose and were completely unafraid of the MGB agents among them. In one of their houses, members of the Orthodox, Unified, and Jewish faiths took turns holding daily religious services, and the various congregations lived in perfect understanding—you could see the Archbishop of the Unified Church walking arm in arm with the chief rabbi of Stanislau. I often asked myself whether it was necessary for people to go through hell in order to learn how to live peacefully together. The same mutual tolerance prevailed in the cemetery near the village, where Russian, Polish, and Jewish gravestones stood side by side.

My first wages after two weeks of work in the forest, minus the fifty rubles I had been given in advance, amounted to two hundred and forty rubles—less than I could live on. I decided to look for another job. I tried my luck in Maklakovo, six kilometers south of Novostroika, where I had been told there was some industrial activity. I used my first free day to take the bus that went back and forth between Yeniseisk and Maklakovo. The bus stopped at the marketplace. It didn't take me long to find the administration building for construction works. As I walked into the building, an old acquaintance from Tayshet came up and embraced me. This didn't surprise me, for there were many former prisoners from the camps living here. I told Trifunov—that was his name—why I had come.

"There's plenty of work. Come, I'll introduce you to the head of personnel." Then he reflected for a moment and said: "It'll go a lot more smoothly if we discuss it over a glass of vodka." He suggested I wait at the inn. He would come back with the head of the personnel department.

I sat down in a corner, ordered half a liter of vodka, and waited. At last, Trifunov appeared at the door, followed by a man whose left leg had been replaced by a prosthesis; he supported himself with a large crutch. Trifunov introduced me as an "old friend." The two men joined me at the table. I filled their glasses with vodka, and we drank to our "old friendship." Soon I had to order a second half-liter of vodka. Before we finished drinking, the head of personnel had promised to hire me as a construction worker as soon as I moved to Maklakovo.

Pleased with my success, I drove home and went to the MVD officer to ask permission to move to Maklakovo. He said that only the regional MVD leadership in Yeniseisk had the power to authorize such a move. The officer was reluctant to let me go to Yeniseisk, but after some pleading and wrangling, I succeeded in getting permission. The next day, I went to the man in charge of questions of exile in Yeniseisk, Captain Tsarkov, and presented my request to him.

"I cannot grant you a permit to move to Maklakovo," he said, "but if you can't find suitable work in Novostroika, I suggest you go to Ust-Kem. It's just ten kilometers from here, on the other side of the Yenisei. There you might get a supervisory position in the lumberyard."

I tried in vain to soften him with pleas. I decided to drive to Ust-Kem. As soon as I was back in Novostroika, I handed the MVD officer the paper I had been given by Captain Tsarkov in Yeniseisk. He then entered a note in my passport stating that I was authorized to move to Ust-Kem.

UST-KEM

I packed my things the next day, took leave of my comrades, and waited by the side of the road, hoping to hitch a ride to Yeniseisk. The driver of a loaded truck offered to take me along for twenty rubles. Two hours later, I was in the port of Yeniseisk. From there, I went by motorboat ferry to Ust-Kem. It took a half hour to get to the other shore. I walked to the lumberyard, which was up on a hill. The director, a grumpy-looking individual, gave me a decidedly sour welcome. After questioning me thoroughly about my background, very much in the manner of an interrogator, he said he would have to think about it and would let me know the next day. He gave me a form which entitled me to find lodging in a barracks.

The long barracks building contained twenty rooms, which were inhabited by both single and married people. I was lodged in a room with ten field cots, all of them occupied by Abkhasians, members of a Caucasian minority. A cleaning woman brought in an eleventh bed and pushed the other beds closer together to make room for mine. When the Abkhasians came back and saw me, they made faces as if a giant bedbug had dropped into their midst—as if they were of a mind to squash me to death. But when they learned that I was a foreigner, they became friendlier. We talked, and soon not a trace was left of their initial hostility. I learned that there was a German living in the barracks. His name was Arnold Arno, a native Berliner, and he was very pleased when I introduced myself.

Arno had been a communist and had fled to Moscow after Hitler seized power. There he worked for the *Deutsche Zentralzeitung*, a German-language newspaper, until he was arrested in 1938 and was sentenced to ten years in camp. After serving his sentence, he was exiled to the Bolshaya Murta district. In 1951, he had been transferred to Ust-Kem. Arno told me about conditions and work in Ust-Kem. When he heard that I had applied for a job as a foreman in the lumberyard, he counseled me against it: foremen were badly paid and were replaced every two or three months.

Eighty percent of the population of Ust-Kem, he said, were exiles. Half of them were Germans from the Ukraine who had joined the German

Wehrmacht during the war, had been captured by the English in Styria, and had then been handed over to the Russians. They were all deported to southern Siberia. I soon got to know most of the Germans and their families living in Ust-Kem. They had set up house here, and it was obvious that they expected to stay in Ust-Kem for the rest of their lives.

When I went to see the director the next day, I told him I would be satisfied with any kind of work. He didn't seem to regret that I had withdrawn my request for a foreman's position.

My most urgent goal was to let my wife know that I was "free" and that she could write to me at my new address as often as she pleased. I had some trouble finding a sheet of paper and even more trouble finding an envelope. What to write now? To say I was actually free would have been a lie. I wrote that I had graduated from camp life to exile.

It took only ten days for her answer to reach me. So there was a difference: in the camp, it had taken months for mail to be answered, and often you would never receive a reply. Sonya wrote that she was glad my situation had improved; she wanted to visit me and had sent off a package of clothes and various little things. I was overjoyed that Sonya wanted to visit me, but I was firmly intent on discouraging her from undertaking the long trip. It wasn't the five-thousand-kilometer railroad trip that worried me so much as the three hundred and seventy kilometers by land and water from Krasnoyarsk to Ust-Kem.

It was the beginning of the early Siberian winter. I worked in the lumberyard at forty degrees below zero—at night, since there were no openings in the day shift. My partner was a Siberian peasant with the strength of a bear; together we loaded railroad track onto a cart that was pulled by a horse from the saw to the storage site. For this hard work, I was given twenty rubles a day; my partner, who was not an exile, received thirty rubles for the same work.

Arno and I bought food together—it was cheaper and more practical that way. Arno and I became excellent friends. During our free time, we went out for walks and talked about our past in Vienna and Berlin. We often visited Germans who lived in houses they had built themselves, had vodka with them, and exchanged memories. The Germans couldn't forgive themselves for having been captured, and they cursed the Englishmen who had delivered them to the Russians. I hardly had any contact with the native people, since they generally didn't want to have anything to do with foreigners. Some of them worked on a collective farm; others were employed as woodcutters.

In the beginning of 1954, I received a letter from a friend in Maklakovo; he asked if I would accept a suitable job there. Given the terrible living conditions and the grueling work I had to do in Ust-Kem, I couldn't leave this opportunity unexploited. The question was how to get the necessary permission. The local MVD officer would not hear of it; he wouldn't even let me go to Yeniseisk to talk to the authorities there. I decided to go to the regional capital without permission. One day, when the MVD officer was visiting the neighborhood villages to inspect the exiles living there, I asked a German who was going shopping in Yeniseisk to take me across the frozen river on his sled.

YENISEISK

It was five in the morning. Everyone was still asleep, and I was lying on the sled, wrapped in a horse blanket. Arno was the only one who knew where I had gone. On his recommendation, I was going to visit a woman from Berlin who had been living in exile in Yeniseisk since the beginning of the war. Her name was Adele Herzberg. She had been a communist and had fled to the Soviet Union after Hitler's rise to power. She had found a job in Moscow. She was lucky: when Stalin carried out his counterrevolutionary coup and exterminated the core of the Bolshevik Party, she escaped persecution. Only after the outbreak of the war was she sent into exile.

Adele received me very warmly when I conveyed Arno's greetings to her. Over a cup of tea, I explained the reason for my visit to Yeniseisk. She reassured me: I had nothing to fear, for the captain who dealt with questions of exile was an obliging and agreeable man. We went to see him together. I made my request, and without asking many questions, he gave me a document which I was to present to the MVD officer, stating that I had permission to leave Ust-Kem.

I returned the same day, picked up my wages at the sawmill, and said goodbye to everyone. Arno was sorry that he was being left behind; we wished one another a happy reunion in Europe. On Adele's invitation, I stayed in Yeniseisk for two days as her guest. I welcomed the opportunity to get to know this ancient city. Adele even advised me to stay in Yeniseisk and not to go on to Maklakovo.

I wandered through the city in search of a room. Before the construction of the Trans-Siberian Railroad at the beginning of the century raised Krasnoyarsk to its present importance, Yeniseisk was the most vital city in Siberia. It wasn't just that the governor's office was situated there. This town was the center of the gold industry and the fur trade, a city where people made fabulous fortunes overnight and lost them as quickly in the gambling casinos. The newly rich merchants built magnificent palaces in Moscow and Petersburg. There they installed their women and children, so that they would learn elegant manners, and so that the merchants could indulge themselves and their lovers with banquets and orgies in the beautiful houses they had built in Yeniseisk. They didn't forget to build schools either, for they wanted their children to be educated folk, not illiterates like themselves. The splendid former high school, a primary school today, still graces Lenin Street in Yeniseisk. A full dozen churches held services in various parts of the city.

A long, arrow-straight main road runs through the city, and smaller roads branch off at a ninety-degree angle. Today, there are only meager remnants of the old splendor. Yeniseisk is no longer a city of rich merchants, gold hunters, and fur traders. All that remains of the town's former population are some old people who live behind closed doors and drawn blinds. I knocked on many doors in search of a room; usually I wasn't even allowed inside. Once, a young girl opened the door; when I asked if her family had a room I could rent, she hesitated for a long time and then led me into the courtyard and said she would ask her sister. Thereupon, a woman appeared, about thirty-two years old, a beauty such as one rarely encounters, of medium height, with a round face, and long, dark blond hair which she wore pinned up in a knot. She looked at me with her large eyes and asked: "What do you want?"

I was surprised by the question, for I had assumed that the younger girl had told her the purpose of my visit. "I'm looking for a room," I repeated.

"Ah, I don't know what to tell you. I have nothing against it, but my mother . . ." She considered for a while; then she invited me in.

The apartment was crammed full of old furniture. The room I had stepped into contained two large armoires, an oval table, a large mirror, several chests; there were icons on the walls. A candle was burning in the corner in front of an icon of St. Nicholas.

The mother came in. At first, she was speechless with astonishment at finding a strange man in her apartment. "Mama, the gentleman wants to rent a room, what do you think?" asked the older daughter.

"No, no, we don't take strangers into our house."

I concluded from this that the woman had had unfortunate experiences with other boarders. "You don't have to be afraid of me," I said.

"You're an exile, am I right?"

"Yes, I'm an exile."

"Look at her," the mother said, pointing at her older daughter. "A man came from the camp and rented one of our rooms. He liked my daughter, he was a decent person, I had nothing against it, they got married. Then she had a child, and three years later another child. We were glad to have a man in the house. He worked as a bookkeeper. One night in 1948, they came in here and chased us all into the stables with the animals—all of us except him. When we came back after a few hours, the place looked as if there had been an earthquake, and he was gone. We never heard from him again."

Two charming boys, four and seven years old, peered in from the courtyard. "They look just like their father," the old woman said.

I beckoned to the children, but they were afraid and hid behind their grandmother. I tried to persuade the woman to accept me as a boarder.

"No, no, please understand this, we simply can't, it's impossible."
I stood up and left.

There isn't a house in Yeniseisk that does not harbor a tragedy like this one, for it is a city of exiles and former exiles. The children of Yeniseisk play the following game: one child walks with his hands behind his back, and another child follows behind, with a piece of wood representing a rifle. The "soldier" shouts at the "prisoner": "If you try to escape, you'll be shot!"

There's a museum in Yeniseisk. Ten percent of the exhibit is devoted to the history of this center of Siberian commerce and trade, and ninety percent deals with the time Stalin lived in Siberian exile—despite the fact that he didn't live anywhere near Yeniseisk but three hundred kilometers away, in the village of Kureika. For a long time, the museum was directed by Professor Dubrovsky, who had been on the Solovetsk Islands and in Norilsk when I was there. His successor was Yelkovich, a former associate of Zinoviev.

I had gone to the museum in the belief that I would learn something about this interesting city's history, but instead I found numerous objects and documents that supposedly had something to do with the history of Stalin. I turned to Yelkovich, whom I had also gotten to know in camp: "Comrade Yelkovich, is this all you're showing about the history of Yeniseisk?"

He spread his arms. "What can I do? The exhibits are sent here by the central museum administration in Moscow; my job is to display the stuff."

"Are you saying that all museums are supplied with the same exhibits?" I asked.

"Not all. Only those museums that offer an opportunity to relate their exhibits to Stalin's life in that particular region."

"But according to the *Short Course on the History of the All-Union Communist Party*, Stalin never lived in Yeniseisk," I objected.

"Not according to the first edition, but this has been corrected in the second edition."

"And you go along with this?"

"What else can I do? I'm sixty-two years old. Do you expect me to work in the harbor unloading flour and cement? I have to live!"

I didn't know what to reply to that.

When I told Adele of my lack of success in finding a room, she was very disappointed: now I had to go to Maklakovo, after all. We took leave of each other, and I promised that I would visit her soon.

MAKLAKOVO

I took the bus to Maklakovo. Once again, I stood in the dirty marketplace. My friend had found me a place to sleep, which hadn't been easy. However, the bed reserved for me in the sawmill workers' domicile had been taken, so I had to share a field bed with another man on the first night. It didn't matter much; I was used to it.

The next morning, I had breakfast in the *chainaya* and set out in search of a room. I found an acquaintance who was willing to let me spend a week in his room. Consequently, I was able to sleep better on the second night, even though I was sleeping on the floor. Then the temperature dropped sharply, and I was still sleeping on the floor. I chopped wood and kept the stove heated in exchange for my friend's hospitality. There was plenty of wood, so I did not have to be sparing with it. Now the room was nice and warm.

Twice a month, I had to report to the MVD command. Each time I went there, an officer would ask me where I was working and how much I was earning. MVD and MGB people frequently came to the mill as well to see if everyone was in his proper place.

I didn't get the job I had been promised by the head of personnel. Someone else had treated him to more vodka than I had. I took a job in a carpentry shop. My first partner at the band saw was Alexander Drechsler, a bohemian character from Leningrad. His long, gaunt figure reminded me of the baron in Gorky's *Lower Depths*. Drechsler treated his job as if he were playing a role on the stage. When the director of the company, Siper, introduced us, Drechsler greeted me with a verse from Pushkin's *Eugene Onegin*.

I liked Drechsler right away. The ten years he had spent in the camp hadn't broken his spirit. He was forty-four years old and very interested in young women—he "consumed them with pleasure," as he put it. He told me later that he spent a considerable part of his wages on young women, so that just a few days after payday he had to make do with a piece of black bread for dinner. He wore the same suit on workdays and Sundays, but he turned the suit inside out when he wore it to work. Drechsler and I became good friends. He's living in the Ural Mountains today, near Sverdlovsk, directing a small theater. That's a much more fitting occupation for him than operating a band saw.

Another colleague was the Bulgarian peasant Petkov, who worked in the room next to ours. We sometimes talked, but he was so taciturn that he never said more than he absolutely had to. This man had grown old in the camps, and he rarely exchanged a word with anyone. That's why I was very surprised when on the way home from work one day he invited me to join him for dinner. I had no other plans and gladly accepted the invitation.

His wife, a Jewish woman from Bessarabia, was young but not pretty. As we sat together in his kitchen eating herring and potatoes, I learned that the little house, consisting only of a room and a kitchen, belonged to him and that the potatoes came from his garden. He told me how he had acquired his house. One day, a fire broke out in the sawmill and destroyed the greater part of the plant, along with the boards that were stored there. Petkov was among the workers who rebuilt the plant. The director allowed the workers to take home the charred boards and use them for firewood. The Bulgarian bought a small plot of land at the edge of the forest and started to build himself a little house with the charred boards—and sometimes he took boards that hadn't been touched by the flames. Because he had built it in his spare time, he was especially proud of his achievement. He told me with tears in his eyes how hard it had been for him to carry the heavy beams on his old back. Now he was happy to have a roof over his head in his old age.

Petkov suggested I live with him. I accepted the offer. The next night, I slept in the Bulgarian's house on a bed he had prepared for me in the kitchen. It was pleasantly warm there, and I didn't have to fetch wood. There was so much left over from the building of the house that we didn't have to worry about using it up. I was witness to daily quarrels between the stingy old man and his young wife, who wanted to go to the movies or buy herself silk stockings, which struck Petkov as frivolous and irresponsible.

I lived with Petkov all winter. When spring came, he bought himself two piglets, which he kept in a corner of the kitchen. He assured me that the pigs wouldn't bother me. For two months, I put up with their stench and their squealing, and finally I had enough. My friend Drechsler, who knew about my four-legged tormentors, introduced me to the head of the housing bureau, Shevchenko. After I spent my entire monthly wages on a Sunday of drinking with Shevchenko and Drechsler, he gave me a room to live in.

I started to set up house, for I expected my wife to visit me; she had written that she would come in May 1954. With the support of the director of the company, Siper, I built a double bed and a kitchen table. For two hundred rubles, which Sonya had sent me, I bought a second pot for cooking and two plates. Now I had almost everything an exile in Siberia would need for his household, and even some things people who had lived here for years hadn't been able to acquire. I could tell from my wife's letters that she had mistaken notions about life in Maklakovo. To reassure her, I wrote a description of the place:

"I can see from your last letter that you have an unrealistic conception of life in Siberia. It may have been like that thirty or forty years ago, but it's not that way today. First of all, you don't have to be afraid of being attacked by bears or wolves on the way from Krasnoyarsk to Maklakovo. Ever since the NKVD settled deportees from the Baltic countries and elsewhere along the road, the wild animals have retreated far into the taiga. I have never heard of a person being attacked by wild animals here. It's people you have to watch out for, not in the forest, but in the teahouse. There you'll find people who expect a traveler to buy them a glass of vodka; if he doesn't, they'll insult and abuse him. The best thing under these circumstances is to compromise one's principles and pay the bill.

"What other advice can I give you? Above all, that you postpone this trip and so spare yourself all these hardships. But if you insist on coming, I hope nothing bad happens to you.

"As for life here, you must be prepared for some very primitive conditions. I do have a good room, and I hope you'll like it. However, you'll be sleeping on a straw sack, not a down mattress—but I don't think that will disturb our happiness! You could cook for the two of us, or we could go and eat at the inn for twenty rubles. The peasants sell vegetables, pork, and milk at the market. There are many stores, too, where you can get various kinds of food. But it's hard to get sugar; it would be good if you brought some along.

"Maklakovo is a large village with more than ten thousand inhabitants. Some of them live in peasant houses; others in recently built barracks. Everyone here is of course either a deportee or an exile, just as everywhere in Siberia. Half of the people are Lithuanians; the rest are Latvians, Germans, Russians, Ukrainians, Poles, Jews, and Rumanians. The circle I move in consists of intellectuals of all these nationalities. There are many interesting people here. Don't be surprised that I don't write about the Siberians themselves—I haven't had a chance to meet any yet.

"There's a bathhouse in town. It's dilapidated, but it has two cabins that can be used by married couples. A movie theater in an old barracks serves the people's cultural needs. There's a promise of improvement, and this helps to brighten one's outlook: a new bathhouse has been under construction for three years, and people still hope that it will be operational someday . . ."

I waited impatiently for the month of May. I worked hard, not just to have enough to live on, but in order to buy little things for the apartment. All my thoughts were with Sonya; I could hardly believe that I would soon be holding her in my arms again—Sonya, who had suffered so much on my behalf and to whom I owed so much. I was worried, too. What if we were strangers when we met? What if we felt disappointment instead of the great joy we had anticipated? Might it not be better to keep her from coming here and preserve the illusion that we belonged together?

May finally came. On the tenth, I received a telegram from Sonya telling me that she was leaving on the fifteenth and already had her ticket. I was afraid of going mad with happiness. I rushed off to tell my friends the news. I had to take sleeping pills; otherwise, I would have lain awake all night thinking of Sonya. Two days later, another telegram came: "Vacation postponed because of urgent work. Trip impossible. Letter follows." When I read that, my heart stopped. I thought I would die. My whole body shook.

Drechsler happened to be passing the post office and was frightened by my appearance. "What on earth is wrong with you? You're pale as a sheet!" I handed him the telegram without a word. He tried to calm me down and led me to the nearest teahouse. I drank a glass of vodka, but that made me feel even worse. Drechsler took me home.

I was physically sick for a week and couldn't go to work. I didn't calm down until Sonya's airmail letter arrived. She wrote that she had started her vacation and was ready for the trip when an urgent message came from her office: the boss wanted to see her. She was told that her vacation had been canceled because of urgent work that had just come in. Sonya protested, but the boss threatened to fire her if she refused.

At first, I was angry at her for giving in. I thought she should have left, no matter what. But after some reflection I realized she had done the right thing. It would have been senseless to give up her job, which was her means of supporting not only herself and her mother but me, too. I could also tell from her letter that she was suffering no less than I was, and I felt sorry for her. She assured me that she would do everything possible to come and see me.

I tried to find consolation in my work, but it was physically very taxing, and I could feel my strength waning. Also, I no longer enjoyed my circle of friends. The basis of friendship among the exiles was one's social position rather than common interests. Everyone was afraid of attracting the attention of the MVD and the MGB, who kept a close watch on the activities of the exile community. Any talk about politically touchy subjects was carefully avoided. Our entire social life consisted of card games, drinking vodka, and singing. Once people got sufficiently tight, they would start to dance. To make life a little more interesting, the men would flirt with each other's wives, and sometimes much more serious involvements developed.

Suddenly, like a heaven-sent gift, I heard that my friend Josef Berger was living close by. About fifty kilometers from Maklakovo was the village of Kazachinskoye, an old exile center, and that was where Josef had been living since he was released from the camp. I wrote to him immediately; there wasn't another time in my life when I stood more in need of this wise and good friend's advice. I received an answer very soon—Josef was just as happy as I was that we had found each other.

We wrote several letters back and forth, discussing how we could arrange to get together. Josef's life in Kazachinskoye was even more desolate than mine in Maklakovo, and we agreed that he should move to Maklakovo. The only problem was how to get the necessary permission. By chance, at the inn, I met the head of the construction company's personnel department. I treated him to two liters of vodka, and he promised to find a job for Josef. The next day, I received a written confirmation of this agreement and sent it to Kazachinskoye. After long and frustrating efforts, Josef finally obtained permission to move to Maklakovo. Our reunion after so many years was a great event for both of us.

ON A SIBERIAN KOLKHOZ

In June 1954, our company was shut down for two weeks and all the employees had to help harvest hay on the collective farm on the other side of the river. Two hundred and eighty of their three hundred and sixty sheep and eighteen of their forty-five cows had starved to death during the winter. For this reason, it was especially urgent to harvest all the available hay; and since the kolkhoz didn't have enough hands, the workers of our company had to be brought in.

Our group was sent to an unpopulated island in the Yenisei. During the summer, the grass there was cut and stacked; in the winter, when the river froze solid, the hay was transported to the village on sleds. Every morning at seven, we assembled on the shore and were taken to the island on a large motorboat. There the brigadier of the kolkhoz divided up the work: some mowed the hay, others raked it into small mounds, and a third group piled these mounds into large stacks. We had to bring our own food. When it rained, we took shelter in sheds we had built ourselves. In the evening, we were taken back to Maklakovo.

One evening, we waited in vain for the motorboat to pick us up—it didn't come. At ten o'clock, we asked the lighthouse keeper—the only inhabitant of the island—to take us ashore in his boat. Only ten people fit into the boat, so we had to go in shifts. I was part of the fourth group. We were about twenty meters away from the shore when we discovered that the boat was leaking. Some women leaped up screaming, and there was a certain amount of pushing and shoving, in the course of which my trousers got caught in the open motor and I suffered a severe injury to my left leg. Fortunately, the motor was shut off immediately; otherwise, I would have lost the leg. Laboriously, we rowed back to the island. I took off my shirt and bandaged my leg, which was bleeding profusely. At midnight, the motorboat came and took us home.

I was bedridden for ten days. The company paid me fifty percent of my salary during that time. By law, I should have been given my full salary, but my injury was not counted as a work-related accident.

Two months later, we had to go back to the kolkhoz, this time to bring in the grain harvest. Here was my opportunity to learn about life on a Siberian kolkhoz with the lovely name *Put k sotsialismu*—the Road to Socialism. The kolkhoz administration was located in a one-story wooden building. We crossed the muddy yard and entered a large room containing several rows of wooden benches. There were slogans on the walls:

"Bring in the harvest on time!"
"Not a grain must remain in the field!"
"Mobilize all forces to produce the livestock's winter feed!"

The head of our company negotiated with the chairman of the kolkhoz to arrange for our work and lodging. We were distributed among the houses of the village in groups of ten to fifteen. I was put in the two-room house of an old peasant couple. The woman gave us a friendly welcome and pointed with her hand to the small room where we would all sleep. After a while, the peasant crept down from the stove and walked past us as if we didn't exist.

We were to begin work the next morning. Before going to sleep, I took a little walk with Drechsler to see how the others had been lodged. The houses didn't differ from other Siberian houses I had seen. Most of them were made of barked tree trunks. Almost all the shingle roofs had large holes in them; some of the roofs were covered with moss. In front of every house, there was a garden where the peasants grew potatoes, onions, herbs, and some vegetables. You could see beds and chests in the houses, but only a few bureaus.

When it started getting dark, we returned to our house. Our hosts were having dinner when we walked in. They were eating potato gruel from a large wooden bowl, using wooden spoons, and chewing pickled cucumbers. A little later, the two daughters came home from their day's work in the fields and sat down to eat without washing their hands. The old woman put some additional potatoes into the bowl. After the girls finished eating, we tried to engage them in conversation about their work on the farm. All we could find out was that they were drying out the wheat. After a little while, the girls went into the next room, sat down on a bed, cast off their muddy boots, and crept under the featherbed without taking off their clothes. I assumed they were embarrassed by the presence of strange men in their house and would undress under the blanket.

We lay down on the naked floor and covered ourselves with our down jackets. I was the only one who had brought along a blanket, and also a pot and a spoon. The others had made fun of me for being so cautious; they were sure the kolkhoz would supply us with everything we needed. Now they praised me for my foresight.

We got up early in the morning and went to look for milk and bread for our breakfast. We bought milk for four rubles a liter; there was no bread. Some of us had been wise enough to bring some bread from Maklakovo. We had finished breakfast and were setting off for work when we saw the old woman waking up her daughters. All they had to do was put on their boots; they hadn't taken off any of their clothes.

Two kilometers from the village, there began a seemingly endless wheat field. The wheat stood nearly six feet tall, with the heavy heads of grain bowed to the ground. Those of us who had some farming experience took the sickles and mowed; the others bound the sheaves. My job was to collect the bound sheaves.

We worked until twelve o'clock. Then we went to eat lunch in the village. On the first day, each of us got a kilo of bread and a pot of herb soup. The chairman of the kolkhoz apologized for the meager meal and promised us a plentiful dinner. It consisted of millet gruel, potatoes, and curd. During the following four days, we were served horse meat. We had no choice but to buy additional food from our own wages; otherwise, we wouldn't have been able to keep up with the hard work. The kolkhoz peasants ate no better than we did; however, they worked less. We started work at seven; they didn't come to the field until nine, and on Sunday they didn't come until noon. We reproached them for that: "You should be ashamed of yourselves! We as your guests have been working since six, and now here you come, six hours later!"

A young peasant woman answered very calmly: "You're getting fifty percent of your salary for working here, in addition to room and board. And we? It's two years in a row now that we haven't gotten a grain of wheat from the kolkhoz. Last year, we got two hundred grams of maize and four kilograms of potatoes for a day's work. So why break our backs? We have to devote some of our time to our vegetable gardens; that's our main source of income."

We didn't believe her. In the evening, when the brigadier came, we asked him how much everyone got for their day's work. He made a deprecating gesture with his hand and said: "*Pochti nichevo*—Almost nothing."

"How come?"

"Last year, almost half the harvest was left on the field."

"How did that happen?"

"We don't have enough people. Almost all the young people have left the village; they prefer to work in the woods or in the sawmill. The men who were drafted didn't come back. You can see for yourself who's working here—old people and adolescents." It was true. There were only a few young adults in the village, and they looked as demented as our hosts' daughters.

It took us sixteen days to harvest the section we had been assigned to. The chairman of the kolkhoz was satisfied with our work; he gave the head of our company a note confirming that we had exceeded the quota by twenty-five percent. This note, it turned out, was the ticket entitling us to be ferried back to the other shore; without it, no one was allowed to cross the river. We were glad to leave the village and marched to the river singing in chorus. We climbed into the boat and returned to Maklakovo.

HOW GEORG BILETZKI DIED

I needed two new photographs for my passport. There were no professional photographers in Maklakovo. A friend recommended an amateur photographer who made passport photographs for a fee. He lived near the new school in one of the many prefabricated buildings. A young woman opened the door when I knocked. I told her why I was there, and she asked me to wait a moment—her husband would come home soon. It wasn't long before he arrived. He greeted me like an old friend: "Why, hello, how are you? How long have you been here?"

I couldn't remember ever having met him.

"Have you forgotten me?" he asked.

"I really can't remember our having met before."

"Sure we did, in Norilsk, in section 6! We were in the same brigade."

"Are you Karpov?"

"Of course I am. How could you forget me! When I saw you, I was convinced someone had given you my address and you were here to visit."

I told him why I had come.

"Certainly, we can take care of that right away," he said.

His wife brought tea, and we talked about Norilsk and mutual friends. "Did you know Georg Biletzki?" I asked Karpov.

"Of course," he said. "Biletzki—he was a doctor, he wore glasses, everyone knew him."

"When was the last time you saw him?"

"Why, don't you know?"

"What?"

"Something terrible. I don't know if I should tell you."

"Speak up. What happened?"

"Georg Biletzki worked for several years as a doctor in camp section ROR—that was an open nickel mine. He was the most popular doctor. He helped thousands of people, saved hundreds of lives. But there were people who didn't like him, especially criminals he'd refused to give sick leave to. One day, one of these bandits threatened to do him in. Biletzki was used to threats like that, so he paid no attention. The criminal came back. Georg was sitting at his table—he didn't even see the man come in. The guy had an ax—he hacked Biletzki in the back of the head several times. The news spread over the camp instantly. Some prisoners found the killer hiding in a barracks and damn near beat him to death—the guards saved him at the last minute. He was given twenty-five years by the camp court; but since he had twenty-three more years left on his first sentence, all he got for murdering Biletzki was, in effect, a two-year sentence."

I was so shaken that I couldn't pose for my pictures. I went home.

THE STRUGGLE FOR POWER AFTER STALIN'S DEATH

After Stalin's death, none of us doubted that large-scale changes were imminent in Russia. There was no way to predict what direction these changes would take, but one thing was certain: the state's extermination campaign against its own people had to come to an end. The reason no one could make a prognosis was that Stalin had killed all the people who might have been qualified to lead this huge country. He had surrounded himself with mediocrities. The younger generation was our only hope.

When the 1953 anniversary celebration of the revolution failed to bring the expected amnesty, the disappointment among the millions of prisoners and their relatives was enormous. Experienced people expressed the opinion that, contrary to the repeated claims of "collective leadership," a bitter struggle for power was unfolding in the Kremlin, and that this was the reason that no noticeable political change had taken place.

After my rehabilitation, when I lived in Moscow for four months, I spoke to people who were close to the leadership; they told me about the first phase of this struggle for power. The changes that were instituted immediately after Stalin's death were supposed to secure a portion of power for each member of the party leadership: Malenkov as Premier; Khrushchev as General Secretary of the party; Molotov as Foreign Minister; Zhukov as Defense Minister; and Beria as Minister of the Interior. Party unity seemed assured. Only—how to go on from there? Molotov, Kaganovich, Malenkov, and Beria were all in favor of leaving things as they were; Khrushchev, Zhukov, Shepilov, Bulganin, and Mikoyan realized that it wasn't enough to secure power—something had to be done for the people. The main thing they wanted was to make Russia a country where the rule of law prevails; they demanded reparations for the monstrous crimes that had been committed on Stalin's orders. After a fierce struggle in the Politburo, they succeeded in pushing through a decision to review all the MGB's and the MVD's judgments and to instruct those organizations to stop using Stalinist methods in future arrests and trials.

Many lovely resolutions were passed, but they weren't put into effect. Beria had voted in favor of the resolutions, but he was not at all eager to put them into practice. Instead, he prepared for a coup d'état that would make him Stalin's successor. His secret supporters in this effort were the MGB and the MVD, and he had agents in leading positions in various party organizations. Beria was just waiting for the right moment to settle with Khrushchev, Zhukov, Mikoyan, and Voroshilov. The only power opposing him was the army, under Zhukov's leadership. Of course, Beria and the MGB had infiltrated the General Staff as well, but there existed a long-established antagonism between the army and the MGB apparatus. The army had not forgotten that they had been robbed of their best generals by the secret police. Zhukov was preparing for a counter-coup.

One day, at a meeting of the Politburo, Beria thundered against the "enemies of the people" in typical Stalinist style, but no one contradicted him, and the chairman closed the meeting. Beria saw this as a bad sign; he stood up with the intention of going to his office, setting the machinery in motion with a code word over the telephone, and having his enemies arrested and tried in traditional fashion. But he had scarcely left the conference room when several generals led by Serov, a confidant of Marshal Zhukov, surrounded and arrested him, led him to the Kremlin yard, where an armored car was waiting, and drove him to the Defense Ministry. Twenty minutes later, Beria was a corpse; forty of his closest collaborators suffered the same fate.

With this stroke, the MGB was decapitated. General Serov became the new chief of state security and moved into the Lubyanka building. Henceforth, the fate of the Russian people was in the hands of Marshal Zhukov. Beria's fate served as a warning to the Malenkov–Molotov–Kaganovich group. From now on, they supported the new measures.

One of the main goals was to make reparations for the crimes committed against Yugoslavia in 1948. The first measure toward this end was to remove the MGB agents from leadership in the Soviet satellite countries—Enver Hoxha in Albania, Viliam Široký in Czechoslovakia, Matyas Rakosi in Hungary, Viko Chervenkov in Bulgaria. Khrushchev and Bulganin went to Yugoslavia to ask Tito's forgiveness. Foreign Minister Molotov didn't want to participate, so he had Shepilov replace him. The reconciliation with Yugoslavia made Khrushchev an extremely popular man in Russia. This was very evident when hundreds of thousands of people filled the streets to welcome Tito on his visit to Moscow. For the first time in thirty years, millions of Russians were demonstrating against the Stalinist policies that had brought such suffering both to themselves and to the Yugoslavian people.

I HAVE BROUGHT YOU YOUR WIFE!

Part of what is produced in the lumberyards on the banks of the Yenisei is exported. Every year, during the brief shipping season, from mid-August to mid-September, freighters from every conceivable country appear on the Yenisei. They cross the White Sea, the Barents Sea, and the Kara Sea, enter the mouth of the Yenisei, and move upstream past Ust-Port and Dudinka until they reach Igarka, the final loading site for the precious lumber from the sawmills.

The principal task of the sawmills is to meet the projected export quotas. Many a manager has been jailed for failing to meet these norms. There are not enough transport workers to load the ships and barges in the brief time that is available. For this reason, the sawmills call a complete or a partial halt to their production, and all the laborers and employees are sent out to help with the loading.

We had scarcely returned from the kolkhoz when we were put to work on the pier of the Maklakovo sawmill. Several hundred soldiers from the nearest garrison were also assigned to work there. Thousands of people labored at a murderous pace day and night. A special delegate of the Ministry of Forest Industries supervised. During this time, the workers were able to buy goods that were usually unavailable: cheese, sausage, fruit—but as soon as the last barge was loaded, all those fine things disappeared from the stores.

I was glad to be able to get back to my usual work as a carpenter. I had advanced to a brigadier's position there. Once again, I had survived a hard winter. The March sun was casting its first rays on the dirty snow of Maklakovo. A woman was cleaning the floors and windows in my apartment. A big event was about to take place: I was going to see Sonya again, for the first time after eighteen years! This time I knew that nothing could intervene: my wife was already on the Moscow–Peking Express, on her way to Siberia. I had asked friends in Krasnoyarsk to pick her up at the train station there and help her get around the city. She would be arriving in Krasnoyarsk on March 9; I expected her to be in Maklakovo the next day.

The head of the sawmill had granted me a few days of vacation. I went to bed early so that the time would pass more quickly—that's what I thought. I couldn't fall asleep for a long time. But finally I dozed off. Suddenly I was awakened by loud knocks on the door. I jumped up and turned on the light: it was 1 a.m. Could she be here already? I rushed to the door.

"Who is it?"

"Does Steiner live here?" a man's voice asked outside.

"Yes, I am Steiner."

"Open up!"

Frightened, shivering, I opened the door. Before me stood Savanin, the head of the sawmill. "I have brought you your wife."

"Where is she?" I cried.

"She's waiting downstairs, by my car."

I was about to run down as I was, in my nightshirt and slippers. Savanin held me back. "Are you out of your mind? It's forty degrees below zero! Get dressed."

I quickly slipped into my boots, threw my coat over my shoulders, and ran to the street with my hat in my hand. I recognized Sonya from far off, pacing back and forth in front of the car. I ran toward her. She heard my steps, turned, and came running to me. We embraced, and then she murmured: "At last!"

Savanin and his driver watched us in silence. I took Sonya's valise, and we went back into the warm room. We looked at each other for a long time. Then she said: "You haven't changed."

Dawn was breaking when we finally went to bed. After nearly two decades, we held each other in a tight embrace, swearing that only death would separate us now. The following days were the most beautiful in my life. We walked in the brilliant March sun by the edge of the woods, talking and talking. Sonya stayed for fourteen days, enough time to get an impression of life in Maklakovo. Desolate as it seemed to her, she decided to leave Moscow and join me until I had a chance to choose where I wanted to live.

It was with a heavy heart that I accompanied Sonya to the bus that would take her to Krasnoyarsk, from where she would go on by train to Moscow. I consoled myself with the thought that she would come back soon.

One of Stalin's craziest ideas was the building of a railroad line from Vorkuta through the tundra via Igarka to Yakutsk, up to the bank of the river Kolyma. Another line was supposed to connect Igarka and Norilsk. The Baikal–Amur line was almost finished; the Tayshet–Lena line was under construction. Immense stretches of land were as yet unexploited, but in the places where new railroad lines and roads were most needed, there was hardly any construction. The new railroad, meanwhile, was being built by hundreds of thousands of workers and with a huge investment of technical equipment. Millions of ties and track were needed to realize this dream of a half-mad tyrant. Any rational person had to ask himself what was the purpose of this railroad. It was useless from an economic point of view, since it led through completely uninhabited regions; neither did it serve a military purpose. Its only conceivable use was to keep millions of prisoners busy in an area where they were bound to perish after a few years of work.

After Stalin's death, the construction of this railroad, large parts of which were already completed, was halted. The prisoners had to tear down what they had built, and tens of thousands of railroad cars filled with ties, track, and machinery were sent back across thousands of kilometers. Some of this material was brought to the Yeniseisk area, where a railroad was going to be built between the regional capital and Achinsk. Near Maklakovo, you could see the barbed-wire fence and the watchtowers of the camp where the builders of the new railroad line were locked up. I avoided passing there, so as not to be reminded of the worst time of my life.

MY LAST MONTHS IN EXILE

I was very surprised one day when I received a summons from the Public Prosecutor's office in Krasnoyarsk. I went to the MVD office and requested permission to visit the regional capital. The officer read the summons, nodded, and said: "Come back day after tomorrow."

I objected that the summons required that I report to the Public Prosecutor without delay, but the officer replied: "*Nichevo*–Doesn't matter."

When I left the MVD office, I thought it would probably be best if I took the next bus to Krasnoyarsk. If there was a control, I could show my summons—there probably wouldn't be any serious consequences.

The head of the company gave me a written permit to take a two-day leave from work. I went to the bus stop. I felt safely hidden among the many people waiting with me in the teahouse. When the bus came,

I watched through the window while everyone else got in, and then jumped in at the last minute. At each stop, I was afraid there would be a control, but everything went smoothly. Twenty minutes before Krasnoyarsk, the bus suddenly stopped on the open road. Two officers stepped in. One of them called out in the door: "Have your papers ready!"

When my turn came, I gave the officer my passport and the Public Prosecutor's summons. To my great surprise and relief, he returned my papers without comment. There were no further delays.

The Public Prosecutor, Solovyov, a robust, blond man with a large head, gave me a markedly friendly reception. He asked me to sit down and offered me a cigarette. "We have received instructions from State Security in Moscow to check your files and send in a character evaluation on you. I asked you to come here so that I could get to know you. I can't make an evaluation of your character on the basis of the MGB records alone."

"May I ask why they're asking for all this?"

"I don't know that myself. I assume someone has interceded on your behalf. Or else the KGB [Committee for State Security] is acting on its own initiative. They're reviewing all cases from the Yezhov period."

"Is there any reasonable hope, then, that something will finally be done for us?"

"Yes, indeed. I can even tell you that we have already taken some steps in your case. We have questioned the only witness from your second trial who is still alive, Larionov. Here is his testimony." He pointed to a stack of documents. "Larionov has retracted all his accusations; he says he incriminated you only because he was pressured by the chief of the NKVD in Norilsk, Polikarpov."

Solovyov asked me a few more questions, took notes, and then allowed me to leave. This was the first time I had ever walked out of an official building in the Soviet Union without the feeling of having participated in a charade. I had the impression that the Public Prosecutor was trying to make amends for the great injustice that had been committed against me.

When I told my friends in Maklakovo about my experience in Krasnoyarsk, all of them were convinced that I was about to be rehabilitated. Of course, I immediately informed my wife of the great event. She had by now taken steps in Moscow to reactivate my case. She had succeeded in obtaining an interview with the military prosecuting attorney, who had promised to speed things up.

Despite these indications of an imminent change in my status, Sonya remained determined to join me in Maklakovo; she still didn't believe I would be rehabilitated in the near future. My friends, on the other hand, considered it senseless for her to move to Siberia under these circumstances. Sonya quit her job and made the long trip to Siberia for the second time. On June 5, 1955, I drove to Krasnoyarsk to pick her up at the station and also to talk to the Public Prosecutor again. Solovyov assured me that my case would be closed very soon, and he expressed surprise that my wife still doubted it.

Sonya could scarcely believe her eyes when she saw me waiting for her on the platform. It was only three months since her first visit; when she left, it was inconceivable that I would be picking her up in the regional capital. My presence in Krasnoyarsk was an important sign that a new era was dawning. We spent the night in Krasnoyarsk. The next day, we were given a ride in a truck that was bringing young workers from the apprentice school in Krasnoyarsk to Maklakovo. Once again, we were together in our modest apartment. Sonya wanted to try to find work in Maklakovo, as we would not have been able to live off my salary. The primary school needed a German teacher; when Sonya applied for the job, the principal used some lame excuse to avoid telling her that he didn't want the wife of an exile working in his school.

I had planted potatoes on a small plot of land. In the fall, we harvested ten sackfuls. Every Sunday, Sonya went to the market and sold some of the clothes she had brought with her. That way, we could buy some fat, vegetables, and other foods and didn't have to go hungry.

I thought the time had now come when I dared write to the Yugoslavian embassy. An answer came promptly, with the ambassador's signature. He informed me that he had taken the necessary steps to ensure that I would be allowed to return to Yugoslavia very soon. A letter from the military prosecuting attorney came almost simultaneously, saying that my case was being looked into and that I would be promptly informed of the results.

We drove to Yeniseisk, where I visited Adele Herzberg with Sonya. Adele was glad for us and told us that she, too, had received good news and hoped to be able to leave Yeniseisk very soon. (She's back in Moscow today.) On that occasion, I also showed Sonya the city, which she had only read about. She was very impressed.

After four months together in Maklakovo, we agreed that she should go back to Moscow to urge the authorities to speed up the review of my case. I gave her a letter to Molotov, in which I asked him to intervene on my behalf, so that I could return to my country. Sonya would try to deliver the letter personally to Molotov. And so I accompanied Sonya to the bus for the second time. This time we both hoped she wouldn't have to come back to Maklakovo.

Sonya tried to see Molotov in Moscow, but this proved as easy as swimming the ocean. One of Molotov's secretaries was indignant that the wife of an exile dared make such a request. He promised, however, to bring the contents of my letter to the attention of the "highest authority" (that's how he put it), and he gave Sonya a date on which she should come back to his office. When she returned a month later, the official told her that the "appropriate authority"—in other words, the KGB— was handling my case.

From eight in the morning until two in the afternoon every day, my wife walked up and down stairs, from office to office, from the KGB to the party, from the military prosecuting attorney to the Supreme Court. In all these places, people crowded the hallways and waiting rooms, hoping to be received by a high official so that they could ask him to put in a good word for their exiled or imprisoned relatives. Now people dared to make known their connection with Stalin's victims; no one had to fear being arrested by the NKVD upon leaving the building, and ending up in a prison camp themselves.

Once again, the harsh Siberian winter set in, and I was still in Maklakovo. The communications I received from Moscow were hopeful, but everything was still up in the air. Good news came in from all sides: we heard that the Central Committee had determined that the cases of condemned party members were to be given priority. I had reason to hope, therefore, that my turn would come soon. I waited patiently.

One cold winter morning, I was on my way to work when I saw a group of people standing around a truck in front of the MVD headquarters in Maklakovo. What sort of people were these? I hoped to God they weren't new exiles!

I stepped up closer. About a dozen men, women, and children were standing by the truck, and two soldiers were handing them their luggage. Someone asked the newcomers: "Where are you from?" He received no answer. That surprised me; usually newcomers welcomed the opportunity to make contact with the old-timers and learn something about local conditions. One of the women in the group put a question to an officer who came out of the building. Her Russian had a Georgian accent, and somebody commented: "They're Georgians!" People assumed they were Georgian followers of Stalin who had attempted an uprising and were now being sent into exile.

It wasn't long before the riddle was solved. After the many suitcases had been removed from the truck, the officer began to read off the newcomers' names: "Beria!" A man stepped forward and stated his first name. That explained it. These were the hangman's relatives, and now they were here to share the fate of his victims. No one felt sorry for them. I heard someone say: "We came here with miserable little bundles—take a look at those suitcases."

December 31, 1955. Once again, several exiled families joined together to bid farewell to the departing year and to welcome the new one. Spirits were higher than they had been on the same occasion in previous years. Some friends who had celebrated with us last year had already gone home. Our hour was sure to come; each of us would soon be allowed to decide where he wanted to live.

The women had prepared a sumptuous feast, with the traditional salt herring as an appetizer, and a delicious roast with roast potatoes and pickles (since we had no fresh salad). There was plenty of vodka too, and even a few bottles of wine we had bought in Krasnoyarsk. At midnight, we raised a toast to a truly happy New Year of 1956. We stayed together until 5 a.m. In the end, we were served a marvelous pie and aromatic black coffee.

Sonya sent me a wonderful New Year's present. At 1 p.m. on January 1, the mailman brought me a telegram from her: "Military prosecuting attorney overturns sentence of military court." It had taken twenty years to correct this miscarriage of justice. But I still had to wait for the decision of the Supreme Court.

The largest building on the main square of Yeniseisk had a new tenant. The officials of the MGB, along with their leader, Colonel Moskalenko, moved out, and in moved the new gentlemen of the KGB, with Major Honsalenko at their head. The copper plate with its black lettering: *Ministerstvo gosudarstvennoi bezopasnosti, raionny otdel Yeniseisk— Ministry for State Security, District Department Yeniseisk* was removed and replaced with another sign: "KGB delegation of the Yeniseisk District."

I stood before the new chief, Major Honsalenko, who had summoned me to his office. The almost delicate courtesy with which he received me contrasted strangely with his crude Ukrainian peasant's face. "I wanted to make the acquaintance of the most prominent exile," he said.

I was silent and waited.

"How are you doing?" he asked.

"You must know very well how people in my position are doing."

"I mean: are you content with your work, and do you have a good apartment?"

"Both are bearable."

"Have you received notice concerning your appeal for a review of your sentence?"

"No."

"Something will be coming from Moscow soon. I think you'll be free in a few months."

"It's about time."

"What do you expect to do after you're rehabilitated?"

"I have already applied for permission to return to my country."

"So you want to leave us?"

"Yes, I'm sure you won't miss me."

"You can stay if you wish. After your rehabilitation, you'll receive reparations."

I chose not to dignify that with a reply.

"If you should need anything," the major said, "I will be glad to assist you."

I thanked him and left. Honsalenko accompanied me to the door.

I took the opportunity of visiting the grave of my friend Max Gaber, who had recently died. Gaber had been a Rumanian official in Czernowitz. When the Russians occupied Bessarabia and the Bukovina, he was arrested and sent to a camp for ten years. After serving his sentence, he was exiled to Maklakovo, where he worked in the sawmill. There he met a young girl, a student at the polytechnic institute in Krasnoyarsk who was working in Maklakovo to get her necessary credits of practical experience. They decided to marry as soon as she had finished her studies. Suddenly Gaber fell ill, and shortly afterward he died in great pain in the Yeniseisk hospital. His friends paid for the burial; Josef Berger even had Max Gaber's name and the dates of his birth and death engraved on a tombstone. I gave the graveyard attendant some money, asking him to see to it that the grave was kept in good order. I left with a heavy heart; perhaps I would be the last to come and lay flowers on my friend's grave.

In the beginning of March, the regional party secretary in Maklakovo sent a messenger to summon me to his office. He told me he had received a telephone call from the Central Committee in Moscow. Comrade Ponomaryov's secretariat had instructed him to find out what my financial situation was. I told him I was healthy and that the six hundred rubles a month I earned were enough to keep me from starving. He thanked me, and I left.

Two weeks later, I was called back to his office. This time, he told me that my country's embassy was very interested in me. Now I could be reasonably sure of a favorable decision in the near future. On April 2, 1956, I went to the market after work and bought cabbage, pickles, and meat. On the way home, I had a sudden impulse to go to the post office. I asked the mail clerk if there was any mail for me. He said there wasn't. I was about to leave when the mailman, who knew me, called out: "There's a telegram for you!" I opened it with quivering fingers and read: "Congratulations on complete rehabilitation stop happy as never before stop Sonya."

This was the long-awaited day. I counted my money—it was enough for a bottle of wine. I ran to share my joy with my friends. We raised our glasses in a toast to the triumph of justice.

A few days later, Josef Berger received the same notice from Moscow. He left Maklakovo a few days before I did. Today he lives in Israel with his family.

Many people came to congratulate me before I left Maklakovo. It took me three days to distribute my "household" among my friends and acquaintances. A small farewell celebration marked the end of a long and tragic period of my life.

THE ROAD TO FREEDOM

On April 5, 1956, I stood with my valise in front of the teahouse, waiting for a truck that would give me a lift to Krasnoyarsk. By "chance," the head of the KGB, Honsalenko, and his deputy, Vasiliev, were in the teahouse as well. They invited me to join them at their table and expressed surprise at my early departure. They would have gladly driven me to Krasnoyarsk, they said, but unfortunately their car was being repaired; however, they could call for a taxi from Krasnoyarsk. I thanked them for the kind offer but said I would prefer to hitchhike; and at that moment a truck loaded with lumber came along and stopped for me.

The driver put my valise on the back of the truck and I sat next to him in the cabin. We stopped at several teahouses along the way to warm up. The driver didn't take so much as a nip of vodka, which was something rare in that part of the country. I was glad he didn't; this way, I could be sure of reaching Krasnoyarsk.

At the train station, I took off my Siberian clothes and gave them to a ragged boy who was wandering around the station. He was so astonished that at first he didn't want to accept the gift; he thought I was making fun of him. A man who had been watching us said: "Go ahead, take them, he's giving them to you!" Only then did the boy reach out with both hands.

The Peking–Moscow Express would be coming in an hour. I had no difficulty buying a ticket for this train, which had only first- and second-class sleeping cars. I sat in a compartment with a female official, who had also boarded the train in Krasnoyarsk; a Chinese diplomat on his way to the embassy in Moscow; and a high railroad official from Chita. For the first time in twenty years, I was sitting in a train as one free human being among others. It felt strange to be able to leave the compartment, go to the bathroom and even to the dining car as often as I wished.

We passed through the great Siberian cities: Novosibirsk, Omsk, Sverdlovsk. In my memory, these were just names representing transit stations en route to the many camps of the Gulag. I was full of conflicting emotions: hatred for those who had robbed me of a large part of my life, and love for the woman who was waiting for me and to whom I owed so much. I tried hard to think only of her.

When the train came into Moscow, my heart leapt into my throat and my knees shook. I got out and searched for my wife in the crowd on the platform. There she was, running toward me; we embraced without a word. Sonya's relatives had come, too. We drove by taxi through the brightly lit streets of Moscow. As we passed by the MGB building, I couldn't contain myself and spat out a curse.

My first surprise in Moscow was the response of the chief of the militia (police) in the city's eighth district when I applied to register as a resident. He said that although I had lived in Moscow before my arrest, I didn't have my own apartment now, and my mother-in-law's apartment was only twenty-one square meters in size and therefore too small for three people to live in. I said that thousands of Muscovites would be very happy to have that much space; he ignored that remark.

I assumed there had been an ordinary mistake, and that I could clear it up by going to the central militia on Leningrad Boulevard. There was a sign on the door of the chief of the militia: "*Nachalnik ne prinimaet*— The Chief does not receive visitors."

"Does he not receive visitors today, or ever?" I asked the secretary.

"He doesn't receive anyone," she said.

"To whom can I take my case?"

"You could take it to the chief's deputy on the first floor."

Hundreds of people were waiting in a large room and out in the hallway. I asked a militiaman how I could reach the deputy of the chief of the militia. "Everyone is waiting. You have to wait, too" was his answer.

I asked several people why they were here and learned that all of them were applying for permission to live in Moscow. After more than three hours, my name was called. An MGB officer was in the office. I told him I had returned from Siberia after being rehabilitated and that I was living with my wife and mother-in-law. He perused the judgment of the Supreme Court concerning my rehabilitation and then asked me to wait outside in the hall.

I waited patiently for another hour. Then the officer I had spoken to came out, read off a list of names, and handed out forms, some of them white, most of them green. Mine was green, and printed on it was the following message: "Your application for residence in Moscow has been rejected. You are to leave the city within twenty-four hours. We advise you that the city comprises all localities within a radius of a hundred kilometers. Failure to abide by this order is punishable with three to five years' detention in a camp, according to Article 35 of the Criminal Code." I was only too well acquainted with Article 35—I had met thousands of people who had been sent to the camps on the basis of this catchall page in the Criminal Code.

All the pleasure of my rehabilitation and my return to Moscow was gone. How could I go home now and tell my wife that our suffering was not yet over? I stood on the street and didn't know where to turn. I'm not going to accept this, I told myself then. How could a decision of the Supreme Court be treated like a worthless piece of paper by the chief of the Moscow police?

It was 2 p.m.; the offices would be closing in an hour. I went into a telephone booth and called the Central Committee. The secretary of a leading party official answered the phone; I knew her by name. She connected me to her superior, and I told him briefly what I had experienced at the militia.

"Did you talk to the chief?" he asked.

"The chief doesn't talk to anyone, I couldn't get past his secretary."

"Who did you talk to?"

"The chief's deputy. He gave me a green form saying that I have to leave Moscow within twenty-four hours."

"Go back to the chief of the militia. By the time you get there, the matter will be settled."

When I returned to the militia headquarters, the secretary received me with a smile and immediately led me into the chief's office. He offered me a chair. I explained the purpose of my visit—knowing, all the while, that his questions and my answers were merely pro forma. Then the secretary came back and led me into another room, where, after a few minutes' wait, I was given a letter addressed to the head of the militia for the eighth district. That same day, I was officially registered as a resident in the city of Moscow.

The repatriation department of the Soviet Red Cross was supposed to obtain travel visas for my wife and me. When I presented myself there, the head of the department informed me that a leading official of the party's Central Committee wanted to speak to me. I went to the Central Committee offices on the Staraya Ploshchad. In the waiting room, a high-ranking KGB officer asked me the reason for my visit. I told him the name of the official who wanted to see me, and the officer directed me to one of several counters. A noncommissioned KGB officer stuck his head out, and I repeated my request.

"Your name?"

I told him my name.

"Sit down and wait."

I sat down. During the fifteen-minute wait, I was constantly observed through the window of the counter. Then the noncommissioned officer summoned me back. "Gate 5," he said.

Once again, I stood outside on the large square, looking for the right entrance. A man in civilian clothes came up to me and said: "What are you looking for?"

"Gate 5."

"That's on the opposite side of the street."

I found the entrance. A KGB major stopped me as I walked in, and I told him who I was looking for. He directed me to a counter, where I was given a telephone number. There were ten telephones in the room, and there was a line in front of each. Finally, I was in the booth and dialing the number I had been given. A woman's voice answered; I told her that Comrade X was waiting for me. "Hold on," she said.

Several minutes passed. The people waiting for the phone were showing signs of impatience. I was relieved when the woman's voice told me to go to the second counter in gate 2 and ask for a pass. I went back outside, found gate 2, and announced myself at the second counter. The uniformed official wrote down my name. "Your passport!" he said.

I handed him my papers.

"Sit down and wait."

While I waited, more and more people came to the counter and then sat down near me. Finally, the official behind the counter called me and handed me a pass. He kept my passport. Then he told me how to get to my destination. I wandered around the immense complex of buildings with my pass in my hand, searching for the building number I had been given. At last, I found the place in a narrow side street. Again, I had to wait. Finally, an officer led me across a courtyard and past dozens of brown Pobeda and SIS limousines. On the first floor, I was received by a voluptuous young woman who led me into an office and from there along a hallway to another waiting room. She knocked on a door; a voice called "Come in!" She opened the door, let me into the room, and closed the door behind me, leaving me alone with the official.

He stood up from his armchair and offered me his hand across the desk. "Sit down, comrade!"

I sat down in an armchair in front of a smoking table, and he took a seat across from me. "What is your impression of Moscow after your long absence?"

To give some kind of a reply to his question, which didn't interest me at the moment, I said: "Yes, certainly, it's a big city."

"Indeed, a great deal has changed. We are investing large sums of money in the beautification of the city." Then he seemed to notice my indifference and asked: "What was your life like out there? I'm sure it wasn't easy."

"I couldn't begin to describe what my life was like. It would sound so unbelievable that my own mother would probably doubt I was telling the truth."

"Well, that's all over now. What are your plans?"

"I want to get back to my country as soon as possible."

He tried to persuade me to stay in the Soviet Union, but I said: "My decision is final."

"As you wish. You are free to go wherever you choose."

"I would like to ask you to speed things up a little."

"Why don't you stay in Moscow? I would really urge you to do so. You'll have your own apartment, and you'll have an interesting job."

"I'm not going to change my mind."

"Very well, you can leave in two weeks."

I stood up and said goodbye.

MOSCOW, 1956

Foreigners visiting Russia usually content themselves with tours of Moscow, Leningrad, or one of the other big cities; having done this, they think they know Russia. Some will come home with positive, others with negative impressions. They do not know that their reports are misleading, even deceptive, for the big cities are not characteristic of Russian reality.

How did I see Moscow after coming back from Siberia? A four-month stay, meetings with old friends, and visits to various government offices enabled me to see the capital of this gigantic empire as it really was. The first thing I noticed was that you no longer risked your freedom or your life by walking (let alone stopping) on Red Square. An experienced eye could spot numerous phony "civilians" among the crowd, but they avoided looking the passersby in the face. The area around Dzerzhinsky Square hadn't changed, except for the giant MVD building, which had been enlarged. But, in contrast to past times, the guards with their blue caps responded to the questions of passersby. Kuznetsky Most, Neglinnaya, Sretenka, Trubnaya Ploshchad are still MVD and KGB streets, and their offices are still carefully guarded by visible and invisible soldiers. The "bread trucks" for prisoners, with their inscription *Khleb—Pain—Bread—Brot,* are no longer in use. There are bread trucks with Russian inscriptions only, and when they make their deliveries to the stores, you can be sure they are in fact carrying bread. Gone are the long lines of people waiting with bundles in front of the prisons to deliver a little food or some clothes for their arrested relatives. On the other hand, the number of people waiting in the anterooms of the Public Prosecutor's office and the Supreme Court—the two offices empowered to revise or reverse a legal judgment—has increased.

Next to the Kremlin (which is accessible to everyone now) are five tall apartment buildings that have become veritable landmarks of the city. I was curious to know who was living in them. When I attempted to walk into one, a liveried porter stepped up to me and asked me who I was looking for. I told him I was interested in the architecture—couldn't I at least have a look at the stairway? "That's forbidden" was his answer.

But on another occasion I succeeded in penetrating one of these buildings. I noticed on the ground floor that no one who lived there was below the rank of major. Later I discovered that, in a building where majors live, there are no residents below that rank, only higher. If one of the tenants is a captain, none of the other tenants is of a lower rank than lieutenant or a higher rank than captain. The same ranking system prevails among privileged civilians: wherever party and union officials live, there can be no "ordinary" tenants. Each caste is kept carefully separate from the others. The rent alone takes care of that. No blue- or white-collar worker would think of renting a room there, for a year's salary would scarcely pay a month's rent.

So where do the workers of Moscow live? In basements and in old, dilapidated apartment buildings, six to eight people to a room. New buildings for workers have been constructed, but only on the outskirts of the city.

The stores and shopping centers of Moscow are always full of buyers—or, rather, of people eager to buy, for only a fraction of those who besiege the counters for hours on end succeed in getting what they want. I wandered from store to store in search of a pair of pants that would fit me; after a few days, I finally accepted what was being offered. It was no different in the food stores: to buy a few sausages, I had to stand on line for two hours. Most people regretted the elimination of the rationing system. When people still had ration cards, the satisfaction of their minimal needs was guaranteed; now you had to spend several strenuous hours to obtain the most necessary goods.

Foreigners visiting Moscow are always surprised by the abundantly stocked stores, never realizing that each of these stores serves an average of fifteen hundred people, whereas a typical European store serves two hundred fifty. On the other hand, radios, television sets, and other technological equipment are available in limitless supply. What a strange country, I thought—no shoes, no sausage, but TV antennas on every barracks!

The government sees to it that a foreign guest does not suffer undue privations. He can eat as well in any one of the Intourist hotels as he could in his own country, and without having to stand on line. There are charming young ladies to brighten his days in Moscow—he will not be bored. There are nightclubs and bars where people dance to jazz music until morning. Long after the Muscovites have turned off their lights, the places that cater to foreigners are brimming over with amusement and excitement. Returning late to his hotel, the visitor often runs into girls looking for a way to add a little to their meager factory wages. And during the day he will meet with beggars who hold out their hands, crying: "Give, for the sake of Christ!"

It was nearly four months before I was granted an exit visa. The promises that I would be allowed to leave without delay proved to be lies. It was because of the energetic intercession of the Yugoslavian ambassador that I finally left Moscow on July 30, 1956.

And so at last I was sitting on the train that would take me out of the country where I had been robbed of my youth and where my noblest ideals had been crushed. I didn't find it difficult. When we reached the border after a three-day trip, I couldn't help remembering the day when I arrived in the land of my dreams, young and full of enthusiasm, twenty-five years before. Now I had the feeling of escaping as if by a miracle from a plague-infested land.